RACE, REVOLUTION,

AND THE STRUGGLE

FOR HUMAN RIGHTS

IN ZANZIBAR

G. THOMAS BURGESS

race, revolution, and the struggle for human rights in zanzibar

the memoirs of
ali sultan issa and
seif sharif hamad

OHIO UNIVERSITY PRESS • ATHENS

Ohio University Press, Athens, Ohio 45701
www.ohioswallow.com
© 2009 by Ohio University Press
All rights reserved

To obtain permission to quote, reprint, or otherwise reproduce or
distribute material from Ohio University Press publications, please
contact our rights and permissions department at (740) 593-1154 or (740)
593-4536 (fax).

Printed in the United States of America
Ohio University Press books are printed on acid-free paper ⊗ ™

16 15 14 13 12 11 10   5 4 3 2

Library of Congress Cataloging-in-Publication Data
Burgess, G. Thomas, 1968–
Race, revolution, and the struggle for human rights in Zanzibar : the
memoirs of Ali Sultan Issa and Seif Sharif Hamad / G. Thomas Burgess.
    p. cm.
Includes bibliographical references and index.
ISBN 978-0-8214-1851-2 (hc : alk. paper) — ISBN 978-0-8214-1852-9
(pb : alk. paper)
    1. Issa, Ali Sultan. 2. Hamad, Seif Sharif. 3. Zanzibar—History—
Revolution, 1964. 4. Zanzibar—Politics and government—1964- 5.
Zanzibar—Race relations. 6. Human rights movements—Tanzania—
Zanzibar—History. 7. Revolutionaries—Tanzania—Zanzibar—Biography.
8. Statesmen—Tanzania—Zanzibar—Biography. I. Issa, Ali Sultan. II.
Hamad, Seif Sharif. III. Title.
    DT449.Z273B87 2009
    967.8'10410922—dc22

                                                           2009003322

CONTENTS

part one   WALK ON TWO LEGS

The Life Story of Ali Sultan Issa

ILLUSTRATIONS

Part One: Ali Sultan Issa

following page 168:

Attending the Moscow Youth Festival, 1957
Attending a trade union conference in Hanoi, 1963
Speaking at a trade union conference in North Vietnam, 1963
Speaking at a village rally in Pemba, 1964
Abeid Karume officially opening a new primary school, Zanzibar, 1965
As Minister of Education, 1965
With daughter Moona Ali Sultan, Zanzibar Town, 1967
With Maria at their wedding, Zanzibar Town, 1966
At party at the Chinese consulate, Zanzibar Town, 1969
As a cabinet minister, Zanzibar Town, 1970
Maria in Retford, United Kingdom, with her children and those of Issa's
    first marriage, 1977
Issa following his release from prison, in Saarbrucken, West Germany,
    with Gertrude Gutt of Amnesty International, 1979
Traveling with wife Eshe, London, 1995

Part Two: Seif Sharif Hamad

Following page 312:

As a student at Beit el Ras Boarding School in 1960
With Fourtunah Saleh Mbamba on their wedding day, Malindi, Zanzibar
    Town, 1968
Aweinah Sanani Massoud on her wedding day with Hamad in Kizim-
    bani, Wete, 1977
Returning to Zanzibar from medical treatment in London, Chake
    Chake, Pemba, 1987
Being interviewed at home in Mtoni immediately following his release
    from prison, 1991

PREFACE

I first met Ali Sultan Issa in 1996 while conducting doctoral research on the Zanzibari Revolution. We met for a number of interviews in his flat in Zanzibar Town and at his cottage on the sea north of town. I was deeply impressed by his candor and the depth and precision of his memory. His personal engagement with history was evident as he recalled past episodes and conversations with remarkable passion, frequently raising his voice and rising from his chair, often to act out dialogues with people now dead. When, in 1997, he asked if I wanted to write his biography, I did not hesitate to volunteer. We accomplished very little, however, until I realized that a first-person narrative, an oral memoir, would be more interesting and authentic. The recording of his life story began in 2001 and continued through two subsequent summer visits to Zanzibar. I stayed in rented rooms close to his flat in Zanzibar Town, near the old Majestic Cinema, and we spent a few hours every day in the recording process. Issa lived with his wife Eshe and youngest daughter Natasha; in his early seventies and semiretired, Issa did not lack energy or enthusiasm for the project. And I looked forward to our visits, continually fascinated by his recollections and taken in by his rather indecorous sense of humor.

Issa's company can only be described as lively; in our many hours together he moved effortlessly in and out of various roles and performances: revolutionary, penitent, playboy, patriarch. He offered me fatherly blessings as often as he cursed me, because of my citizenship, as a capitalist imperialist. A heavy drinker, Issa in his cups was both shameless and discreet. He was free with several of his favorite Swahili obscenities. In our walks around Zanzibar Town he was continually recognized and saluted in the streets by old friends, acquaintances, and those who knew him by personal reputation as much as by memory of any specific services he had ever rendered to the revolution. Issa was and is a notorious local personality as much as an icon of Zanzibar's revolutionary past. He is also a friend.

At first, the aim was simply to exhaust his repertoire of stories; later, I composed lists of questions to provide details and transitions and to illuminate larger historical themes. Issa's recollections traversed time and space; the only logic to the flow of his memories was provided by my list of randomly ordered questions. As in any oral history project, the questions asked guided and shaped the answers received. Issa shared stories he had preserved and rehearsed in memory for decades, but our interviews also provoked him to explore spontaneously less traveled areas of the past. It was eventually necessary in the process of compiling and editing the manuscript to convert, with Issa's permission, his spoken sentences to the standards of written English. My intent was to preserve as much of Issa's thought and language as possible, yet in order to provide the reader a compelling narrative, I had to compose and order his memories for the printed page. To meet the publisher's length requirements, I also had to omit significant amounts of material.

Issa took multiple opportunities to carefully read draft copies of the text as it evolved and to make corrections where he thought necessary. The end result is a memoir published with his full consent and approval. It is, however, incomplete; Issa did not reveal all he remembers of his own past or that of his islands; nor did I ask all the questions I might have. Issa, in fact, did not answer certain questions, either to protect himself or others; he specifically asked me to stop recording when he wished to confide in me personally. Yet as the perspective of an insider willing to criticize, his memoir of the Zanzibari Revolution is unique. Issa did not set out, I am convinced, to recount selected incidents in order to satisfy a particular community or to inoculate himself from public scorn. Nor did Issa merely provide recollections that conformed to the contours of public rhetoric—marking his memoir as somewhat exceptional in Zanzibar. Yet, clearly, Issa's own convictions color his interpretations of the past; unsurprisingly, his is not a memoir that transcends subjectivity.

Confident that Issa's account would, when published, aid in understanding the revolution, I accepted a request in 2004 from Ismail Jussa Ladhu to record the life story of Seif Sharif Hamad. Since Hamad was by no means retired and was in that year, in fact, preparing himself and his party for another election campaign, I was initially uncertain of what our interviews would yield. Until then, my personal contact with Hamad was limited to his brief visit to the United States in 2002. I had a few Zanzibari and Western friends who were close to him and sometimes told stories; I'd also seen his image on countless campaign posters around Zanzibar Town. I was familiar with the ebb and flow of the islands' ongoing political drama and knew him to be revered by some as "Seif the Liberator," as someone of almost mystical stature, who provoked equally profound passions among his political foes.

That said, I entered the research process with little idea of what kind of document would emerge from our sessions. I quickly found, however, that we could work together according to the same methods employed with Issa, with both their strengths and weaknesses in terms of absences and subjectivity. I discovered that Hamad equaled Issa in his memory and engagement with the past and that he possessed a surprising openness about his personal history. Hamad was not interested in producing a mere formulaic tract or political manifesto but wanted to give an account of his life and times of interest to anyone wanting to know about Zanzibari history. The Civic United Front's secretary general impressed me by his warmth, good humor, and doses of modesty rare in high political circles. Indeed, his criticisms of the revolution are mild compared to those I have heard from many Zanzibaris. Nor does Hamad come off on a personal level as an opportunist, an unscrupulous demagogue, or someone motivated by thoughts of revenge. My only regret is that his very busy schedule allowed little time for leisured conversation. I recorded the bulk of his life story in a series of marathon interviews in December 2004, with additional sessions taking place in July 2005 and July 2006. Throughout, his manner was nearly always serene; despite the rough and tumble of Tanzanian politics, Hamad exuded the confidence of a man proud of his achievements when in power, and certain that his principles would someday prevail.

Like Issa, Hamad has provided a life story whose accuracy will, without doubt, be evaluated over time as others may come forward to offer their own memories and insights. Hamad's narrative of the revolution's first decade is new and valuable yet not entirely exceptional in that it reflects the views and experiences of many islanders, available to any future researcher collecting oral histories of the revolution. Hamad's insider perspective on Tanzania's national history of the 1980s, 1990s, and 2000s is unique, a record to be reckoned with. It reveals Tanzanian high politics in an age of liberalization, when elites were compelled to recognize the failures of *Ujamaa* socialism and one-party rule and to confront the issue of Zanzibari nationalism. Schooled in a political culture that since Julius Nyerere's time has tended to defuse ethnic and sectarian tensions on the mainland, politicians of Tanzania's ruling party have, however, proved rather inept when it comes to such conflicts in Zanzibar, and unwilling to sacrifice their allies within the ruling party there in order to recognize the will of the electorate.

Neither Hamad nor Issa, moreover, shies away from the inevitable ethical ambiguities of any revolutionary project seeking to benefit one element of society at the expense of another. Their stories engage our most basic assumptions about social justice and human rights and shed light on a host of themes key to understanding Zanzibari history that are also of universal relevance: identity; the legacies of slavery and colonialism; the origins of political conflict, poverty, and underdevelopment; public discipline and private corruption. Their stories suggest how a cosmopolitan island society negotiates multiple influences coming from Africa, the Middle East, Asia, and Europe and how Zanzibar continues to occupy an ambiguous position at the crossroads of different cultures. It is to be hoped that their memoirs will encourage many others to come forward and share their own life histories.

Cosmopolitanism and Its Discontents

THE ZANZIBARI REVOLUTION OF
January 1964 was the climax to years of growing racial, ethnic, and
partisan tension in the islands and a violent rejection of Zanzibar's
cosmopolitan heritage. Probably one-third of all Arabs on Unguja Island
were either killed or forced into immediate exile; for those Arabs and
other minorities who remained, the next years witnessed the confisca-
tion of most of their lands and urban properties, as well as their mass
exclusion from government employment. A new African nationalist
regime espoused socialism and, for two decades, found means by which
to transform privileged minorities into second-class citizens. The revolution ended 150 years of Arab and South Asian economic and cultural
hegemony in Zanzibar.

Many hoped the revolution would heal or reduce communal tensions
in island society, but any observer of Zanzibar's contemporary politics
can see that it did not. Three elections since 1995 have served, among
other things, as popular referenda on the legitimacy and legacies of the
revolution. One legacy is the political union of Zanzibar and Tanganyika
and the creation of the United Republic of Tanzania in April 1964,
barely three months after the revolution. Initially, the island government
retained nearly all aspects of its national sovereignty, including control
over its finances and armed forces. Starting in the mid-1970s, however,
the mainland began to assert increasing control over island affairs, so
that today, although Zanzibar retains its own presidency, cabinet, and
parliament, the archipelago is utterly dependent on the mainland for its
security, finances, and even its electricity. Zanzibari presidents are now
nominated and kept in power by a Tanzanian ruling party and army
dominated by mainlanders. While Tanzania enjoys a reputation for
political stability, such stability is purchased only through rigged elections in Zanzibar. Ruling-party elites justify such measures as necessary

to preserve the revolution and to ensure the islands remain part of Tanzania.

Thus, Zanzibar constitutes by far the most turbulent part of Tanzania today, a direct result of the revolution in the 1960s. Officials of Tanzania's ruling party recognize that, if they face a serious political challenge, they do so in Zanzibar. Since the 1990s, the ongoing political impasse in the islands has resulted in violent crackdowns on political demonstrations and the flight of thousands of Zanzibari refugees. The Zanzibari "crisis" has called into question Tanzania's respect for human rights: does *Chama Cha Mapinduzi* (CCM), meaning "Party of Revolution" in Swahili, actually intend to allow opposition parties to win elections, or are they permitted to exist merely to appease Western donors?

MEMORY COMMUNITIES

How Zanzibaris remember the revolution—as either the original sin or the triumph of the independence era—often determines whom they call their friends, with whom they share a cup of coffee, or whom they welcome to their homes as in-laws. Many Zanzibaris continue to trace their present fortunes to the revolution; it assumes center stage in discussions of how present conditions came to be. Defenders of the revolution claim it was good for Africans and describe the violence in 1964 and afterward as minimal and justified in order to right a century of wrongs. They often speak the language of African nationalism, whereas their opponents espouse the language of human rights and regard the violence as neither minimal nor justified. These latter remember the revolution as a long era of arrests, empty shops, and an ever-present atmosphere of isolation and fear. They claim the revolution reversed the social and economic development of the previous century and reduced what was once a proud and independent sultanate into a powerless appendage of the mainland.

Politics in the islands is not merely a contest common within contemporary Africa over such issues as government corruption and promises kept or broken; rather, it is about memory and identity. The revolution in the 1960s, in the name of African unity, largely repudiated Zanzibar's cosmopolitan past and ended the islands' independence. It promoted an African nationalist discourse of racial grievance, which, when wedded to socialist ideals, justified an assault on the wealth and exclusivity of minority communities and the punishment of Pemba as an island of "counterrevolutionaries." Opponents of the revolution, meanwhile, embrace Zanzibar's multicultural heritage and the idea that such a heritage makes islanders a unique people, possessing a set of interests that ought to be defended within the Tanzanian union. In their efforts to rally islanders of all backgrounds against the ruling party, they employ a language of human rights that has attained a global currency as widespread as that of socialism and of African nationalism in the 1960s. Thus, not only do Zanzibaris contest the legacy of the revolution in their lives, they also disagree on the language through which it is to be understood.

The two memoirs contained in this volume may be read as opposing arguments for and against the revolution; as such, they provide rare and contradictory insights into Tanzania's postcolonial history and current political stalemate. They demonstrate how conflicts within Zanzibar have become issues of national importance for Tanzania. The memoirs also demonstrate the differences between the language of socialism and that of human rights. Ali Sultan Issa supports the revolution on socialist principle as an event that liberated islanders from a colonial system of class exploitation. Seif Sharif Hamad, however, regards the revolution as a disaster in terms of human rights, an event to be regretted deeply. While each man served for years as a minister in the revolutionary regime, each was also imprisoned and forced out of the ruling party. Neither espouses African nationalism nor advocates the politics of race. Each, in fact, specifically deplores the habit of some Zanzibari politicians to manipulate racial or ethnic identities in order to achieve political ends. They both, furthermore, dispute official claims made for decades in the schools, in the media, and at public rallies that, since 1964, the islands have seen rapid social and economic development.

Official claims that reflect African nationalist currents of thought should be understood in order to grasp the historical and intellectual context of the memoirs presented here. Salmin Amour, who served as president of Zanzibar (1990–2000), completed his doctoral dissertation at Karl Marx Party College in East Berlin in 1986. "Zanzibar in the earliest days," he writes, was "a totally classless society." Unfortunately, it was not "left to prosper smoothly over time."[1] Arabs came and introduced slavery, something Amour claims was until then completely unknown, ignoring considerable historical evidence to the contrary.[2] Arabs denied Africans the chance to evolve their own forms of socialism: had Africans "been left to follow their life styles smoothly," they would have developed "into a higher form of the African collective mode of living."[3] Africans possessed no desires to exploit one another, and it was only the infiltration of foreigners that produced "evils" such as class divisions in the islands.[4]

Amour's portrayal of precolonial society in Zanzibar as protosocialist and egalitarian is familiar; it reflects the intellectual influence of Julius

Nyerere and his vision of African "familyhood" as the basis for socialism in Tanzania. It also serves very important functions in contests over memory more specific to Zanzibar. By asserting the fundamentally moral nature of precolonial African society, Amour inverts distinctions commonly drawn in coastal East Africa between "savagery" and "civilization."[5] Amour does not reject the language of civilization but merely recasts the assigned roles, with Africans now representing civilization and Arabs—through their role in the slave trade—the forces of savagery. Amour's image of the precolonial past makes possible his claim that the revolution restored island society to its former moral equilibrium and reestablished a society of tolerance and mutual respect. Amour's claims thus reflect what Liisa Malkki observed about oral histories in general: they represent "not only a description of the past, nor even merely an evaluation of the past, but a subversive recasting and reinterpretation of it in fundamentally moral terms."[6] On moral grounds, Amour and other African nationalists award Africans status as an advanced people, justify the revolution, and reject the worthiness of Zanzibar's mixed cultural heritage.

The argument against cosmopolitanism is carried further in Omar Mapuri's *The 1964 Revolution: Achievements and Prospects*, which is perhaps the most significant clue to understanding the extremist edge of racial politics in contemporary Zanzibar. Mapuri served Amour for years as his deputy chief minister in the 1990s and was an outspoken defender of the ruling party, the CCM.[7] Published in the aftermath of Zanzibar's 1995 elections, Mapuri's book inflamed opinion in the islands. He called on the African majority to maintain racial unity in the face of what he regarded as Western intrigues and resurgent Arab influence.[8] Such unity was as essential in the 1990s as just before the revolution, when, in a series of election campaigns, Africans confronted an imagined alliance between the British colonial government, the sultan, and Arab politicians. The British were not neutral referees; they wanted to leave behind "an Arab state" in Zanzibar[9] and employed all kinds of "well designed political maneuvers, deceptions, intimidations and humiliations," intended to divide Africans.[10] Unfortunately, Mapuri offers few specifics, none of which is convincing, and relies overwhelmingly on a secondary school history text for his information.[11] Throughout, Mapuri's intent is not so much to convey historical realities as to encourage unity among CCM supporters around a series of shared suspicions, including suspicions toward Zanzibaris of African ancestry who do not support CCM.

Mapuri also sets out to defend the ruling party's record over the past decades. The party did not permit plunder and violence in 1964; although "following centuries of oppression . . . a climate of retribution and revenge would have been explicable," the new regime "nipped all attempts at retribution in the bud."[12] Such a conciliatory policy, along with alleged revolutionary success in education, health, and housing, were responsible for forty years of tranquility. Peace and progress did not entirely heal old divisions, however. Public dissent was, regrettably, allowed to resurface in a new and "dangerously premature" era of multipartyism. Mapuri records his deep distrust of democracy, a distrust that pervades the ruling party in Zanzibar today:

> Karume [Zanzibar's first president] understood well that the legacy of centuries could not be swept away overnight and that a true Revolution needs time to take root in the hearts of people accustomed to tradition. Karume's foresight and wisdom in his declaration immediately after the Revolution that no election should be held in Zanzibar for fifty years was to prove prescient.[13]

Mapuri's readers cannot help but wonder, however, how old habits of thought have survived in the islands. He denies the reality of mass killings in 1964 and instead claims the existence of documents that reveal the genocidal intentions of the "Arab" government the revolution overthrew. He claims that, as retribution for the deaths of sixty-five Arabs in the June 1961 election riots, the government planned to kill sixty Africans for every one Arab fatality and to expel and confiscate the wealth of all Africans of non-Zanzibari origin. Those remaining would be enslaved and have Arab culture imposed on them. Zanzibar would be "proclaimed a land of Asians and Arabs." Furthermore, "all male African babies would be killed, and African girls would be forced to marry or submit to Arabs so that within a few years there would be no Africans to remember the vile treatment of their ancestors."[14] Thus, according to Mapuri, the revolution in 1964 did not unleash anti-Arab and anti-Asian violence in Zanzibar; it was instead a relatively peaceful intervention that protected Africans from their own genocide and forced assimilation into Arab culture. Would-be sins of the past extend, in fact, to the imaginary sins of the present. In 1997, referring in a work titled "Zanzibar under Siege" to the CCM's main political rival, the Civic United Front (CUF), Mapuri claimed that "had CUF won the [1995] elections, they would have massacred people with impunity in revenge."[15]

It is hard to imagine claims more corrosive and inflammatory and hard to see how the CCM's language of protection is *not* actually a language of incitement. Mapuri invents his own massacres to justify the revolution and any means necessary to preserve the political status quo in the islands. No clearer example can be conceived of how actors in Africa and elsewhere manipulate memory and identity to produce mass fear and suspicion, to be exploited by political elites for their own antidemocratic purposes. Mapuri and other CCM officials feel they represent the interests of the islands' allegedly embattled majority and regard the threat of Arabs' seeking retribution as very real, yet it is never clear who or where the Arabs in question are—are they a small minority of rural Pembans or Arabs living in exile far away in the Middle East? Regardless, readers cannot possibly miss Mapuri's conclusion: Africans must not "continue to be victims of their humility" or "continue to be harassed in their own land." They "must prepare themselves for bigger tests ahead [than the 1995 elections] so as to ensure that the Great 1964 Revolution remains for ever and that Zanzibar remains African."[16] Tanzanian scholar Issa Shivji has recently noted that CCM claims that CUF intends to restore Arab power in Zanzibar "may sound somewhat fanciful to any scientific observer, yet [they continue] to be the substance of the ruling party's position in Zanzibar, supported even by some establishment scholars."[17]

CCM claims of African victimization can make sense only if slavery in the nineteenth century and colonial-era racial inequalities are projected onto the present; Mapuri's claims begin to persuade only if one is willing to ignore the revolution as an era of major historical transformation. However, in *The 1964 Revolution,* a book ostensibly about revolutionary achievements, Mapuri has very little to say about the period between 1964 and 1995 or how the revolution actually impacted the lives of Zanzibaris. He pauses briefly to cite a few numbers intended to suggest social and economic development, figures that do not impress: for example, that life expectancy increased from forty-three years in 1964 to forty-eight in 1988.[18] Nor does he consider how effective the revolution actually was in forcing into exile tens of thousands of non-African minorities or in ending Asian and Arab domination of the island economy. Mapuri seeks to awaken his audience to colonial-era injustices, when many islanders of all races and ethnicities find their memories of the revolution more traumatic than memories of British or Arab domination. Mapuri is far more at home in the "racial war of nerves"[19] of the late colonial period than he is in any time since. Careful readers can only assume that he—and others—value the revolution more for its negative than positive consequences. Unfortunately, Amour made Mapuri's book required reading in Zanzibar's secondary schools, a move apparently intended to impart to students a firm understanding of who their historical enemies are, or at least were conceived to be a half-century ago.

Students in Zanzibar need to look elsewhere for an understanding of their history, yet no text speaks with any authority to all islanders about their past. Where can they read an assessment of the revolution that allows them to analyze it on its own merits, rather than the perceived evil intentions of its critics? For decades, critical voices remained oral; they survived in an atmosphere of storytelling and private performances, in which the object was often as much to entertain and provoke as to instruct and in which a series of revolutionary incidents were continually recounted as outrageous abuses against God and humanity. Such voices have asserted fundamentally moral claims, arguing that the revolution empowered individuals to act according to their worst vices: cruelty, pride, and ignorance. For decades, the only dissenting voices to appear in print were those of Zanzibaris living in exile, of whom Abdulrazak Gurnah emerged as the most compelling. In *Admiring Silence*, Gurnah refers to "the incompetence of the [revolutionary] authorities, their mindless bullying, the endless fiascos, their irrational vengefulness."[20] In *By the Sea*, a political prisoner is forced night after night to listen to government radio sermons "by one personage or another, haranguing and hectoring, rewriting history and offering homespun moralities that justified oppression and torture."[21] Speaking through his character Amin, Gurnah seeks in *Desertion* to convey how residents of Zanzibar Town responded in 1964 to a new revolutionary age:

> We have to find a new way of speaking about how we live now. They don't like to hear people say certain things, or sing certain songs. . . . People have been killed. I cannot write these things. They have frightened us too much, and it would be stupid to be found scribbling what we are required not to know about. . . . They want us to forget everything that was here before, except the things that aroused their rage and made them act with such cruelty.[22]

Gurnah is unique in the Zanzibari context for his capacity to suggest how any hegemonic language locates and catalogues the horrors of the past in order to legitimize present excesses. The memoirs contained in this volume are two separate and very different attempts to convey, through the idiom of personal experience, how Zanzibar's revolution either helped or harmed island society. They allow readers to begin to assess the revolution on its merits, rather than the alleged malevolence of its detractors.

The first memoir is that of Ali Sultan Issa, an icon of Zanzibar's revolutionary past, whose life is thoroughly cosmopolitan, but not in the centuries-old sense of close ties between Zanzibar and the world of the western Indian Ocean. Issa's connections are more distant; his most influential experiences came in London, Moscow, and Beijing; and he even expresses open contempt for the "backwardness" of aspects of Arab, Indian, and African societies that do not measure up in his estimation to the enlightened ways of more "scientific" lands. His Arab ancestry and allegiance to scientific socialism meant that only through a remarkable chain of events did he come to wholeheartedly serve an African nationalist regime and to seek new ways to impose the revolution. His inclusion in the cabinet and even his physical survival were rather fortuitous, given the execution, at Karume's order, of four of the other original nine cabinet ministers serving him in the 1960s.

Issa's life story has value on a number of levels. It provides unity and coherence to the abrupt transitions of the last half-century of Zanzibari history. Issa's life, it can be said, has come full circle in many of the same ways as his island society. His life reveals how socialism enjoyed allure in a colonial society and came to influence a revolution of have-nots. His story illustrates how socialism was closely associated with the youthful years of a post–World War II generation from across the islands' racial spectrum, endowed with the unique privilege of imagining a new future. The worldview of Issa and his like-minded contemporaries was more expansive than that of their elders and more dismissive of the familiar than the exotic. It was nurtured by the stories and experiences of friends who seized opportunities to see the world, of which Issa may be regarded as exemplary. Setting out at the age of eighteen, he spent two years as a seaman and stowaway, spending months in Calcutta, Cape Town, and Vancouver. Arriving in London, he assimilated into the circles of East African workers and students in the city but ultimately gravitated toward the multiracial but predominantly white society of the British Communist Party. There he gained access to a world of secular intellectuals thousands of miles away from the colonial and qur'anic schools of his youth. He studied political economy and absorbed the vocabulary, class taxonomies, and views of world history espoused by his socialist mentors. He attended the Moscow Youth Festival of 1957 at his own expense and then returned to Zanzibar and took up full-time work for the Zanzibar Nationalist Party (ZNP).

As his party's representative overseas, Issa obtained and distributed hundreds of scholarships to Eastern Bloc colleges and universities, intent on influencing a rising generation of nationalists. In doing so, he and a few others literally put Zanzibar on the socialist map of the world. In their time abroad, Zanzibaris reflected on island history and came to believe they understood its essential injustices, contradictions, and medievalisms. They learned to regard themselves as a cosmopolitan elite with access to a ready-made template to erase all the ills of island society. They adopted a general historical sense that socialism had and would continue to be adopted by the planet's most progressive nations. They began their analysis of island history not from the moment Arabs first civilized or enslaved Africans, but from an imaginary future when Zanzibar would fully realize its capacities for development. They sought to convince others that Zanzibar could become something completely different and better by radically departing from centuries of its own historical evolution. Issa and his comrades adopted an imported future that forced their secession from the ZNP and compelled their support for a revolution they sought and failed to control.

Issa's story, then, provides intellectual context to the revolution. Issa's stated intent is, in fact, to suggest that he and his comrades were a vanguard responsible for nearly all that was enlightened about the revolution and that had they been able to influence leaders like Karume to genuinely follow socialism, the revolution would have succeeded. In this respect, Issa echoes his life-long associate, A. M. Babu, who claimed the comrades intervened to broaden "the objectives of the uprising from a narrow, lumpen, anti-Arab, anti-privilege, anti-this and anti-that perspective into a serious social revolution with far-reaching political, social and economic objectives."[23] Given time and influence, the comrades could have fully developed the nation's productive forces. They were thwarted, however, by "novices" who ruled the islands "with the caution of a bull in a china shop" and who relegated Zanzibar to "permanent stagnation."[24] Zanzibar, once "a brilliant revolutionary star of Africa, was henceforth to be reduced to one of the worst bungling and tyrannical petty-bourgeois despotisms in Africa."[25]

Issa endorses selected aspects of the revolution and exonerates himself from others. His narrative is at times a confession, a polemic, and a dispassionate account of revolutionary events. He distances himself from the racial politics espoused by the regime he served, yet he helped introduce socialist purge categories like "capitalists" that served as popular labels for Arabs and Asians. As a cabinet minister for eight years, Issa enforced a quota system that ended Asian and Arab domination of secondary education. He nationalized Arab and Asian properties in Zanzibar Town and established youth-labor camps in the countryside. Though one of the most controversial personalities the revolution ever produced, Issa makes no apologies. He sees himself as the wise and incorruptible civil servant, trying to build the nation, yet continually undermined by the public's "unscientific" habits and worldviews.

In this sense, he represents a generation of officials whose ideas of revolution were deeply embedded in their ambivalent views toward island society. If Zanzibar wasn't exactly "the laziest place on earth,"[26] as one visiting Western journalist put it in 1962, it was a culture in need of reform according to socialist precepts. Specimens of what Frantz Fanon referred to as "underdeveloped humanity,"[27] Zanzibaris needed to renounce "the gentle life" for a heavy dose of revolutionary discipline. Like British colonials, the comrades wanted to instill the work habits of industrialized society, yet the "crooked timber" of humanity could not always be made to conform to the socialist ideal.

The discipline that Issa preached in public did not always extend to his private life, as his story abundantly reveals. He moved in a world of hotel lobbies, nightclubs, and international conferences. As a minister, he enjoyed a relatively lavish salary, land in the countryside, a seaside villa, servants, and mistresses. Rather scandalously, he married an English woman without revolutionary convictions, who gave him four children. While he survived and even benefited from the revolution, Issa became increasingly disillusioned with Karume's regime, which either failed in its nation-building imperative or was simply too cruel and capricious.

Eventually, the wrath of the regime came down on Issa's head. His arrest, torture, and death sentence following Karume's assassination in 1972 provoked considerable reflection on his part. While in prison, he read the Qur'an three times and reembraced Islamic beliefs; and upon his release, he devoted himself to reconstructing his life through trade and entrepreneurship, rather than politics. In the 1980s, he thoroughly accommodated himself to the realities of a new world order. Don Petterson, former U.S. ambassador to Tanzania, remarked in his memoirs that "in 1964, there was no more zealous Marxist in the whole of Zanzibar [than Issa]."[28] Yet at a reception held in 1987, Issa "showed up wearing a three-piece suit and presented me with his business card," his appearance suggestive of the new "entrepreneurial spirit" in the islands.[29] This spirit has ever since been dedicated to turning Zanzibar into a place for fun and relaxation more than for work: with Italian financing, Issa opened Zanzibar's first beach resort hotel.

Today, Issa exudes almost equal amounts of pride for his part in the development of tourism and for his role in constructing socialism in the 1960s. Instead of touring the island with Che Guevara, ticking off for his visitor visual signs of Zanzibar's revolutionary development, the intent is now to obscure from the gaze of hotel guests anything that is industrial or not quaint. Yet he still retains more than a nostalgic belief in socialism; this may be witnessed, as I have seen, when he sings revolutionary songs in Spanish, Russian, and Chinese to his slightly disoriented Italian hotel staff. In 1996, he went on a pilgrimage to Mecca and then made another to Cuba, to attend a socialist youth festival. When interviewed by a Cuban television crew about his memories of Che, he wept uncontrollably, until the crew was forced to end the interview. Issa would probably say, quoting Mao, these are all "non-antagonistic contradictions;" and in a way, he is right. The historic appeal of socialism in Zanzibar, as in Ethiopia, may be attributed to the power of "a story of how a weak and backward collection of nationalities, located outside of Western Europe, attained unity, wealth, and international respect: the allegory of the Russian and, later, the Chinese, revolution."[30] Yet socialism also responded to universal desires for grandeur and destiny. An Argentine journalist writing about the Zanzibari Revolution in 1965 claimed it offered the latest evidence that revolution was changing humanity: "The armed struggle breaks up the old routine life of the countryside and villages, excites, exalts. . . . Life acquires a sense, a transcendence, an object."[31] Issa's life and exploits should at least partially be understood through his pursuit of such transcendence on both a personal and a communal basis. If Issa can freely recollect episodes from his past, without regret or conscious irony, events that are scandalous by local standards, it is perhaps because the God he came to accept in midlife is the kind of nation-building god that is sympathetic or forgiving of such pursuits. If there is anything clear about his memoir, it is that the eye of Issa's memory is turned toward both the past and the prospect of a future judgment. Having escaped the worst punishments of man, he is preparing to meet a socialist-minded deity.

SEIF SHARIF HAMAD

If Issa's account is one of complexity and contradiction, reflective of the kaleidoscope of values embraced by residents of cosmopolitan Zanzibar Town, the life story of Seif Sharif Hamad suggests a more undeviating course, adopted by one who never found any ideology or belief system more compelling than the rural Islam of his youth. Hamad has not sought to transform the conservative countryside of his youth through values at least partially adopted from overseas; he has asserted himself as a defender of that society from what he considers a harmful revolution instituted by outsiders. If Hamad has spent much of his adult life as a counterrevolutionary, he has been motivated to do so largely as a result of his satisfaction, so apparent in his memoir, with the Zanzibar of his youth.

From a family in the island of Pemba that in colonial times produced a series of landowners, schoolteachers, and civil servants, Hamad was a rural notable years before he entered politics. A product of a political culture in the islands that accommodated itself to British colonialism, Hamad sometimes comes across in his account as extraordinarily pragmatic, even devoid of ideology. And yet, as Abdellah Hammoudi reminds us, such an impression is only accurate if the concept of ideology "is restricted to systems of social and political ideas engendered by the European humanist revolution. . . . Let it not be forgotten that Islam provides the faithful with a theory of the ideal society and its economic and political structure" that is acted out in "Muslim daily life." Ideology "is thus not a coherent system of ideas and concepts, but rather a concrete set of comportments [prayer, almsgiving, fasting, etc.] which the faithful display as rallying signs."[32]

Yet Hamad's pragmatism does have an analogue in European humanism. Hamad asserts an Islamic social vision that overlaps and associates with village notions of honorable behavior and global discourses of human rights, all of which he feels were promoted or protected by the colonial state more than by the governments that followed. Hamad's family prospered under British rule, and as a youth, he achieved distinction within the meritocratic culture of colonial boarding schools. In such favorable circumstances, Hamad looked forward to following his father into the civil service. His initial willingness in 1964 to allow the new regime to prove itself soon ended, however. Denied government permission to attend university overseas, he was posted as a teacher to a country boarding school in Pemba, where like most Pembans he became thoroughly disenchanted with the revolution. Hamad's account of conditions in Pemba in the 1960s may explain better than any other printed source the genesis of postcolonial discontent in Pemba, including the rationing, constant surveillance, and punitive punishments that broke his father's health and forced many of his close friends into exile.

Hamad's account also illuminates the thaw experienced in Zanzibari society after Karume's death in 1972. A less suspicious president, Aboud Jumbe, adopted a more inclusive attitude toward Pembans and educated people in general and gradually dismantled much of the islands' coercive security apparatus. Jumbe allowed Hamad to attend the University of Dar es Salaam, where the young man was unimpressed by the socialist views espoused by his lecturers, both Tanzanian and expatriate, including the famous Walter Rodney. Hamad read widely, excelled academically, and continued to embrace pragmatism and reform. In 1977, Jumbe appointed him minister of education, despite his Pemban origins and heterodox views. Hamad was a leading light of a new educated elite—cultivated by Jumbe—responsible for "introducing a modicum of rationality in the government."[33] In a complicated and controversial series of events, Hamad soon emerged as the ringleader of a circle of reformers who outmaneuvered the revolutionary old guard in the CCM and forced Jumbe's resignation in 1984. The new president, Ali Hassan Mwinyi, appointed Hamad chief minister, and the two pushed a reformist agenda: liberalizing trade, initiating a new, more liberal constitution, and abolishing Karume's system of People's Courts.

Despite the popularity of these measures, the pendulum then swung against the reformers: in 1988, CCM's old guard managed to oust Hamad as chief minister, and the next year he was arrested for sedition. Hamad's political exile provided the latent popular opposition in the islands with its most potent leader. By 1992, he was out of prison and, in a new era of multipartyism, serving as the spiritual leader and organizational genius of the Civic United Front. Since then, Hamad has campaigned for the Zanzibari presidency three times—in 1995, 2000, and 2005—and served as CUF's secretary general for over a decade. The issues and personal conflicts that now separate CUF and CCM in Zanzibar stem from the disputes of the 1980s between reformist and old-guard politicians. The rhetoric has become more heated, however, as the stakes have risen and as the opposition has aired a generation's worth of grievances.

One contest is over memory. Hamad has disputed the ruling party's version of the past, asserting that Africans participated in the slave trade and that the British did not oppress Africans. Most important, according to Hamad, the revolution was the beginning of Zanzibar's current problems. He claims it did not sweep away a regime of privilege and servitude so much as it did late-colonial institutions that imposed checks on the accumulation of despotic power. He asserts that mainlander politicians have over the decades sought to make the island chain a dependent appendage of the mainland. If, in the 1970s, many Zanzibaris welcomed mainland influence in Zanzibar as a force for moderation, by the 1990s the union had become in their eyes the chief obstacle to Zanzibari desires for democratization and better governance. The use in recent election cycles of Tanzanian security forces to maintain minority CCM governments in power has further encouraged such sentiments.

The solution, according to Hamad, is not secession but rather reform of the Tanzanian union. Yet Hamad also insists, contrary to considerable archival evidence, that the revolution was actually a cleverly disguised invasion from Tanganyika, encouraging islanders to blame their post-colonial problems on Nyerere and the mainland. CCM officials fear that a CUF electoral victory will mean the union's dissolution, since many in CUF support Zanzibari independence. "Losing" Zanzibar to CUF will, in CCM eyes, allow the islands to receive large infusions of aid from the Middle East, which will set Zanzibar adrift from its ties to the African continent. Such fears have provoked national CCM leaders to rig elections repeatedly and intervene militarily in island affairs. In 2001, a violent crackdown resulted in dozens of civilian deaths, an unknown number of rapes and attacks on personal property, and thousands of refugees.[34]

Hamad's account also reveals how Tanzanians continue to be divided over issues of identity. His calls for unity in the islands under the banner of Islam have, in an age of global terrorism, opened his party up to CCM allegations of dangerous sectarianism. Hamad also provokes controversy when he expresses unambiguous pride in Zanzibar's cosmopolitan heritage and in his own Shirazi ethnic identity. He locates Zanzibar as much in the western Indian Ocean world as in Africa. While CCM officials like Mapuri equate nation with race, Hamad's nationalism is based in part on a *celebration* of cosmopolitanism in the islands. Zanzibari nationalism is also generally grounded, for better or worse, on local pride in the regional influence that the islands exercised in the nineteenth century, on cultural chauvinism, and on a shared sense of victimization within the Tanzanian union, a victimization often conceived in sectarian terms.

Hamad's memoir, thus, illustrates some of the most profound tensions in contemporary Tanzania and gives the only account anywhere of how a political party in Tanzania gets off the ground and survives government opposition and internal factionalism to emerge as the nation's largest challenger to CCM rule. It reveals how CCM functions on its highest levels as neither a true despotism nor an open democracy, how it values consensus and moderation yet is capable of authoritarianism when it feels its interests are threatened. Hamad's memoir is a rare window, therefore, into one of the many versions of "African democracy" that have emerged since the 1990s.

Hamad's account, finally, is a fitting counterpart to those of both Issa and Mapuri. For Hamad, Zanzibari history is not so much the story of the struggle of any particular class or race as the story of human virtues and vices in perpetual opposition. It is not so much the story of how so-cial groups employ various strategies by which to protect their interests and assert or maintain their dominance as about how and why individuals, as autonomous moral agents, exercise power to either promote or violate human rights. Hamad's version of human rights is anything but contingent; though informed by the village norms of his youth, it is not parochial. It resists subordination to either the power of a revolutionary agenda or claims for justice by a community that has historically been excluded and enslaved. His version of human rights is guided instead by the view that Islam teaches a set of ethical standards that apply to politics: in his account, Hamad repeatedly refers to the alleged deceit, folly, and foul play of his rivals—and their theft of elections—as violations of a community's trust and as offensive to God.

One of Hamad's arguments against the revolution is that it provided a language and view of history through which men could and did set aside Islamic ethical standards, not to mention codes of human rights; when African nationalists view politics as a "racial war of nerves," they obscure any ethical component of elite decision making. For Hamad, the only way for islanders to move forward from their traumatic memories of the past and to end the divisive politics of race is to remember and commonly embrace Islamic sensibilities that speak to the worthiness of an individual—and a community—more than do labels of race, ethnicity, or class. In this way, Hamad employs a language of virtues and vices, confident of its explanatory power. He remembers his life story as a mission to convince leaders to apply Islamic notions of decency and civility to political institutions derived largely from Western experience. Hamad's memoir, thus, illustrates how democracy and human rights can be strengthened rather than weakened by appeals to Islam and how Islam can be employed to realize the European humanist revolution better than some of its ideological descendants.

COSMOPOLITANISM

A guidebook published by Zanzibar's colonial government in 1931 noted, "The population of the Protectorate (235,428) is one of the most cosmopolitan in the world and there are few races of which representatives may not be found in the two islands."[35] For over a millennium prior to the 1930s, Zanzibar figured as a small part of a vast Indian Ocean world of trade, monsoons, and Islam that had fostered a nearly uninterrupted flow of goods and people across the sea and at least three continents. This world was multicultural and multilingual; it produced a number of diasporas and a patchwork of ethnic enclaves in islands and port cities along its ocean rim. Along the coast of East Africa, Arab and Persian merchants and settlers gradually assimilated into local Swahili-speaking society, which, though predominantly African in ancestry, was unique from societies of the interior due to its reception of peoples, ideas, and commodities from overseas. Michael Pearson expressed well the current scholarly consensus: "inland people" "moved to the coast, and there were subject to more foreign influences" than those "who remained inland."[36] If anything was distinct about Swahili coastal towns, it was their cosmopolitanism.

The islands of Zanzibar were, until the beginning of the nineteenth century, a relatively insignificant portion of this Swahili-speaking chain of settlements. In the next few decades, however, the islands were transformed when an Arab dynasty of merchant princes from Oman decided to make Zanzibar Town, which until then was little more than a fishing village, the capital of a sultanate that exercised political hegemony over the Swahili towns of the coast, as well as commercial dominance over much of the East African interior extending to the Great Lakes. Through trade in slaves, spices, and ivory, Zanzibar Town became the largest and most powerful metropolis of the region. The enormous influx of African, Arab, and Asian migrants, whether voluntary or involuntary, swamped Zanzibar's indigenous population, some of whom lost their lands during the Arab conquest. Zanzibar Town became East Africa's leading trading emporium, and the islands led the world in the production of cloves, a tree crop grown for the most part on Arab-owned plantations sustained by African slave labor and South Asian credit.[37] The new wealth of the era supported the consumption of the products and adoption of the cultural fashions of the Indian Ocean world.

British colonialism brought the abolition of slavery starting in the 1890s but not the eradication of inequalities. Africans commonly remained as squatters on Arab-owned plantations or moved to villages on the margins of plantation society where they engaged in fishing and subsistence farming. Many Zanzibaris experienced, on a very personal level, the close correspondence between identity and access to wealth, status, and opportunity in the islands. The British accepted a social hierarchy in which the different economic roles performed by Zanzibar's various communities were perceived to be natural and even complementary since, colonial officials maintained, each existed in various stages of enlightenment and civilization.

It is easy, however, to overstate such divisions within colonial Zanzibari society. Allegiance to Islam was overwhelming, creating something of a spiritual brotherhood. There were large numbers of poor Arabs and South Asians, as well as Africans who owned considerable numbers of clove trees. Each of the communities also experienced its own sharp divisions; South Asians, for example, were Hindu, Sikh, Parsee, or members of semiexclusive Muslim sects such as the Ismaili and Bohora communities. Africans were divided by ethnic identity. Former slaves in both Unguja and Pemba sought inclusion in island society by acquiring land and by adopting the dress and manners of wealthier islanders. They sometimes adopted ethnic markers, such as Swahili, Hadimu, and Shirazi, which obscured their slave origins and identified them as free and established members of coastal society; such markers also distinguished them from more recent African migrant workers from the mainland.[38] Zanzibar's two principal islands, Unguja and Pemba, were also remarkably dissimilar: communal relations were more harmonious in Pemba than in Unguja. In Pemba, longstanding cultural and economic ties, along with high levels of intermarriage, tended to diminish the importance of racial or ethnic differences, whereas, on Unguja, African grievances toward Arabs over land and labor were especially acute. As a result, Africans in Unguja were more willing than those in Pemba to transcend their ethnic differences in order to oppose Arab political objectives.

Times, furthermore, were changing. The long-term trend in both islands was for Africans to improve their position gradually in the agricultural sector relative to Arabs, who commonly mortgaged their plantations to South Asian creditors, lived in continual debt, and were increasingly "peasantised."[39] The gains made by African small landholders were not matched, however, by sizable gains in either education or employment in the colonial administration. By the 1950s, Arabs and South Asians, aside from a few hundred British expatriates, dominated the civil service; and in the increasingly important sphere of Western education, Africans were dramatically underrepresented. If colonial schools were the means by which many Africans sought to access the knowledge, skills, and positions of more urbanized and cosmopolitan communities, progress was slow and a matter of frustration.

Empires by their nature encourage cosmopolitanism, and the islands continued to receive migrants throughout the colonial era from around the Indian Ocean rim: mainlander Africans, Arabs, Goans, and Comorians. Outside of Zanzibar Town, the British didn't undertake any revolutionary schemes, satisfied for the most part to collect taxes, enforce the law, invest in public works, and manage the clove industry. Rural life was often slow and isolated. Life for town residents, however, was often a cosmopolitan feast of the senses: cafes offered African, Arabic, Indian, and Chinese dishes, and cinemas packed in audiences nightly to see everything from American Westerns to Egyptian dramas and Indian musicals. Congolese music competed with calypso, jazz, Latin bands, *taarab*, Bing Crosby, and rock and roll. Shops displayed imported and locally made items, enticing not only to islanders but to the increasing number of day tourists deposited on the streets by passing cruise liners. Over a dozen newspapers appeared in Swahili, Arabic, English, and Gujarati, and they reported on the development of nationalist movements in India and other imperial outposts. Under local pressure and in order not to fall behind the pace set by other territories, administrators in Zanzibar initiated a series of constitutional reforms that, within a few short years, extended the franchise and the principle of "one person, one vote" throughout adult island society. In doing so, the British committed themselves to a course of democratic development that challenged the privileges of Zanzibar's minority communities.

NATIONALISM

In the nationalist era, the British role was overwhelmingly one of referee in an increasingly antagonistic dispute over the colonial inheritance. Although nationalists of all varieties have criticized, both then and now, the British for engaging in "divide-and-rule" tactics, it was always in British perceived interest to reduce and not exacerbate communal tensions.[40] The British wanted to avoid a costly and embarrassing outbreak of violence within the islands. They wished to hand power over to a party that represented a voting majority, espoused "moderate" politics, and rejected communism. If the British ever manipulated their own rules to suit their own interests, it was not to undermine either of the nationalist parties per se but to eliminate what they regarded as the communist virus in the islands.[41] They did not play favorites to such an extent as to affect the outcome of any of the elections preceding independence, despite allegations from all sides to the contrary.

The British did, however, sanction a very public and acrimonious debate about the nature of Zanzibari society and its cosmopolitan heritage, which revived old wounds, fears, and hatreds. Zanzibaris disputed a series of interrelated questions: Are the islands outposts of the mainland, extensions of East Africa, and is Zanzibar largely an African cultural space? Or are the islands to be regarded as part of a multicultural Indian Ocean world, with allegiance to Islam being one of its primary distinguishing features? Who should and should not be considered a true Zanzibari? Who are natives, and who are alien intruders? In reviewing the past, could islanders claim the creation of a culture of peace, tolerance, and civilized living or instead a long history of cruelty, slavery, and exploitation? Would an independent Zanzibar see further inequality and an inevitable clash of communities, or could islanders work together toward an end, like development, considered by all to be good?

Founded in 1955, the Zanzibar Nationalist Party (ZNP) attracted the support of nearly all members of minority communities in the islands, as well as a substantial number of Shirazi, who identify themselves as Zanzibar's indigenous population. Shirazi identity, however, was and remains highly controversial since its widespread usage began only in the 1930s and because the percentage of islanders who identified themselves as Shirazi by the 1960s dwarfed the actual indigenous population. Many Africans claimed Shirazi identity to obscure their slave ancestry, to mark their status as landowners, or to gain access to World War II rations distributed by the colonial state along ethnic lines.[42] To complicate matters further, the Shirazi usually regard themselves as primarily of Persian ancestry. If it is not always clear what the label represents in a positive sense, its negative claims are more consistent: Shirazi are neither Arabs nor "mainlanders"—recent labor migrants from the African mainland. As indigenous Zanzibaris, Shirazi claim exemption from the stigma of slave ancestry; those who claim Persian ancestry do not, furthermore, claim racial kinship with Africans and regard their unique ethnicity as being more significant than their African birth.[43] The circumstances of Shirazi identity render it extremely difficult for scholars to even say if the term represents *racial* or *ethnic* tensions in island society.

The ambiguous nature of Shirazi identity lay at the very center of Zanzibari politics prior to the revolution, since, according to the 1948 census, 56 percent of islanders identified themselves as Shirazi; 21 percent, mainlander; 19 percent, Arab; and 4 percent, South Asian.[44] Shirazi did not vote as a bloc; they split over which community—Arabs or mainlanders—presented a more natural ally. The ZNP sought to attract Shirazi voters through an appeal to Zanzibari nationalism that promoted the islands' cosmopolitan and largely Muslim heritage as a positive good and differentiated "native" Zanzibaris from allegedly less civilized mainlanders. The party preached multiracialism, while paradoxically denigrating mainlanders as uncouth newcomers intent on burying Zanzibar in a federation with much larger East African nations, none of which possessed a Muslim majority. Through an alliance with the smaller Zanzibar and Pemba People's Party (ZPPP), based among Pemba Shirazi, the ZNP emerged by 1961 as a serious contender.[45]

The Afro-Shirazi Party (ASP), as the name suggests, was established as an alliance of mainlander and Shirazi voters who found common cause in a struggle against the ZNP, which they painted as more of a threat to their interests than the colonial power. The ASP regarded the ZNP as a vehicle for Arabs to defend their privileges and subjugate the African majority. Convinced their constituents would never receive fair treatment, ASP leaders wished to impose their own settlement that would protect their supporters from future exploitation. The politics of race the ASP espoused was based on the premise that cosmopolitanism had not produced wealth and harmony but a deceptive facade for cultural chauvinism and racial injustice. In a fictionalized account of the revolution, Gurnah's protagonist recalls:

> We liked to think of ourselves as a moderate and mild people. Arab African Indian Comorian: we lived alongside each other, quarreled and sometimes intermarried. . . . In reality, we were nowhere near *we*, but us in our separate yards, locked in our historical ghettoes, self-forgiving and seething with intolerances, with racisms, and with resentments. And politics brought all that into the open. . . . So when the time came to begin thinking of ourselves in the future, we persuaded ourselves that the objects of this abuse [Africans] had not noticed what had happened to them, or had forgiven and would now like to embrace a new rhetoric of unity and nationalism. To enter into a mature compromise in everyone's interest. But they didn't. They wanted to glory in grievance, in promises of vengeance, in their past oppression, in their present poverty and in the nobility of their darker skins.[46]

The ASP won little support among minority communities but received huge voting majorities in rural Unguja, as well as in Zanzibar Town's largely African neighborhoods. By rejecting much of the islands' cosmopolitan heritage as a disaster for African interests, the party lost access to the skills and international ties of the most educated elements of Zanzibari society, the reality of which African nationalists were keenly aware. Front and center in the ASP campaign against the "Arab" ZNP was Abeid Karume, formerly a professional seaman of limited education, who knew how to move a crowd. Salmin Amour noted that Karume was chosen as president of the ASP because, through his travels as a seaman, "he was more conversant with the overseas world" and so "could give better guidance to the masses of Zanzibar."[47] Through his travels, he could see "the hard lives of so many innocent masses, in a number of countries."[48]

After election riots in June 1961 claimed more than sixty lives, nearly all Arabs, the British imposed a state of emergency. Michael Lofchie, who conducted doctoral research in Zanzibar from 1962 to 1963, described the manner in which politics came to pervade nearly every aspect of island life. All social relations, he noted,

> became a battleground in which every individual act was invested with highly symbolic significance as a demonstration of party membership and solidarity. Performance of the most routine daily tasks—marketing, working and commuting, for example—was viewed as an integral facet of the national political struggle. . . . By early 1958 no dimension of social behavior remained politically neutral. Even private quarrels and disputes which had long preceded the formation of modern political parties were absorbed into the pattern of partisan conflict.[49]

In the last elections before independence in 1963, the ASP captured more than 54 percent of the total popular vote, yet lost eighteen of the thirty-one seats contested in the Legislative Council, often by narrow margins. ASP supporters could not help but feel cheated. The only significant setback for the ZNP-ZPPP was the defection of A. M. Babu, for years the ZNP's secretary general and most talented grassroots organizer. Babu and a number of his supporters, such as Ali Sultan Issa, seceded from the ZNP in 1963 to form their own Umma Party, which espoused socialism as its official creed. Instead of looking to Gamel Abdul Nasser for aid and inspiration as had the ZNP or as the ASP to African nationalists like Julius Nyerere, Umma claimed that Mao and Stalin possessed the answers to Zanzibar's underdevelopment and inequality. As the party cut its ties with the "petit-bourgeois" leaders of the ZNP, Umma allied itself with the ASP, whose leaders it had formerly ridiculed as members of the unprogressive "lumpen-proletariat." Umma represented a small but influential and well-trained cosmopolitan cohort, composed overwhelmingly of young men from Zanzibar Town, many of whom had visited or undertaken studies in Britain, eastern Europe, China, Egypt, and Cuba.[50]

Only one month after Zanzibar celebrated its independence from the British in December 1963 and colonial army units withdrew, an insurrectionary force organized by the ASP Youth League launched an attack on the night of January 11–12, 1964, on two police arsenals located on the outskirts of Zanzibar Town. The rebels took the police by surprise, even though Karume, on the day prior, had lost his nerve, warned the ZNP government of imminent violence that night, and then fled to the mainland.[51] The rebels quickly gained control of nearly all the government's weapons supply; from the morning of January 12, Umma members were active in the revolution. Within a couple of days, the sultan fled on his yacht, and the prime minister and his cabinet surrendered. Within a couple of weeks, the rebels exported the revolution to Pemba. What might have initially been a fairly bloodless seizure of power soon became a fairly systematic campaign to round up, detain, and punish supporters of the ZNP-ZPPP regime, in which Arabs and South Asians, regardless of class, were singled out for the harshest forms of vengeance: plunder, rape, execution, ritual humiliation, and exile. Zanzibari historian Abdul Sheriff describes the net effect of weeks of violence in 1964 as "genocidal in proportions."[52]

While the revolutionaries had overthrown an elected government, they were in no way united as to how to proceed next. Few members of the hastily erected Revolutionary Council possessed, like Babu, both political skill and radical nation-building ideas; most commanded deference, however, as a result of their leading roles in the uprising and supported Karume as chief, since he still commanded mass popularity. Babu urgently advised Karume to adopt socialist policies and lean on advisors from East Germany, China, and the USSR; he gave the impression to some he wanted to supplant the older man. If so, Babu was outmaneuvered; in a few short months, Karume removed from the islands a series of individuals whom he regarded as untrustworthy, including Babu and a number of his Umma colleagues.[53] The union agreement between Tanganyika and Zanzibar in April 1964 meant, for Karume, little actual interference from the mainland and a strengthened position from which to assert his primacy and purge his political rivals.

Yet Umma's influence continued, at least indirectly; an influx of socialist foreign advisors made Zanzibar into something of a regional showcase for revolution. The CIA reported in September 1964 that "Babu and his colleagues have brought Zanzibar further under Communist influence, or at least for the time being, than has been the case in any other African country."[54] British administrators, who had for decades introduced ideas and ruling practices from other imperial territories as far away as Guyana and Malaya, were replaced by hundreds of East German, Chinese, and Soviet teachers, doctors, and technicians. Karume saw in their various proposals the means by which to fulfill African nationalist desires for racial development. Such development would be achieved through the establishment of multistoried apartment complexes, factories, and youth labor camps, paid for through the imposition of socialist austerity measures, such as forced labor and food rations. Socialist nations continued for two decades as sources of foreign aid and as patient tutors in the techniques of authoritarian rule. Socialist vocabulary expressed old ideas in new words; new terms gave old antagonisms—and the revolution itself—a new legitimacy by including them in a global conflict against imperialism and injustice.

For most Zanzibaris, regardless of ethnicity, the initial violence in 1964 affected them less than the series of policies that followed. They experienced the revolution less as a sudden outbreak of violence than as more than a decade of confiscations, shortages, surveillance, and fear. Ali Mazrui observed in 1972 that the revolution caused "a devastation of the polity, a dislocation of the economy of the country, a general sense of insecurity in the population, a lack of sense of direction in national policies, and a rapid erosion of human values."[55] The revolution swept away much of the substance of the legal, bureaucratic order of the colonial state and inverted a social pyramid present in the islands since the Omani colonization. Karume's regime was dedicated to redistribution and the idea of "the first shall be last, and the last shall be first." Most minorities left who could possibly afford to do so and who had survived the initial bloodletting. As, in Nyerere's eyes, the "new sultan"[56] of Zanzibar, Karume sat atop an extensive, East German–trained security apparatus and was able to rule by personal decree.

For supporters of the revolution, however, these were years, despite the hardships, when the regime extended access to Africans in education, health care, land, and housing. For nearly all Zanzibaris, and for better or worse, these were years of discipline; in contrast to the routine corruption of more recent times, civil servants were afraid to steal. In an era of "Cultural Revolution," the ubiquitous security apparatus routinely punished displays of "decadence" or "idleness," such as wearing miniskirts or bell-bottom pants or avoiding political meetings or forced-labor assignments. Cultural forms like *ngoma* dances were designated as indigenous and promoted, while others such as *taarab*, Western music, and cinema were repressed. Tens of thousands of Zanzibaris went to labor camps and learned to march, drill, and handle guns like good soldiers. While Zanzibaris experienced social and commercial isolation, the islands for a brief moment captured the imagination of a generation of Cold War warriors. While largely cut off from its connections within the Indian Ocean world, the archipelago achieved international recognition as a link in a global chain of socialist revolutions and received a series of esteemed guests such as Malcolm X, Che Guevara, and Chou En Lai. With the merger of the ASP and the Tanganyika African National Union (TANU) to form the CCM in 1977, islanders ceded control over the selection of their presidents to the mainland.

Living conditions bottomed out in the early 1970s and again in the 1980s due to serious agricultural decline and government neglect and mismanagement. Clove harvests of the early 1980s were on average less than half the size of those of the early 1960s.[57] The islands produced less wealth than they did under the British and, in the 1980s, were increasingly dependent on Western aid and remittances from Zanzibaris living abroad, most of them exiles from the revolution. In 1994, per capita income was reportedly a mere $125, less than a quarter the continental average.[58] When and if the ruling party looked for solutions to years of stagnation and deteriorating infrastructure, it did so through rolling back its former policies and obtaining aid from overseas. The boom in clove prices had come to an end, there was little left to nationalize, and the state's efforts to promote industrialization had failed. Increasing corruption, years of food rationings, and constant shortages desensitized citizens to calls to sacrifice to build the nation.

Reformist policies of the 1980s—many of them instituted during Hamad's time as chief minister—slowed the outward flow of talented individuals. The state relinquished control of commerce and imports, . ending shortages and stimulating economic activity, at least in Zanzibar Town and areas most affected by the growth in tourism. If conditions have improved since then, they have as a result of the state's new willingness to accommodate foreign and private investment. The state now accepts the accumulation of personal wealth—beyond a few politically embedded extended families—as a legitimate motivation. More capital and more commodities are in circulation now that Zanzibar is no longer a place where it is nearly impossible to do business. Infrastructure has improved, yet the islands have not kept pace with the mainland's relatively rapid economic growth since the mid-1990s. Pemba in particular continues to languish.

Under Western pressure, Zanzibar adopted multiparty politics in the 1990s. Some, especially in the CCM, assert that current political rivalries are identical to those of the days before the revolution, yet the correspondence between wealth and race is no longer nearly so obvious. Zanzibar's minority communities in no sense exercise their former dominance over the islands' resources and commercial life. If African nationalists in the islands once earned credibility for their advocacy of the cause of the downtrodden, it is more difficult for them to do so now.

Poverty in the islands, where it is most severe in rural areas of Pemba, for example, does not exist due to racial exclusion but rather as a result of decades of misrule and the appropriation of that island's clove revenues for investment elsewhere. Pembans claim they are poor because the ruling party continues to punish them for their support of the political opposition. Their marginalization has encouraged the emergence of separate ethnicities for Pemba and Unguja islands; indeed, Zanzibar may be taken as an example of the narrative construction of identity, where allegiance to shared memories of the past and stories of the present promote in each island a sense of collective uniqueness and destiny. For Mapuri and others, the frame of reference continues to be the indignities and inequalities of Arab and British colonialism. It continues to be racial nationalism. Writing after the CCM victory in the 2005 elections, CCM minister Muhammed Seif Khatib exulted that "lovers of peace and stability were overjoyed . . . because we are now assured that the respect and dignity of the black man in Zanzibar will be defended, respected and honoured. *Waswahili* [Africans] will continue to receive equal treatment without being turned into slaves and labour-migrants."[59] And yet for those who support the opposition in Zanzibar, stories of post-colonial injustices have more power than do CCM allegations of Arab guilt and Western guile.

part one

WALK ON TWO LEGS

The Life Story of Ali Sultan Issa

PREFACE

My reason for writing this book is for people who will come after me to understand, because I will not live forever. I have included these stories from my past so they may know what type of a person I am. Each individual has many faces, and I cannot say that I am virtuous and that I have done nothing wrong and only paint myself in positive colors. I do not regret, however, any of the things I have done because, at the time, I did not know they were wrong.

I started in hardship, but I worked very hard and exposed myself to the world. I am a self-made man, with very little assistance from anyone, who came to know all the greatest revolutionary leaders of my generation. And after our revolution here, I served the people as a cabinet minister for eight years.

Perhaps some will learn from my experience, but it will depend on their conditions and environment. I want to bequeath my story to my family and my country; and if anyone from outside is interested in our struggle here in Zanzibar, he or she will have to read my story because I am part of that history. He will understand how our revolution in Zanzibar inspired other countries and why the Americans in all their reports were so disturbed that this country was known as the Cuba of East Africa. Some will benefit from reading my humble contribution, but I am not conceited—I know others will not bother, saying "Who knows Ali Sultan? He's just an old man sitting at home, waiting for his day to come." It is true that I am an old man now and that I have become lazy; but in my heyday, I was not afraid.

I am telling my story as a contribution from all of us Umma comrades, because some have written we did not contribute anything to the revolution, when actually we worked very hard to build Zanzibar. Umma was unique in Zanzibari history because we were a tiny seed, but a very good seed. We comrades planted that seed, and it bore fruit.

In the Umma Party, we espoused a Marxist ideology and were mixed ethnically. We did not commit ourselves to the struggle because of race; but for others, the struggle was about race. To this day, there are some people in

Zanzibar with racial prejudices; we keep fighting against this attitude, but it is a long struggle. Our revolution was also a conflict between the haves and the have-nots, and in history, the contradictions between these two groups have been decided by the barrel of a gun. That is what happened here. A revolution is not a tea party. You are playing with life; you either kill or get killed.

But each country has its own conditions, and we managed here to minimize the time of violence. Our country was small, so our revolution did not take very long. During our time after the revolution when we were implementing our revolutionary policies, I believe we were very successful. We may have made some mistakes. I will not say we were perfect. We killed each other, which was regrettable. But only when we departed from our revolutionary policies did we corrupt the country. That is what happened eventually, and that is what is happening now. If we are not careful, our people's lives will soon become even worse than now, and the dream will be lost. Unfortunately, since the fall of the Soviet Union, the whole world has gone back to capitalism, and now everyone is trying to get rich. Even I am now a petty capitalist. Now I do not belong to any political party; to paraphrase Lord Palmerston, I have no permanent friends and no permanent enemies, only permanent interests.

I believe God has given very few of us here inspiration to be leaders. Either you are born a leader, or you are not. I hope I have not let my people down too much. There is a saying, I believe, in all religions that perfection is the prerogative of God. And there is another saying that to err is human, but to forgive is divine. I believe that, whatever I've done, especially the good things, God inspired me to do.

I buried my uncle the other day. I spoke to him at 5 p.m. and joked with him over the phone, and he was fine. At 7 p.m., I got a call from the hospital that he was dead. I had had a few beers, but immediately I sobered up. The distance between life and death is so thin, like a razor's edge. You may pass somebody in the street, and the next thing you hear he has passed away. Death does not wait when the time comes. As a Muslim, I believe there will be a day of judgment, and all of humanity will be gathered to be judged, each one accordingly. God knows the past and the future, and I will be either forgiven or punished for what I have done in my life.

 **ORIGINS**

I WAS BORN ON MARCH 4, 1932, in the small town of Wete, in Pemba. Pemba and Unguja islands are together known as Zanzibar. Because the islands are so near the African mainland, there is no doubt that Africans were the earliest settlers in Zanzibar. They lived in small villages as farmers and fishermen. They were mainly Muslims; they called themselves Shirazi and claimed at least partial descent from settlers who came from Persia. They call themselves Shirazi also to differentiate themselves from Africans who came to the islands in the last few generations as either slaves or migrant workers. The Shirazi regard themselves, proudly, as having never been enslaved.

The people of Zanzibar have always been known for their seamanship. Every year dhows from India, Persia, and Arabia followed the winds to come to and go from Zanzibar. For centuries, these travelers came to stay in the islands for almost six months, from December until June, when the monsoon winds would change.

In Oman in the nineteenth century, there was constant feuding, so Sultan Seyyid Said [1806–56] moved his court to Zanzibar Town. The sultans were quite powerful in the nineteenth century, and many Africans came to the islands to live, either as free men and women or as slaves. Most of the influx came from close by on the mainland, but we had slaves come from as far as the Congo because the influence of the sultans went right up to the lakes. There was once a saying, "When one plays the pipes in Zanzibar, they dance on the lakes."

Seyyid Said was responsible for bringing the clove tree to Zanzibar. We were lucky the soil here was so good for cloves. Even today our cloves are the best in the world. Seyyid Said gave land to different Arab clans; my clan, the Ismail clan, was given land near Wete in Pemba. I do not think anyone was living there already; it was still bush, and if a man cleared the bush and planted clove trees, then according to our legal traditions, after five years the land was considered his. That was how my ancestors came over in the 1800s.

The first sultan who really built Zanzibar was Barghash [1870–88] because, for a time, he was exiled from Zanzibar to India, where he was exposed [to other cultures]. He built almost all the palaces here in Zanzibar, like the Beit al-Ajaib, which had the first elevator in East Africa. He was also the first in East Africa to introduce electricity and the railroad, and he gave Zanzibar Town a piped supply of clean water. My great grandfather was one of his principal advisors. In those days, Zanzibar Town was the principal town of East Africa.

It was during the period of Barghash's rule that, due to British pressure, the slave trade was abolished—not slavery itself, because we still had that in one form or another until it was abolished during the colonial period. Did slavery leave a lasting legacy in our society? No, I do not think so; it ended when it ended. I have even known some ex-slaves who still worked in their former master's household, instead of leaving as they were permitted. My uncle inherited an ex-slave from the household of my grandfather. By the time I was born, all the family slaves were gone, apart from this one. He was employed to do errands, to slaughter a goat, to chop firewood, or to bring water. He had a room in the house, ate the same food as the rest of us, and was paid. He stayed with my uncle until the end of his life, saying he would not leave the house until either he or my uncle died, whichever came first.

Zanzibar was a very tolerant society; before politics came to the islands in the 1950s, we lived like brothers without much ethnic tension. The society was also tolerant when it came to religion. Islam was predominant, but we did not discriminate against Hindus, Parsees, Buddhists, or Christians. That is the reason I can say even now that we are not fanatics or zealots; we are not ready to fight a jihad and to go to heaven.

Zanzibar was a feudal society up to the early twentieth century, and then boof! A lot of Arabs lost their property to Indians because the Indians were the merchant class, created by the British, who gave the Indians credit. The Arabs came to the Indians and bought things on credit until the harvest season came; sometimes the harvests failed and their property was confiscated. The majority of Arabs were, in fact, rather poor. Very few were rich. Many from Yemen worked as water carriers, called *maarass* in Swahili. They would collect water at a communal tap and carry it to people's homes, most of which lacked running water in those days.

In Pemba, there was more land for Africans to own. There was also a lot of intermarriage between Africans and Arabs, so many people in

Pemba considered themselves arabized. Pemba also had fewer migrant workers come from the African mainland; those who came on labor contracts during the clove harvest season left when the picking was done. Pemba was more homogeneous than Unguja, and more traditional. Pemba got electricity for the first time only in 1960.

Migrants from the mainland mostly went to Unguja, but the fertile land was concentrated in the west and difficult for them to acquire, forcing them to work as laborers and squatters. The Arab landlords lived in town and sometimes sent their children or their cronies to supervise the harvest. They wanted their lands weeded, though, and would allow Africans to live on their plantations and cultivate cassava and bananas and thereby keep the bush cleared. The squatters kept what they produced in their gardens. They did not pay rent but periodically sent gifts to the landowner, like some bananas or breadfruit. That was the system, and it was bound to break down. It lasted until the revolution in 1964.

As far as my own ancestry is concerned, I was not asked into which family or womb I wanted to be born; nor was I consulted about my race. My maternal side originally came from Yemen, and my paternal side from Oman. Both sides of my family, however, were mixed. My great grandmother on my father's side was a Zaramo from Tanganyika, and my grandmother from my maternal side was from the Nandi tribe in Kenya. Since the slave trade, the society here in Zanzibar has been very mixed. Even our sultans were very dark; very few were of pure Arab stock. My family, I can say, was African Arab. We lost the Arabic language and spoke Swahili as our mother tongue.

I was brought up partially by my maternal grandmother, who was very dark. Because of that background, color or race did not influence me at all; I was brought up by my grandmother who was an African, so how could I look down on Africans? I was colorblind and had no problems with Africans. My own people insulted me, but Africans did not, and I lived with Africans on an equal basis. To this day, race means nothing to me, only how you live with your fellow beings.

My maternal grandmother was named Bibi Ruzuna Binti Tamim, and she was once married to Sultan Ali bin Hamoud [1904–11]. He was the first sultan to have been educated outside of Zanzibar, at Harrow in the U.K. My grandmother lived in the palace with him and gave him three children. Then in 1911, the sultan traveled to Europe to attend King George V's coronation in London. When he arrived in Paris, he received a letter from a friend who advised him to abdicate because the

British were going to force him out. If he abdicated, he would get a nice pension, so he did and stayed in Paris until he died.

After my grandmother left the palace, she met my grandfather, named Ali Muhammed Bakashmar al-Abbassy, who was among the first teachers at Zanzibar's first secular school. Later he became Zanzibar's chief *kadhi*, a Muslim judge who decides issues of marriage, divorce, and inheritance. I was very proud of my grandfather. I would greet him, and he would always give me a penny. But he was very strict and very clean; sometimes when I wanted to shake his hand or to kiss it, he would pull his hand away.

On my father's side, my grandfather was named Issa Salim Ali bin Nassor el-Ismaily; he was a respected landowner in Pemba. I never knew him since he died before I was born. I knew only my grandmother who helped raise me. Whenever I went to Pemba, I spent more time with her than with my father. I was very fond of her, and because I was her only grandson, she was very fond of and favored me. I went to her farm and ate fruit all day and talked to her and climbed the mango, tangerine, and orange trees. She would do a little weeding in her cassava garden and chase the monkeys that would come to uproot the cassava with their tails.

Although my father was from a family of landowners, he could not read or write. While he waited for his inheritance, he learned how to drive a car and then became a taxi driver in Zanzibar Town. That is how he met my mother. He had a nickname, *Kibeberu*, meaning a he-goat, because he had a beard and used to stammer. Later, a British district commissioner in Pemba wanted a driver, so he hired my father. The government then appointed my father a district overseer, responsible for all the bridges and secondary, unsurfaced roads on the island; he had a labor force under him. He had an office on the ground floor of a government building and earned about fifteen British pounds a month. This was when our people considered it very respectable to work for the colonial government.

Despite his success, my father was a man of the people. He would joke with the people and swear with them and was very popular. The whole island knew him: he mixed with all classes of people, rich and poor, and whenever a poor person asked for help, he gave it willingly. That is the reason that, when he died, people from throughout the island converged at Wete for his funeral.

My father influenced me; I also joke and swear with people, but not in a bad way. I get my jovial nature from my father's family and my strictness from my mother's side. My mother had a very strong character, very *mkali*, which influenced me a lot. She always fought for her rights; when she wanted something, she got it. She was named Harbuu, which comes from the word for *war* in Arabic, because she was born during World War I.

My mother did not work, never went to school, and could read only a little from the Qur'an. Her first husband was her cousin; her second, my father. I was the first born and then my sister, Dalila. Later, I looked after my other younger brothers and sisters, but Dalila and I were only a year apart, so we grew up together and were very close.

My parents did not stay married very long. I remember Thabit Kombo's telling me the story that, when my mother was eight or nine months pregnant with my sister, she held my father by the throat with one hand, so that his feet dangled in the air. My father pleaded for Kombo to help him, but Kombo just took me, a baby, out of my mother's other hand, to protect me. My mother then held my father up with both hands, demanding a divorce.

After the divorce, my mother took us children to live with her family in Zanzibar Town. My relatives owned two houses just behind the Ijumaa Mosque in Malindi, a heavily Arab neighborhood close to the waterfront, an area of fishermen, sailors, and dock laborers. Malindi, although not the wealthiest or oldest part of town, was proud of its history. But because my mother had frequent arguments with her family, we sometimes had to move elsewhere. Or sometimes we moved when my mother failed to pay the rent. So, I lived all over the capital, in neighborhoods such as Kajificheni, Vuga, Baghani, Mchangani, Mbuyuni, Kikwajuni, and Miembeni. I lived among Africans, Arabs, and Asians, among Muslims, Hindus, and Christians. I have always said a true Zanzibari should be able to speak four languages: Swahili, Arabic, Hindi, and English.

In the 1930s (and even now), however, Zanzibar Town was divided into two main areas, Stone Town and Ng'ambo. The well-to-do people lived in Stone Town, and the less well-off lived in Ng'ambo. Ng'ambo started as a poor man's land on the other side of the creek from Stone Town. That is what *Ng'ambo* means in Swahili, "the other side." Stone Town had stone buildings three and four stories high, but Ng'ambo mostly had ground-level buildings constructed of mud, cement, and thatch. The more prosperous had roofs made of corrugated iron.

Mostly Arabs and Indians lived in Stone Town; very few Africans lived on that side of the creek; they would come for work in the day and return to Ng'ambo in the evenings. Ng'ambo was more ethnically mixed than Stone Town. There were Arabs and Comorians living near the creek, but the further you went into the interior, the more Africans you encountered.

I had to keep moving with my mum when she could not pay the rent. I lived in probably seven or eight different places in Stone Town and about five in Ng'ambo. My mother also remarried several times, so I had a number of stepfathers. These were short marriages: as soon as the husband tried to dominate her, she asked for a divorce. My mother married several men from the mainland, in Dar es Salaam, Tanga, and Mombasa, giving birth to four more children.

My mother caned me for little things, and I feared her because she was huge and strong. Once she sent me to the shop three times to get different things for our dinner. After the third time, I said to her, "Why don't you decide what you need first, so I can get everything in one trip?" She got mad and took a piece of firewood from the fire and hit me on the head, and I bled. She tore off my shirt as a bandage, and she cried over the wound. I laughed and said, "You hit me, and now you cry."

As a young boy, I was rather naughty. I would not be bullied, and despite my small size, I was often chosen as a leader. As children, we played ping-pong, cards, and dominoes. We also went swimming, but sometimes my mother would beat me because she thought I was going to drown. At high tide, we would jump off the waterfront at Forodhani or in front of the old English Club. Cinema was also very popular in those days. We'd go to the Majestic Cinema, the Empire Cinema, and the Sultana Cinema. I saw Bogart, Sinatra, Dorothy Lamour, Ava Gardner, and Elizabeth Taylor. I liked Western films more than Indian films because I could not understand what was happening in the Indian pictures.

I spent most of my years attending primary school in the home of my grandmother in Ng'ambo. She was very strict, tidy, and clean; she would sweep outside the house, and anyone who came, she would chase away. She had the cleanest toilet around, which everyone in the neighborhood knew about. Since she once lived in the sultan's palace, I used to walk and play in the palace, but I also played with the local African boys. I had no established roots and no allegiance to one part of Zanzibar Town or any particular racial community. I was proud of myself and of my family, but not of my race. I did not belong to the school of thought that Arabs had achieved great things in Africa. What had they achieved? Nothing, except the accumulation of wealth for some and poverty for others. Whatever progress was achieved in Zanzibar was the product of historical accident.

Once when I was very young, I dreamt my grandmother took me to Pemba and introduced me to old ladies standing in a vast clearing, all with their earlobes pulled down to their shoulders. This was at Giningi, a place famous in Pemba for where *wachawi* [witches] like to congregate. There, in front of that gathering of *wachawi*, she asked them to protect me from evil for the rest of my life. In the morning, I told her about my dream, and she said "Shhhhhh, don't tell anyone." I was very young, an innocent boy less than seven years old, but since then I have been a survivor.

My friendship with [Abdulrahman Muhammed] Babu began at a very early age. Babu, who became the brains of our political struggle here in Zanzibar, was several years older than I and lived just across the alley from our house in Malindi. He would tease me whenever my family served rice because he could see I liked to eat *ukoko* and *matandu*, which was the rice crust that would collect on the earthen pots after boiling. I liked to dip the rice crust in curry, but Babu would joke with me about that because normally people would not eat the *matandu*; they would just leave it for the servants.

I was seven when World War II started, and food was very scarce since most of it was imported, except cassava and bananas. Ships did not run during the war, so bread and other imported foods were rationed. The British made it compulsory for each family with land to plant some sweet potatoes and cassava, and if the family did not, they were arrested. Around five in the evening, we had our meal, which was our last food until the next day. In the mornings, we had just a cup of tea. I never knew how my mother managed to support us; maybe she received money from her boyfriends. I never asked. I think that is why later I became more sympathetic with the working people, because of that experience of hardship.

It was during the war that racial discrimination became very apparent in Zanzibar. According to the colonial rationing system, the Africans did not receive any imported rice or bread, but the Asians and Arabs got rations of rice and wheat flour of equal quantities. I remember because my mum sent me to the shop with the ration card. Because of this system, I think the British were responsible to a great extent for racial prejudice in Zanzibar. If, when the British came, Arabs were already predominant, they continued Arab dominance for their own ends.

TWO STUDENT DAYS

I ATTENDED JUNIOR SECONDARY school at Dole, a boarding school outside Zanzibar Town. There were about 160 students, roughly 60 percent African and 40 percent Arab. Very few Indians went there because they went to their own schools in town. I was small for my age, but when I was fifteen, the school principal at Dole, Mr. Lang, appointed me prefect. I was the youngest student in the history of the school to be appointed prefect. The teachers worried about my ability to control the other students because of my small size, but I believe Mr. Lang wanted to see if I had leadership abilities. I was placed in charge of dormitory number seven.

Eventually, it was my turn to shout out *"Bismilahi"* [By the name of God] to begin the meal in the cafeteria. When I did so, some of the big boys laughed—they thought it funny that a small guy like me was supposed to lead them in this prayer. So I ordered them all to go outside and stand and wait for five minutes. When they returned, I again said *"Bismilahi,"* and no one laughed. They all repeated after me, and then we ate. I had proved that I would not be pushed around or mocked by anyone, regardless of my size. And the teachers no longer worried about me.

At school, I played football, hockey, and cricket. While in primary school, I considered myself something of an athlete, but in boarding school, I had skin ulcers, which became very septic. We have a certain poisonous grass here; we call it *mpapura pumbu,* which means "testicle thrasher." If it cuts you, and the poison gets in your blood system, then boof! We did not have any antibiotics in those days; penicillin did not come until the 1950s, and it took me almost two years to heal. I was the worst infected of all the students.

At Dole, I was in the choir and learned to recite *qasida* in praise of the Prophet Muhammed. During the Maulidi celebration, there was a competition between different schools, and those who sang well received presents from the Ministry of Education. We performed on the Mnazi Mmoja football ground, in front of the sultan. I also observed the Ramadhan fast. In the afternoons, to kill time, we would go sailing out to Bawe and Changuu islands. We would leave the waterfront after the 3:00 prayer, and by the time we returned, it was almost sundown and time to eat.

Sometimes, though, we boys ate fruit together during the daylight hours, breaking the fast. We hid ourselves because we would not get food in the evening if we were caught. I was naughty, I tell you. My mum sometimes took me as a young boy to my uncle and gave me a tort of brandy or whiskey, whatever was available. Then in 1945, I started drinking on my own, usually coconut palm wine. It was just for the excitement, but that was why I was not being bullied—no one would dare. I was young in age but reckless and no longer a child.

My friends and I would run away from the boarding school around midnight to go to dances and return by the morning prayer at 4:00 a.m. We had no torch, so we moved through the bush risking our lives with all the snakes, to come to Maruhubi to see a seasonal dance called *sum sumia*, which was mostly for gay people. We came to watch and maybe try and seduce a gay chap if he was a nice-looking man. But I did not seduce anyone, of course. If we ran, it would take us about forty-five minutes to get there, and we were able to stay for only about an hour and a half.

Or we went to Dole village, where the girls started dancing about midnight and continued until morning. They performed traditional African dances like *mbwa kachoka*, meaning, "the dog is tired." Men would come and dance in rows facing the girls, hoping to seduce one. In fact, while I was at Dole, my number one pastime was dancing and seducing. I was a young man and virile, and that was the pride of a young man, to have as many girls as possible, to have girlfriends wherever he went. Still, I managed to pass my entrance exams for secondary school.

I first went to the boarding school at Beit el Ras, just north of Zanzibar Town. The British had just opened the school; it brought together different boys from the rural areas, and the discipline was sometimes harsh. The school officials put us to work in the afternoons and on the weekends clearing land for football grounds. We could stay in town only one weekend a month; otherwise, we had to work. But I had already been indulging myself in the town's pleasures and wanted to play. You might say I was a rebel; I did not like harsh discipline, though I came to appreciate it later in life. Without discipline, you cannot organize; you cannot have a political movement without discipline.

After the war, the world was clearly changing. The war made the world smaller; soldiers from Zanzibar serving in the British army went to Burma and Egypt, and when they returned, they would talk about their experiences. Zanzibar was a cosmopolitan place, a seaport that attracted all the ships passing between Cape Town and Aden. As a young man I felt that I was free, that the future was there for me, that the world was open for anyone who dared. I never felt oppressed or inferior in Zanzibar because of the colonial system. I was an Arab, we had an Arab sultan here, and my family had land in Pemba.

My first political ideas did not come until 1949. By that time, Indians and Pakistanis had obtained their freedom from the British, and we had a lot of them here celebrating their independence. We Zanzibaris felt left behind. Then the news came that Palestine had been divided into two nations, one Jewish and one Palestinian. One day we had Palestine on the map, and on the next day, Israel was on the map. I was incensed by what I thought was British complicity with the Jews to take away Palestinian—Muslim—lands in the region.

Otherwise, I did not have many specific complaints about the British. My complaints came only later in life; back then, we were humble, docile, and subservient. My father was actually quite fond of the British; whenever the British Resident visited Pemba, he would arrange a tea party for him, the district commissioner, and other colonial dignitaries. My father did the same when the sultan came to Pemba for an official visit. Sultan Khalifa bin Haroub [1911–60] was very popular because he was old and his lifestyle was not extravagant. He received a salary and spent his time in his palace or visiting people in the evenings. A few times a year, he would have meetings with representatives of all the ethnic associations in Zanzibar, but, otherwise, he led a quiet life. During the Idd, our celebration marking the end of the Ramadhan fast, he would give presents to the poor who went to the palace, whether ten cents or half a shilling, and people would queue for hours until everyone had received something personally from the sultan.

In the schools, we'd call England *home*, just like the British teachers who went there on leave. They would tell us they were going home, so, for us, *home* was synonymous with Britain, and we all aspired to go there to see what it was like. In fact, the values the British taught imbued us with subservience. When I was in Arabic class, I learned a poem about a parrot reciting a poem in a cage. The parrot said prison is not my character, so that, even if you put me in a gold cage and feed me, I prefer to be free in the bush fetching my own food and drinking water from the dew of the leaves. I came to realize the inner meaning of that poem only later on in life because, in Standard 4, the teachers just translated the poem literally and did not teach us that we must struggle to liberate ourselves. They did not instill in us that desire to strive for our independence. Still, I do not regret going to colonial schools because they broadened my mind.

I passed my exam to get into Ben Bella School, the government secondary school in town. By then, I was very good at geography, history, and English. Since my mother was away from Zanzibar at the time, I stayed with her family in one of their houses in town. My uncle, Ahmad Rashad, paid for my food at the Dagger restaurant in Malindi. The Indians were the majority in that school, then Arabs, followed by Comorians and Africans. Aboud Jumbe, the future president of Zanzibar, taught biology and history. I adored him. He was very meticulous; when he explained things to you, they got into your head.

I was quite handsome at the time and very promiscuous. In those days, I had a girlfriend named Zuwena. I met her one day as I was coming from the football grounds to a place called the Victory Bar. She knew I had an appointment there with Babu, so she was there, waiting for me. She took me to a mutual friend's house, and that is how it started. She could not take me to her parents' house since her father was very fierce. I was seventeen, and she was maybe twenty. She would give me half a bottle of brandy every night. She already had been married and was divorced and had a daughter. Later, Babu was not upset about this affair, even though he had been running with her. We were freethinkers; we did not indulge with someone's wife, but with girlfriends, we were free.

I left Ben Bella after my first term in Form 2, not because I failed, since I was in the top ten of my class, but because I drank and came to class with a hangover; that interfered with my education. When my uncle found out, he stopped paying for my meals at the restaurant, forcing me to leave school and go to work. Aboud Jumbe halfheartedly signed my school-leaving certificate, saying, "Why do you want to leave school? You are all right to carry on." I said, "I cannot. I want to work, so I can drink and fornicate."

I found employment at the docks as a checker. They used to call me *maova* because I worked so much overtime, usually a hundred hours a month. I would allow myself one weekend off a month to drink and party, usually at the Victory Bar. After six months, I left for Pemba to work on a government project studying the sudden death of clove trees. We took notes on the location of the trees and their level of infection. I met Babu again in Pemba; he was working for the Clove Growers Association [CGA] and was headed to London for more studies. That was when we conceived our plan to meet up in the U.K. We wanted to learn how the British managed to rule us. We were inquisitive; we wanted to find out how a small island like Great Britain could rule the world, an empire where the sun never set. We thought, "What is there? They must have something, so let us go there."

This was in 1951, and you could not compare Zanzibari with British society since the British were far more advanced, which is still true today. I was just a young man who wanted to get somewhere in the world. I wanted to see what I read about in my lessons. My geography textbook taught about the minerals of the world, where the produce and the beef came from. I liked to learn about other countries and wanted to see them all someday. I wanted to go "home," since that was what we called the U.K. in those days, and meet Babu there. Babu and I had that inclination to go to the U.K., and it was only there that serious political ideas began to influence us.

Babu, for example, had never entered secondary school; he went as far as Standard 8. After that, he took English classes with Father Driscoll at the UMCA [Universities' Mission to Central Africa]. He was already twenty-five years old, but he built himself up and later became the brains of our political struggle. I believe each society creates someone; each society produces one of its own children to become a leader. For us in Zanzibar, it was Babu.

three AN EXPANDING WORLD

SO, IN 1951, MY FATHER GAVE me one hundred British pounds to travel to the United Kingdom. I left Pemba with Babu with this money in my pocket, enough when I arrived in Zanzibar Town to pay for my passage to the U.K. on a steamer, tourist class. Babu and I agreed that, within two months, we would meet in London; instead, I met my mum in town and gave her part of the money, which she requested for some personal reasons. She was in difficulty, and I was duty-bound since she was my mum and had looked after me. Instead of taking two months to travel to the U.K., I took two years.

My father refused to send more money, so all I could afford was a passenger ticket to India, my first step, I thought, to get to the U.K. In India in those days, it was possible to obtain work on a ship and earn the same wages as any British seaman, unlike in East Africa where there were rules that enforced lower wages for colonial subjects like me.

I first arrived in Bombay, where I stayed for three weeks and found no work. So I went to Calcutta, where I stayed for a couple of months. Calcutta was not a place where one wanted to live, especially without money. The poverty was appalling, unlike anything I have seen anywhere else in the world. I stayed in a guesthouse with a toilet and shower but saw people sleeping outside on the road at night or chasing rats out of their houses to eat when it rained hard and it was flooding.

To be honest, I looked down on the local people and considered it below my dignity to waste my time on them. I completely ignored them and spent my time with other East Africans. Every morning I went down to the docks and looked for a ship that needed a crew. Sometimes I helped clean ships in the harbor to get some money and something to eat. If I could find a racially mixed crew, I could get some food. The code of comradeship between seamen was that, if you had work, you helped someone who had none. All over the world it functioned this way.

Eventually, I discovered a ship with some Zanzibari crew going to Chittagong, in East Pakistan, so I took a train there, and by chance, there was a position for me. The ship's captain promised to give me work, but he could not legally do so in East Pakistan since I was not a Pakistani, so he told me to wait for the ship back in India.

While in Chittagong, I wanted to see if my geography lessons were true and if the pictures I saw in our books actually conformed to reality. My teacher in Zanzibar who had served in the British army said it smelled like shit in Chittagong because the people had no pit latrines and they built their homes along a river where all the sewage went. So when I went there, I wanted to see if what he had imparted to us in school was correct because, here in Zanzibar Town in Funguni, at one time people had no pit latrines, and they used to poo in the ocean or on the beach during low tide.

I traveled by train south to a place known as Vakpatnam. I never paid for train tickets in India; I just stowed away. In Vakpatnam, I slept outside in a garden. I found the ship from Chittagong and was hired, and before leaving India, I gave my cash advance to some of my East African friends. I worked as a galley boy helping the chef in the kitchen, and I taught English lessons to the ship captain's son.

We eventually came to Maputo in Mozambique. We stayed there a month, until we got an order to go to Casablanca and load up our ship with phosphate. It took us thirty-one days to reach Morocco, where I wanted to jump ship and go to the U.K., which was still my dream. I was ready then with my earnings to pay for a ticket from Morocco as a regular ship passenger to Great Britain. I thought, "I'm so close!" But the British consul refused me permission to travel to the U.K. He threatened me, saying "Go back to your ship, or I'll tell the French, and they'll arrest you."

So we took the phosphate to South Africa. When we arrived in Cape Town, I jumped ship, thinking from there I could stow away on another one headed for Great Britain. Later, my ship went to Zanzibar, and I heard afterward that my mum was there at the docks waiting for me. She wanted to take me home, and legally she could force me to do so since I was still under twenty-one.

I stayed in Cape Town with a domestic servant named Sophia, who boarded my ship with several other women, looking for men. Through her brother-in-law, I managed to find work as a waiter at the Marine Hotel at Sea Point in Cape Town. This was during the apartheid era, so it was necessary to pretend to be "Cape coloured." The headwaiter was a former seaman from Malta, and he helped me. I learned a few words in Afrikaans but still feared being arrested as an illegal alien.

I stayed with Sophia for three months. It was sort of an accidental affair, a transitional period; I knew I could not stay with her very long. I did not have much feeling for her, but I had little choice. She was coloured and wanted to run with white people. I even came home once and found her with a British sailor. I let him stay the night; then, early in the morning, I let him out discreetly since, in those days under the Immorality Act, it was illegal for Sophia as a coloured to sleep with a white man. She had an inferiority complex—she wanted to have children with whites because, in those days, if you could prove you had 90 per-cent white ancestry, then you could be accepted into white society. Sophia wanted to purify her blood, so to speak.

It was a horrible system. Even the coloureds, the Malays, and the Indians were separated from the blacks. We did not have that system here in Zanzibar, though we were under a colonial regime. We only had a few exclusive clubs, like the English Club.

My father sent me another one hundred pounds from the clove harvest from our lands in Pemba to pay for my passage from Cape Town to London. But I was in South Africa illegally, so how could I buy a ticket? Instead, I spent the money and enjoyed myself. I decided to marry Sophia, who converted to Islam and changed her name to Saphia for me. But I married her only to keep her mouth shut about my status in the country. I thought that, otherwise, if I ran away, she might report me to the police.

Eventually, I realized my secret could not last. It was fun for me in Cape Town, but I wanted to legalize my life, so I had to come back to Zanzibar and start over again. And I could not take the restraint in South Africa for long; to go with even an African girl, not to mention a white girl, was very difficult. I spent all the money my father had sent me and then took a train to Durban, leaving my new wife, promising I would send for her later. I met some Zanzibari seamen in Durban who stowed me away on a ship called *Sofala* going to Dar es Salaam. All the crew who knew of my predicament agreed. I stayed under the bed of the petty officer of the engine room crew. I spent all day like that; if I needed to pee, I did so into a container. At night, my friend brought me some food, and I went to the loo and emptied the container. I sneaked around like that for eight days.

I left the boat in Dar es Salaam and met my friend [Ahmed] Badawi [Quillatein], and we came back together to Zanzibar. That was in March 1952. I was still only twenty years old but had seen so many places. I was becoming something of a novelty in Zanzibar. I was more exposed to the world than was the average person, and the way I dressed was completely different; I wore dungarees and t-shirts with printed images on them. In Cape Town, I had learned to dance the jitterbug, which was completely unknown in Zanzibar. We had the waltz, rhumba, tango, and fox trot, but the jitterbug came originally from the American South. I also developed a taste for Nat King Cole, Perry Como, and Frank Sinatra and could sing many of their songs.

I stayed a few months in Pemba, helping to build my uncle's house. I wanted money from my father, so to please him, I tried to be a good Muslim, but I was not very sincere. I would call for prayers at the local mosque, especially the *magharibi* prayer at 6:30 p.m. In those days, all the young people would come, saying, "If Ali Sultan is calling for prayer, then let's go." Yes, before I lost my teeth, I had a lovely voice.

My father took my return to Pemba as an opportunity to marry me off. He wanted me to stay in Zanzibar as a family man, to be more stable. I did not tell my father I was already married to a woman in South Africa. I said to him, "I really don't want this, but if you are serious, then get me this one," a sister of my father's friend. She was nice looking and came from a good family, and I believed she liked me. But my father's proposal was rejected; instead, she married a rich Arab from Burundi with no intelligence. A real dummy, as far as I was concerned. She could have had fun with me because I came back from South Africa jiving, and that was very new here. I taught her to dance the jitterbug, and I sang Nat King Cole songs to her, like "Mona Lisa" and "Too Young." Of course, she fancied me, but in Zanzibar in those days, marriages were arranged. It was a very bad system.

I eventually went to Dar es Salaam and found work at the port as a clerk, earning money for a ticket to the U.K. I was about to turn twenty-one, so my mum could not stop me from going. My wife in Cape Town sent me letters saying she was pregnant, but I knew I was not going back to South Africa. I sent her letters of divorce and never saw her again. I do not know if the baby was actually born or not.

In January 1953, I took another ship to India. All I could afford was a ticket as a deck passenger, which meant I slept on the deck without money even to buy food, until I met a clerk on the ship who let me stay in his office at night. During the days, on deck with the other passengers, I used to recite three *suras* I remembered from Qur'an school. A group of Muslim Indians from South Africa in tourist class noticed me reciting and saw that I was not eating. They asked the clerk how I got my food, and the clerk told the Indians that I did not have any money.

They asked me the same question; when I answered that I trusted in God, they were moved and said, "Since you trust in God, we will pay for your food." They instructed the steward to feed me at their expense.

Then around five in the afternoon, a chap from first class would take me to the promenade deck where he paid for my drinks. We ordered Coca-Cola and rum and Coca-Cola. I would be served the Coca-Cola, but we secretly switched drinks; it was sort of a camouflage, to disguise my consumption of alcohol to the Indians.

We stopped for two days in Colombo, Ceylon. While there, I saw a Hollywood movie being filmed called *Elephant Walk* with Elizabeth Taylor. By chance, I actually saw her as she passed in a convertible. She wore a white dress and a sun hat. I thought she was beautiful.

When we arrived in Calcutta, I helped the Muslims from South Africa pack their things in their cabin, and I discovered they had left behind a small bag of gold coins, which I returned to them, and they were very grateful.

I stayed in Calcutta for two weeks, living like a pauper, sleeping everywhere, even on the docks. If I managed to get one and a half rupees a day, I was all right. Because I had already been there the previous year, I knew where to go. Every morning I went to the docks, helped crew members clean the ship, and made friends with the crew working in the pantry. I could get breakfast, lunch, and dinner that way.

Then while walking one night in an area of Calcutta called Kidarpoor, near the Ganges River waterfront, I met an old Zanzibari seaman. It was a pretty tough area for lower-working-class people, with cheaper brothels for the seamen who came from the ships. When I asked where he was from, the seaman claimed to be from Mombasa, but I could tell from his accent that he was Zanzibari. This countryman of mine could not read or write and for years had been a coal shoveler in the days when ships burned coal. It so happened that his ship needed another fireman, so I was trained as a fireman and then signed a two-year contract. Greeks owned the ship, but it sailed under the flag of Panama. There were only three of us who were not Greek on that ship: myself, my Zanzibari friend, and a sailor from Sudan.

We first traveled to Japan, to take scrap iron to Kawasaki. I wanted to join the American army and fight in the Korean War, so I went to the American base at Hanida to enlist. I did not know the politics of the Korean War—it was not in my head in the least! I asked the American officer there to allow me to enlist, but he told me, "You are an alien. If you can go to Canada, you can enlist yourself as a British subject, but you can't enlist here." I said, "But I am right here, and Korea is right there!"

The ship traveled empty to Vancouver, Canada, where I decided to jump because it was supposed to return to India, and I wanted to go to the U.K. I had quite a struggle with the Greek ship captain, but after a month, I was eventually able to receive all the wages owed me and to stay in Canada. I moved to the British Mission to Seafarers, where I cut grass and helped out around the place. The superintendent was a hunchback, and his driver was on holiday. One day the hunchback put the car—an old British Hillman—into second gear, when he wanted to go in reverse. I watched him and laughed because my dad had a Hillman, then a Vauxhall, and then a Morris. I told the superintendent, "I can drive better than you," so he hired me as a temporary driver.

There was a Spanish chap staying at the mission, who had also, like me, left his ship. He wanted to go to Guatemala and fight against the United Fruit Company. Someone at the mission accused him of being a communist sympathizer, but the Spaniard did not even know what a communist was. That was when I first heard the term *communist,* and I was curious. I asked, "What is this communism? Tell me!" He said he did not know. Imagine: I left my country when I was twenty years old. Communism had existed from the 1840s, but for me, it waited all those years until 1953 when I first heard of that word. Can you imagine? Nor did I understand the word *exploitation,* which I came to know only later in London when I studied Marxism.

I liked Canada, but my whole objective was to go to England because Britain, not Canada, was ruling Zanzibar. I wanted to go there, study, and then return home and struggle for our emancipation. Who gave the British the right to rule us? In my heart, I felt that colonialism was wrong, especially when other colonies like India were already independent. So, one day after about three months in Vancouver, it was our turn at the mission to collect books for the ship libraries. I drove the superintendent around in his car, taking bundles of books to certain ships. It was my luck that a ship in need of a fireman was leaving that day, and in two hours, I was gone. We went through the Panama Canal to Curacao and then on to Liverpool, England, where we discharged our cargo of timber. From there, we went to London, where I was paid off and finally "home." This was in August 1953.

four LONDON

I RANG BABU WHEN I ARRIVED IN London and took a train to Shepherd's Bush, where I rented digs in the same house where he stayed. I immediately started looking for employment, and my first job was as a dishwasher in the Great Eastern Hotel. Then I took another job at the Mount Royal Hotel, where I was a silver man; I had been upgraded to the one who cleaned the silverware. I worked from 7 a.m. to 3 p.m., six days a week, and made five pounds, ten shillings a week, after taxes and health insurance.

Babu worked at the post office and attended courses at a local college. He had a girlfriend named Mary and was active in the British labor movement. In those days, though, he considered himself an anarchist. Mary and I would argue with Babu about his anarchism; we had many discussions because, after all, at the end of the day, we had to come back here to Zanzibar and commence the struggle.

We Africans also went to a club in London paid for by our colonial governments called the East Africa House, at the end of Oxford Street, close to the Mount Royal Hotel. All of us from Kenya, Tanganyika, Uganda, and Zanzibar came after work hours for drinks and endless talk of liberating our countries from the British. There was food there, and since the colonial government subsidized the beer, it was cheaper than in a regular bar. The British were trying to gather us to create an elite subservient to their interests, but it did not turn out that way.[1]

My mind in those days was open, a recipient of what was happening in the world. In those days, there were the Mau Mau Emergency and later the Suez Crisis. I went to the Marble Arch on Sundays, to Speaker's Corner, where each man who wanted to would stand and speak on a box. There were speakers from the British Communist Party; being a colonial subject, I liked the communists' ideas on freedom for the colonies. Even though there was a Labor Party wing trying to help the colonial people, the party in general had reservations about granting us freedom. But the communists were outspoken on the matter, saying, "If we get power in Britain, the colonies will be immediately free."

When I first arrived in London, I was impressed by British freedoms and development, but my intellectual reorientation took only a few months. On May Day 1954, I formally joined the British Communist Party, mostly because it was the only party wanting to give up the colonies. The party suited my temperament, that of a rebel.

Although there were many African students in London ready to discuss the struggle against colonialism, I spent most of my time with my comrades in the party. I did not join any Pan-Africanist associations; in fact, I ignored Pan-Africanism because its adherents just used the color of their skin and the name of their continent as an ideology. Some of them were very nice, but the majority were racists. I did not want to work with people like that, to try and change them when they should have changed themselves. If I found a nonracist Pan-Africanist it was because he was a communist or was willing to work with communists. Communism taught that not all white people were bad; it eradicated in me any element of racism. When I accepted Marxism, it oriented my thinking completely toward the class struggle and away from racial politics.

Of course, at that time, my progressive Zanzibari friends and I in London had no thoughts of violence. We knew we could not fight the British. On the other hand, some of us came to accept the Maoist admonition to "walk on two legs"—that is, negotiate for your freedom but keep armed struggle as an option.

I also liked the socialist idea of collectivizing the means of production, especially for a small country like Zanzibar, rather than having economic fragmentation. And I wanted land reform—I did not care that my family was landowners because, like many others, my relatives were in debt to the Indians. The Arab plantation owners exploited the Africans, the Indians exploited the Arabs, and the British banks exploited the Indians. I came to realize this during my discussions with party members in London. I saw the system in my youth, so it was easy for me to analyze it dialectically to my comrades.

I had my reservations, though, about atheism. I knew I could not come to the same conclusion as Marx, that religion was only a drug for the working people, intended to keep them as slaves and serfs. When I read Darwin, I accepted his theories at the time, though according to Islam, God created Adam in his image, not that of an ape. There was a conflict within me on that point because I could not accept that we originally came from apes.

Nevertheless, I took it all seriously. I wanted to read anything I could get my hands on. I participated in Communist Party summer classes and often visited the Karl Marx Memorial House in Ferringdon, where there was a good library. I attended classes through the evening school of the University of London. I did not sit for exams because I just wanted to learn. But what I found in college was not radical enough for me. All the institutions of Western countries had a system where they conditioned the students. The politicians did not really want radicalism, so they molded the thinking of the people.

Eventually, I moved from Shepherd's Bush to a flat in Swiss Cottage with Khamis Abdallah Ameir, another Zanzibari. Khamis was working and studying and had joined the Young Communist League; we were comrades. Swiss Cottage was an upper-class area of London where I paid over a third of my wages on lodgings. I could have lived in the East End where rents were less expensive, but I preferred to live in a more intellectual area and to participate in the more sophisticated discussions at the local party branch in Swiss Cottage than were possible in a working-class neighborhood. All the intellectuals were there in Swiss Cottage: professionals, Jews, gentiles, lawyers, and doctors. I met many fine people—it was like the Swahili saying, *udongo na waridi,* or clay and rose. I was the clay, and I wanted the scent of a rose.

The party was under Russian domination but very lively and full of activity. Most of my friends were British and were very warm. Here I came from the colonies and was not white, but I was not segregated and was made to feel welcome in all their homes. We organized meetings, classes, and lectures. People from the Central Committee or from the trade unions lectured to us, and they were very impressive. I knew after my training in the party in the U.K. that I would know how to work and organize when I returned to Zanzibar.

In the summers, though, I looked for a ship. I wanted to make more money during the school holidays when there were no evening classes. I was part of a unionized labor pool and found ships suitable to my time and interests. On the *MV La Laguna,* for example, I was a senior ordinary sailor, making about twenty-three British pounds a month. Wherever I traveled, I would always talk to the common people. I sat with them, asked how their lives were, and what they earned. I always went down among the lowest of the masses because it was there I knew I would learn. I wanted to see how people lived in other parts of the world and how they were exploited.

I went once to Rosario, Argentina, and there was an old Arab fellow from Yemen, once a sailor like me. He had jumped ship and now had three beautiful girls. He invited me home and begged me to marry one of his girls because I was a Muslim and there were not many Muslims in Rosario. I said I was still on the move and was not ready to marry. I left, feeling sorry for him, but told him it was his own fault because he had left his ship and had married in that distant land.

I also remember going to a pub on a late Sunday afternoon in Bahia Blanca, Argentina. Inside we saw two policemen arresting an Argentinean. I said to my three friends, "Come on, let's let this guy go free. There are only two of them and four of us." We jumped the police, and the guy ran away. One of us was an amateur boxer, so he did most of the fighting. We managed to run away, but the police arrested the boxer, so I had to go back to the station to get him out. The police pulled their guns on me, and I challenged them to shoot me, a British subject; instead, they kicked me and gave me a scar over my left eyebrow and then locked me inside. The boxer was the ship's assistant cook, and there were only two cooks in the ship's galley. So he was released on bail after just one night inside, but I remained there for eleven days. I was only a deck hand, after all.

I did not do anything in jail, except to learn a little Spanish in order to go to the toilet and so on. Eventually, I was let out on bail; but when the ship sailed, I jumped bail, so I could never again go to that port. The captain fined me fifteen pounds to pay for the lawyer.

I went with *La Laguna* to Maseo in Brazil where we loaded sugar and bananas to take to Santos, the port of São Paolo. It was a very nice little place; it was like Zanzibar, where the poor lived somewhere opposite the port, frying fish, cassava, and *mishkaki* [meat roasted on a kebab]. And most of them were dark, like us in Zanzibar. In fact, I met an exact replica of a girlfriend I had in Pemba, working as a disc jockey in a pub in Maseo. The only difference was the language: the girl in Zanzibar spoke Swahili; this one, Portuguese. At the time, I had a friend on the ship from Pemba, who happened also to have had the same girlfriend. I asked him to come to the bar and see the disc jockey for himself. He also thought it was the same girl—the same gap in the teeth, the same figure, and the same skin. She was the Pemban's exact twin. Later, she called me to her room, and she did not ask for money.

I did not stay very long in Uruguay, but I found the mentality of the people very interesting. In a bar once, I bought a girl a drink; after a while, I touched her arm and found that she was wearing an amulet. She said it was to protect her from people's evil eyes. I laughed because it was the same superstitious mentality as at home. Only in highly industrialized countries did such unscientific ideas fall away. Africa was full of those ideas, except among the intellectuals, the ruling circles, and the rich elite. Once I spent eight hours in the United States, in Norfolk, Virginia. We had the evening off to enjoy ourselves and see the place, but we had to be fingerprinted before we went ashore. I went out with a Welsh friend, but we reached a point where the police told me to go to the side of a street for coloreds. One area was for whites and the other for non-whites. I was told to go to the left, my friend to the right. I said, "Oh, my God, there is no freedom here." I had heard this about the Deep South but was surprised that all the way up in Virginia the color bar was like that. There was no color bar among the workers on a ship. There was only the comradeship that develops when you work together, for your safety, for everything.

That is how I managed to survive until I had the chance to go to Moscow in 1957, for the International Youth Festival. I had my dreams about that festival, and to get there, I was willing to pay the British Communist Party fifty British pounds I had earned on one of my trips to South America.[2] On the opening day of the festival, as the only Zanzibari delegate, I was put in an open Land Rover all by myself, to be driven through a stadium full of thousands of Russians. Each country had its own delegation and its own car, but I passed alone under the rostrum, where stood Khrushchev, members of the ruling politburo, and other Communist Party officials. I was wearing my white *kanzu* and my *kofia*.[3] The car was outfitted with a poster saying, "Zanzibar" and the flag of the sultanate: a solid red flag that turned out to be very appropriate for a communist festival.

I noticed that each delegation would stop for a few seconds in front of the rostrum where the microphones were very sensitive. Beforehand I had memorized a couple of lines in Russian, which I delivered from the car as it paused under the rostrum: "Long live the friendship of the people of Russia and the people of Zanzibar! *Za mir y druzhba!* For peace and friendship!" I shouted this as loud as I could, and the microphones caught my voice. The whole stadium erupted in applause and cheers. They responded saying, "*Kharasho!*" "Good!" It seemed as if there were over a hundred thousand people in the stadium.

I believe that is the reason that later that day Khrushchev called me over at an official reception and requested that I open the Kremlin Ball that night by dancing with a member of the Communist Party's Executive Committee. Her name, I remember, was Madame Furtseva.

Imagine: here is Ali Sultan coming from Zanzibar, dancing with a member of the politburo and the Central Committee of the Soviet Communist Party! A huge lady! You know the Russians, the way they eat! My interpreter was very impressed. That was my first impression of the Soviet Union, or any socialist country, way back in 1957. I was the first Zanzibari to visit Moscow. If there were Zanzibaris working in the ships, they went to Leningrad or the other seaports, but not to Moscow.

I spent two weeks attending seminars, concerts, and dances. I met youth from all over the world and had a girlfriend who was a member of the Norwegian delegation. We went to museums together. I was also taken in by the hospitality of the Russian people. I would walk into a pub alone, and the Russians would invite me to drink with them. They had seen me on that opening day, with my *kanzu*, my *kofia*, and my red flag, and had heard what I said there.

My best memory of the festival, however, was seeing *Swan Lake*, by Tchaikovsky, at the Bolshoi Theater. The authorities invited all the delegates; it was my first experience with ballet. I saw the dancers Raisa Struchkova and Alexander Lapauri, and I was mesmerized by the choreography; it was something completely new to me. And the lighting was amazing, the way the technicians would play with the light to simulate waves or a swan's swimming on a lake, as if there were a real lake in the background.[4]

When I returned to England, I discovered my father had sent me a ticket to come home to Zanzibar. In those days, I enjoyed my life and did not want to save money, and that is why I had to ask for his assistance. I worked a few more months in London; then at the beginning of 1958, I finally left to come home. Before doing so, I resigned from the British Communist Party, telling my comrades that I was only safeguarding my interests since, in the colonial system, you could easily be imprisoned for your membership. But, deep in my heart, I was still a communist. Those five years in London had changed me completely. I was ready now for action back in Zanzibar, ready to commence the struggle against colonialism.

# five THE STRUGGLE

THE BIGGEST CHANGE IN ZANZIBAR since I had left was the introduction of political parties and the beginning of our independence struggle. We did not know how long the struggle would take; I personally thought it would take a long time, at least ten years, because I had followed the Mau Mau struggle in Kenya and knew how bitter a conflict that was.

Babu had returned from London the year before and had been appointed secretary general of the Zanzibar Nationalist Party, the ZNP. Babu turned out to be a brilliant and subtle strategist and tactician. He was also friendly and generous, a real man of the people. He drank a lot, sometimes a full bottle of whiskey a day, but all us comrades drank in those days. Babu wanted me to join the ZNP right away, even though the party had lost the elections the previous year to the Afro-Shirazi Party, or ASP. I told him I first needed to see my father in Pemba, and then we would see.

In Pemba, I attended the rallies of each party. I went to the ASP and asked to see the party constitution, but it did not have one. The ASP appeared to be an agglomeration of individuals all following their leader, Abeid Karume. Karume was a very strong man; he spoke Swahili, some Gujarati, some Arabic, and some seaman's English. He was a very good orator in Swahili and could move people and command an audience. And his words just came to him spontaneously—he never read a speech, just spoke from the heart. Karume was very popular among the working people because he came from them and was a simple man willing to talk and joke with everyone, especially the poor of every community.

But the ASP was too patriarchal, and in those days, it did not criticize colonialism. I could never join a party that did not want to get rid of the British immediately. Our society was divided into different ethnic associations, through which the British played the old game of divide and rule. Now we had a party called the Afro-Shirazi Party, which contested politics on a racial basis; since I was class conscious, I knew we had to break racial politics in Zanzibar.

The ZNP, on the other hand, had a party constitution. It also criticized colonialism, which I thought was the most fundamental contradiction. I did not agree with all the constitution—for example, where we swore allegiance to the sultan—but I knew the first task was to get rid of the British; we could deal later with the sultan and the feudalists, the big Arab landowners. The first struggle was to achieve our independence since socialism could not come under colonialism. The class struggle was not the immediate priority; rather, we had to unite the people of all the ethnic communities.

I could see that the ZNP was a very heterogeneous party, that it included all the ethnic groups, workers, peasants, and landowners. Although the feudalists in Zanzibar all supported the ZNP, the party also attracted nearly all the young intellectuals of the islands, people like Babu and others who had studied overseas. I could see the contradictions within the ZNP but was willing to cooperate with the feudalists for the time being in order to achieve victory against colonialism, and the ZNP was the only party then fighting colonialism.

Since we socialists were so few, it was foolish to organize our own party. Our adversaries would have branded us atheist communists. Of course, that is what I was in those days, but we socialists had to be subtle about it; we had to bury ourselves in a mass movement and then try to politicize from within. Even then, the British hardly tolerated us communists.

So I joined the ZNP and was very soon elected organizing secretary for Pemba. In March 1958, we called a mass meeting at Mkoani for the whole island, just one month after my arrival from London. I had a lot of work to do because the ZNP had lost the elections the year before and was a very young organization and unscientific in its methods.[1] We had to have an organization and needed to instill discipline in our members, so I started recruiting members and establishing branches everywhere in Pemba, following the party constitution to the letter. I began in the south; it took almost six months to get the island organized. We started with the youth because they are the ones who matter the most and can be remolded. We organized the men first, but later also the women since they knew we were pressing the British for women to be able to vote.

I worked very hard for the Nationalists. I was lucky that my first assignment was in Pemba where the ASP was weak. The Shirazi and the

Arabs considered themselves kin to one another, and however much the ASP tried to instigate racial tension, it could not succeed in that region. We were saved from that curse. In Pemba, things were relatively quiet and harmonious, and that is the reason we never had much violence there, even during the revolution.

Only in Unguja did the people experience deep social divisions because of politics. The ZNP instigated a campaign to evict African squatters on Arab-owned plantations in retaliation for their support of the ASP. The evictions deepened racial enmity, so that, for a time, people did not even attend the funerals of members of the other party. Village wells, once open to all, were closed to members of opposing parties, all depending on the whims of local village leaders. It was not, of course, in the interests of progressives to see such worsening divisions. We had to speak the same language and to confront the British with a united front.

I met my first Zanzibari wife, Aysha Amour Zahor, during that year in Pemba. She was a matron in a girl's boarding school, and she and two other teachers would come in the afternoon to visit my stepmother. I invited all three to go swimming with me, but Aysha was the only one who came. She was of the same clan as I, and I knew her father from the party. She had already finished secondary school and had been through teacher's training.

We first met in February 1958 and were married in June of that year. I was twenty-six years old, and she was twenty-one. At the time, we were opening a women's union in the party, and I did not want the men to be suspicious of me, to think I could not be trusted around their wives. I decided I should marry, so they would not be jealous and restrict their women from joining the party. Aysha was open and agreeable, though not the most beautiful among the three I had invited swimming. She wore glasses and was asthmatic. She was very simple in her tastes and had many friends among her schoolmates. I decided she met my criteria.

But when I asked my father for his permission to marry, he would not consent, and I still do not know why. I asked my uncle to make the marriage proposal to Aysha's parents, but he would not go without my father's permission. Since my family did not approach her parents, they refused to give their consent to the marriage. Her father and I were both members of the ZNP Executive Committee, but he was in Unguja, and I was in Pemba. I heard later that he did not cooperate because I did not believe in religion, but at the time, he told me it was because my father had not personally come to propose.

So Aysha and I took our case to the *kadhi*'s court, something very new in Pemba in the 1950s. Aysha protested that she wanted to marry me, but her father would not consent. Her father was asked to come to the court to explain, but he did not respond to the first summons, or the second, and so the *kadhi* gave us his permission to get married. I paid my wife only a token amount of one hundred shillings as a dowry, and we had a small wedding party in my friend's house, with *taarab* music. Aysha was open-minded about the dowry, but even if she had wanted something more, where would I have gotten it? I was a politician with no salary.

Eventually the leaders of our party came to reconcile my father and me. They spoke to him first and then came to me; they asked me to bow down, touch his feet, and ask forgiveness. I refused, saying that he was the one in the wrong, so he should beg forgiveness and bow down. They said that kind of thing did not happen in our society, so eventually I agreed. All of us walked to my father's office. As I was bowing down to beg forgiveness, my father stopped me, saying it was not necessary.

It was a happy marriage, and Aysha was very good to me, very quiet, kind, and docile. We had a very good understanding. I indoctrinated her, and in time, she became very progressive in her ideas and very active politically. My wife would address the women at ZNP meetings. She almost caught me cheating once, but I did not confess. I was just like Bill Clinton: I repudiated the affair. But then one time I caught Aysha speaking with an Indian boy on the street, one of her former classmates. It was not an affair, but I warned him I would beat him if I ever saw him speaking to my wife again.

My wife gave birth to our first child, a daughter, in April 1959. I named her Raissa, after a Russian ballerina I had seen perform in Moscow in 1957. Another daughter, Fidela, was named after Fidel Castro [1961]. The third daughter was Maotushi, named after Mao Tse-tung [1962]. She later became known as Moona. The last of our four children was a son I named Stalin [1966], who later changed his name to Sultan.

So, in those days, we dared to struggle. I would be out on party business all day and come back late at night sometimes. We depended on friends for our food and shelter. We stayed with different people. From Amour Abdalla al-Kiyumi, we received rice, beans, cooking fat, and sugar. From Saleh Salim Shirgah, we obtained soft drinks, bread, and meat. They knew we had nothing, that my father had thrown me out for marrying my wife, and that I was not earning a shilling for my work with the ZNP. My wife and children learned to accept these conditions;

there were no luxuries, but neither were we deprived. In those days, I had no personal ambitions whatsoever; I was not thinking I wanted to be a candidate and be elected to the Legislative Council—no. I was the ZNP's organizing secretary in Pemba until 1959, when I was promoted to acting secretary general during Babu's absence on one of his trips overseas. And I was only twenty-seven years old.

Since the British were formidable, we had to find a way to reason them out of Zanzibar. Of course, time was on our side; after World War II, India became independent and then Ghana in 1957. The issue that united everyone here in Zanzibar was liberation from the colonial yoke, not emancipation from economic weakness. Early on, we foresaw there would be neocolonialism because, even though we might become independent, we could still be manipulated economically.

We also knew before we achieved our independence that there would be a breakup of the movement, because the ZNP was a temporary union of different forces. We progressives were the intellectuals, the organizers, and the blood of the ZNP. We had ideas acceptable to the majority of the people who were poor, and we spoke to them in a very simple way. When I spoke in town, I appealed to the workers, pointing out their exploitation. When I spoke in rural areas, I appealed to the squatters, saying they were doing a service to the landlords by clearing their farms without any return. I explained to the peasants why, when their harvests failed, they were losing their *shambas* to the court.

Ali Muhsin, a leading personality in the ZNP, could not speak to the people in this way. Once in 1960, he and the Executive Committee stopped me from speaking at mass meetings. Muhsin knew that, at the end of the day, I was aiming for a socialist Zanzibar, so I was banned from public speaking. Muhsin said my speeches were exactly like Karume's, the only difference being that Karume was an African and I was an Arab. The content was the same. That was his accusation, but it was those speeches that convinced people to join the party.

I went to Ghana in 1960 with Babu and Hussein Mubarak to attend a conference meant to protest France testing their bombs in the Sahara Desert. Kwame Nkrumah, who received our delegation for half an hour, was strong and energetic but not ideologically inclined to my standards, like most African leaders. He gave the impression of being an intellectual of the Westernized world, not a fully committed socialist. He theorized for a long time with us—but it was just blah, blah, blah. He did not have much of an influence on me. I had already formed my radical opinions and thought most African leaders were too bourgeois, too willing to perpetuate the same system.

From Ghana, I flew to Guinea, for a much more substantial and international Afro-Asian Solidarity Conference, which grew out of the Bandung Conference of 1955. Babu headed the delegation and gave a speech about our struggle in Zanzibar and asked for support, whether moral or material. I had been to Conakry before as a sailor and knew the city when it was under the French, so I took Babu and Hussein around to the naughty places I had been in those days. We stayed a week or two, and Sékou Touré invited us to his palace, where he had a state banquet for us. Sékou Touré had a lovely wife, and he was actually nearer to me ideologically than was Nkrumah because he had come up through the trade union movement. Under Touré's leadership, Guinea was the first French colony south of the Sahara to gain independence.

Babu and Hussein Mubarak returned to Zanzibar, while I went off to China, where I stayed for almost a month, attending a trade-union conference. I was asked to give a speech on socialist liberation and made the front page of the *People's Daily* in China. I attacked Tito's revisionism in Yugoslavia, unaware that the Chinese were using my comments in their rhetorical war with the USSR, because, by then, the Chinese were accusing the Soviets, and not just Tito, of revisionism.

After the conference, my hosts wanted to show me the story of the communist struggle and to indoctrinate me, so they took me on a tour retracing the steps of the Long March. I had read about the Long March in London and was really impressed, so I was ready to learn. I traveled with an official interpreter, sometimes by train and sometimes by plane, all the way from Jiangxi through Hunnan and eventually to Shaanxi, near Inner Mongolia, a province of hills and caves, the cradle of the communist resistance.

The tour opened my outlook and broadened my horizons, to see how the communists had made huge sacrifices and how, wherever they went, they confiscated lands and gave them to the peasants. I was not as interested at the time in iron smelting or coal mining or in their heavy industry and armament factories. I wanted to understand the history of their party and how they had struggled. Our slogan here was "*Uhuru* 1960," and though I knew freedom would not come in 1960, I also knew it would not take as long as it had taken the Chinese.

The Chinese took me to many cities. Poverty was not as visible as in India; everyone had food and something to wear. People were neither naked nor in rags, and although the houses were old, I never saw people sleeping in the streets. The country was huge. It had been left behind for so many years that, had it not been for socialism, it would not have caught up as quickly as it did. Of course, now the Chinese blame Mao, but they should not; it is the same as how the Russians blame Stalin. Developing a backward country into an industrial country in a short period of time is not easy—no wonder a lot of people died in the process. But the sacrifice of lives was justified; if I had that same power, I would have done the same as Mao or Stalin. If I had a huge country to bring from backwardness to modernization, I would have done the same things, yes.

Mao Tse-tung gave us an audience in Wutan and compared the Chinese struggle to the Algerian struggle, which then was the foremost struggle in Africa. I remember that Mao was a chain smoker and that one of his arms was weak, as if he had suffered a stroke. I also met Chou En-Lai: a great man, meticulous, and very well briefed. In general, although I had been a member of the British Communist Party for four years and had visited Russia in 1957, I had not been as impressed by the greatness of the Russians as I was with the Chinese. Life is a constant state of change, and I was free to develop and put all ideologies to the test, to see which was most viable and most suitable to our own conditions in Zanzibar. In China, I was deeply impressed by the vast and formidable country, by the people's sacrifice and their achievements, so when I returned to Zanzibar, I was in complete agreement with Babu about China, that this was the ideological line to follow.

After returning from China, I was made director of the ZNP's International Department. I was sent to Cairo, where the ZNP was opening an office and where the party was already sending many students on scholarships offered by the Egyptian government. When I first arrived in Cairo, there was a delay in setting up the office, so in the meantime, I attended North Vietnam's independence day celebrations. I went because I was intrigued with the North Vietnamese's zeal and also because I wanted to meet Ho Chi Minh, who at one time was a seaman like me. Ho invited us to his palace to discuss his experiences and teach us how to apply what he knew to our own liberation movements. I remember he had the common touch; once we were at a formal dinner, and it was a very, very hot day. Ho walked in wearing a worn-out khaki uniform and sandals made from tire treads, the kind you see in the street on children. He opened the dinner by removing the top of his uniform, wearing only a t-shirt underneath, and asked the rest of us to do the same. Of course, it was so hot that we all took advantage of this.

Ho was very simple. In fact, I have never seen a president like him in my life: he moved through the streets without any guards, walking among the children. He loved children, though he did not have any of his own, and all the kids surrounded him in the streets, calling him "Uncle Ho." I was being driven one day through the streets, and there he was walking in his tire shoes and wearing a faded khaki tunic. I had never seen such openness before or since—no protocol! All the other heads of state I have seen have moved around with an entourage and bodyguards, as if they were the enemy of the people or were afraid. Ho impressed me very much.

 CAIRO

CAIRO IN THOSE DAYS, UNDER
Colonel Gamal Abdel Nasser, was a center for liberation movements in
Africa and Asia. The whole country was politicized. Nasser in those years
was the spokesman for the entire Arab world, and he encouraged libera-
tion movements throughout Africa. Nasser had enormous influence, especially in Zanzibar because of the ethnic makeup here, because the
sultan was an Arab, and because of Radio Cairo. My uncle Ahmad
Rashad arrived in Egypt around 1957 and was well established at Radio
Cairo, sending out Swahili broadcasts to East Africa and agitating for
independence. He had a special program called *Sauti ya Uhuru wa
Afrika* [Voice of African Freedom]. Everybody in East Africa who spoke
Swahili tuned in to that program, and in Zanzibar, we listened to his
programs in all the cafes. My uncle was a radical in those days, wanting
to get rid of the sultan. His broadcasts infuriated the British, but they
gave us inspiration.

I was supposed to obtain support for the ZNP cause among the various foreign delegations. I had access to the embassies of all the socialist
nations—even the Soviet Union was represented. In those days, the
Soviets had no information and no representation in colonial territories;
they only had their clandestine sources. So I went to the Chinese, the
North Koreans, the Czechs, and all the other socialist embassies and
explained our struggle in Zanzibar and requested material aid, scholarships, literature, or whatever else they could give us.

I was also expected to supervise the Zanzibari students studying in
Cairo on ZNP scholarships. In 1960, there were already about a hundred, and I think that, until the revolution in 1964, in total about eight
hundred Zanzibaris studied in Cairo.[1] The students stayed in a hostel in
Heliopolis, and Ali Muhsin's sister acted as sort of their matron. They
also provided us with an office in a building in Zamalek, which we shared

63

with other African liberation organizations, like the ANC [African National Congress] and PAC [Pan Africanist Congress] from South Africa. It was like a diplomatic office, and we had certain immunities, like any diplomatic mission.

I rented a house near the office with my wife and eldest daughter from a stipend we received from the Egyptian government, about one hundred Egyptian pounds a month. And I made other friends, and they also subsidized us. The Chinese labor movement gave me another hundred pounds a month; and whenever we wanted to travel, these international organizations always paid for our plane tickets and expenses. I had become used to a certain standard of living in Zanzibar; I had my drinks, my food, and my fun without any difficulty. In Cairo, I went out with my uncle Ahmad Rashad almost every weekend to various nightclubs. He had been there much longer and advised me where to go and where not to go.

Meanwhile, life was hard for the students in Cairo, but they did not starve. Life was harder for the ordinary people in Cairo than for most of us in Zanzibar. One time I went to a hospital in Cairo to visit three of our students, and I would not even sit down because it was so dirty. After that, I immediately gave all three new scholarships to get out of Egypt. If the hospital was like that, then what were the living conditions in the student dormitories? You can imagine.

In those days, I was an agnostic, rather than an atheist. I doubted the existence of God. I would argue and joke with my uncle, saying, "You are all wasting your time. I will put my hand up and count to three; after that, I'll drop it. If there is a God, let him try to stop me."

"You think God will take your challenge?" My uncle said. "You think God is immature like you? He will just give you time and enough rope, and you will come to learn of His existence one day."

Years later, I came to believe that patience is one of God's virtues. He can wait, and He will punish us for our sins in His own due time. Otherwise, there is no meaning or justice in this world. If you are strong, then you can do anything, even slaughter others. We must have the fear of God in order to restrain our actions. That is the most fundamental element in all religions.

But when I was involved in Marxist politics, I was ignorant of Muslim belief because, in school, we were never taught the meaning of Islam. Since Arabic was not our mother tongue, we never knew the meaning of the words we learned; we recited the Qur'an like parrots. The only people who learned Arabic in their homes were the Washihiri [Yemenis in Zanzibar]; after just one generation in Zanzibar, all the other Arabs spoke Swahili. By the time I left Zanzibar, only three chapters of the Qur'an had been translated into Swahili. So when a person is exposed to a new philosophy without a solid basis in Islam, it is easy to doubt. We were just like parrots and monkeys.

Our party had no specific program for the political education of our students in Cairo; the students simply absorbed Egyptian politics. They were free to make up their minds: some were conservative, while others wanted to get rid of the sultan in Zanzibar just as Nasser had thrown out King Farouk. The majority was loyal to ZNP leader Ali Muhsin, who supported the sultanate, but a vocal minority followed my uncle. Even before I arrived in Cairo, a crack appeared among the students. I was sent by the party to try to repair the division, which I thought was just a childish dispute. It was secondary actually since the first issue in 1960 was to bring an end to colonialism; nothing else mattered.

I solved the dispute by sending the more leftist students for further studies in socialist countries. Anyway, I thought that Cairo was moribund and decadent and that the young people would be better off studying elsewhere. It had been the decision of the Communist International in 1960 to invite our students to their communist universities in order to train the next generation of political leaders. The socialist nations paid all the airfares and gave the students free tuition and living allowances.[2]

Although we organized the scholarships through the ZNP, they were open to anyone who wanted to study overseas and who met certain minimum qualifications. Ethnicity or party status meant nothing; if I had one, I would offer a scholarship to anyone from Zanzibar who wanted one. But the ASP also had its own connections and scholarships for its members. The majority from Zanzibar went to the East because we were offered scholarships there; only the elite obtained a chance to go West. But we sent ordinary people to the East, workers and peasants; they reached a secondary-school level and then boof! They went to a technical institution or a college or university in a socialist country. Even if one of our boys in London was hard up, we could arrange a scholarship for him in a socialist country.

I wanted to send as many students as I could to foreign universities because I knew that, at the end of the day when they came back to Zanzibar, they would help push our independence struggle. The main idea was to expose them to different ideas. The Russians offered all kinds of scholarships, in medicine, engineering, law, and dentistry, many of them at Lumumba University in Moscow. I would say that at least two hundred Zanzibaris were there in those years, at colleges and universities in

Moscow, the Ukraine, and Byelorussia. East Germany was second in intake, offering short courses in trade unionism and cooperatives and full degrees in fields such as medicine, engineering, and telecommunications. The trade union and cooperatives courses were short, from six months to one year maximum. We sent over three hundred students to East Germany, but they usually did not stay as long there as the students in the Soviet Union.

Then there were about thirty Zanzibari students in Czechoslovakia and a few each in Hungary, Romania, and Bulgaria. Almost all the European socialist countries accepted our boys. Europe was more popular than the East because our boys could not take the Asiatic lifestyle. Chinese society was too monolithic. We sent eighteen students there, and I think all except one left early; it was the same in North Korea and Albania. I sent three students to each, and none of them stayed very long. The society was too tough, and the social life was very bad; the students were not allowed to mix with the Chinese. Our boys wanted their freedom to drink and have sex, but in China, everyone's eyes were watching you, as if asking, "Why do you want to fornicate?" Also some students did not really want to study Marxism–Leninism.

Even though some students did not last very long in China and other places, most of them returned to Zanzibar, and that was how we managed to politicize the whole island. In our struggle against colonialism, we had to take the young men because the old people were just dying and not in a fighting mood. They were a spent force, cold blood. It is the youth, the students, who are the most important element in every country.

But this was a long struggle, one we knew would not end on our achieving independence. What next? To emancipate ourselves from the colonial economic yoke, to build our country from scratch. We knew we could not change everything in a day: the infrastructure, the mentality, the training, and the education all had to be dealt with. Because the colonies were meant for only what? For raw materials and cheap labor and a market for the finished products of the metropole.

From Cairo, it was easy for me to set up ZNP missions in other countries. London was easy—we just rented a flat there and selected volunteers to run the office, people like Salim Rashid. I also had discussions with the Cuban ambassador to Egypt, and he agreed to help us. To Havana, we sent Ali Mahfoud, Salim Ahmed Salim, and Muhammed Ali Foum, comrades carefully selected for their socialist beliefs and loyalty to Babu and me. They were attached to an organization called "Friendship of all

People," an umbrella organization for liberation movements, but which at the time only included two: the ANC from South Africa and our own. Our office in Havana published a newspaper, *Sauti ya Jogoo*,[3] which was more radical than our own *Dawn in Zanzibar* in Cairo. Eventually the British banned *Sauti ya Jogoo* in Zanzibar.

The Russians, the Vietnamese, the Cubans, and the others in Cairo were very approachable when we needed financial help to run the office or to publish our newspaper—or to feed my family and me. And then I would also house the students who came on their own to Egypt, some even traveling overland. It was that kind of life, and that is how we cemented our comradeship. I gave some of my countrymen scholarships to other countries, while others I put to work around the office; and some, about twelve, I sent for military training in a desert camp organized by the Egyptian army. They learned how to handle explosives and how to shoot a gun. We needed, as Mao used to say, to "walk on two legs" and be prepared for any eventuality.

For myself, in every country I visited in the East, I asked for training in intelligence, in sabotage, and in weaponry. I obtained all three kinds of training in China, in Czechoslovakia, and in Vietnam. I would be taken to a secluded place to practice with firearms, hand grenades, and plastic bombs. The training was for short periods of time, between one and two weeks. I would have preferred to stay longer, but I could not be away from my station in Cairo for very long. It was easier to travel from Cairo than from Zanzibar, where the British would have stopped me.

We heard the news in 1961 of the death of Patrice Lumumba in the Congo. In protest, all the African organizations with offices in Cairo organized an assault on the Belgian embassy. But the Egyptian government stopped us and arrested some of our activists. I went to the Ministry of Interior to ask for their release, but Egyptian security intercepted us. Through security, however, we contacted top Egyptian government officials, who offered to work with us to plan another demonstration in front of the Belgian embassy. We agreed, even though we knew it would not be as spontaneous as we wanted.

When we eventually demonstrated, there were about ten thousand of us, mostly Egyptians, who mobilized youth, students, and workers. With their support, we broke the gates and ransacked the embassy, and the police did not stop us. No one was seriously hurt; the diplomats had already run away. They must have been tipped off, which was good, because they would have been killed had they remained. Emotions were very high that day.

Some of us got inside the embassy and took classified diplomatic materials. We gave the documents to the Czechs, the Russians, the Chinese, and the Egyptians. But we gave the Egyptians only the rubbish, the unclassified documents, so they complained, and were very displeased.

At that point in mid-1961, I decided I had done enough in Cairo. The Egyptian authorities were unhappy with me, so I decided to come home. The struggle, anyway, was back in Zanzibar.

seven EXPULSION

SINCE THE 1957 ELECTIONS, the ZNP had been organizing and mobilizing the people. The next election took place in January 1961, while I was in Cairo. The ASP won ten seats; the ZNP won nine; and a new party, the Zanzibar and Pemba People's Party (ZPPP), won three seats. The ZPPP was a breakaway party from the ASP, led by Shirazi politicians who did not like Karume's leadership. Most of its support came from Pemban Shirazi who considered themselves closer in kin to Arabs than to Africans from the mainland.

After the elections, the ZPPP split, with two members forming an alliance with the ZNP and the third joining the ASP. Each side now had an equal number of seats, producing a stalemate and forcing the British to schedule new elections for June that year. They carved out one more constituency, so the total number of seats would be odd, not even. In the June elections, the ZNP-ZPPP alliance won more seats [thirteen] with less than a majority of the votes, while the ASP won fewer seats [ten] with a small majority of the votes.

I returned to Pemba in time for the June elections. It was quiet in Pemba, but in Zanzibar Town, riots started in Gulioni in Ng'ambo and spread from there to the rural areas. Rumors spread among ASP members that ZNP members were voting twice. Sixty-eight Arab members of the ZNP died in the rioting, but only a couple of ASP members were killed. It was a precursor of the revolution in 1964.

After the elections, the British arrested Babu and some leaders of the ZNP youth organization, called the Youth's Own Union. They accused them of arson. When the authorities could not prove arson, they charged Babu with sedition. They did not like what he had printed in his newspaper, *ZANEWS,* when he criticized the British over the contents of an official commission's report on the election riots of 1961. The report spread the blame for the violence among both the victims and the

69

perpetrators of the violence. According to Babu, it did not adequately condemn those in the ASP who had killed members of the ZNP. The British said they were just trying to reconcile the two sides, but Babu objected, so they charged him with sedition, saying he was trying to incite the people against the government.

Babu was let out on bond to attend the Lancaster House Conference in London as an observer for the ZNP. The conference was convened in 1962 to decide how and when the British would leave Zanzibar and whether there would be a final round of elections before independence.[1] I went to London with Babu for that conference and stayed with him in the same hotel; every evening he would explain what happened that day. Babu slowly began to realize then that Ali Muhsin and Muhammed Shamte, the leader of the ZPPP, were going to sell us socialists in the party out to the British. The British told the ZNP leaders that they would not receive power unless they purged the party of socialists. And the old guard, Muhsin and Shamte, were prepared to collaborate with the colonialists to get us out of the way.

For a long time, we heard—even in the bars in Zanzibar Town—that the party leadership wanted to purge us socialists. I remember that one day even Ali Muhsin told me he was happy the British were building a new prison at Langoni because, he said, "they would have a place to put [you] radicals." I was shocked by what he said and by the disgust with which he said it since we had been working together for years. I could not believe my ears. I told him, "You are my leader, so you will go first, and I will follow," and this turned out to be the prophetic truth.[2]

I told Babu in London that, if the British were going to put him "inside," then I would go to Cuba and get military training for our youth cadres. I obtained his blessing because, as I have said, we were guided by Mao's dictum, "walk on two legs." We needed to prepare ourselves to employ both peaceful and revolutionary methods for taking power. There is also a saying in Swahili, *"Ukiujua huu na mimi ninajua huu,"*— basically, "If you are going to do this to me, then I will be forced to respond by doing that to you." Also, we had studied Russian and Chinese tactics and knew how to undermine the opposition.

So, after the conference, Babu returned to Zanzibar, and I went to Havana. The Cubans put me in the Riviera Hotel where I was told Frank Sinatra once had shares. Before Castro nationalized the hotel, it was apparently a Mafia-owned establishment.

I went around in the evenings to the nightclubs; I was fond of Cuban music. Between the Riviera Hotel and our ZNP office in Havana, there was one nightclub I frequented, well known throughout Cuba, called

Los Violinas. It had a huge auditorium and staged a floorshow. It was a twelve-story building right on the waterfront, where, I was told, under the Batista regime, prostitutes would line up, waiting for the tourists to come.

My hosts took me all around the island to show me their efforts to eliminate racial discrimination in Cuba. They had a type of affirmative action in Cuba because, before the revolution, the blacks were less advantaged than the whites, so the new government wanted to give them an opportunity. Even today, the people who defend the Cuban revolution to the last are the black Cubans because they obtained their liberation through the revolution and are very thankful for that.

The Cubans also had, I would say, the best health services in all Latin America. The WHO [World Health Organization] has even acknowledged them as superb. Today we have Cuban doctors in Tanzania helping us, as in most African countries, because the Cubans have a surplus of doctors and can afford to export them. Unfortunately, I did not fall sick in Cuba; otherwise, I could have sampled the fruits of the Cuban revolution as far as health care was concerned.

I took a trip from Havana to Santiago Oriente, in the eastern part of the island. It took twelve hours driving in a car, and we stopped in two towns along the way. I tell you, even in the late hours of the night, the Cubans really enjoy life—they dance and drink up to the early hours of the morning. The music goes for twenty-four hours. You would think that these people did not work during the day.

Santiago Oriente was just like Africa. I saw a complete difference between west and east in the island. There were more dark people in the eastern province than in Havana, maybe because of the climate or the agriculture there. In the east, there were profound similarities with society in Zanzibar: the people were selling *madafuu* in the streets, young coconuts they cut open and drank. They roasted maize on charcoal, and fried *mishkaki* on the street corners. I found this all over Latin America; wherever the population was so mixed that Africans were predominant, I found such a situation, and it really made me feel at home.

And we were free to mix with the Cuban people in their homes—even in Russia it was more restrictive. I do not remember ever being invited to a Russian home, though the girls mixed with us and came to the flats where our boys were living. But in Cuba, it was an open environment; once you befriended a Cuban, he would invite you home to sit and talk and drink together.

I remember I did voluntary work cutting sugar cane one Sunday. I spent the whole day in the field, from six in the morning until two in the afternoon, working and drinking cane juice. It was hot and sweaty work, but we enjoyed ourselves. It was like a picnic to me—I sang and enjoyed the beautiful girls. There were beautiful girls there, oh, my God! I went for one, but I restrained myself out of a sense of socialist discipline; but I liked her nevertheless, and she would have responded.

I could have married there, had I not been married already. They were very simple people, full of sympathy, "*simpatico*" they call it in Spanish. Well, I regret that I did not have much time in Cuba; I think I would have been a Cuban by now because I liked the culture so much. But I knew I had an obligation to my country, and we had to struggle for our independence, just as the Cubans had struggled for theirs.

I wanted training for our boys, so I asked for a meeting with Raul Castro, the minister of defense. One evening I was with some delegates enjoying dinner at the Habana Libre, which had been the Hilton Hotel before it was nationalized.[3] As Ali Mafhoudh and I were leaving, I was whisked away and taken to a room where Raul was seated with his entourage. I explained my desires and described the nature of the security forces in Zanzibar. Raul estimated that we needed only twenty people to overthrow the government. We agreed that twenty boys would be enough. After I returned to Zanzibar, I found eighteen young men ready to go to Cuba for military training, which we described to the colonial authorities as a course in trade-union organization and leadership. Some of the eighteen were my comrades who had already received military training in Egypt.

After meeting Raul Castro, I remained in Cuba for two more weeks. One night I was drinking in Havana at the bar of the Club Tropicana when I was informed through the Ghanaian ambassador that, back in Zanzibar, Babu had been convicted of sedition and sentenced to fifteen months' imprisonment. I immediately told the bodyguard assigned to me that I wanted to take the first plane out the next morning.

The flight stopped in Cairo, where I told the boys at the ZNP office there—Amani Thani Ferouz, Suleiman Sultan Malik, and Mbarak Khalfan, for example—that when I returned to Zanzibar, I would tell everyone that Babu's imprisonment was a result of Muhsin's and Shamte's collaboration with the British. I wanted their support, but they warned me that I would split the party. They begged me not to say anything, but I was convinced the truth needed to be told.

From Cairo, I flew to Dar es Salaam where I heard rumors that the British intended to apprehend me upon my arrival back in Zanzibar. After all, Babu was now imprisoned, as well as several of our youth comrades. To outmaneuver the British, I held a press conference in Dar es

Salaam, at the Arnautaglu Hall. I told the reporters of the rumors and said that, if they were true, I was ready to go to prison and become yet another mouth to be fed by the exploited taxpayers of Zanzibar, to join the other political detainees of our party. I did this to put off the British because they never liked to act according to expectations. If I predicted my own arrest, they would wait and find some later pretext to put me inside. I was trying to gain time, you see.

When I arrived in Zanzibar Town, I went to the offices of the Federation of Progressive Trade Unions, or FPTU. The FPTU was an umbrella trade-union organization affiliated with the ZNP, where some of my socialist comrades were in leadership positions. The FPTU had already scheduled a public meeting with the government for that same day, obtaining permission for several speakers to be on the program, including me. I told my comrades in the FPTU that I wanted to publicly discuss Muhsin's collaboration with the British, but they overruled me. I could not remain silent about Babu's imprisonment, however, and I blew up as I finished my speech. I related the whole story and all the past conversations that together made it very clear it was Muhsin's and Shamte's intention to get Babu out of the way.[4]

That same day I was called to a meeting of the ZNP Executive Committee. I was not certain what would happen, so I came armed with my Browning pistol, with the trigger cocked and one bullet inside. I had obtained the Browning that year through my Czech contacts who purchased it for me in Belgium. I took the seat nearest the door because I thought that, if anything happened, I could take out my pistol, shoot a bullet into the air, cause mass fear, and then run for the door.

In the meeting, I once again denounced Muhsin and Shamte. Muhsin was in Morocco, but Shamte was present. I said I was ashamed to be working with people like them. How could Muhsin be roaming around Morocco when the British had just imprisoned his secretary general? I had felt it necessary to take the first plane home, but where was he? I also asked how it was possible to collaborate with the British and to sacrifice one of their own.

Of course, the members of the committee did not like to hear that kind of talk. One branch leader attending the meeting said to Shamte, "Allow me to hit him." He did not know I had my pistol cocked under my shirt. And then Ahmed Seif Kharusi, the editor of *Mwongozi,* told me I was expelled from the party. I said, "You cannot do that. You have forgotten your own party constitution. You have to have a general party conference to expel someone. And anyway, I do not care because I personally do not have the heart to work with you anymore."

Later Shamte and the others expelled me from the Executive Committee; they pressured the FPTU also to throw me out, but the FPTU refused to do so. I convened a press conference, where I delivered the following statement entitled "Condemn Me Now, But History Will Absolve Me," a title I had taken from one of Castro's speeches.

All students of history both contemporary and medieval will not fail to recall that what is taking place now in our country has taken place elsewhere on earth.

What is taking place now in Zanzibar has not surprised me at all but confirms the belief I have always held since I started to think and use my intelligence, to differentiate right and wrong, just and unjust. . . . The ZNP is not a party in the real sense but a liberation movement . . . a mass movement comprised of different sections and stratum of the people. This is an objective reality and anyone who tries to deny this is just fooling himself.

Concretely, we have within the ZNP the following main features: a section that cherishes capitalism and abhors socialism, the capitalist class, and the landlords who prosper and grow fat by exploiting the working people. They live like parasites, while others toil and sweat. And a section of proletariats, peasants, small farmers, small shopkeepers, individuals who through their own labor manage to make two ends meet. We have also the professionals, the intelligentsia, the students, the youths, and the women.

The characteristic feature of such a movement is that while you will no doubt notice that the interests of the toiling masses are diametrically opposed to the interests of the parasites, yet under colonialism there is something that unites all these different social stratum. . . . Though the parasites oppress the people, they are in turn also oppressed by the colonialists and imperialists. Hence, you get a united front movement such as ZNP. . . .

We must be ruthless and wage a determined struggle against the enemies of the people, expose them for what they are, and not flirt and appease them, hoping that they will change and be good. It is the U.S.A., Britain, France, West Germany which represent the imperialist powers . . . while the local reactionaries are nothing but imperialist running dogs.

I also believe that the Afro-Shirazi are not my enemies but my friends. If today there is misunderstanding between the ZNP and Afro-Shirazi, it is because of the reactionary tendency of certain elements both within the ZNP/ZPPP and the Afro-Shirazi.

I cannot compromise with opportunism, for he who compromises with opportunism is bound to be an opportunist himself. Now since the challenge has been launched against me, I say this openly: that it will be . . . the progressives who shall lead the ZNP and so achieve real independence, or I shall not support the reactionaries who I know very well are ready to sell the interest of our people, and for that I shall oppose them to the end.

I am confident that we shall win in the end, and by "we" I mean the progressives, not only in Zanzibar but throughout the world.

VENCEREMOS, VENCEREMOS, VENCEREMOS.

After the press conference, the British Resident, Sir George Mooring, called me to the State House. For the same meeting, the Resident called the commissioner of police. I had a cousin working there as a clerk who was certain I was going to be put inside since that was what usually happened when the commissioner of police was called in.

In his office, the Resident threatened me, saying, "You talk too much." By that time, I had lost the support of the party, so I had to be humble. But I still told him, "I have not committed any crime, but if you want to, I will be another mouth for the taxpayers to feed in one of your prisons."

"You be careful. Watch what you say," the Resident said.

"Okay, yes, sir," I said.

My cousin the clerk was surprised when I walked out of there a free man.

 THE VANGUARD

AFTER MY EXPULSION FROM
the ZNP, I had no income. I worked for the FPTU, but there was no
allowance. Whatever we could raise as membership dues, we would use for
office rent and for printing costs; but there was no personal allowance,
nothing. So my wife went to China, taking our two daughters with her.
She lived in Beijing and taught Swahili at the Chinese Foreign Language Institute for two years, from 1962 to 1964.

I stayed with friends in a house in Malindi. There were four of us:
Badawi, Farouk Muhammed Said, Anwar Ali Said, and myself. I lived
very simply. The rent was free, but I helped pay for the electricity; all I
wanted beyond that was food. In those days, I had a moderately rich
English girlfriend, Miss Suzanne Dixon, who sent me money. She came
to East Africa for a visit in 1961, and we happened to leave Zanzibar on
the same plane. After spending the night in the same hotel in Nairobi,
we started speaking on the plane to Entebbe, in Uganda, and from there
we traveled on to Khartoum.

We drank on the plane. It was dark; I wanted to kiss her, but she refused. In the seat in front of us was another English girl with a child,
just coming from the Seychelle Islands. When Miss Dixon refused to
kiss me, the girl in front said, "If she doesn't want to be kissed, then
come here with me!" She was actually more physically attractive than
Miss Dixon, so I put her child in my seat and went to sit next to her.
After a few kisses, I returned to my old seat and then dozed from all
the booze.

When the flight reached Khartoum, it was time for me to transfer to
another plane. Miss Dixon woke me up, and because she liked my cigarette case so much, I deliberately left it in the seat for her. It was from
China, and the lighter was inside the cigarette case, a new thing at the
time. But as I was leaving, she ran out of the plane onto the tarmac to

remind me of the case. I said, "Just keep it because you like it." She said, "No, you take it, and when you come to England, you'll give it to me."

She gave me her telephone number in England and was my girlfriend for years. She was not as beautiful as some women I have known; but she was kind, and she had money. Her family was in the wine business and had a couple of shops in London. She had a sports car, a Carmen Ghia, which I drove when I was in London. Whenever I needed money she sent it—she was very generous.

Eventually the British released all the ZNP youth cadres from prison, but Babu stayed inside until 1963. While he was imprisoned, I discussed the idea of forming a third political movement in Zanzibar [the Youth and Students Union]. I discussed this with trade unionists, young people, my old comrades in the ZNP, and people I knew in the ASP who were progressive in their ideas, people like Hassan Nassor Moyo, Abdulaziz Twala, and Kassim Hanga, socialists who had studied in the Soviet Union. Of course, I had no intention of doing anything without getting Babu's blessing. But we wanted to present him when he came out with a *fait accompli*.

I was summoned suddenly to Cuba because one of our boys there wanted to leave the camp and report to the British that Zanzibaris were receiving military training. He cracked, I think, because he smoked a lot of marijuana. I knew his family very well, and as children, we used to play together. By the time I arrived, the Cubans had locked him in a cell inside the camp. I asked him, "Why did you do this?" He was apologetic, but I said "Listen, I can kill you here and bury you, and even your mum wouldn't know what happened. Will you behave yourself if I order your release?" He said yes, and I told him that, if he attempted the same thing again, there would not be a cell, there would be a grave. Then I told the Cubans to release him because we had come to an understanding. He behaved himself after that.

On that second trip to Cuba, I was invited to an official function where suddenly Fidel Castro arrived. I was holding a plate of cassava and pork, and he came and joked with me, saying "*Yukka con poyo,*" cassava and pork. He was just moving about and giving each of us a few words with the cameras following him. The function took place in the garden of a huge palace. I did not have a chance to speak with him as I had with his brother Raul; anyway, as a young man, I found Raul fiercer and more serious than Fidel, more of an agitator, I would say. Of course, they were from a well-to-do family; middle-class intellectuals have, in fact, led most of the revolutions in the world. Lenin, Marx, and Engels:

none of them was from the lower echelons of society. All of them sacrificed their class origins to fight for the downtrodden. To change a society, you must create history.

Another significant event happened just nine days before Babu was released from prison. Our house in Malindi had a leaky tap, so I asked a plumber to come and repair it; he said he would come the next day. Badawi refused to wait for the plumber, saying the leaky tap did not bother him. So, halfheartedly, I went home to wait during the day, a time when I was normally out. I unlocked my bedroom door and boof! On my bed, I found a bundle wrapped in brown paper that someone had thrown in from the window. At first, I thought it was *maandazi* that maybe my girlfriend in Zanzibar had sent me. I opened it up and started to shake.

The bundle was copies of personal letters supposedly signed by me and addressed to Jamshid, the prince who would later become the sultan; to Ali Muhsin; to Muhammed Shamte, who was then the chief minister; and to Karume, leader of the ASP opposition. In those letters, I informed them that my group of comrades and I were going to kill them.

I showed the letters to my house servant, who did not know anything. Then I rushed to the FPTU office and showed them to Khamis and Badawi, who were writing the daily worker's paper we published. Khamis said "Burn them." By the time they were ashes, Suleiman Sisi came and said the police had surrounded our house. Badawi worried that my pistol might be found in my room, so he came back to deal with the police. He watched as they searched my bed, broke open my wardrobe, and forcefully opened my briefcase. It was a miracle that they did not unwrap my Browning pistol. They failed miserably. God was on our side because, if the authorities had managed to plant those letters, Babu would not have come out of prison and our boys would have all gone inside. It was an obvious ploy by the colonial government to frame my comrades and me and to give them a reason to lock us up. The leaky tap saved me; had it not been for that, I would not have gone back to the house at that unusual hour.

When we returned that day to our place in Malindi, we put mosquito wires on all the windows to stop the government from doing the same thing again. And then in the evening, around five o'clock or so, a cable and wireless messenger came to the house, saying one hundred British pounds had been sent to us from friends in China. I said "*Al-hamdulilah!*" Badawi cashed the money through an Indian merchant, and we shared it with about twenty other comrades. I went with some friends for drinks at the airport, and we enjoyed ourselves; the next day there was nothing left at all. That was in early 1963. After that, I kept my shutters closed.[1]

When Babu was released from prison, the ZNP organized receptions for him every day for a week all over Zanzibar. He was a hero to the nationalist rank and file, but I immediately pressured Babu to leave the ZNP. He said "Let's work first for unity and reconciliation and bring you back into the fold." I said this tactic would not work with those people.

Babu wanted to compromise until the last day, yet he prepared a strategy to test the party's good will. At a ZNP conference that summer, he demanded three safe seats for progressive candidates. Babu was already promised a safe seat in Pemba, but he wanted two others for our comrades, who would not just keep quiet, who wanted real change. Three safe seats in Tumbatu, Nungwi, and Bumbwini were to be given to Babu, Muhsin Abeid, and Abdulrazzak Mussa Simai, who was called "Kwacha." The last two were Shirazi candidates who were progressive in their thinking.

At the same time, we were meeting with Hassan Nassor Moyo in the ASP's labor movement, who, at his own party's conference that summer, had also demanded three safe seats for progressive candidates. There was an understanding between Babu and Moyo that, if each side succeeded, then the progressive members of parliament would hold the balance of power and could force the creation of a government of national unity. Or they could form a third party of socialists across racial lines to act as a bridge between the larger parties. We wanted our own party, and we hoped Moyo and other ASP progressives would join us.

Of course, the reactionaries in the ZNP-ZPPP did not want that. They refused Babu's demands, so he and other progressives walked out. Had they accepted Babu's proposal, we would have formed a national government, and the revolution would never have taken place. Instead, some of us comrades were waiting to welcome Babu and ready to establish our own organization. We went to Mbuyuni and held a meeting on a rooftop, where we decided to form the Umma Party. In Arabic, *umma* means the Islamic community, including everyone from India, Indonesia, and so on. But here it just means "the people." We wanted to call our party the People's Party, but in the local language so people would understand.

We founded the Umma Party in June 1963, but some of us blame ourselves for waiting too long. Since 1958, we had been the vanguard and had organized the ZNP at the grassroots, mobilizing all our national forces. The reactionaries could get the support of other reactionaries, the *petit bourgeoisie* and the landlords, but we were the ones who mobilized the majority rank and file: the workers, peasants, students, and youth. We split from Ali Muhsin and his clique because we blamed them for conniving with the British to put Babu in prison. Ideology also played a very big part; we needed to have an organization of like-minded socialists and progressives.

The workers from the FPTU were the first to join Umma. The ZNP youth were split; the more active and revolutionary minority, ready and determined to fight, went over to Umma. These young people came from the working class or peasant families and were pliable. In fact, we relied almost completely on the youth. We concentrated more on them than the peasantry or, for that matter, on the urban *petit bourgeois* shopkeepers.

I was a member of the Umma Party's Executive Committee. There were about fifteen of us on that committee, but Babu was clearly the leader. Only Badawi, Khamis, and I were able to debate with Babu ideologically because we had been more exposed than had the others. All four of us were pro-Chinese, although we eschewed the "Maoist" identity and simply called ourselves socialists. We were the four leaders of the Umma movement, a quartet, and Babu never did anything without our support. He came to us before presenting ideas to the rest of the party. I had known him since childhood, and we had been in London together; sometimes I could read his mind. Sure, we had our debates, but they were not divisive. One of our slogans was "Unity, Criticism, Unity." It was a socialist doctrine that you criticize not to break but to strengthen unity. Though we were united and wanted our unity to remain strong, we still had our differences; some of us were more exposed and thus more advanced in our thinking.

We had cell meetings, rather than mass meetings, and we enrolled members discreetly. We advised our supporters to vote according to their conscience. We knew we could not win the elections, so we did not ask them to vote for this or that party. I voted for the ASP in the Malindi constituency, in protest. I would not give my vote to Ali Muhsin. In the 1963 elections, unsurprisingly, the ZNP–ZPPP alliance won more seats with less than a majority of the votes, while the ASP obtained fewer seats with a majority of the votes. The voting percentages were 54–46 in favor of the ASP.[2] The British agreed to withdraw in December 1963, turning power over to the ZNP–ZPPP alliance.

This situation came as no surprise to us in the movement. We had faith, and we knew it was a matter of time. By working closely with all the opposition forces, including the ASP, we knew we would have a solid base.[3] We said, "Once the euphoria of independence has passed, the people will see; they will open their eyes." The reality of where the ZNP was taking Zanzibar would be obvious to all those who could see. Muhsin was not interested in land reform, only in capitalism. He could not see there was another side to the coin or even imagine any compromise between the two systems. His thinking was just to bring in some kind of Nasserism, Islamism, Arab ideas, and all that; and yet we were surrounded by African nationalist secularist states in Kenya, Tanganyika, and Uganda. It was inevitable that Zanzibar would move toward a collision course with her neighbors, and we were ready to exploit that contradiction when the time came.

The ZNP threw stones at us, saying we fornicated with our mothers and sisters; they said we held parties where we exchanged wives, like orgies. None of that ever happened because we were very strict. And then the party said, "Look! They want to bring in communism! They're atheists; they don't believe in God." Religion was actually a major cause of the split. Ali Muhsin would say, "Look at them! They don't say their prayers, and they don't fast." If we were not fasting, we ate only at home, not in front of the people. If we wanted to work in that type of society, we had to be shrewd and to observe local customs. The Communist Party had enough wisdom to train us that way. We were quite disciplined; even when we were fornicating, we did it discreetly. I was a rebel against colonial institutions but not a rebel against Islamic morality. I was never decadent, just very discreet. We were taught that, if you sinned discreetly, then God would punish you discreetly. If you sinned openly, then God would punish you openly.

I continued to stay with Badawi in Malindi, even though it was a ZNP stronghold. My wife was in China, so I employed someone to cook for me and my comrades who had been thrown out by their families. They were chased away from getting food at home as a sort of punishment. It was like, "Okay, if you rebel, then find your own food." It happened mainly among the cadres I recruited for military training in Cuba, Arab boys from Stone Town.

So we cooked a big dish of cassava, and I asked every one to bring his own *kiteweo*, the vegetable or meat sauce you add to the cassava. And because they were Stone Town boys, they could go down to the waterfront and be given a small fish. There were about eight or ten of us, and we had at least one heavy meal a day. We even shared cigarettes; when someone would light up, another would come over for a few puffs. They were outcasts, and Badawi's house was like a commune— until, that is, some ZNP youth came one night and poured dung in all our windows, except my own since I was the only one who bothered to close his shutters ever since the police dumped those forged letters into my room.

I was so furious that I refused to clean up afterward. Since my room was the only one that remained clean, all of us slept there until we found a new place to live. I moved with Badawi to a house in an African neighborhood in town named Mitiulaya, where we would be protected from such incidents. But still the FPTU offices were in Malindi, so when we walked there, the ZNP youth—just young boys—you could just spit and they would run away—would wait for us. When they saw us, they would clap their hands and sing in Swahili, "You motherfucking comrades!" If they had a chance to kill us, I think they would have done so. And these were the same youth whom Babu had once recruited for the Youth's Own Union, since that was one of his projects in the ZNP. It was like that until I left the country.

Since 1956, I had been suffering severely from duodenal ulcers, and the party decided I should go to China to seek treatment and also to be with my wife and daughters. The nucleus of Umma was already established, and I had confidence in my comrades' ability to continue to organize. Mind you, I did not want to leave, had it not been for my ulcers; but our Executive Committee made a decision that I should go. Since the British had impounded my passport, I had to leave the country illegally. We paid a crew of four men to row an outrigger at night for four hours to reach Bagamoyo, on the Tanganyikan mainland. Unfortunately, we arrived during low tide, and the water was out. We waited for another two hours, and by the time I reached land, it was around 3:00 a.m.

I surrendered myself at the local police station. I later explained to the area commissioner the reason that I had left Zanzibar and that I was en route to China, and he invited me to breakfast. Later that day, I traveled to Dar es Salaam, where I met Babu and, through his assistance, obtained the necessary emergency travel certificate from the Tanganyikan government.

 REVOLUTION

WHEN I CAME TO CHINA, I WAS
very happy to see my wife and two daughters. Fidela only spoke Chinese,
so when I went to take her from my wife's arms, she shouted out, "*Wo
bu yao ni!!*" I had to ask my other daughter, Raissa, who was then four
years old, what she was saying. She told me she was saying, "She doesn't
want you." *Wo* = I, *bu* = no, *yao* = want, *ni* = you. Fidela was two years old
and dressed like any Chinese girl, and she had a round face, so she could
pass for a Chinese girl. My daughters stayed in a boarding school in Beijing because my wife was working and could come to visit them on the
weekends. They were fed there, and they played with the other expatriate children from Russia, America, Germany, Australia, and so on. Our
third daughter, Maotushi, remained in Zanzibar with my wife's parents.

We stayed in a flat designated for Russian expatriates, in building
Yo Yee Ping One, room 2235, or in Chinese, *ah ah san woo*. I was content and never demanded anything extra. I was a disciplinarian; I never
flirted with any girl and never begged for anything. But I had access to
a car; and in a period of rationing, I had plenty of food, clothing, and
gasoline. I also received treatment for my ulcers, but the Chinese doctors did not operate.

I was in the flat during the day, reading mostly Maoist revolutionary
works. Sometimes I would ask a friend to take me on day trips to visit
historical places, instead of remaining idle. I met with dignitaries from
the Chinese trade unions since we had been working together since my
first trip to China in 1960. My wife and I and Muhsin Abeid attended
a trade-union conference in North Vietnam organized by the World
Federation of Trade Unions, in support of the struggle in South Vietnam. Ho Chi Minh hosted a huge banquet; since my wife was the only
woman delegate present, Ho invited her to be seated next to him at the
main table. She had that privilege. As an appetizer, we were served a

snake cut into small pieces, which tasted like a kind of fish we have here in Zanzibar called *ngogo*. I told my wife in Swahili, "You are eating snake, but eat it and don't vomit." But she had been living in China since 1962 and was used to eating all kinds of concoctions.

Ho gave a toast and gave my wife a hug and kissed her on the cheeks. They flushed afterward—Ho and Aysha both became red—and we all clapped because we were very happy.

At the beginning of January 1964, just three weeks after Zanzibar had obtained its independence, the ZNP government banned the Umma Party and confiscated all our property at the party headquarters. The authorities wanted to arrest Babu under the false pretext that they found a pistol in his compound. The police had planted a gun in his home, forcing him to flee Zanzibar for the mainland in a canoe.

As soon as I heard the news, I wanted to return to Africa to carry on the struggle, which I knew was reaching a climax. I had discussions with the Chinese for a week on how to organize as an illegal party because, for most of their history, they had worked underground. How did they work under such conditions? They taught me from their own experience; I was being groomed, so to speak. I made preparations to move my family to East Africa, but in those days, it took some time to book a ticket from Beijing to Dar es Salaam.

Then on January 12, 1964, around five in the evening in China, we received the BBC news relay from Hong Kong. It announced a revolution in Zanzibar. I remember I had a high temperature on that day and had my sweater on, but when I heard the news, all of a sudden I was well. My temperature, boof! Gone! My Chinese friend heard the news over the wireless, and we both came out of our rooms at the same time, to inform one another. We embraced, and to celebrate, we opened a bottle of Chinese champagne, known as Mao Tai.

That night I did not sleep because I thought we were going to be suppressed by colonial forces. In fact, for three days I did not sleep; I just listened to the radio, expecting British intervention at any moment. I could hear my comrades in Zanzibar, the ones I had sent to Cuba for training, shouting in Spanish, *"Aki esta oi, Zanzibar proklama ente Afrika e el mundo Zanzibar primero pais libre d'Afrika."* [Today Zanzibar proclaims in front of Africa and the world that Zanzibar is the first liberated country of Africa].[1] *"Nos otros sobrenia nunka negociables!"* [Our sovereignty is not negotiable] *"Patria o muerte!"* [Our fatherland or death] and *"Venceremos!"* [We shall conquer] These were Cuban slogans the comrades remembered from their time there; they just substituted *Zanzibar* for *Cuba*, and since that time, we have greeted each other in this way, using these words. Eventually I managed to book tickets to return home, and we left China on January 15, 1964.

Later in Zanzibar, I was told how the revolution took place. The ZNP-ZPPP government refused any defensive agreement with the British because Ali Muhsin's policy was to wait instead for a treaty with the Egyptian government. He was a racialist, naïve, and stupid because he should have first agreed with the British for a limited period and then phased them out in favor of the Egyptians, if that is what he wanted. If he had had foresight, he would have signed a temporary pact, but he did not. I think it was because God wanted the revolution to happen.

When the ZNP banned the Umma Party, the ASP thought its turn would be next. There is a Swahili expression that when you see someone having his head shaved, it is time to water your head, to prepare yourself to follow: *Ukimwona mwenzako ananyolewa wewe tia maji*. The government started with us comrades because they feared us more than they did the ASP, though we were much weaker in numbers. They could not believe the ASP was capable of launching any kind of attack, but, in reality, the leaders of the ASP Youth League organized the revolution. They were men of very little education, some of whom had not even finished primary school and were doing manual work around town as tradesmen, dockworkers, and tailors. Babu had a phrase for these elements: the lumpen proletariat. Umma comrades had been in discussions with the Youth League about the need for a revolution, but the ASP had the support of the majority of the population, and we did not.

The government received intelligence reports of a possible uprising among the police rank and file, who generally supported the ASP, while the officers supported the Nationalists. Many of the rank and file were Africans from the mainland who were rapidly being dismissed and replaced with island recruits more loyal to the regime. To counter the threat of a police mutiny, the government decided to collect and dismantle as many weapons as possible and put them in the armory at Ziwani. Information was leaked to the Youth League that, at Ziwani, only the sentries were armed and that each sentry was limited to just five bullets. Seif Bakari and other Youth League leaders decided to mobilize a considerable force of men armed only with clubs and machetes to attack the armory at Ziwani and also the police barracks at Mtoni, both located on the edge of town.

On the night of January 11, the Youth League organized a dance concert at Raha Leo in Ng'ambo in order to distract the police. While some people were dancing, others secretly approached the armories. They escaped notice and attacked around midnight, taking the government completely by surprise. They were led by people like Yusuf Himidi, Said wa Shoto, Abdullah Said Natepe, Khamis Darweshi, Ramadhan Haji, Pili Khamis, Seif Bakari, and Saidi Iddi Bavuai. By 2:00 a.m. both Ziwani and Mtoni were in their hands, and probably no more than fifty died in the attack.

The revolution came as no surprise to the comrades. The Youth League first brought the captured guns to a taxi stand near Mwembeladu, in Ng'ambo. Within a couple of hours after their capture, Badawi called the boys I had sent to Cuba to come and assemble the guns and give them out because very few people in Zanzibar had ever handled a gun. So the comrades cooperated with the revolutionaries from almost the very beginning, though Babu was in Dar es Salaam at the time for his own protection. I was told that Karume also went to Dar es Salaam.[2] Although Karume did not organize the revolution, he must have known about the plans and given his blessing and then went to Dar es Salaam in case they failed.

The only real government resistance was at the Malindi police station, where I was told there were a few losses among the revolutionaries. But once the revolutionaries arrested all the ministers, the sultan sailed away on his yacht. He could have gone to Pemba where he had much support, but he did not. I do not know why. Maybe the British advised him not to.

Had they wanted, the British could have intervened militarily and defeated us, but I think it was a plan. A week later there was an army mutiny in Dar es Salaam, and the British intervened there; so why did they not intervene in Zanzibar? Here in Zanzibar, they had a number of British expatriates; even some principal secretaries in the government were still British.[3] But it was a blessing because, if they had not stayed away, we would not have succeeded. *Al-hamdullilah!*

With all those guns now in people's hands, thousands of people died, generally Arabs. I cannot say how many. A revolution is not a tea party; things like that are anticipated. The arrogant ones suffered after the revolution; for certain things, there were repercussions. It was a day of reckoning, based on how you had treated your fellow being. If you were a good Muslim, you had no fears. If you lived nicely with your neighbors, you were all right. If not, then some people might have a grudge against you, and when they got the upper hand, they could be nasty. There were some Arabs hidden in African homes, so it all depended on how you had lived with your neighbors.

It was not so much a genocide as it was revenge killings or a chance to steal and rape. Sometimes the killing was accidental because the revolutionaries could work whimsically: they might be nasty one minute and nice the next. Criminals whom we released from the prisons murdered people, but at other times, people were killed for political reasons. The violence was conducted primarily by men from town who went to the countryside with guns. Stone Town was too congested for the revolutionaries, so few people actually died there. They died mostly in the *shamba* or in Ng'ambo where they were more isolated and where there was little chance of resistance. Outside of Stone Town, few people had guns with which to resist.

Some Arabs were killed immediately, while others were rounded up and detained either in town or on Prison Island. Eventually ships came from the Red Cross to take them to Oman. After I returned from China, I did not visit the island to see their misery, but I knew they were there.

I do not know if any central authority directed the violence in those days. There was a revolutionary headquarters at Raha Leo where John Okello claimed over the radio that he was field marshal of the revolution, but that was just rubbish. In fact, I remember when Okello first came to the islands in 1958 from Kenya. He was a stone breaker, and I secured a job for him in Pemba. I sent him to a fellow named Mazrui who had a quarry in Vitongoji, and I forgot about him until he wanted to see me after the revolution to thank me for finding him work in those days.

The Youth League recruited any element prepared to fight, including John Okello. Later he claimed to be the field marshal, but if he really was, then how a couple of months later did we manage to throw him out of the islands just like that? The other revolutionaries used him because people did not know his name, and it frightened them. It was easy to believe he was Mau Mau, with a name like that. "What monster is this?" they asked. The names Seif Bakari or Yusuf Himidi would not have inspired such terror. Okello was really a naïve, simple fellow who was used to frighten people. So it is rubbish that Westerners believe John Okello planned and organized the revolution.[4]

The violence lasted about ten days, and I would estimate that about one-third of the Arabs in Unguja were killed or forced into immediate exile. I personally supported the revolution completely and had no reservations about the government's being overthrown. Good riddance! For us who had nothing to lose but our misery, we welcomed the revolution. The authorities had banned our party, and they had confiscated our property; but we got it all back after the revolution, whatever little we had, even including a table fan.

I may have sympathy for some unfortunate ones who died in the process, but in a revolution, those kinds of things happen, like in any war. I cannot condone it, but it happened.[5] My own uncle, an Arab land-lord, was killed in Mfenesini. But let me tell you: I warned him before I left Zanzibar, saying, "I'm leaving for China, and I'm asking you not to spend your nights in the *shamba*. Move your family into town and go every day to the *shamba* to do your business, but please sleep in town. Never mind if you think you have a gun, that it can protect you. Do this until I return from China."

There was already hatred in the country when I left in 1963, and that is why I warned my uncle. "If these people in the ZNP can turn against me, those with whom I've worked for years, then why can't the Africans in the countryside turn against you, my uncle?" He just laughed and did not follow my sincere advice; the result was he was killed. I heard peo-ple set fire to the thatch of his roof, and he fired his gun until he ran out of bullets. I do not know what happened after that. I did not ask the de-tails from those who survived. Painful. I was not very close to him, but he was my uncle, after all. His name was Nassor Issa, and he had quite a bit of land, planted mostly with coconut trees.

But I warned him, and he did not listen, so he was meant to die. He must have lived badly with the people around him. He was the only one we lost in my family; I had brothers and sisters in Unguja, but they were well known as members of my family, so no one would touch them be-cause they knew of my role in the Umma Party. During those days, comrades distributed photographs of Babu around town to our members or sympathizers, so that, when men with guns came to their door, they could show them Babu's picture and the gunmen would know they were comrades and not to be harmed.

I was blessed by being away because sometimes I was unpredictable. I really do not know how I would have reacted, how I would have con-ducted myself during that month around December and January, during independence and revolution. I missed that part of my life, but it was a blessing. Today no one can blame me or say anything because I was not there. No, my desire when I returned home was for no further excesses.

The revolution took place on January 12, 1964, and my family and I left Beijing on January 15. We stayed in Hong Kong for a couple of days because my wife was interested in doing some shopping. My idea was to return home as fast as possible, but I had to consent to her wishes. She wanted to buy some clothes for herself and the children and gifts for friends and family at home. Hong Kong was more stylish than the

Chinese mainland, and since we were Western-oriented, we had that stupid mentality. Even I, as a seaman staying in London, would go to a Jew in the East End, opposite Aldgate East tube station, to have my suits tailored. We in Zanzibar had imported materials like gabardine, linen, khaki, and silk. We had our suits made during Ramadhan so that by *sikukuu* [celebration marking the end of fasting], they would be ready to wear.

After Hong Kong, we spent a night in Bombay. The next day we were ready to leave for Tanganyika, but the management of Air India informed me that the airport in Dar es Salaam was now closed because of an army mutiny. A revolution in Zanzibar, and now a week later an army mutiny in Tanganyika!

I asked where we could go closer to Zanzibar and was told we could go to Nairobi, where we managed to arrive on January 19. In our hotel were the wives and children of British expatriates fleeing from Zanzibar. One of them said to me, "Why are you going to Zanzibar? You are an Arab, and you are taking your small children there to be butchered." I said, "Don't worry. I'm part of this struggle."

I met Babu where he stayed at the New Stanley Hotel, and he gave me his condolences. I said, "Don't give me your condolences because we've won the revolution." But then he told me that my mother had passed away a week earlier in Dar es Salaam. So, despite the mutiny, I had to go to Dar es Salaam first rather than to fly directly to Zanzibar. No commercial planes were flying, but I flew the next day on a government plane with Babu.

The army mutineers wanted to Africanize the higher echelons of the army and sack all their British officers. They wanted to capture Julius Nyerere and make their demands to him, but he was hiding in a house somewhere in Dar es Salaam. I thought this situation was clearly the effect of the revolution in Zanzibar: when the soldiers on the mainland saw that, in one day, we had turned our world in Zanzibar upside down, it gave them the idea to mutiny and to demand changes. A few days later there were mutinies also in Kenya and Uganda.

The soldiers controlled the airport and their two barracks but nothing else, so I could drive through town and visit my mother's grave. In the evening, I went to drink at the Dar es Salaam Club, a place for the African elite that, in colonial times, was the European yacht club. I was there with Lawi Sijaona, the minister of home affairs, and some other ministers and ambassadors, when some soldiers involved in the mutiny approached and asked the ministers why they were talking to an Arab. After that, Lawi advised my family and me to stay in our hotel room and not to drink with ministers like him in public places. I was not surprised; we had racism in Zanzibar, so why would there not be racism in Tanganyika?

On the fourth day in Dar es Salaam, a Czech intelligence officer awakened me early in the morning, saying he had heard gunfire and wanted me to find out what was happening. I took a car and went to the home of Oscar Kambona, the minister of foreign affairs and defense. Kambona was gone, but I met Lawi Sijaona there who informed me that Nyerere from his hideout had asked the British to intervene and suppress the mutiny. Lawi told me to return to my hotel and rest and by noon the airport would be open. The mutineers surrendered without a fight; and on that day, January 25, my family and I were able to fly to Zanzibar Town.[6]

I went immediately to report to the State House. Karume welcomed me and said, "Look, there's a boat going to Pemba tonight with some forces. And that man John Okello is already in Pemba. You'd better go and have a look and see which points are the weakest, from where, in your mind, infiltration from outside might come." So that night I left for Pemba; it took me three days to follow his instructions. I located all the strategic points and all the good harbors with deep water, any place where people might land by sea. The vulnerable places were formerly used by smugglers, where we had to strengthen our positions.

After returning to report, I stayed less than a week in Zanzibar Town before I was dispatched again to Pemba as an area commissioner over Chake Chake, the central area, even though I was originally from Wete. I had to move my family to Pemba; I had three young children, four younger brothers and sisters, and I was taking care of the five children of my deceased sister Dalila. There were fourteen of us in total, including my wife and me.

When I arrived in Pemba, I found the people dejected; they had surrendered without a fight and showed no open hostility to the revolutionary government, though the island had been a ZNP-ZPPP stronghold. Okello was going around frightening people, moving with a jeep-load full of men with guns. People were afraid of this Okello because he had a strange name and spoke Swahili with an accent, as I said.

It was chaos almost, but I have seen *Gone with the Wind*, and I am sure you saw the same thing in the American South after the Civil War. The Asians and Arabs who wanted to leave Pemba for Kenya or Tanganyika had to surrender their jewelry. We did not ask for anything else, just their jewelry. Of course, they were also afraid to take any currency out of the country. We would search them before they left, confiscate their jewelry, and send it to the central government coffers in Zanzibar Town. What the government did with the jewelry after that, I do not know.

There was a spirit of revenge in Pemba, which I think was wrong. It was a revolution, so it was like any revolution in the world. We tried to tell the people to work together and forget the past, but still there was a day of reckoning, and the arrogant ones suffered. Again, there were certain repercussions, depending on how you treated your fellow human beings.

There was a breakdown of law and order; people would not take their cases to the court, only to administrators like me from the revolutionary government. At the time, a decision came from Zanzibar Town that was sent to the regional commissioner in Pemba, Rashid Abdalla. Instead of putting people in jail, all offenders were to be flogged and then released. That was the decision. I thought it better than sending them to prison because if you send a bread earner to prison, you ruin the whole family. When he is gone, the family invariably disintegrates. When the man is inside, people can do anything to his family, like rape his wife and plunder his goods.

So I sat in a chair in the marketplace, and I dispensed punishments. We did the caning openly, for people to see, so they would behave themselves. Any offense would lead to flogging. I prescribed a maximum of twenty-one strokes, mostly for thieving, not for political reasons. I never caned a woman, but I did order seven strokes for a homosexual who dressed like a woman and even wore beads around his waist. This was an open violation of our customs. We have a saying here: *Ukifanya kwa siri, Mungu atakuhukumu kwa siri.* If you do something in secret, God will judge you in secret. He was openly dressing like a woman, so I ordered him to be publicly caned.

I tried in most cases to reconcile those who came to report offenses. There was a case, for example, of a wife's reporting her husband for having taken and sold her jewelry. I knew both the husband and the wife, and I used all my persuasive arguments in asking the wife not to prosecute. Eventually I won her over because I said the man had sold the jewelry to buy a lorry to earn money and to maintain the house in which she lived.

One night my father telephoned and wanted to see me after work. I was on my way to Wete when I reached a point on the main road still under my jurisdiction where I saw a group of people. I stopped my car; just two or three houses away from the road I found an old man whom they wanted to lynch. I intervened and told the old man, "Don't worry. No one will touch you because I have witnessed this. If anything happens to you, I know the culprits." And I told those young boys, "If anything happens, I will hold you responsible." I checked again that night, and in the morning I called the local *sheha* and told him, "I don't want this kind of thing in my area. You people are taking the law into your own hands, and this I will not tolerate."

I was also very strict about looting. I had the Youth League in my hands, and they respected me. Were they responsible, or was I? If anything happened, who would be blamed? There was no looting, as far as I remember; but, of course, our boys got out of control sometimes. One of our soldiers raped a girl, and we flogged him in front of the whole town and threw him out of the army that same day. There were excesses, but we tried also to have a semblance of a society based on the rule of law. I was appointed to create an administration out of chaos; actually, I thank God I did not stay longer in Pemba because I do not know what kind of cases I would have faced later on.

So I worked and listened to people's grievances; then one day I heard Babu announce over the radio that all Umma Party members should join the ASP. I knew immediately that Karume had pressured Babu to dissolve the party because normally there would have been a meeting of the Umma Party Executive Committee, of which I was a member, as I have said. We should have had a resolution for the party to be dissolved, but there was none. My reaction was just to follow the stream—that is all. I decided to work within the ASP because it was not antagonistic to my ideas since it was the party of downtrodden peasants and workers. We socialists had to work in whichever way possible. We were not in the time of Lenin, and the only possibility for us was to work within the ASP. The merger was permissible since the Chinese Communist Party had once joined with the Goumingdang, though they remained separate. The advanced countries may have a different way, but we had just come from being a colony and had to follow a different path. So after listening to Babu over the wireless, I went the next day to buy my ASP membership card.

 MARIA

I STAYED IN PEMBA FOR LESS THAN
two months, and I do not remember doing anything I now regret. I
would act exactly the same way today. I never went around frightening
people; anyway, in my society, if I did, they would report it to my father.
But there was no need because the people of Pemba were already subservient toward their fellow countrymen in Unguja. Before the revolution, if anyone came from Unguja, there would be festivities and a big
welcome. Life in Pemba was tranquil and the people very generous and
humble. Of course, these days they are trying to undo what happened to
them in the past; but back then I just called to them, and they came; I
spoke to them, and they listened.

If I have any regrets, it is over the conduct of John Okello. He provoked fear among the people, and he thought he was superior to us administrators and beyond our control. His orders contradicted our own
and those of Karume, and there was even a point when he threatened to
have all us area commissioners flogged. Another time he forced the head
of the Clove Grower's Association to give him money to pay off his
men. Karume permitted his request for funds, but he was supposed to
take the money from the treasury in Unguja and sign for it. But Okello
instead went early in the morning to the CGA without authority. It
should have never happened because, once you do that, there will be
thieving, and we wanted to put a stop to that kind of behavior.

Mind you, I was very disciplined and dedicated to the cause, and I
did not go in to enrich myself. I wanted to instill socialist morality in
Zanzibar and to fight against the corruption bred by capitalism. I
wanted to change the mentality of the people and to create a "New
Man." This was an idea from socialism that I came across in my studies
in London, to build a society where everyone is hardworking, honest,
humble, and sincere, where no one looks down on his fellow human

93

being. In capitalism, people always want to accumulate, especially when they come from the bush and they start with nothing except their shoes. They want to accumulate quickly so that, if they fall down again, at least they have something for the future.

One way of creating a New Man, I believed, was to change the environment. By changing the environment, we could change the mentality of the people. That is one reason why I wanted Zanzibar to industrialize rapidly after the revolution—in order to change the work habits of the people. I wanted to build factories and engage in heavy industry not only because we needed to produce tractors and guns but also because an individual cannot remain lazy if he is working on an assembly line— the conveyor belt does not wait. If you plant only cassava, you wait for six months for it to mature, and you become stagnant. But when I worked in a factory in the U.K., we were like machines. The bosses would start the conveyor belt slowly in the mornings to allow us to warm up a little, and then they would speed it up. We were being conditioned to work like machines. Machines can change human behavior.

I wanted to accelerate work and production and to achieve abundance in Zanzibar that would, in turn, help our people to live better and more happily. Why should we in Africa lag behind if we have all the resources to industrialize? Are we able to send only raw materials to the factories in the metropole? No, we needed the industrial life here in the islands because it requires more discipline and conditioning. You have to be on time and to perform your work according to the machine's speed and rhythm. Otherwise, if you cannot conform, you will be thrown out of a job, and no one will employ you. The bosses will sack you, and you will have to struggle because you have nothing but your labor power to sell.

Under socialism, bosses cannot sack you, but they can set certain production quotas. As an incentive, the best workers can receive honors and material rewards. But the socialist mode of production relied for the most part on self-criticism within each worker. Self-criticism means you are motivated to ask yourself questions like "Why am I backward, and why can I not perform?" That kind of motivation should just be within you; a human being can perform formidable things if he or she works hard. And nothing is better than self-criticism because, if another person criticizes you, you are sometimes unwilling to listen. That is the reason we wanted a New Man who could be pushed and encouraged to conform and who, without threats, would constantly desire to improve.

In this way, we could build a socialist paradise in Zanzibar. We only had a quarter of a million people, but we could do wonders, like mechanize farming, develop small agricultural industries, and provide work for our people. We could establish a classless society. It turned out that our ideas were different from those of President Karume, however, so we had to follow him or at least try to influence him.

So I mobilized people in Pemba to work and not just wait for the clove harvest because the opposite of mobilization is stagnation. I convinced people to work by speaking to them; there were no armed guards forcing the people. They would come to listen, especially because they knew me. I was well known in the whole island: I had worked in Mkoani and in Wete, and I had danced in Chake Chake. The people from top to bottom all knew Ali Sultan. It was not hard for me to mingle; I would go into any hut and sit with them and eat with them. I was not an aloof old colonial administrator who would not come down to the people.

Normally, we would explain the government project in their area and encourage people to participate. In Chake Chake, we had to eliminate the sewage problems and the stagnant water so we would not be infested with mosquitoes. We organized labor in such a way that it would not be a burden, so people also had time for their own work. I did not like forced labor, but rather voluntary labor with some encouragement. Of course, maybe there was a certain amount of fear that motivated people, but I did not tend to rely upon fear. But, yes, there is no doubt some people had fear in their hearts since Pemba was predominantly pro–ZNP or ZPPP, and the majority of the people felt cowed by the new revolutionary government.

Sometimes I would even take a cane through the streets and chase away anyone not working, not building the nation. So many people in Pemba just sit under their clove trees and wait for the harvest time to come. I would first speak to them and try to mobilize them through words; but after that, I did not hesitate to cane people if I found them sitting around when it was time to work.

So, any project came with the people's participation. Without that, we could do nothing. We spoke to them in order to invoke in them a spirit we progressives wanted them to possess. And that was Marxism, to involve the people. I went down to their level and volunteered my own labor, and that is the reason they followed me wholeheartedly. You can see how subtle we were. We could not go straight to the people and say, "This is Marxism." With the common people, you have to find the common denominator. If you want to build a school, you say it is for their own children; if you want to build roads, it is so they can have access to the market for their crops. It was necessary to build an infrastructure and to clean up the environment so we were not living in the bush. We knew that, by changing the environment, we could change the people's mentality.

It was also in Pemba that I met Frank Carlucci, the American consul. Before his arrival in Zanzibar, he was well known to us for his work for the American government in the Congo during the days of Patrice Lumumba; years later he became President Ronald Reagan's national security advisor and then secretary of defense.[1] Babu, in fact, rang me in Pemba and warned me about him. Carlucci came to Pemba to investigate the looting and the question of whether Indians had been mistreated in the island. I was assigned as his host. I told him, "I am your guide, your driver, and your bodyguard. You tell me where to go, and I'll take you, and I won't listen in on your conversations." I took him in my car from Mkoani in the south all the way to Wete in the north. He followed me around to my public meetings because I wanted him to see what we were doing in Pemba—all our nation-building projects.

Carlucci even stayed with me in my house, and we drank whiskey and argued until 4:00 a.m. I asked Carlucci, "You are Italian, so why are you helping the Americans to push us around? Why do you support imperialism?" He said, "You are an Arab, so why are you helping the Africans communize their country?" By the time we had consumed about three-quarters of a liter of whiskey, we agreed to disagree. Luckily, my wife was away for a conference, so I told him we could share the same huge bed, seven feet wide.

[The following is Carlucci's report to the U.S. State Department about his visit to Pemba:][2]

> March 26, 1964
> . . . Issa is capable, personable, dedicated Communist, Peking variety, even tried convert me. . . . decorates house with pictures Mao, Stalin, Lenin and has named daughter "Fidela."
> Issa came direct from Peking to Pemba after outbreak of revolution, has since been mainspring of Pemba Communist movement. Proud of his handiwork, Issa treated me to demonstration of how Communists can use popular revolution to indoctrinate people. We attended youth cadre meetings, people's mobilization meetings, party rallies and even danced in mud with work battalion. Issa gave out with Castro style Communist line simplified for Africans, once had crowd shout to me

"tell American people we building peoples paradise in Zanzibar and Pemba."

On tours of island people came out of houses to wave and shake hands. Over 2,000 at airport see Issa off. . . .

While not difficult whip up enthusiastic African demonstrations, Issa's performance all more impressive since armed forces nowhere in evidence except at Mkuani pier for ship landing. Freedom fighters, estimated at about 100, keep to barracks and 200 police are concerned primarily with traffic problems. Public corporal punishment instituted and favorite sport of officials is seizing "capitalist" money and jewelry at airport and distributing loot at mass rallies. . . .

Only consolling [sic] factor is that Karume has been able remove Issa, even refusing request for him for one day postponement. On other hand Babu may have agreed in order have Issa keep watch on Othman Shariff in London. Although he has departed Issa has trained his subordinate so well and trend he initiated unlikely be reversed without major counter effort. Such effort does not appear in the making.

I spent less than two months in Pemba, and then boof! I was sent away to London. After I left, I heard that, in Pemba over the years, the political die-hards suffered hardships depending on their status in the society. The higher they were before the revolution, the lower they were brought, even, say, to sweep the streets. Men had their beards shaved, just to humiliate them. It was rather excessive, and had I been there, I would have protested.[3]

When reassigned to London, I was ready to serve my country overseas, considering it an honor. I was to work in the Zanzibari High Commission in London as a councilor under Othman Shariff, the high commissioner. I was to be second in command and to keep an eye on Shariff, who was at loggerheads with Karume. Shariff had been intriguing against Karume for years, and I was supposed to watch his every move.

While I was away in Pemba and in the U.K., the revolutionary government banned all ethnic associations. Even the African and Shirazi associations were eliminated. The authorities banned rickshaws and had them burned in the streets because Karume did not like seeing an African pulling another human being. He thought it degrading. They banned independent newspapers and took over the printing presses. They closed down the Indian-owned pawnshops and returned all the possessions to the original owners. The people were very happy, especially those who had pawned their gold in the shops because they now received everything *gratis* from the government.

And according to the government decree of March 8, 1964, the land was now declared the property of the people and nationalized. This was socialism: the owners possessed the trees but not the land. The root issue of the revolution after all was land since we did not have mines or factories in Zanzibar. Even my own family's lands in Pemba were eventually redistributed and given away to peasants.

In April 1964, the government announced the union between Zanzibar and Tanganyika. It all came as a surprise to us. At the time, Babu, our minister of external affairs, was in Indonesia and Aboud Jumbe, the minister of state, was in Pemba. While they were away, Nyerere came to Zanzibar to sign the articles of union with Karume. Normally, it would not have been done in such an improper way, in the absence of Babu and Jumbe. So we knew there was outside pressure. Britain and America worked very hard with the East African leaders to get Zanzibar into their fold, to stop Zanzibar from becoming another Cuba or from falling into the hands of the Chinese or Russians. Their desire was to create a union in which we communists would supposedly be buried and neutralized.

I was later informed that everything happened between Nyerere and Karume at the State House in Zanzibar Town, and then the agreement was presented to the Revolutionary Council [RC] while Babu was still away. Salim Rashid, an Umma comrade, tried to raise questions but was told to keep quiet. The union was presented to the council merely as a *fait accompli.*[4]

I personally agreed with the union, although Babu and most of my other comrades did not. Although Nyerere wanted to hold us and swallow us in Zanzibar, I saw the federation as a larger platform for our ideas and as a chance to spread the revolution to the mainland. I wanted the whole of East Africa to be socialist since I was a socialist internationalist, after all. So I did not see it as a defeat, like Babu and the other comrades. They just wanted to work on Zanzibar, keeping it as a small base and showcase for socialism. But it would not have happened that way; we would not have survived. Because of the union with Tanganyika, we could now expound our ideas on the mainland as well and carry on the struggle there.

The idea, after all, was to revolutionize the mind. We had to get our Umma boys in the administration, depending on their qualifications. If we had a chance to put trained socialist cadres in the administration, we were pushing our ideas as well. We had to take these people from within and push them. We were committed, but we were just a minority, just like a pinch of salt.

We had been planting the seed of socialism within the ZNP since 1958. We had formed our own party, arranged a united front with the ASP, and made a revolution. Of course, Carlucci believed we now wanted to overthrow Karume because he was too moderate for us. This is what he told Karume in 1964, and it was really sinister.[5] I was not around, but this was related to me. At the time, there was no thinking like that at all. We thought we could work together. Anyway, the time was too short to throw him out. And Karume was formidable; to overthrow him, we would have had to have the support of Seif Bakari, chairman of the Youth League. Bakari had the African youth, and they would not have supported an Umma takeover. We were like salt; if you put too much salt in your food, how does it taste? If Umma was as strong as Carlucci believed, then why did we dissolve the party? Because Babu was coerced or threatened by Karume and then told us all just to go along.

After the union, how could we throw Karume out, with Julius Nyerere there? As time went on, Karume entrenched himself. In the early years, Nyerere could manipulate him, but later Karume resisted, and Nyerere himself was afraid to come to Zanzibar. If we had any business with Nyerere, we went to the mainland.

While I was a diplomat in London, I first stayed in a hotel called the Linster Towers, where I met Paul, an African American actor who lived in the basement. I invited Paul to a party I was organizing, as well as a woman named Lee Akbar working with the British Guyana embassy very near our High Commission, just opposite us on Trafalgar Square. Paul and Lee met and hit it off, so you could say I brought them together.

Afterward, Lee invited me to join a foursome, including myself, the two of them, and Lee's friend Maria Neil, a British girl. I said okay, but I asked Lee if her friend was nice looking. Could I be enticed to spend my time with her? I said jokingly, "If she looks like you, I won't bother." Lee said, "Okay, this will be a challenge. You come, and if you like her, then you can stay."

I went home and took a bath and changed into an evening suit. I lied to my wife, saying I had been invited to a function at the Russian embassy, where they had beautiful girls to entice the men so they could get information. When I arrived at the Linster Towers, Paul was still in the shower, but he said, "The girls are in the bar upstairs, so have a look."

As I entered the bar, Maria was facing me, and I thought, "My God! I'll take the invitation!"

I went back to Paul and said, "If you fool around with Maria, I'll shoot you. Don't forget I have my Browning automatic pistol and my diplomatic immunity." I rolled a thin one because I could finish it quickly, and then Paul and I joined them at the bar. From there, we went out in my car; I drove a Ford Valiant and had a small bar in the boot. I always had my drinks there, and all my alcohol was duty free. We first went to Mayfair, to a club called Club 21 where I was a member. We had dinner, I paid, and then Paul said he wanted to take us to a nightclub in Leicester Square where he was a member.

We danced and drank there, almost up to three in the morning, and then we drove back. I dropped Paul off first, Lee second, and then I took Maria home. Before we got to her house, we stopped at a traffic light; I wanted to kiss her, but she refused, telling me, "I am not a girl to be kissed in the street." I said, "Okay, there will be another time, another chance." But at her house, she made it very hard to make plans to see her again. And that is how she hooked me—by making it very hard. It was a challenge.

I later invited her and Lee to a diplomatic function during the visit to London of Kenneth Kaunda from Zambia. Kaunda was attending a constitutional conference in preparation for Zambia's independence. After the two women arrived, I wanted to leave, so I asked my wife to take over my duties. I left alone, but later met Lee and Maria in a hotel room I rented in London on a weekly basis in case I wanted to indulge myself. We drank there, and then Lee deliberately left us two together, and that is how our love affair started.

For a period, I was alone in London: my wife was in Cuba celebrating May Day, and my children were in Cairo attending school. So I took Maria to Paris for a week, where I had a good friend, a communist like me named Jacques Vergès who took us around.[6] I told her, "This is our honeymoon, if ever we get married. So don't claim later on we never had a honeymoon." I left her in London with a promise that we would correspond or telephone whenever we had a chance.

When I returned to Zanzibar, I was informed that my father-in-law, Amour Zahor, had been executed as part of a group of men accused of counterrevolution. The accused never went to court; I heard he and the others were simply taken to a place and shot. The bullet did not actually kill him, however, so my father-in-law pleaded to be finished off. Instead, his executioners just buried him alive with the others. He was a reactionary, so the news of his death did not surprise me or slow me down; I still wanted to serve the regime.

After the union with Tanganyika, however, most of my Umma comrades were sent away. They were usually, like Babu, given positions in the union government in order to remove them from Zanzibar, the so-called Cuba of East Africa. The few comrades who remained in Zanzibar were ones like me who supported the union, including Ali Mafoudh and Khamis Abdalla Ameir.

When I reported to Karume, I did not know what job he would give me, but I knew he would give me something. Karume was sympathetic to me—he knew me my whole life, knew about my struggles in the ZNP, and knew about my dislike of Muhsin and the old regime. At first, Karume asked me to go to Indonesia as an ambassador, but I knew that would be a problem because I was already supporting so many children, my own and five that my deceased sister left me to raise. I asked Karume for an assignment at home, and in August 1964, he appointed me minister without portfolio.

I also served as chairman of the committee responsible for nationalizing urban housing. In this capacity, I went to the town planning office and looked at the registration of each deed. I found out the owner's financial status to decide who did and who did not get to keep his house. I never actually went to visit the houses themselves: I just looked at the legal documents, found out how many houses each chap owned, and then confiscated what I thought was necessary.

In the four and a half months I served on that committee, we nationalized hundreds of houses, most of Stone Town's residential properties. Some houses were already empty because the Arabs had run away; those who remained could do nothing. They had to come into the fold, or we had places for them to go. They could not even say boo to themselves. They were all cowards, and there was no resistance to the confiscations— who would dare? Only one person came to object, a good friend of mine, and I told him that, even though we were nationalizing his home, he could continue to stay there.

According to the law, I just needed to sign a document, and I could take someone's house. But even if I nationalized a house, I did not immediately throw the owner out on the street because he had the right of appeal to the president. If he thought I had exceeded my power or that I had confiscated his property out of spite just to deprive him of his livelihood, he could appeal. If Karume was favorable toward him, he revoked the nationalization, and the owner got his property back.

There was never any compensation. We did it as Fidel Castro did, without compensation. We compensated only one or two people, for their good work for us before the revolution. We compensated a Jewish family that owned a fishery, for example, and an Indian merchant in Pemba named Mastar, but that was all.

Even when it came to land in the rural areas, we would take some and leave the owners the rest. The idea was to share what little we had and to allow the person to keep something. "Live and let live. Give us a little, and you carry on." Those who criticized could not see the larger context; otherwise, they would have seen it was not my fault because I was not taking their property for personal gain. I have never taken one penny that was not due me. I had my salary and my allowances, and that was all.

After I returned to Zanzibar and was appointed as a minister, I wrote to Maria and asked her to visit me. I wanted her to come to Africa to see my island and to see if she could adjust. I met her in Nairobi in December 1964, and we first traveled to Uganda, where I attended a conference. We stayed in the Entebbe Lake Hotel, and we had a car and a chauffeur to take us around and to my meetings in the afternoons. After about a week, we flew to Mombasa where I needed to help reclaim the sultan's yacht, which he had abandoned on his flight from Zanzibar to the United Kingdom. I needed to see if the Kenyans had released it to our government.

While we stayed at the Oceanic Hotel, I went to visit my Zanzibari girlfriend, who was also in Mombasa at the time. She was a few years older than I, but I admired her nevertheless. When I was sixteen or seventeen, we lived in the same neighborhood, and I would always stand at a certain spot on the street corner and look up at the window of her sitting room on the second floor, hoping to catch sight of her. She must have known I was standing there and of my admiration for her because, after the revolution, when her husband was imprisoned, she called and asked me to provide her a place to stay. So I rented a place for her in Zanzibar Town, just behind the Ministry of Education. I called her place "Sanctuary" because it was where I could go and hide: a private room for my private fornicating. Sanctuary was much better than a hotel where people could see you come and go.

Eventually her husband, a teacher by profession, was released from prison. I had actually gone to secondary school with him years earlier; when he came out in 1966, I told him, "I looked after your wife in your absence, and here she is. I am returning her to you."

When I went to see her in Mombasa, she told me that she was pregnant and that I was the father. I told her to abort the child and to see me later in Zanzibar. I was then a communist and did not follow Islamic law. And she aborted the child. She had the money somehow from a British boyfriend of hers, so she was not economically desperate.

After a few days, Maria and I came to the islands, and she stayed for about three weeks in the Africa House Hotel, once the old English Club in Zanzibar. We avoided detection by my wife the whole time; when we went out in public together, people thought Maria was a guest of the government, but those near me knew of our relationship.

I took her around to both islands, Unguja and Pemba, because I wanted her to see our home and our way of life here. I introduced her to my family in Pemba. She was impressed with the islands, the people, and, no doubt, with myself. And I was in love with her. She was extremely beautiful, like a movie star. She was not extravagant but kind and considerate, especially to my family. These are the characteristics one needs in a partner.

We attended a New Year's dance at the Africa House Hotel, and then she was supposed to return to London and her old boyfriend. At the time, Maria was living with an older scientist who invented a new form of lightweight concrete. He had an artificial arm, and from what I heard, he was kind to her, though I never met him.

We drove to the airport for our flight to Dar es Salaam, but the plane was delayed. My wife was somehow informed that I was with Maria, and she came to the airport and confronted me. I was caught red-handed. My wife decided that she wanted to join us in Dar es Salaam, so she drove to town and got her passport; and because of the delay, she managed to board the plane with us. Maria pleaded with my wife in the plane, saying, "Let me have this last day," but she would not hear of it.

My friends Ali Mafoudh and Salim Said Rashid met the three of us at the airport in Dar es Salaam, and they could immediately see my predicament. I had already booked Maria's hotel, and I told Maria to follow my friends through the VIP entrance, while I took my wife through the ordinary gates and put her in a different hotel. I had to spend part of the night with my wife and part of it with Maria because she was leaving the next day. I had to try to please them both.

My wife left early the next morning, on a 7:00 a.m. flight, and I stayed behind with Maria. I took a plane for Zanzibar later that day, around 6:00 p.m. Since Maria was leaving at 8:00 p.m., we went to the airport together.

When I returned to Zanzibar, I rushed to the rooftop of my private flat, my "Sanctuary," and I watched as her plane passed overhead. I cried because I did not know when I would ever see her again.

From the day she left in January 1965, I started writing her every day. I do not know where the words came from, the inspiration. Normally, it took three days for a letter to travel from Zanzibar to London. Every morning Maria would get a letter from me. She showed my letters to her mum, who said, "This chap must love you deeply." Maria wrote many letters, but she was not as regular as I was.

eleven NATION BUILDING

IN JANUARY 1965, I WAS
appointed minister of education, youth, and culture. We had only six
ministers and were highly centralized in our administration, unlike now.
One of my first assignments was to act as a host to Che Guevara, who
came to Zanzibar that month for our annual revolutionary commemo-
rations. He arrived suddenly from the Congo and stayed for only three
days. I had met Che originally in Cuba in 1962 and again at an UNCTAD
[United Nations Conference on Trade and Development] conference in
Geneva in 1964, and he remembered me. I tried to make sure he was
comfortable and to be a friend. I told my principal secretary to vacate his
house for our official visitor.

We had a long private discussion one night, for about two hours. Because he had asthma, Che was not fond of drinking. He mainly told me
about his plans for organizing a tricontinental conference, an assembly
of delegates from Latin America, Asia, and Africa to promote unity
among our nations so we would not have to confront imperialism piece-
meal.[1] He said there was opposition to this conference in Cuba, but we
agreed that the struggle against American imperialism should be waged
on three continents simultaneously, not just in Asia now and Africa later.
I thought Che was sincere about world revolution.[2]

For all those years as a minister, I never abused my power. That is, I
never took anything without paying for it. When I first took over the
ministry, I called in my principal accountant and principal secretary. I
put my Browning pistol on the table and said I had made a vow in the
Revolutionary Council to be ready to die if I mishandled the finances. I
asked them to make the same vow. Corruption was actually minimal
under Karume, not like what it is now. Today they will not do anything
without getting a bribe. If someone has come from nothing and wants

to accumulate wealth immediately because he is not sure how long he will remain in power, then he will be corrupt. But during Karume's time, if you were reported engaging in corruption, you might lose your life. You were supposed to serve the people and not demand anything from workers or peasants because they had nothing. Of course, if you took something from the Indian or Arab merchants, the exploiting class, you might be forgiven. My own deputy minister would take things from Indian-owned shops on credit and never pay. He had four wives and left behind twenty-six children. Karume, however, said to the RC that, if any of us were in hardship, we could come to him and he would authorize the Ministry of Finance to give us what we needed. But he would first consider whether our needs were reasonable or not.

As a minister, I dealt with Frank Carlucci to obtain American aid for a technical school. We managed to build it eventually at Chukwani, south of town. I also worked with the East Germans, who sent us teachers for a low price, whom we placed in the secondary schools. We wanted to emphasize the sciences, so I asked the East Germans to give us nuclear physics teachers, but they refused. Otherwise, the East Germans were very good; they had their own problems, but they were very good. They were the first to build housing as a grant in Kikwajuni and later in Michenzani and Kilimani.

The Chinese assisted in agriculture and health. They were more sincere in wanting to help than were the Russians. For instance, when the Chinese and the Russians gave us arms, the Chinese gave us new weapons, while the Russians, old ones. The Russians once sent us a one-engine plane they had used to spray their fields with insecticide and four pilots for that one single-engine machine. Another time in Moscow, the authorities gave us all kinds of propaganda books to take back to Zanzibar. They wanted us to pay freight charges, but I refused, and they eventually paid. Another time I asked the Russians for some teachers, and do you know what they told me? They said they wanted to be paid in gold. I said, "We don't have any gold here; we have cloves." And then they told me that, if a Russian teacher were to die in Zanzibar, then we should pay for his coffin to be sent back home. I said, "Your colleagues the Chinese cremate their people here. I think if your comrades die, you should pay for their remains to be sent home yourself."

I always relayed such conversations to Karume; that was my style. Of course, he knew my affinities were with the Chinese, but Karume could see himself who was the more sincere and generous between the Chinese and the Russians. But, at the time, we had to work with both. We renamed the hospital in town "V. I. Lenin Hospital," but the Russians sent only sporadic shipments of medicine. Meanwhile, the Chinese sent us a full team of doctors, and they remain even now at two hospitals, one here and one in Pemba. We should have called the hospital "Mao Hospital."

There was no comparison. Here the Chinese were backward; they wanted to develop their country first, but still they helped. Here the Russians were advanced with Sputnik and everything, yet they were stingy. They were very mean and arrogant, I can say. The Chinese cultivated rice with the people, but the Europeans would not, so the people accepted the Chinese more that the Russians. Each country helped in its own way, but the Chinese were more akin to us: they lived in the fields, planted with us, and won the hearts of the people.[3] So it was through our experience and our contact with the Chinese that we looked for our solutions through the Chinese way. In the end, however, we were the masters of our own destiny—not the East Germans, not the Russians, not the Chinese. They would give us advice we could accept or reject; if any mistakes happened in Zanzibar, they were our own.[4]

In my ministry, we had certain goals in mind. We wanted all children to go to school and for schools to be free for everyone, so that no one would have to pay any longer, like in the colonial period. We also wanted to achieve 100 percent literacy. Each child should be able to develop according to his or her own intellectual capacities. We also wanted to focus on science instead of art.

We started planning how we could send education to the people. That was the policy: to go and reach the people where they were, rather than to expect them to come to the urban areas for education. We planned that, in every village of four thousand or more, there would be a school. It took years to implement this plan, but in my four years as minister, the number of schools mushroomed, both in Pemba and Unguja.[5] And with each school, we later tried to build a clinic also.

Within one year, each area was building its own school. We were ready to provide the material, and the people were ready to provide their labor because they knew it would benefit their children. They knew no one would come from outside to build schools for them. Once we started to bring schools to the people, I did not slow down, whether we had money in the budget or not. Of course, any decision had in the end to be made by Karume himself. Before you could execute any decision, you needed his consent.

Karume had a personal dislike for educated people because they always gave him problems within the ASP; they always challenged him because he himself was not educated. But he did not look down on education as such; and once I explained to him what I wanted to do, he understood and sided with me in the RC. If all went well, he would tell me, then he would take the credit; if it failed, then I was to blame.

Of course, the schools took time to develop. We first built to take Standard 1 students and added rooms as the years passed, so that, in eight years, all the primary classes were completed. We established a system of compulsory education up to Standard 8. We had to push Africans [to go to school] because, in our society, they were the least educated. During my tenure, there was no coercion; instead, we encouraged people to send their children to school, starting at five years of age.

I traveled a lot in those days giving speeches and mobilizing the people to work and to build the nation. For two days of every week, I would be out in the villages, to be near the people, listening to stories of how they lived and how they endured hardships. In my speeches, I would talk about the local area and its history. I went to Pemba and explained what it was like under colonialism. All the seventy years the British were there—what had they done? How many schools had they built? People who worked and toiled at their labor, what was their return? Normally in these functions with the broader masses, we would not go very deep because this was a predominantly Muslim country, and we did not want to give our opponents bullets to shoot at us. Only when it came to denouncing imperialism, and particularly the United States as head of the imperialist camp, did we really become ideological. Instead, we would speak more ideologically at party seminars and at meetings of the youth organizations.

I also spent one day a week at ASP headquarters because the people felt more comfortable going there with their problems than to the ministries, where there were certain bureaucratic procedures to follow. The headquarters was open to the public, and people came with their complaints and requests. Sometimes they brought a little present, maybe some mangoes, cassava, or bananas; I had the habit of taking note of these gifts and instructing my driver to bring the person who had given me a gift rice and sugar from town in return.

In the new educational system after the revolution, everyone reached Standard 8, but after that, every student took qualifying exams in order to continue. There was a bottleneck since there were only a few secondary schools in the islands. We imposed racial percentages in the secondary schools and started promoting students according to their race and their exam results. Each race was given seats according to its overall population numbers, and no more.

At first, we used the old colonial census, which gave us racial percentages. Then in 1967, we had our own census, and everyone registered according to four classifications. I cannot recall the exact percentages, but it was something like Comorians 1 percent, Indians 3 percent, Arabs 5 or 10 percent, and the rest of the seats in the secondary schools were awarded to Africans. I was much criticized for this. Africans benefited, while Indians, Arabs, and Comorians lost their traditional dominance in education. When I was at Ben Bella before the revolution, for example, Indians had the most seats and Africans the least.[6] People criticized me, but I told the Comorians to register themselves as Africans. They were proud, though, and refused to do so.

We had to establish this system because the majority of our people were Africans from rural areas with the least chance to get into the schools. They were less developed because their environment was not conducive to learning, unlike in town, where the majority before the revolution went on to secondary schools. Before the revolution, there were only three government secondary schools. The Indians, meanwhile, had four private secondary schools: a Hindu school, an Ithna Asheri school, a Memen school, and an Ismaili school. For those Indians who could not get into a government secondary school, they could enter one of their private schools. Because of financial help from overseas, they had an advantage over the local people. It was unfair, so we nationalized all the private schools and gave more opportunities to the rural people. Of course, Africans were happy with the system because the mid-level civil servants for years and years had been mostly Comorian, Indian, and Arab. That was the old colonial system.

Our new system was like the system you also adopted later in America. I was blamed for this; my critics said we were not taking people according to merit but on a racial basis. But when affirmative action came up in the United States, I felt exonerated.

We also continued to send students overseas for education. I still wanted to plant the seeds of socialism among young people, so most went to the Eastern Bloc for studies. I actually wanted them to go everywhere; wherever an opportunity was open for us, we would send them. Listen, there is a dictum of Mao: "Let the hundred flowers blossom, and every school of thought contend." Once you open up the mind, it is an inquisitive organ. Though I knew foreigners wanted to indoctrinate our students, if America in particular had offered us scholarships, we as a poor country would have sent our young people. There were very few scholarships coming from the West, however.

We had our own system of indoctrination here in Zanzibar. We taught politics in the schools because it was the compass to where we wanted to go in the future. It was necessary to properly orient our young boys who did not otherwise have much exposure, so they could conform to what we were building in Zanzibar, the society we were creating. We set aside two or three class periods a week for political education. The main subject was our own struggle in Zanzibar. Students read Karume's speeches in the primary schools, in little booklets we published every year. In the secondary schools, they read the works of Marx, Engels, Lenin, Stalin, Mao, and Nkrumah. Political lessons were compulsory; to pass an exam, students had to be politically minded and accept African nationalism and Marxism.

Of course, we also had to have politically minded teachers, so we organized refresher courses through the Teacher's Training College. I even once lectured the teachers on the entire history of the world, beginning with primitive communism and continuing through slavery, feudalism, capitalism, and eventually socialism and communism. I had problems with the teachers, however. There was a period when we had to reduce their salaries, at the same time as we rapidly increased enrollment, especially from the rural areas. After the salary reductions, a teacher in Zanzibar earned about the same as a policeman or a soldier, a starting salary on average around three hundred shillings a month.

I appealed once to the teachers for their wholehearted support and patriotic devotion, and I almost cried. I even told them they could speak their grievances; but maybe that was a mistake, to give them that freedom on that particular day. In those days, even the student boarders cursed me because I cut margarine and eggs from their diet, but Karume told me the British had purposefully given them eggs and margarine to spoil them.

In the beginning, any new thing is hard, and people tend to be conservative. They do not want to change. Those teachers who did not approve of our politics eventually went away. Those who remained would not say anything because they were afraid of being called racialist or reactionary. But many educated people left who did not want to serve Africans or the revolution. They left because of ideology; some of them were racialists, I dare say. They were mainly British-educated. They would not serve us, and we said, "Good riddance," because we wanted to bring the Africans up and educate them in our own way. Of course, naturally, boof! There was a brain drain, and the standard of efficiency dropped because any change like that takes time. But losing so many talented people after the revolution was not a serious obstacle for development because we replenished our numbers with Africans who came with degrees from socialist countries.

When it came to religious education, we did not interfere. For a time, we closed down the Qur'an schools in order to check the qualifications of the teachers, but that is all. Otherwise, we continued to offer the same amount of religious instruction in the government schools as under the British—two periods per week. We did not interfere because we were sensitive, and it would have been wasting time. We had to keep peace with the people, and so we left it as in the colonial days.

Those stories about my interfering with religious education are crazy. And I never saw a Qur'an burned in the streets. Who would burn a Qur'an in the streets? That is a lie! We were not stupid; we understood the people's feelings about religion, and I was very careful since I did not want to be considered an atheist opposed to religion. It is true, however, that Islamic scholarship in Zanzibar declined after the revolution because most of the religious scholars left the country. We progressives saw this as a good thing; the whole bloody island was already predominantly Muslim, so what more did they want? Instead of scholars coming here, they should go to places where people want to be Islamized.[7]

Maria returned to Zanzibar in 1966, and I put her up in the Africa House Hotel. After a week, we were having lunch one afternoon at the hotel with some friends, and I again proposed marriage to her. She accepted, so at that very moment, I said, "Let's go and get married." As witnesses, I took two of my friends drinking at the bar, Ahmada Shafi and Muhammed Abdalla. We went to an old member of the RC, Mzee Daud Mahmud, who performed the ritual that very afternoon.

Maria volunteered to convert to Islam for me, though she did not need to in order to marry me. She said, "I bear witness that there is only one God and Muhammed is his prophet." Maria became known as "Mariam," and we changed her passport to reflect her new name: Mariam Sultan Issa. I do not think Maria ever read the Qur'an or became very religious, however. I was not saying my prayers, so how could I ask her to? At the time, I was not a Muslim in the real sense, only by birth.

When I told Aysha about my marriage, she asked me, "Why do you want to marry again when I've already given you a son?" In 1966, she gave birth to our son Stalin. Nevertheless, Maria became my second wife, and I put her in "Sanctuary," my private flat. At first, I spent one day with each, but I could not split my affections; when I spent time with Aysha, my heart was still with Maria. So less than a month after I married Maria, I told Aysha, "I cannot live with two wives; my heart is with her, and you are like my sister now." Aysha cried, but she accepted. According to Islamic law, I just had to say, "I divorce you, I divorce you, I divorce you."

I agreed to give Aysha a third of my salary every month and secured a flat for her in Stone Town where she stayed with our children and one of my sisters. Then the Chinese wanted someone for translation work, so I recommended her. She went to China with our three daughters, while Stalin stayed here in Zanzibar and was raised mostly by my father and his wife. Since Aysha earned her own money in China, I stopped sending her a third of my income.

Maria loved me, and I am very grateful because, otherwise, she would not have left a rich man in England to venture out here to live in an unpredictable continent. It was not an entirely new thing for a Zanzibari to marry a European, but some people in the Youth League went to Karume and complained, especially when I divorced my Zanzibari wife. They said I would tell Maria all our state secrets, and then she would tell the British, and then we would have no more secrets in Zanzibar.

Karume called me into his office, and I said to him, "Listen, you are the one who offered me this job as minister. I am free to marry anyone. If I cannot be free in my own country, then I would rather die. Either you trust me, or you don't. Why should I tell her secrets? I have a lot of other things to talk about with my wife. Give me another job, make me head of the street sweepers, so I will know no secrets, but I will not leave my wife."

Karume said, "Carry on, and do your work. They are fools."

My family accepted Maria, especially my father, who had been very fond of the British since colonial days. Whenever we came to Pemba, he wanted to please Maria as much as he could and to make her feel at home. And Maria loved Zanzibari society and its openness. She adapted to the environment and went to the market and the port to buy produce and fish. She would take a car and go to the rural areas by herself or with one of her friends. She learned Swahili and could speak it pretty well, so you could not fool her. She was friendly with the wives of the Revolutionary Council members and with those of my friends. She had people with whom to speak English, but she never missed the U.K., going only once for a couple months to show off our son Omar when he came along.

Maria did not want to stay in the old house where I lived with Aysha, so we took a house at Beit el Ras, at the time occupied by two East German teachers. I asked them to move to alternative accommodation, and they accepted. It was a nice house meant for colonial expatriates, right on the sea front, with a balcony and four bedrooms, enough for six of my nieces and nephews to stay with me. We lived at Beit el Ras for two years, from 1966 until 1968, and we were very happy. In that period, Maria gave birth to our first child, Omar.

Maria never bought unnecessary things and was never extravagant. She would make inexpensive dresses made from *kanga*, our local material. She would design the dresses herself, and they would look nice. But I did introduce her to certain shops, certain perfumeries in town. She loved expensive perfumes, and one month her bill surpassed my monthly salary. In those days, my salary went straight to my principal accountant who paid my bills, kept all my receipts filed away, and just gave me a summary of what he had done.

I said to him, "Listen, tell me my deficit, and I'll pay in full." I had about five hundred British pounds in traveler's checks left over from my months working in London in 1964. I signed a couple of checks to pay the debt and told the accountant to put the rest in the bank, so the bankers would not worry. From that day, all the Indians in Zanzibar respected me because my Indian accountant told all his friends, saying, "Don't play with Ali Sultan." I was brought up to be grateful to God for what little I received.

That was in 1966, toward the end of the year, because in 1967 we nationalized all trade in the islands and all the Indians were forced to leave the country.

twelve DISCIPLINE

ON THE DAY OF THE
revolution in January 1964, the government opened all the prisons and
released all the convicts. They gave guns to any Africans who came and
asked at the revolutionary headquarters. For a period, the social fabric
was ruined: burglaries, rape, and murder were rampant; there was no law
and order. Eventually, the authorities recruited some of the criminals
into the army and collected the guns from the people.

Afterward, we in the Revolutionary Council observed that the youth
wanted to test the new freedom and to speak their minds. We watched
as girls turned toward prostitution and showed signs of feeling emanci-
pated. Girls went to pubs and fornicated, as if the whole fabric of society
were breaking down. We had brothels during the colonial period when
our women were more restricted, but formal prostitution died out around
the revolution as women experienced more freedom. They could go out
more openly, so there was no need.

We in the RC had many discussions about young people's declining respect for elders, knowing that once respect went—respect for elders was
part of Islam—the whole social fabric would break down. It all started in
the home; if you were rude and disobeyed your parents, then you would
be the same with other people. For the state to restore order, we needed
to use force to restrain those youths who would not obey any code.

And there was a problem also with idle youth, whom we wanted to
make more productive. We had to contain the multitude of our young-
sters swarming from the rural areas into town after the revolution. We
could not have them roaming the streets, doing nothing, so we decided
they should go back to the country and cultivate. We should put them
in labor camps, like in the socialist countries.

We comrades originally had the idea of youth camps from our time
spent in socialist countries, but I wanted the Youth League in the ASP

to get this idea on their own. I wanted to send them outside so that they could see for themselves and then want on their own to try to implement here what they saw in socialist countries. So when we sent delegations to socialist countries after the revolution, I discussed with the diplomats from these countries what they would see. I requested they be shown this, this, and this, to impress upon the youth delegates certain things so that, when they came back to Zanzibar, they would try to imitate the good things from socialist countries.

Eventually, the Youth League came up with the idea to organize labor camps in the countryside, and I supported them since youth was under my ministry. These camps already existed in China, Ghana, Cuba, Israel, and other places. We comrades had China as a model, but others who had not traveled as much did not necessarily have that example in mind. We brought over a Ghanaian expert named E. A. Hawkson to run the youth camps along lines already developed in Ghana.

The camps would take youth off the streets, organize and discipline them, train them with practical skills, and, finally, give them ideological and military training. From the Chinese, we also had the idea of sending people from the town to the countryside, so we could break down urban and rural differences. How can we have a more homogeneous society and more unity? How can urban people know the hardships of the rural areas if they do not go there? The intelligentsia here looked down on the peasantry as inferior, but they relied on them for their food.

Starting the camps was a collective decision within the government. I was an Arab trying to push Africans; if I had given orders alone for Africans to go into the countryside and farm, I would have been called a racialist. That would have been the reaction. Whatever innovation I had, my job was first to convince Karume; when he was convinced, I knew he would defend me in the RC.

The first camp was at Kama; the other three started during my time were at Chechele, Bambi, and Chejuu. My budget in the ministry was not enough for this venture, however, because we had to feed the young people before they could produce their own food. I managed to buy them a little maize meal, a little rice, dried fish, sugar, and tea—no luxuries. We bought cassava from the prison farms and sent it to the camps to augment their rations.

We ran the camps on a minimal basis because most of the youth were from the rural areas. Do you know what they ate there? Hot water in the mornings and then nothing until the evening. But we did not just send them there and dump them. We built *mabanda makuti*, thatched shelters, and later they had tents. Later, we provided uniforms contributed by the East German youth organization the Frei deutsche Jugend. At first, we did not have blankets, mosquito nets, or even pit latrines; but as we progressed, we became more organized.

Some camps were for rice cultivation and some for cassava, depending on local soil conditions. We had to heavily subsidize the ones producing cash crops because we were experimenting unsuccessfully with wheat, peanuts, and cotton, for example. The camps producing cassava, sweet potatoes, bananas, and rice took care of themselves in terms of food, but each youth also received a stipend from the government, and each camp required other assistance such as for transportation and camp infrastructure that their harvests could not support. So the camps were never self-reliant.

At first, the Youth League selected youth activists known for their past sacrifices and behavior. They did not choose just anyone to go; the young person had to have stamina and the right party history. They did not just round up unemployed youth; these boys volunteered through the Youth League and were sent to camps where they mixed with people from different areas. No doubt they saw it as a chance to be near the eyes of the government because, whenever we had opportunities to recruit staff according to their ability and test results, we started from the camps and gave those youth priority. The morale was high in the camps; the boys were hopeful about getting jobs in government. Many of them went into the army, the police, and the prison department since that kind of work was suitable for them. Those sectors had more opportunities than did the ministries.

I visited the camps to encourage the young people or to sort out any problems or contradictions. I went often during the harvest period to volunteer my labor. They sang nationalist songs and drilled, and later they received army training. There was a phobia here about a counterrevolution, so we wanted a reserve to be called on in time of need to defend the nation.

The youth had to stay in the camp during the week, and only some were permitted on a rotational basis to go home on the weekends. Usually they had a monthly visit home. On the whole, they observed the discipline. If they did not like the camps, they could always leave, but I did not have a major problem with that. We sent these young people to do tough work, to learn how to be productive, and to be indoctrinated. And after staying in the camps, they were employed, or they went back to the village as leaders because now they were organized and disciplined.

Of course, the youth from town hated to go. They thought that the people from the bush were inferior and that their going to the rural areas was degrading to them. The rural youth thought it was a picnic, though, for which they volunteered, but the ones from town tried to resist. Later, we instituted a system where, if secondary school students did not go to the camps, they would not pass their exams and graduate. It was compulsory for a student after graduation to work for two years in the camps in order afterward to obtain any kind of employment. We made them go because they had to differentiate between rice and grass. They had to learn how to use a hoe. We had to minimize the differences between the rural and urban youth, so the contradictions would be eliminated, so the people from town would not look down on the peasants.[1]

And I can say that, after the revolution, all our young men, at least from the rural areas, were very enthusiastic. We could rely on them; we could call on them, and they would respond.

Youth camps, along with land reform, managed to contain the influx of people from the villages into town in the years after the revolution. We also tried to build modern blocks of flats designed by the East Germans, but the people did not like the flats. They also did not like working on them, saying it was forced labor.

But who forced the people to build? We volunteered our labor. I was a minister, and I went myself to contribute my labor to build the flats at Michenzani. Our people were sometimes very lazy, and they liked to have things given to them on a silver platter. We had to mold them, to change their attitudes; we had to use certain means to make them do certain things. Any organization must have discipline, like the army. Once the center has decided on something, you have to agree, and you cannot rebel. Whatever has been decided, you must follow.

I used to really dislike manual work. In Standards 7 and 8, we went early in the morning for an hour to cultivate the school farm. But later in life, especially after my training in the U. K., I came to appreciate discipline and to enjoy voluntary work. I went willingly, but only after I had joined the party, after I had learned discipline. I went to Michenzani three times a week for an hour or two, and the other ministers did the same. We arranged a schedule, saying, "If we don't go and show an example, the people will react." We had no cranes, so we carried bricks in a line. Of course, when you mobilize people, there will always be some resistance, but it encouraged our people to see a minister doing that kind of work.[2]

And then on Sundays sometimes, the whole town would go to work or attend a mass rally to receive its new orders. We also encouraged school children to go to the countryside on the weekends to cultivate. They did not like it very much, but as they say, "*Revolucion tene mucho sacrificio,*" and we were revolutionary and had to sacrifice part of our leisure. Sometimes we had to forgo certain luxuries and have only necessities. That is the reason our government only paid in cash and never took loans. We managed to balance our budget and even have a surplus. How could that have come about in a poor country, without discipline?

So, slowly in those years, we began to develop Zanzibar. Water and electricity came to the villages, where before there was only darkness and fornication. In the beginning, we were lucky because the price of cloves was good on the international market, but as time went on, the price dropped.

I have been smoking marijuana on and off since 1945. Smoking in the mornings when I was a minister gave me energy and the capacity to think. When I wanted to write something, I would smoke a stick, and then the ideas came. I also found that using a small stick in the loo in the morning helped my motion. But here people look down on someone who smokes marijuana; they despise you. They associate marijuana with madness and hallucination, but I would say tobacco cigarettes are worse than marijuana because they are more addictive. Anything you use to excess is dangerous. I have never tried harder drugs, and if I go to a place where there is no marijuana, I do not crave it. If marijuana is available, I will use it moderately and discreetly. It is just grass, a natural thing; and fortunately, I have never been prosecuted.

My first wife was furious once, and she wanted to report me to the colonial police in Pemba. I said to her, "You'll ruin me!" But she did not listen; luckily, my friends managed to persuade her not to report me. That was in 1959—crazy girl! Later, I tried to introduce Maria to marijuana, but she did not like it. And then after the revolution, they passed a law in the RC to send people to jail for marijuana. I said to my colleagues, "Now that we're passing this law, are we ministers also going to jail for ten years?" Karume answered no, that it was just for the sellers. But they used the law indiscriminately, against the user and the seller, locking people inside for ten years.

Once there were some students caught smoking marijuana in the school toilet at Lumumba, in their last year, just before their exams. The school principal wanted to expel them, but I pleaded with him, saying, "Cane them, but forgive them. Otherwise, you are going to ruin their lives." I heard the students' confession; they asked to be pardoned and were ready to receive corporal punishment. The principal was adamant, but I overruled him.

Also in those years, the government wanted to stop our young boys from wearing very narrow pants, a style common in the 1960s. My trousers were the narrowest of all the members of the RC. I brought the Italian style into Zanzibar; I had been wearing Italian suits since my days as a councilor in London. That was the fashion, but the government passed a law that our trouser bottoms had to be a minimum of eighteen inches in circumference. Anything less was considered *suruali ya chupa*, or "bottle pants," which the Beatles were known to wear. As a test one day in an RC meeting, I was asked to unbelt my pants, and then someone dropped a beer bottle down one of my trouser legs. If the bottle could pass all the way through, even through my cuffs, then my trousers met the official standards. The bottle passed through, fortunately, and, of course, we all laughed because it was sort of a joke.

That happened in 1966 or 1967 before bell-bottoms came in. I always disliked bell-bottoms; in fact, they appalled me. There was a clique in the Youth League headed by Seif Bakari against both bottle pants and bell-bottoms. I do not know who gave them the idea that we should not adopt such foreign fashions. Maybe they thought that it was cultural aggression and that we should not allow our youth to be corrupted by the foreign styles.

While I was a minister, my personal lifestyle was far above that of the ordinary people. The starting salary for a government teacher was three hundred shillings a month, while I received three thousand a month. And then from 1964 to 1967, I was also a member of the Central Legislative Assembly in East Africa, which gave me certain allowances and more income. But I never saved any money; I spent it all. Even though the car, the driver, fuel, rent, water, electricity, and telephone were free, when I was taken out of the ministry, I had an overdraft of two hundred Tanzanian shillings at the bank. I had a huge family, and I supported a lot of people in those days. I was eating well, and I kept my family well. I looked after my four younger siblings, as well as my sister's five children. Maria and I would travel together around East Africa. And during those years, Maria and I had three children of our own, starting with Omar in 1967, then Salim in 1969, and Johanna in 1971.

I also helped my friends who came for parties at my house. Since I was a man of the people, my house was open to all, whether comrades or just friends in the government. Respectable people usually like to stay in private when they indulge themselves, rather than be seen in public. I was on good terms with everyone on the RC; there was no one with whom I refused to speak.

I would not observe Ramadhan but was careful not to eat openly in the streets. I would conceal my smoking as well. I had an ulcer, anyway, which made fasting very difficult. In those days, I also had a private flat if I wanted to fornicate. I had my separate place for my indulgences. We are in Africa; and as a Muslim, I am allowed to have four wives, so it is permitted and accepted in our society. It is not like in your society where, if Clinton decides to kiss a girl, it is in the newspapers the next day. People should have their privacy; if they are discreet, they should be forgiven.

Still, my lifestyle as a minister was not ostentatious; it was very humble. I knew who I was, so I did not have to be pompous, and Maria on her part was very frugal. She never asked how much I earned. No, Maria just liked to go around with her friends and go to official receptions, and that was all. I gave her the Browning pistol to keep in her bag when she went out alone, to give her confidence. I trained her to shoot, and people were afraid of her. I had two cars: a Vauxhall that was the government car and a Renault for her private use, so she could go swimming on the east coast.

Our women here were ostentatious, wanting a new dress for every function. They spoke of her when she wore the same suit to every function, a beautiful silk suit she had brought with her from the U.K. They would laugh at her, but do you know what Maria told me? She said, "This dress of mine cost three or four times what theirs cost. To every party they wear a new dress, but if you go in their homes, you see the way they eat." In our house, we ate very well, and we had about ten people to feed. So you see their thinking and ours.

Maria and I lived at Beit el Ras until 1968, and then when Karume removed Abdul Aziz Twala, the minister of health, I was given his ministry. We moved from Beit el Ras back into town, to a house in Stone Town at Mizingani, near what is now Mercury's Bar. The house had three floors and had been constructed by an old Arab family on the sea front, with thick walls and mangrove poles supporting the ceilings. Maria and I lived on the top floor; below us was a huge room and sitting place occupied by the children, and the ground floor had a kitchen, a dining room, and a room for the big boys.

Next to our home was a big old banyan tree, which is still there today. An Arab boy about ten years old would climb the tree and onto the branches only a few feet from the windows where my children slept. He would sit in the branches and make jokes and tease my children, until one day I grew tired of this and ordered the police to arrest him and throw him in prison. Or course, the police took special action because I was a minister. After about a week, his mother came to me and begged for his release; I said okay, and he was released.

We ministers in those days could arrest and imprison anyone we wanted. We were representatives of a revolutionary government, after all, so we even had the power to kill. But I did not kill anyone, and I did not abuse my power. Many members of the RC, however, abused their power by putting husbands inside when they wanted to sleep with their wives. Eventually, Karume said, "You can put them inside, but if you want to release them, I need to give my permission. You need to come and explain first why you want them released."

I personally only imprisoned two—the Arab boy and an Indian chap to whom we gave training as a lab technician. Afterward, he did not want to work for the government, so I ordered his imprisonment. Eventually, his father and his teacher both came and pleaded for his release. I consented on the condition that he work for the government. And he did; he had learned his lesson and later became a very good friend of mine.

We lived in that house until 1970, when we finished building our own beautiful home at Migombani, on the ocean just south of Zanzibar Town. Maria and I designed the house ourselves, with a balcony and a wonderful view of the sea and a footpath right to the beach. We had seven bedrooms, two bathrooms, and a garage. There were two kitchens, one indoor and one outdoors, and servants' quarters with their own toilets. We had a flat roof, so if we had parties, we could host them up there.

Upstairs we had a study, a library, a kitchenette, and a bar. The furniture was built into the walls and very modern looking. On the outside facing the street, I put up a sign that said to all who passed, *Azimio la Mapinduzi*, which translates roughly as "Fruits of the Revolution," because I felt building houses of that style and proportion was what the revolution was all about.

At first, we were alone, and then Karume came and built one of his several houses there. Behind Karume's on the main road was Seif Bakari's house. And then Jumbe also came and built a house close by. On my right was Karume, and on my left was Jumbe.

We were very happy in those days, and after work, unless there was an official function, I spent most of my time with my family. We had no television, only radio and cassettes. Maria spent a lot of time reading novels, quite a lot of them actually. To me, it was a lot of rubbish, but I never tried to indoctrinate her or make her into a Marxist. She was apolitical. Instead, we went to the cinema or for a drive or a picnic in the countryside. Sometimes we went out dancing at the Africa House Hotel or to the embassy functions. My ulcers were acting up, so I did not drink as frequently.

I never told Maria that I had a son, Malik, who was born out of wedlock in 1961. I had never even told Aysha, my wife at the time, but she managed to find out about the affair through her sister. Since I did not want Maria to know about his existence, I did not spend a lot of time with Malik when he was young. He stayed mostly with his maternal grandmother in Zanzibar Town, and after I became a minister, I started giving her money every month for his upkeep. I had nothing before 1964, but afterward I gave his grandmother something.

Sometimes, though, I would sneak out of the ministry during the day and go to where he stayed with his grandmother. He was my first son, after all. When I went there, he would run away at first because I was a minister and everyone was afraid of me. I grabbed him and played with him a few minutes before leaving. I could not waste too much time. I would say hello to the grandmother, play with Malik, slap him around a little, and then go back to work.

I felt sorry for him, actually. Once I saw him as I drove to my house in Migombani, with Maria and Omar in the front seat with me. Malik was walking home from picking guava in the forest. Our eyes met, and he recognized me as I drove past. He stopped and stood there on the side of the road and watched me pass in my car. I said to myself, in my heart, "There is my son, forced to fetch guava in the forest, and here I am in my nice car with this *mzungu* wife and son, enjoying myself." It pained me in my heart.

I became minister of health in July or August 1968. I tried to bring health to the people by building clinics in the rural areas, and received some assistance from outside. Cuban doctors worked in Wete Hospital in Pemba, and Chinese doctors were assigned to Mkoani Hospital in Pemba and to the V. I. Lenin Hospital with the Russians. The Russian doctors did not last very long, leaving very early in the process. But the Chinese went even to the rural areas with their team and were very close to the people, providing us with free medicine.

In Zanzibar, we did not have a serious problem with malnutrition. It might happen that, due to an unbalanced diet, some of our kids would have bulging tummies. But it was more through ignorance of the parents about what to feed their kids. We tried to encourage good hygiene and had an intensive campaign with posters in the villages to get all the people to dig their own pit latrines. Having a pit latrine was a minimum in the rural areas, instead of just going outside. We also tried to organize traditional healing properly. We knew we could not completely control or stop it because some people in a backward country like Zanzibar had faith in it.

Otherwise, we expanded health services in the rural areas; wherever there was a school, there was now a clinic. The clinics were equipped with outpatient and inpatient beds, a minimum of eight, and for minor treatments, people could be hospitalized there. We trained more nurses and midwives, and doctors even performed small surgeries in the rural areas, for example, for a hernia and appendicitis. Our people were aware that the quality of health care was improving because, in the past, they were forced to come to town, but now we extended services to them in the villages. Also, the hospital was free, and the food there was very good. They had eggs, porridge, bread, and butter, which they would not have had in their own homes. When they were cured, some people did not want to leave, so we had to speak to them and say, "Look, you are already cured, but some people are sick, and they need the bed you are occupying."

So, I managed to survive through eight long years in the cabinet, when some of the other ministers were executed. It was because of my style of work—I always sought Karume's counsel and never took a decision on my own without his consent. After a thorough study and analysis in my ministry, after we prepared a paper to send to him, we sat with him until we agreed. And Karume almost always gave me his support in the RC. I am very grateful for that because, in that way, he was a man of honor.[3]

Karume was from the working class and not formally educated, although he had traveled extensively as a seaman, so you could say he was somewhat exposed. As far as ideology was concerned, he had none. He was a nationalist and wanted rights for the squatters and the working people; otherwise, he was pliant and open to new ideas. Because of his class origins, it was natural for him to understand and even be inclined toward socialism; for this reason, it was sometimes easy for us comrades to work with him. At other times, however, he thought any little mistake on our part was a deliberate sabotage of the revolution. In those days, that word *sabotage* was powerful. It meant that you were a counterrevolutionary and that whatever happened, whatever little mistake took place, it should be investigated. But only God is perfect; perfection is the prerogative of God. We as mortals are fallible, and we make mistakes.

thirteen POWER

MANY PEOPLE RAN
away from Zanzibar, leaving empty houses. Many wanted to go, especially
Arab or Indian youth whom we had sent to the labor camps. Even after
things had stabilized, after thousands had already died in the revolution,
we still had another ten thousand or so leave for other countries.

Older people were allowed to emigrate, but we did not want younger
people to run away, ones we had trained and educated. We thought they
should work here, to serve their country and to show their gratitude. It
was not fair for them to run away and serve another nation—where was
their loyalty, their patriotism? So we imposed travel restrictions: anyone
wanting to travel had to obtain a letter from the party in order to receive
a passport. Sometimes we allowed students to spend Easter on the Tanzanian mainland, but as minister of education, I put a stop to that when
some students refused to return to the islands.

In Karume's time, nearly all the Indians left Zanzibar. That was because, in 1964, we nationalized the wholesale trade, and all the big
merchants went away. We also nationalized the Indian-owned factories
producing ice, soda, coconut oil, and coir. Then in 1967, we nationalized
the retail trade, and that was when most of the others left, the little
shopkeepers. Some continued to work in government offices and as artisans, but all the others lost their factories, businesses, and livelihoods.
They would not go to the countryside to cultivate farms like peasants,
so very few remained.

Karume wanted to get rid of the Indians and saw nationalization as the
only way. On my part, I did not have many friends among the Indians,
only one or two who were professionals, so I did not feel sad or happy
about their departure. Of course, I thought Indians as a group had exploited other Zanzibaris. As a merchant class, how would they otherwise have survived? In any business, the owners must have profit, and

what is profit? According to Marx, it is wages stolen from the workers. We comrades, though, advised against the government's taking over the retail trade. We thought it would ruin our economy, but Karume would not listen.

So, with the departure of most of the Arabs and the Indians, very few remained in Stone Town who had been there before the revolution, maybe 10 percent. Those who remained could do nothing; they had to come into the fold. And with so many gone, many houses in Stone Town were empty and falling down. Stone Town was like a bush, where anyone could hide if he wanted to. If you had nowhere to stay, you could get in and establish yourself. We in the RC saw Stone Town as a vulnerable point and offered people from Pemba the chance to stay in these huge houses that were falling down.

But Karume also wanted to get rid of the Comorians. The majority had sided with the ZNP, and Karume had had a rough time with them. They sang taunting songs and called him names like *manjo*, a wedding singer, a derogatory reference to the speeches he gave to the ASP rank and file. The Comorians wanted to let him know that what he said was meaningless. After the revolution, Karume demolished the area of Funguni in Zanzibar Town, where many Comorians lived, to build the Bwawani Hotel. We also passed a law stating that all the subjects of the Persians, the Portuguese, and the French had to renounce their identity and nationality in order to enjoy Zanzibari citizenship and that their old governments had to agree. The law was intended to apply to the Comorians, the Shirazis, the Goans, and the Baharan, all of whom theoretically were originally from Portuguese or French colonies or from Iran.

Karume did not care about the Goans, who were only a handful, an insignificant minority. Instead, there was pressure on the Comorians and on the Baharan, who were of the Shia sect and from the Gulf. Karume wanted to humiliate them, so in 1968, they were enticed—those who say *forced*, let them say *forced*—to demonstrate in Zanzibar Town, renouncing their identity and paying allegiance to the revolutionary government. They marched across town carrying placards and saying, "We renounce Comorian nationality. We are all Zanzibaris, Tanzanians." Even the Baharan demonstrated in this way, and afterward they were able to keep their jobs. Those who wanted to run away did so.[1]

Karume even wanted the Shirazis—the majority of the population—to be declared aliens. Karume and Bakari were both mainlanders, as well as most members of the RC. Karume said that, because Shirazis claimed partial descent from Persian colonists who came to the islands a thousand years ago, they were not real Zanzibari citizens. He wanted to eradicate

Shirazi identity and have all of them just call themselves Africans, but he failed because they were very proud and very numerous.[2] The ASP remained the Afro-Shirazi Party, symbolizing that there was a mainlander and Shirazi element in Zanzibari society that could not be denied.

In the past, Arabs looked down on Africans. After the revolution, it was the reverse: Africans looked down on Arabs. We ended ethnic associations and completed our land redistribution, but people who did not have any education still espoused racialism, only it was not very open because Tanzania was supposed to be a nonracial society. But deep in their hearts, they still clung to racialism, especially those with no qualifications.

Seif Bakari was a racist, I can say, because he never married an Arab girl, which was the fashion in those days. The government wanted to have a mixed society and to put an end to racial antagonism, so it arranged marriages between Arab women and African army officers or members of the RC. In the past, it was easy for an Arab man to marry an African woman, but it was very rare for an Arab woman to marry an African man. To put an end to such prejudice, the authorities encouraged cross-marriages or what others have called "forced marriages."[3] I did not think anything of the mixed marriages, but Bakari once said to me, "See these people! They're mixing blood!" I said, "What's wrong with that? There's no blood that is pure."

Actually, Bakari and the people in the Youth League were the ones responsible for almost all the atrocities after the revolution. Their idea was to control every facet of life, and to change the mentality of the people, so they established a group known as the Volunteers. Each locality had its own Volunteers to maintain peace and order and to force people to do voluntary work. They were supposed to know everyone in a village, to collect information, to report on petty crimes, and to turn people over to the police. The Volunteers were hardly paid, but they could always extract something from the people through intimidation. The citizens did not like the Volunteers because they wanted to impose their authority, to frighten, bully, and harass.

The people were kept quiet out of fear: they were afraid of the government, the party, and the Volunteers. The country was ruled by decree; there was no constitution or bill of rights. Even though, as a minister, I had immunity from people like the Volunteers, I still had fear. In those days, we could not trust even our own wives because they sometimes informed on their husbands to the state security, trained by the East Germans. And we all know how the East Germans controlled their people, so almost the same system applied here. Of course, my first wife was a very honorable lady, but the peak of fear came after our divorce in 1966, and by then I was lucky to have an English wife.

We used to have a saying that "among three people, one is not yours." We thought the walls had ears, that they could be bugged. For all the years after the revolution, we had to stay on our toes; we had to watch where we went, whom we met, and what we said. We had to think before we spoke. We knew people were missing; it was an open secret that common people were accused of wanting to overthrow the government and were killed. People disappeared and were never seen again. As time passed, the situation grew worse.[4]

Of course, if a person was ideologically oriented, then life under Karume was very good. Otherwise, society was so strict and harsh that a lot of people feared imprisonment and had no freedom to express an opinion not endorsed by the regime. If you want to quantify freedom as more important than food or housing, then life was hard in those days. But then starting around 1969, the physical hardships increased as well.

After the government took control of all imports, clothing and other commodities were sold only in government shops, and because of inefficiency, the people sometimes had nothing. We stopped importing shoes and cigarettes and made our own. We produced our own milk, butter, and ghee from a dairy built by the East Germans. But inevitably there were shortages, and when people went to the mosque, they would sit together and talk. If there was any hardship, they would often help one another, according to Islamic tradition.

But Karume was not satisfied. In 1968, he personally took over the Ministry of Finance and saw the money spent for our imports of rice, sugar, and flour. The government spent a lot of resources on such commodities, and Karume decided that the country had to become self-sufficient in food production. The only way to get our people to produce food themselves, he thought, was to stop importing rice, sugar, and flour, to put our people on rations.

But normally in a planned economy, if you increase production a hundred tons, then you can stop importing a hundred tons. But when you stop importation and the people are not ready, then there is hardship. There was suffering among the people, and our idea after the revolution was originally to stop suffering. Karume, of course, had the support of the rural people who could always eat, but the people in the towns did not have access to land.

So I believe Karume had the right intentions, but the results were negative. There was widespread hunger, although no one actually died because in the rural areas people had cassava and bananas. But in the urban areas, people did not want to eat just cassava; they wanted rice and bread, and all of it was rationed. As a minister, I had to rely on the rations I received, but I also had a farm producing rice, beans, bananas, and cassava. I was given three acres eight miles north of town, where I planted rice and beans. And I was awarded nine acres at Machuwi, a government *shamba* since the time of Sultan Barghash. In addition, when I went to Dar es Salaam for parliamentary meetings, I would buy what we needed at home, even though it was considered smuggling. I had immunity, so no one could search my bags or stop me as I returned to Zanzibar.

What I did not like was all that queuing, that waiting in line for the ordinary person. Why? People had the money, but they could not buy anything. It was unprecedented; it had happened only once during World War II, but now we were not at war. Instead of breaking their fast at the end of Ramadhan, the people waited in line to get a pair of pants or a shirt. People carried baskets at all times in case they saw anything for sale. Of course, I did not have to wait in line because a shop in Kikwajuni was specifically consigned to us ministers and members of the RC. But if any hardship fell on the people, we were all blamed. "They are there," they would say. "Why can't they say anything?"

Maria never commented on the hardship, the rationing, or the long lines. I said to her, "It's none of your business. Just comment to me and no one else." Once we were driving and saw people waiting in line, and even though it was just the two of us in the car, I said "Ssshhh! It'll reach the old man!"

For the vast majority of Zanzibaris, this was Karume's most unpopular action. Rations, combined with the Youth League's iron hand of discipline, were his downfall. In the beginning, the economy was all right, and life was tolerable because the price of cloves was high. But the further we went, the worse things became. From 1969 onward, everything went down, everything deteriorated.[5] We replaced the Indian shopkeepers with cooperative shops, but they did not function due to dishonesty. In any business venture, honesty is one of the basic criteria. And then maintenance of infrastructure was never much of a concern for uneducated people from the bush, who thought, "Our country is rich, so they'll provide a new car tomorrow."

To make matters worse, malaria in those days made a dramatic resurgence. The WHO had a project in the 1960s to eradicate malaria from the islands. Then one day the head of the WHO came and spoke to Karume without first telling my ministry what he wanted to say, a serious mistake. The official told Karume that we could never completely eradicate malaria in Zanzibar—we could only control the disease—because people came and went from the mainland by canoe, and it was not possible to quarantine all the people on the island from the mainland. Karume called us ministers in and said, "Okay, we will now stop our support for the WHO." We were paying the bill for the fuel used by their vehicles and the salaries of Zanzibaris working for the WHO. Karume wanted to stop our support because, he thought, "If we cannot eradicate the disease, then what's the purpose?" That was Karume's mentality.

We pleaded with him, and he allowed us to use our supply of DDT for another six months. After our stocks were finished, of course, there was an immediate and dramatic resurgence of malaria, which we reported to Karume. In the ministry, we had our statistics, and we presented them to the RC. But Karume blamed the official from the WHO, saying, "He told me we couldn't eradicate malaria." He did not understand that, even though we could not completely eradicate malaria, we had seriously reduced its impact. We did not want to criticize Karume—he was the big boss after all—even though malaria once again became Zanzibar's most deadly disease.

I felt the whole idea of the revolution had gone radically wrong, especially when we started to consume our own. I had a seat on the RC and saw a lot of it happen there. Of the first nine ministers appointed after the revolution, four were executed: Othman Shariff, Kassim Hanga, Saleh Sadaalah, and Abdulaziz Twala. These men were more educated than Karume and had a history with him that went back to the 1950s. Karume despised them all and worked closely with Seif Bakari to eliminate them.

The country was run by the gun. The state security used the bogey of counterrevolution to get rid of certain elements, among them these educated ministers. Only after the fact did they inform us on the RC of the killings. Since I was a minority in the government, I watched all that happened to the Africans and Shirazi like a barometer. I asked myself, "If this thing can befall so-and-so, what can happen to me?"

Othman Shariff was accused of plotting against the government when he was our ambassador to the United States. He was removed from that post and reduced to being a veterinary officer on the mainland. But whenever he came to Dar es Salaam, Shariff had meetings with some of his supporters from Zanzibar, who are all gone now, with the wind. Nyerere arrested him and eventually sent him over to Zanzibar, where he was executed.

On a Saturday in 1966, there was a party at the Russian ambassador's residence for all the ministers. Afterward, I left with Saleh Sadaalah, the minister of communications, for Dar es Salaam. I stayed in Dar until early Monday morning but returned to the islands in time to be in my office by 8:00 a.m. Immediately, that morning, a meeting of the RC was called. Karume asked me where I had been over the weekend and why I had not asked his permission to go to Dar. I said there was no standing rule I needed to do so, but I was very polite and answered all his questions. Karume said, "From now on, if any member of the RC wants to go outside the country, he must do so only with my permission."

Karume was not very hard on me, so his anger was meant for someone else. Saleh eventually came back to Zanzibar on Wednesday, and we knew the next day there would be a meeting. I went to his house and told him what had happened. Badawi, who was his junior minister, also tried to talk to him, but Saleh was furious. He said, "Is he my husband that I must ask his permission?" We said, "Listen, Karume is your boss." We tried sending others to him but he was half drunk and would not listen. So we left him, after having done our duty.

In the morning, there was a meeting, and Karume asked Saleh the same questions, but Saleh's response was different from mine: he drew his pistol. Karume's reflexes were sharp, however, and he hit him on the hand with his cane, and the cane broke. Others in the meeting disarmed Saleh; he was immediately imprisoned and eventually executed. Later, I came to know that Saleh had taken his gun to the meeting wanting to shoot Karume, but he was still drunk and did not realize that his girlfriend had taken out the magazine.

Kassim Hanga was still vice president at the time in Zanzibar and also minister for union affairs in Dar es Salaam. When he heard about the incident with Saleh, he came immediately from Dar, and instead of going straight to Karume to ask him what had happened, he went to the prison and asked Saleh first. This infuriated Karume.

Hanga had once been very close to Karume. But while he was in the U.K. in 1957, studying there on Karume's recommendation, he became very close to Oscar Kambona. When Hanga worked in Dar after the revolution, his close friendship with Kambona continued. But then in 1968, Kambona ran away from Tanzania to live in exile in London, and that was the start of Hanga's falling out with Nyerere, who suspected his relationship with Kambona. When Hanga visited Saleh Saadalah in prison, he lost Karume's favor as well, who took the vice presidency away from him.

Hanga by then had married a Guinean lady. Once on his way back from Guinea, he stopped in Cairo and made certain comments that were reported here in Tanzania. I did not see the report from our Cairo embassy, but they were not positive comments about the authorities here. When Hanga returned to Tanzania, he was arrested on the mainland; Nyerere sent him later to Zanzibar, where he was executed.

Abdulaziz Twala, the minister of health, made the mistake in 1968 of applying for a scholarship to study in America. He and I were somewhat close; ideologically, we agreed on certain principles. I asked him, "Did you discuss this with the president?" He said no, and I said, "Ah, you should have done that!" That was the point of rupture because the U.S. consulate informed Karume, wanting his opinion about the scholarship. Twala was removed from the ministry and the government; he managed to stay out of prison for awhile, and then we heard that he had been arrested and sent to a rural prison camp. Twala got desperate and ran away from the prison, but they eventually caught hold of him. We never asked why he was executed. As I have already said, we worked in fear. Such decisions were taken outside the RC, and sometimes we were informed afterward, but never before. What could we do? Nothing, especially when someone had already been executed.

It was easy, then, for someone to fall from favor. Indeed, sometimes I feel lucky to have survived to tell my story.

fourteen ARREST

WE SAW WHAT
happened in early 1972 as a purge of former Umma comrades. Nyerere
dropped Babu from his cabinet on the mainland, and soon after that,
Badawi and I were dropped in Zanzibar. I remember it was February
20, 1972. I had gone to see a matinee in Malindi, a showing of *Madame
Bovary*. After the film, I went home and listened to my Zenith and
heard that I was no longer minister of health.

I said "*Al-hamdulilah!*" I was so relieved! But my friend Ali Mzee was
worried because I no longer had my immunity, and in those days, if you
were dropped from the cabinet, you were put in prison. But I thought,
"Whatever they do now, I am not a part; I am not responsible." For all
those years, I could not come out of the government because, if I had
tried to resign, I would have been sent straight to prison. I thought, "But
now they've taken me out themselves, and they haven't arrested me, so
at least I'll survive. And God will forgive me."

I was lucky to stay a minister for eight long years, four in education
and four in health. And now only two former Umma comrades remained
in the RC, Khamis Abdalla Ameir and Ali Mafoudh. Karume might
have been suspicious of Umma at the time. I do not know his thinking,
but some of the Umma element might have given him reason to doubt
their allegiance.

I did not know how I would support my family, but I knew Karume
would offer me a job somewhere. After a week or so, he appointed me
chairman of the State Fuel and Power Corporation. My salary as a
minister had been three thousand shillings a month, and now I earned
fifteen hundred.

In those days, people remembered the terrible cyclone of 1872, a hundred
years earlier, and people were saying another calamity would happen

that year. For me, it happened on April 7, 1972, a Friday. On that day, I had gone to see a matinee at the cinema in Malindi, called *Lady of Monza*. I was with my wife, Ali Mzee, and his wife. Ali Mzee and I were always together. Everyone in Zanzibar knew Ali Sultan was with Ali Mzee, and Ali Mzee was with Ali Sultan. Everywhere we went, we went together. So after the cinema, the two women went to a friend's house, while my friend and I sat outside drinking coffee with the people who were always there sitting and gossiping. I did not have a car on that particular day.

As we were walking away, we heard a burst of gunfire. At the time, we thought maybe it was the sound of a house falling down not far away. But after the next burst, we ran to an Indian friend's house nearby. We locked the door, and I asked Ali Mzee to roll a couple of cigarettes; after a smoke, I wanted to leave, but Ali Mzee was afraid. We waited for the evening call to prayer from the Ithna Asheri Mosque, and then we walked toward Darajani. My friend said we should avoid the Youth League headquarters, but I said no, that was where we would get our information. I said, "I must go there and find out what has happened, so, if required, I can get my uniform and defend my country." At the Youth League, I spoke to a friend who said there had been gunfire at the ASP party headquarters but did not say if Karume was dead or alive.

I said, "Oh, my God," and then I noticed that everyone there, all wearing their Volunteer uniforms, was looking at me strangely. I could see that the faces of the people had changed. They were all my friends— I mean, we had been working together all that time, for almost ten years since the revolution—and now they were looking at me differently.

We walked to Ali Mzee's house, passing a bakery owned by a Goan named Diaz. At the time, people always had to queue for bread. On that particular day, there was bread available, but nobody was waiting. Everyone had run away to hide. There was fear throughout the neighborhood. I said to my friend, "If someone among us Umma comrades has done this, then we are in hot soup, and all of us will die. And especially if they shoot Karume, and Karume has not died, all of us will be killed. But if Africans have done this among themselves, then we'll be all right."

At my friend's house, I met my wife who said we should go home to look after Johanna, our newborn baby. I was afraid, but Maria told me that, if I did not come, she would go home alone, so we started walking. When we reached Mlandege, someone passed by who called me aside and told me that Karume had been shot and was in the hospital in critical condition. Going further, we found Miembeni full of people, whereas all the areas that were ZNP before the revolution, those closest to Stone Town, were deserted. But Miembeni had always been Afro-Shirazi, and they were all there selling fish as if nothing had happened. Africans lived without fear that day. Here you can feel the tension, and there, nothing at all.

I did not eat my dinner that night. There was no news, only announcements of a curfew starting from 8:00 p.m. At 2:30 a.m., the police came to arrest me. My wife, who was five months pregnant at the time, wanted to make some trouble, but I said, "Never mind!" That was the last time I saw her for the next six years and nine months.

The police took me to the Malindi police station. I had to undress to my t-shirt and boxers. Within a couple of hours, they transferred me to the Ng'ambo police station, where I stayed overnight. They did not give us breakfast, though I suffered from ulcers, and they knew I had to eat every four hours. By 11:00 a.m., we were transferred to the security prison at Ziwani, each one put in a separate cell, but still received no food. Maybe that was the East German system since our security had been trained in the GDR.

Because of my ulcers, I complained about food, knocking at my door, but the guards did not bother to answer. I thought I was finished, that I would not come out of there alive. Of course, the rumors were out that we had already been killed. Even Maria heard that someone had found my body hanging from a mango tree. Eventually, I received boiled smashed cassava to eat, but nothing else. I was kept alone and completely isolated and allowed only twenty minutes in the morning to go to the loo or something, and then another twenty minutes in the afternoon. They took everything away, except some cardboard to sleep on.

My first cell companion was a police officer, Yusuf Ramadhan. He had actually received me at the Ng'ambo station and now was put into my cell. And then Hassan Makame Seif was also put in my cell, an army officer who later accused me of being part of the conspiracy to kill Karume, though I never had met him in my life. Poor fellow, he is dead now.

We reached a point where we were about ten or twelve in that small cell, packed like sardines.[1] In the beginning, we did not even have a bucket or water, just a small hole. When we would get some water, we would try to flush our shit through the hole. Later, the guards gave us a bucket. It was terrible because even the jailers thought we were going to die.

And then I could hear the cries of men being tortured. Once you are sent to prison anywhere in Africa, you are going to be tortured. Your humanity is totally discarded. From April to June, people were tortured. Each one, when he broke down, gave the security people what they wanted. They wanted maximum information, and people were implicated.

My day eventually came, and the jailers took me out for interrogation. When they asked if I knew anything about the plot to assassinate President Karume, I said I knew nothing, and they started hitting me. They said, "We know how to make a person talk." They brought their team of about fifteen to hit me and torment me. Hassan Mandera, who is dead now, was a main interrogator and torturer.

They started caning me and clubbing me, and I fainted. I regained my consciousness, and I kept saying "I don't know," but they kept hitting me. I fainted again and then regained my consciousness a second time. They kept on beating me, and I fainted a third time. When I regained consciousness, I said, "Listen, you are going to kill me for nothing because I don't know what to tell you. Ask me what I know, and I'll answer you, but I cannot relate something I don't know. I cannot tell lies; it's not me. If you want to write something, I'll sign; but if ever I go to court, I'll repudiate the statement and say you tortured me."

For three days, I suffered. I returned to my cell every day, my shirt torn, my back slashed. I slept on my stomach on the cement floor, wrapping myself like a mummy in the cardboard since our cells were infested with mosquitoes.

When they tortured me, I would stand holding my balls while they hit my back. I learned to do that because, at first, there were some who caned me in the balls. Later, when everything cooled down in the prison, say by July or August, I questioned one of them who had hit me in the balls. "Why did you do that?" I asked. "What if I were to go out and be impotent? I wouldn't have taken your girlfriend because I don't want her, nor could you have taken my girlfriend because she wouldn't have accepted you."

He said, "Forgive me."

Years later, after I came out of prison, I got drunk one day and saw this same officer in the marketplace. I blew up in front of everyone there, and he went down on his knees, holding my legs, begging forgiveness. He is still in state security, and now we are good friends because, on that day at the marketplace, I forgave him. I have forgiven all my torturers; even when they come to my house, I give them money. When I see them in the bar, I offer them drinks.

When I told the torturers that I knew nothing and that I would repudiate any statement they would write on my behalf, they allowed me to write my own. I was the only one, of the hundreds they arrested, to be allowed to write my own statement; I believe some of them were convinced I was not involved in the conspiracy to kill Karume. But we have a saying in Swahili, "*Samaki moja akioza,*" when one fish goes bad, then all the fish go bad. It was guilt by association; I was an Umma comrade, and all comrades were under suspicion of killing Karume.

Through conversations with my comrades in prison, I came to know why Karume was killed: Babu and other Umma comrades wanted to overthrow his government. They were angry about the hardships of life in Zanzibar and about all the people who had been killed without due process, and they wanted to change the regime. They wanted to use the material hardship of the people so prevalent in 1972 to pull off a coup. They planned to steal weapons from the armory, capture Karume, and force him to resign officially over the radio. They thought that once they did so, there would be a spontaneous uprising. They assumed the masses were so fed up with the regime that they were ready to die to make changes.

It did not happen that way, and I told my comrades in prison, "This is a most unscientific way of approaching a problem, and look where it has ended. You cannot, therefore, call yourselves Marxists. Anarchists, maybe." It was a stupid idea because you can never rely upon the spontaneity of the masses. Anyway, it was no longer true as it had been in 1964 that, once you captured a couple of police installations, it was all over. Each army unit was composed of soldiers from different rural areas, with its own weaponry. It was not such a professional army, but it was a people's army recruited from the villages and not from town. This meant any coup had to take each region and each district one at a time.

Our army had been trained by Russia with obsolete guns, but in Africa, they were not obsolete. And the Chinese had given us their new weapons. We had artillery, mortars, and submachine guns. We only sent the union government the MiGs the Soviets gave us. So if the rebels planned a coup and expected the whole army to rise up, well, it was wishful thinking and unscientific. You cannot plan people's lives that way. And Karume would never have resigned over the radio, even at gunpoint, as they had planned. Even though he was unpopular with the ordinary people in the street or maybe to the ex–ZNP members, he was not unpopular among Africans, not among the core, and not among the army rank and file. This is the way I saw it, the reason it went wrong: they were unscientific. Had I been involved, I would have at least questioned their plans.

I do not know exactly how many were involved, but eventually twenty or thirty comrades were convicted of conspiracy. They stole weapons from the armory. Within a few days, the government knew the weapons were gone—members of the RC, the army, the security—they all knew they had been stolen, but the authorities were slow to respond. They could have gone straight to the platoon leaders assigned to guard the armory that week, but they were blinded. The assassination was meant to take place.

Some comrades told me that, after they stole the weapons, they waited for Babu and others from the mainland to arrive before instigating the coup. They said Babu and his group from the mainland sailed in a fishing boat from Dar and came within a few kilometers of Zanzibar, but then, for some reason I do not know, they decided to return to the mainland.

Eventually, the conspirators in Zanzibar decided to go through with their plans without any assistance from Dar es Salaam. They selected five men in total to go in two cars to assassinate Karume, and it so happened that, among the five, almost all the ethnic groups were represented: an Omani Arab, an African, a Comorian, a Shirazi, and an Mshihiri [Yemeni Arab]. Later, the government tried to suppress the information that there were Africans in the conspiracy, suggesting it was just the work of Arabs and Comorians.

Lieutenant Hamoud Muhammed was the leader. The group traveled in two cars to party headquarters. Hamoud killed Karume, spraying him with bullets as he played cards with his friends. Hamoud was killed instantly, but the others drove away and went on to spray bullets into the Youth League offices, to frighten people and maybe to get Seif Bakari. After that, they fled and were all hunted down and shot, two in town, and two in Bumbwini. The last one was hunted down a couple of weeks later in the bush near Nungwi.

Well, after I had written my statement, there was no more torture. I had survived.

fifteen IMPRISONMENT

MARIA BELIEVED I WAS
innocent, that I was not part of the conspiracy to kill Karume. Living for
six years in Zanzibar, she had never once expressed her negative opinion
of the government, but now she was furious. She had three children to
support, was five months pregnant, and did not have a penny because we
had no savings. The government took away my twelve acres in the
countryside, so she was very thankful to Rashid Abdalla and his wife for
supplying her with food and to Musa Maisara and his wife for bringing
her milk from the dairy. Life was still hard, so she left Zanzibar two
months after my arrest, with all our children. The government tried to
stop her from leaving the country, but eventually the authorities let her
go back to the U.K.

The first three months in prison were the worst. The conditions were
harsh, inhuman. They call the prison the *chuo cha mafunzo* [training
institute], as if it were a corrective institution, but once you are sent
there, you are forced to suffer. Even today, it is a place of suffering, not
of correction. Two Umma army officers died while awaiting trial.

There was a group of nineteen men led by Salim Ahmed Busaidi who
had landed on Tumbatu Island and were arrested and imprisoned as
counterrevolutionaries. At Maisara Grounds, the old colonial Golf Club,
in front of all the people there, I was the minister who read the judgment of the state on the counterrevolutionaries [May 1971], which was
to tend government cattle in the countryside for ten years. I saw them
in prison because they had a cell facing the toilet.

On the last day of December 1972, the warder opened the window to
our cell to tell us to finish our food because we were going to be taken
out. We spoke among ourselves—we were so worried! A few minutes
later, the warder came again and said, "I'm sorry; it's not you. I made a
mistake." We looked and listened under the door and passed information

138

down the hallway, zigzag, from cell to cell. We found out that the nineteen counterrevolutionaries were taken out and slaughtered.

The months passed, and finally it was time for our trial to begin. The guards took us first to the People's Court, where there were three magistrates without any kind of legal training; they were just elders appointed by the party whose attitude was that a prisoner was guilty until proven innocent. It was our responsibility to extricate ourselves from their accusations. But they never gave us any defense lawyers! Wolfango Dourado, the attorney general, was the prosecutor, but he was also supposed to defend us at the same time. It was a strange system. I still joke with Dourado now about this, calling it a kangaroo court. How can he both prosecute and defend us at the same time?[1]

Early on, the prosecution managed to get nine of the accused to confess and plead guilty, including my old friend Badawi. The judges sentenced the nine to death, and then they used their testimonies against the rest of us. Only one of the nine, Amar Salim Saad, implicated me; the other eight did not.[2] The prosecution claimed I was not just trying to kill Karume but to launch a coup d'état. I was informed that it had been my job to take over the airport. I was "Mr. Airport." I asked, "With whom was I supposed to take the airport? Alone, by myself?"

"That was your job to arrange," they said.

Instead of being at the airport, I was at the cinema with my wife. There was no evidence; even among themselves, my accusers could not corroborate their testimonies.

The court atmosphere was like a cinema with cameras televising the entire proceedings. Television was very new in Zanzibar; each party branch was provided a color television by the government, and some individuals owned their own sets. So people sat at home or came to the party branches to watch us because every evening they broadcast the whole proceedings, even in the rural areas. The whole island followed our case, and all of us detainees became celebrities as a result, though we had the noose hanging over us.

The first trial was like a purge, a political case. The authorities just wanted to get rid of us, to execute the Umma elite. They had a problem, however, in that Nyerere had arrested Babu and some Umma army officers in Dar es Salaam and refused to send them over to Zanzibar for what would have been their certain execution. When we discovered in our prison that Babu was sitting in a prison on the mainland and that we were going to be sent to court and not just taken out and slaughtered, we believed in our hearts that we would not be killed. Aboud Jumbe, a man of some education, and not Karume or Seif Bakari, was now in power, and Babu was still alive.[3] For this, I am actually very grateful to Nyerere. Maybe he had learned his lesson after what happened with Hanga and Shariff; by refusing to hand over Babu and the other prisoners, he saved us all from execution. Had he handed them over, we would have all perished, all of us together. But Jumbe and his government thought, "How can we kill them all, when the leader of the conspiracy is safe on the mainland?"

Once we went to court, we had no fear; we thought the trial was a big joke. In fact, we were very jovial: the television cameras were there, and it was like acting—we were singing and joking and laughing. The people in court were surprised to see us in that mood. Our fear was present mostly in 1972 during April, May, and June, when they tortured us and got us to sign those concocted statements.

Only a few people from outside were permitted in the courtroom. One person per family of the accused was allowed to come and watch. My niece Sweetie came, and she would sit next to a young woman named Aisha, or "Eshe," as she is more commonly known in Zanzibar. Her uncle was on trial, Amar Salim Saad, the same one whose testimony implicated me, accusing me of being "Mr. Airport." Eshe was so beautiful that she caught my eye, and I promised myself that one day, if I ever survived, I would have her. I was not necessarily thinking of marriage at the time. I do not think Eshe noticed me watching her, although she knew who I was. As minister of education, I had been the one who sent her and her classmates into the bush to cultivate farms on the weekends, and she hated me for that. In those days, Eshe and the other schoolgirls would joke among themselves and call me *Waziri wa Makoo,* meaning basically minister of mistresses, because in those days I had many girlfriends.

In 1974, the three judges found us guilty and sentenced us to death. A few of us had sentences of ten and eighteen years, but I was sentenced to death, along with about thirty others. We appealed to the High Court. Ali Haji Pandu was the chief justice then, and he had had some legal training in Yugoslavia. But once again, we had no lawyer. Dourado prosecuted us and then tried to act as our defense lawyer. I said to him, "You have imprisoned me, and you are seeking a death sentence for me. But now you want to undo all that you've done—? This is hypocrisy."

I thought the chief justice had a legal mind, so he would see there was no evidence against me. Dourado argued, however, that there was circumstantial corroboration since I was once a leader of the Umma Party. After a year and a half, the High Court ruled in 1975 that a few of my comrades would be released, but most of our group, including myself, received death sentences. The chief justice essentially confirmed the ruling of the lower court.[4] But we knew it was only a political game, so we appealed to another court, even higher. This was the Elder's Court, consisting of seven judges, who were laymen without any legal training. In the end, they reduced our sentences. Only three were left with death sentences; the others, including myself, were given thirty years.

So, we served our sentences, hoping some miracle would happen. For the first two years, we were in complete isolation. This was the training the government received from the East Germans, to keep us apart. It was a house of torture, and we were lucky to come out alive, when others who preceded us did not. Fortunately, the jailors wanted certain jobs done around the prison, so they recruited us to make doors and windows. I could spend most of my time outside in the fresh air.

In 1974, we were moved to the central prison, where we were not as isolated as we had been during the first two years, but we still occupied the condemned cells, where we did not mix with the other prisoners. We were awakened at 5:00 a.m. to say our prayers; then for the whole day, we were left within our own compound. We created games like draughts and dominoes, but our entertainment was mostly talking and reminiscences.

Prison conditions were so bad that about twenty of us decided to embark on a hunger strike. We demanded better food than just boiled cassava; we also wanted mosquito nets, medical treatment, mattresses, a radio, and newspapers. I only drank water and felt weak and hungry from the fast, but the food they gave us was horrible anyway. I stayed in my cell and just went to the loo, and then, after three weeks, the authorities gave in to some of our demands. We obtained mattresses, but no nets. Our diet slowly improved; in addition to cassava, they gave us *ugali* and then rice. Later, they gave us bread, spinach, milk, and tea. Of course, I could never get cigarettes, but I never craved them. Instead, we smoked *sonyo*—unprocessed tobacco leaves. They brought in a radio, and when we were sick, we were taken to the hospital.

Here they were, warders; they were trained to torture, and I would classify some as animals, but some were actually human. Either through bribery or whatever, they were sympathetic, especially when they could see I was innocent. They could be kind; they did not always have that steel, that bile, that hatred. Still, my health suffered. Normally I weigh about sixty-two kilograms, but I went down to about forty-five. I bled from my rectum when I went to the loo. My ulcers were the problem; when I began eating *ugali* again, I started bleeding inside.

I was an atheist and did not want to say my prayers, but when I was allowed to write my own statement, I began to believe there was a God. Afterward, during my imprisonment, I was with a group of men, some of whom were saying their prayers. Eventually, I requested from outside my personal copy of the Qur'an that I had inherited from my grandfather, the *kadhi*. I decided to read the Qur'an in order to find its contradictions. Muhammed was illiterate, and it took over twenty years to compose the Qur'an, so I thought there were bound to be contradictions.

For three years, I studied the Qur'an word for word. I read through several translations, and I could find only one passage, about Jesus Christ, that disturbed me. There were miracles in his life, for example, when he was born of a virgin. God, however, would not allow His servant to be crucified; otherwise, He would cease to be God. As Muslims, we believe that Jesus was not crucified, that God would not allow his prophet to die as ignominiously as that. No, God sent the Jews an image to believe Christ was crucified and then took him up into heaven.

But there was a saying in the Qur'an that God caused Jesus to die and then raised him up. I did not understand how that could be true if he, in fact, did not die on the cross. On that issue, I was a bit worried, but much later I went to the U.K. where I had a friend who was an Old Arabic scholar, and I posed this question to him. He said that Jesus, or Issa, as we say, died in heaven, not on earth. He died in a lower heaven, and then God raised him up to the heaven of God. There are seven heavens in all. His answer satisfied me.

After my study of the Qur'an, my habits really did not change all that much; but as far as believing in religion, the prison brought my belief back. Though I was born a Muslim, I followed Marxism from 1954 to 1974, and then I studied the Qur'an for three years and returned to Islam. I conformed to my heritage. I denied the existence of God all those years since, as a child, I never understood Islam in the first place because it was taught to us in Arabic, not in Swahili. But when you are in hardship, you begin to contemplate, reason, and reflect. I considered my survival in prison a blessing from God; God had stayed my enemies' hands. And I had a feeling that God actually wanted me to go to prison so that I would go back to Him. Maybe He thought, "How will I get Ali Sultan back into the fold? I will put him in the assassination plot." And it worked—I saw the hand of God when the torturers allowed me to write my own statement.

Prison was a blessing, but it was also a punishment for all the wrongs I had committed: not for anything I did against my people when I was in power, but for the sins I committed against God by denying His existence. I actually do not regret anything I have done in my life because I did not go into politics to enrich myself. I did not originally come straight from the bush with nothing, and I was content. I was not corrupt. I was innocent before God, and He kept me alive because I never put my personal interests before those of my people and my country.

As far as my personal life is concerned, of course, as a Muslim, now I know there are some things I have done that are wrong, like fornicating, drinking alcohol, and smoking marijuana. All these things are forbidden, but until I went to prison, I was not a Muslim except by heritage, and I did not know they were wrong. No: I suffered in prison for no other reason than denying God's existence for those many years. Maybe I will not be punished in the next world since I have already suffered enough here in this world.

Though I am no longer a Marxist, I remain proud of and continue to associate with its good principles: to help alleviate poverty, disease, and backwardness. I find Islam actually very compatible with Marxism, with the exception of Marxist atheism and Islamic capitalism. Marxism is almost like a branch of Islam because it teaches charity, tolerance, forgiveness, and kindness to your fellow human being. All these virtues are espoused in both Islam and Marxism; they are simply two sides of the same coin.

But Islam goes beyond Marxism because it teaches that we will meet God on the last day, we will be judged, and we will be punished. Otherwise, there would be no sense; anyone could do what he wanted, to molest this or kill that, and there would be no eternal judgment, only judgment here in the world. No, no. I resist doing something because of the fear of God and His punishment. Even though I know I can do something, I resist. Why? The fear of God. And we also must forgive each other, or we will be punished. This is my religion: God has given me commandments to follow, that I should not compare Him to any other and that I should not go to a tree and beg. No, this is shit, to associate God with another object of creation. It is wrong.

The outside world was pressuring for our release from prison. Branches of Amnesty International adopted most of us detainees as prisoners of conscience. Amnesty International played a big role, and my wife was very active. When Jumbe came to London in 1974 or 1975 for a Commonwealth Conference, she and Omar chained themselves to a lamppost outside the Tanzanian High Commission, where he was staying. They were there about an hour, protesting and demanding my release. Eventually, the police said, "Please, you've made your point. Please let this man go." Jumbe wanted to leave the High Commission for a meeting at the conference and did not want to see Maria and Omar like that. They were on television because a crew from ITV based in Leeds came and filmed the event.

My only contact with the outside world was through one of my nieces who had married Jumbe's son. She had access to me in prison once a month, and Maria in the U.K. managed to send word to me. Sometimes I received pictures of the family growing up in the U.K. But I was only getting messages without her body being there. Maria could smuggle messages and tell me something I could feel in my blood, but it was not the same.

After Maria returned to the U.K., she obtained council housing in her hometown in Nottinghamshire: a home with three bedrooms and one bathroom for her and our four children. Our last child, Sarah, was born in the U.K. in 1972, and then for two years, Maria also took care of three of my children from my first marriage. My three oldest daughters came to stay with her when Aysha was forced to flee China during the Cultural Revolution and it was impossible for our children there to get a decent education. Eventually, Aysha reestablished herself in the Gulf, where she had family and where there were many other Zanzibari exiles. Three of our children went to live with her there. The fourth went to the United States, to New Jersey, to be with my sister.

And then on April 26, 1978, Nyerere released Babu and the Umma comrades detained on the mainland. And here in Zanzibar a few days later, on May Day, Jumbe followed suit. He announced the future release of all of us imprisoned back in 1972. I eventually came out on December 8, 1978.

sixteen RECONSTRUCTION

I WAS RELEASED FROM prison after being inside six years and eight months. I went in when I was forty years old, and now I was almost forty-seven. I have a picture somewhere of me when I came out. I was so thin you would think I suffered from tuberculosis. You could count my ribs, but I was all right, thank God.

My father and Ali Mzee were there to receive me on that day. In the morning, they took me to my house, and in the evening around five, we decided to go out for drinks. I did not take a beer because I was just coming from prison and I had forgotten about beer. It was not so much for religious reasons as it was a matter of taste and habit. My father gave me a thousand shillings; I thought that was big money because my salary as a minister was three thousand a month. But when the bill came for the drinks, I could not pay for everyone because our money had devalued so much. I thought "Oh, my God, what has happened to us?"

My only thought, though, was just to go and meet my wife and children in the U.K. I wanted to go there and put on some meat so I could come back here and fight for my rights. I was put inside wrongfully, and now did I have to be a pauper and go in the street and beg? I was very lucky because I was a prisoner of conscience adopted by a branch of Amnesty International, group number 88 in Saarbrucken, West Germany, a very well-off committee. They were helping me, but for how long? I had my pride, but no savings.

I stayed around Zanzibar for a few weeks waiting for my passport and for some of the other prisoners to be released. On January 16, 1979, I was able to travel to Dar es Salaam, and a ticket to the U.K. was waiting for me there from Amnesty International. Two days later, I flew to London. When I arrived at Heathrow Airport, two of my friends were there to meet me, Ahmed Rajab, who now works at *Africa Analysis* in

London, and Colonel Ali Mafoudh, whom I had sent to Cuba way back in 1961.

After three days in London, I went north to Nottinghamshire to a town called Retford, where my wife lived with Omar, Salim, Johanna, and Sarah. It was my first time to see Sarah, who had been born in the U.K. Maria was very kind. In those days, after having recuperated a little, I would help my wife in the kitchen and the garden. We had a huge yard with apple trees.

After all that time, I enjoyed spending time with my children. We played together in the yard and went to the swimming pool. The oldest was Omar, twelve years old, a student of karate. He had already won trophies for karate and was very popular in the neighborhood there. He would not let his sister be seduced by other boys, and I heard that, when he first arrived, he fought a boy who had called him an African.

I met Maria's parents for the first time. Her mother was warm, but her father was aloof; I think he did not like colored people. But her mother was very sweet and kind. I would visit her and call her mum, and she would buy me presents, small little things, and embrace me.

I lived there for three months, and then the British gave me an extension for another three months. I visited the grave of Karl Marx in Highgate Cemetery and laid a wreath there. Another time a British television crew from ITV came to visit me in Nottinghamshire, and I gave them the story of my imprisonment. The theme was that I had forgiven but could not forget what I went through. Sarah was on my lap when they interviewed me. People from the Labor Department also came and visited the house and told me I should find a job and look after my family. Maria could not work with so many children and was relying on social security. But I never once tried to look for employment—what kind of a job could I have had? Only rubbish. I wanted to recuperate, to put meat on my skeleton, and then return to Zanzibar to face whatever ordeal came next. So I gained my regular weight back and prepared to return home. I never considered living in the U.K. because my struggle was here, not there. Even though Maria was there with my children, so what? I had other kids who were elsewhere.

Maria knew I had left people here in Zanzibar whom I had politically mobilized; could I run away and leave them while I lived happily in the U.K.? I thought, "I will return to Zanzibar and struggle with them." I thought that, when my country was in hardship, it would be immoral to run away and find refuge somewhere else. I would rather be with my comrades, for better or worse. And Maria agreed; she knew my commitment and never said I should not return.

To be honest, I love Zanzibar, I always have, and I could never really think about making someplace else my home. I feel quite comfortable and at ease here, and you have seen when we walk together through the streets how everyone calls out my name, either positively or negatively. Where else could I get that kind of response? A person should have his roots somewhere, and I knew Maria could not cope with the kind of life I expected to lead back in Zanzibar. And because the kids were in school, I could not uproot them and take them back to Zanzibar.

So I said to the Labor Department, "I'm going home because I have a bigger job there than what you can offer me here. I'm very grateful to you for what you are doing, but don't forget that, during the colonial days, I worked here for five years and never drew anything from the dole."

My marriage with Maria ended in 1980. She asked for a divorce, and I consented. This happened not on the first trip, but on the next trip to Great Britain, the following year. The years I had spent in prison had their effect, physically and emotionally. And for the social security, it was good we divorced, so she could be a single mother, which entitled her to that benefit.

Maria was an angel, really. We were very happy all those years until I went inside. Only once did I make a mistake, in that I took a girl, and she found out. She followed me in the countryside in her car all the way to Bwejuu, on the east coast. But she did not punish me; she never even told me she knew until after I came out of prison.

And then to chain herself to a lamppost outside the High Commission in London—with all my shortcomings—yet she did that for me. To look after our four kids while I was inside, and then for a time three others from my previous marriage—can you imagine an English lady taking care of seven children? I cannot pay her back for all she has done. Even now she uses my name and has never remarried. We are still friends. She is well known and respected in her small town in Nottinghamshire.

Whenever I go to England, I stay at her place. At first, I went to the U.K. every two years to renew my British residence permit. Later when the British changed the law, I went every year, until I decided in 1987 there was no longer any need for such expense. I even had an operation in Wakefield for piles, but I had my gastrectomy here in Zanzibar. The doctors removed three-quarters of my stomach because of duodenal ulcers. Ever since, I have been very careful with bones. Now when I eat, I chew every little bit because bones go straight through me. For years, I kept the remains of my stomach in my house in a little bottle, until, that is, my house was burglarized and someone stole the bottle with my stomach inside.

So, I returned alone to Zanzibar. On the way back, I went to Saarbrucken, Germany, to visit the Amnesty International group that had adopted me. The chairperson, Frau Gertrude Gutt, was my adopted mother, and I paid homage and thanked them for what they had done. I stayed for three days and then returned to Zanzibar, to my beautiful house in Migombani. I had no savings, no pension from my eight years as a minister, and Jumbe had taken my acres in the countryside. I lived in a nice house, but, otherwise, I lived only day to day. I wanted to eat and to eat well, and I wanted my beer. I could not at that age go back to the land and become a peasant cultivating for cassava and bananas. I did not have the physical strength, and mentally I was not prepared. Nor could I become a capitalist, because where was the capital?

Instead, I became a petty trader, buying and selling whatever I could, trying to survive. I went into business importing things from the U.K. and selling them here. I had to live, okay? I knew I was not going to be a capitalist or exploit anyone by buying and selling since I had no factory or shop where I employed workers. I was only buying and selling straight to the people.

Salim Rashid gave me money to pay off my house and gave me another three hundred pounds, and that was my capital. I bought mostly women's garments in the U.K.; they sold like hotcakes because, at the time, the economy was still very tight and there was always a shortage of goods. When I brought the goods to Zanzibar by ship container, the people knew.

I was becoming interested at that time in a woman called Eshe, whom I had first seen at my treason trial in 1973. I noticed her in the court audience and vowed I would never die before I got hold of her. After I was released from prison, I first passed Eshe on the road as she rode her Bravo moped to her parents' flat at Kilimani. At the time, I could not approach her too fast because she was having an affair with a Danish man who worked in Oman and came to Zanzibar periodically. She already had one son, Saleh, from her first husband, a Zanzibari. A daughter, Fatma, came from her second husband. She also had a son through the Dane, but he did not want to marry her because he already had a wife in Denmark.

Later, I heard that Eshe was trying to go to Mombasa, but she could not obtain a government travel permit. So I sent her a note saying I had heard about her problem and believed I could help her. I asked her to please ring so that perhaps we could make certain arrangements. That evening she rang, but I had another girl in my house at the time with whom I was drinking and who was shouting when I picked up the phone. Eshe asked me who was doing all the shouting, and so I handed the girl the phone. Eventually, Eshe promised to come the next evening at 8 p.m.; she also said I should have a drink waiting for her. She arrived exactly at 8 p.m. on the dot, which impressed me very much.

I managed to get her the travel permit, and we went together to Mombasa, in 1979 or 1980. In those days, though, we were on and off because she would come from Oman and stay a month or so and then return to her Danish boyfriend. The Danish chap eventually came to Zanzibar, and I told him he should convert to Islam and marry Eshe. But he said he could not divorce his wife in Denmark since Danish laws required him to split his property in half. I told him, "If you don't marry her, I'll take her away from you, and you won't play with her any longer."

But I had nothing at the time with which to support her: no regular income, only politics. The Danish chap, in fact, said to Eshe, "What can Ali give you, politics? Can you eat politics?" I did not have an income, but I was not a pauper and managed to live well. Eshe said that, if I could guarantee her two thousand shillings a month, she would marry me, but I said I could not guarantee even that.

So we continued as friends for two years, and while she was in Oman, I had other girlfriends. There were three in all, Eshe was Number One, another from Mombasa was Number Two, and then another was Number Three. If Number Two came to my house and Number Three was there, then Number Three had to leave. If Number One came and Number Two was at my house, then Number Two had to leave. They accepted these terms, and all knew one another.

Then in 1982, Eshe came from Oman with her baby and informed me the Dane had finished his contract in Oman and returned to Denmark without her. She was frustrated and accepted my marriage proposal.

When I was first released from prison, I wanted to join the ruling party, which by then was called CCM, which stood for *Chama cha Mapinduzi*, or "party of revolution." It was a union formed in 1977 of the ASP in Zanzibar and TANU [Tanganyika African National Union] on the mainland and was part of Nyerere's attempts to swallow Zanzibar into the federation and lessen our autonomy. The ASP elite agreed to the union with TANU wholeheartedly, in order to curb the excesses of Karume's time. Seif Bakari and his group resisted, but they could do nothing.

I wanted to join CCM because I wanted to be politically active again, and this was the only way. But the party leaders told me I had first to go to Kivukoni College in Dar es Salaam, the party's ideological institute, for training. I thought this was rubbish since I had just come from the "training institute" in Zanzibar, what people called the prison in those days. But because I had been convicted of treason, they insisted.

Instead of resuming political activities, I started hosting parties at my house. It was a good location because electricity was never rationed—I lived so close to President Jumbe that my house always had power. I would invite all kinds of people to my parties—locals, expatriates, even gays. Up to fifty people would come at a time. I did not discriminate—I only asked that they bring their own drinks. We never discussed politics; instead, it was just about music, drinking, and sex. I arranged the music to play one European song, followed by an Arab song, an Indian song, and then a Swahili song.

The expatriates worked for the FAO [Food and Agriculture Organization], and at the time, only they were allowed to hold foreign currency. When I came back from overseas, the authorities told me I could not keep dollars in my pocket. I had to deposit them in the bank and change them into Tanzanian shillings, when the expatriates here were getting all our women because they had dollars. What kind of a society was that? It was stupid to live under such circumstances; that was one reason why I wanted to fight for constitutional reforms.

They even almost arrested me one day. I was at a bar and paying my bill when about five dollars accidentally fell out of my pocket. A security chap said, "I see you have dollars there, so I am arresting you." I said, "Fuck you! Go and arrest Jumbe, not me; this is my hard-earned money!" Then I went to the loo, and the barman said to him, "Do you know this man? He is Ali Sultan Issa." The chap ran away when he heard my name—when I came back from the loo, he was no longer there. He was young and innocent and did not even know his own history.

Deep in my heart, I was still a socialist and did not want to renounce socialist thinking completely. But I wanted to make the system more humane and to put an end to the negative restrictions, the fear, and the discipline. I thought people should be free to express themselves; we have matured enough as a people, I thought, so why should we have a regime that exists by force and fear? Everything was under the thumb of the government, and Jumbe was paramount. He was running the country like his own personal fiefdom.

I had a lot of discussions with my former Umma comrades. A group of us had the same ideas, including some in Zanzibar and some living in exile in the U.K., like Salim Rashid and Ahmed Rajab. We discussed the need for a new constitution. We wanted democracy and the end of rule by decree. We wanted to liberalize trade, so the people could get something, so they could live. The state should allow a mixed economy while retaining control of part of the economy because, if we totally opened up, capitalists from overseas would swallow the whole island. Even China is now a mixed economy. Once China criticized Soviet revisionism, but now China can be criticized for revisionism.

Wanting to open up the country, however, did not mean we comrades ceased to be socialists. Socialism is synonymous with abundance; that is the kind of socialism in which I believe. We did not want our people to starve and Zanzibar to become a nation of beggars, so we had to be pragmatists. I still believe in socialism primarily as a system of social justice. The line between socialism and capitalism is the difference between being humane and a brute.

I thought Jumbe, being an academic, would want to alleviate the hardship in the country and be more accommodating; but he was under the influence of Nyerere, and Nyerere until the end did not want changes. So Jumbe would not listen to anybody. He even made his decisions on the mainland, from his home outside Dar es Salaam. Can you imagine? The cabinet in Zanzibar flew to the mainland to consult with him, when he could have just come here.

Several times I appealed to see Jumbe because I thought I could work with him to bring changes. I said to his son, who had married my niece, "Tell your father I want to see him." Jumbe was once my teacher and a good friend, but during that period, he was like all megalomaniacs and did not want to give me an audience.

My comrades and I sat and argued and agreed we had to do something. I printed up leaflets in Mombasa and distributed them in Zanzibar Town. I was the only one who dared do that, perhaps because I had already been sentenced to death and did not have fear. Prison teaches you not to fear, not to care whether the authorities put you inside again.

The leaflet, called "The Claims of Zanzibaris," demanded free elections for a new president and Revolutionary Council. It said all Zanzibaris wanted their basic citizenship rights. It called on Nyerere to replace Jumbe, saying he was in poor health and should be given his pension and someone to look after him. When the leaflet came out, the security people wanted to arrest me, but Jumbe intervened, saying they must arrest me with evidence that I was actually responsible for the pamphlet.

So after that, I printed t-shirts that had the words *Maendeleo Zanzibar* [Development Zanzibar] on the front. I printed them in Mombasa, brought them by boat, paid the duties, and cleared them through customs. I sold them at seventy-five shillings a shirt or bartered them in the street for fish from the fishmongers. There should not have been any problem since the government had its own ship called *Maendeleo Zanzibar*. I did not think I would be arrested because it was purely a commercial enterprise. *Maendeleo Zanzibar:* what does that mean?

But the t-shirts and the leaflets together were what put me back inside. I never thought the government would be so stupid to arrest me, but in October 1982, it did. There was no questioning, no torture, and no trial. Nothing. I was kept in prison one year; that was my punishment. And I had just married Eshe only a week before my arrest.

The treatment in prison was not bad. This time I had a mosquito net, and I read the Qur'an. When I was released in October 1983, I found that, while I was inside, Eshe had aborted our child and run away to Indonesia to be with the Dane. When I learned she was with him, I divorced her, sending the papers to her relatives, and then I went to recuperate with Maria in the U.K. The same Amnesty International group in West Germany gave me an allowance for almost six months.

I was in the U.K. until February 1984 and then returned to Zanzibar just after Nyerere threw Jumbe out of office. It was easy for Nyerere to uproot him. Jumbe uprooted himself, actually, by living on the mainland. He thought that, after Nyerere retired, he was going to be the next president of Tanzania. It did not work that way; he underestimated Nyerere.

Eshe returned to Zanzibar in 1984, so I grabbed her, and we got married for the second time. I threatened her at the Hilton in Nairobi where we stayed on our honeymoon, saying, "If you run away again, this time I'll kill you. I have a gun in my briefcase. And the Russians taught me how to strangle people without letting them make a sound." But I lied, just to frighten her. I never had that training, nor did I have a gun anymore.

seventeen

BY THE TIME I
was released from prison the second time, everything had collapsed
economically in Zanzibar. We had to salvage the country because the
islands were in ruins. We had to open up because everything was in the
hands of the government. So when Jumbe was taken out, we comrades
pushed for liberalization. We wanted to let people go everywhere and
buy anything, to let trade and tourism come to the islands, as long as we
did not sell the country out completely.

Ali Hassan Mwinyi, the new president, had once worked as my principal secretary in the Ministry of Education. My friend Salim Rashid, a
former comrade, was a London-trained economist and advised Mwinyi
to open up the economy. Under Mwinyi, Zanzibar began to open up, as
all of us wanted. Zanzibar was an experiment because we liberalized before the mainland, still ruled by Nyerere.

After I married Eshe the second time, I imported clothing from the
U.K., and my wife assisted as a model and salesperson. We bought dresses
because the women in our society want a new dress for each party. My
wife was and is very popular in Zanzibar, so she would wear the dresses,
and then we would sell them. But we had very little money, and my wife
sold almost all her gold for our upkeep and our food. In those days,
Eshe's mother did not like me, nor did her elder brother; they both preferred the Dane. The mother would come to Migombani and shout at
us. In fact, it took me some time before we became friends. When Ramadhan arrived, she came and lived and fasted with us; eventually, Eshe's
father said to me, "You really are a politician to win over this woman. I
salute you!"

I needed to try something else to keep us alive, so as soon as the
government opened up the country in 1984, I decided to build a hotel.[1]

At the time, Hassan Nassor Moyo was in the Ministry of Agriculture. He said, "What can I do for you?" I said I wanted land. Legally, he could not give me more than three acres, but I wanted more. Moyo said he would help because he and I had worked together as ministers after the revolution.

I wanted land in Chuini, on the ocean north of Zanzibar Town. We had to petition the new president to get more than the usual allotment. Later that year, though, President Mwinyi gave me twenty-seven acres in Chuini, and told the Ministry of Agriculture that if some people had land there in Chuini, they should be given acres somewhere else. All the peasants already there received plots elsewhere. They were just planting cassava next to the beach, and we wanted land to build a hotel, to create some wealth in the country, so they had to relocate.

After I acquired the twenty-seven acres, I wanted more land in Chuini, so I put in five applications for three-acre plots, since each of my family members was entitled to the three acres he or she never received during the days of land reform in the 1960s. But all I could do was swap my three acres in Pemba for three in Chuini, next to where we built the hotel. I wanted to hold those three acres so that no one could come and build another hotel and compete with us. And it was on that plot by the sea that I built my own cottage in 1987, where I still go today on the weekends.

To build the hotel, I worked with a circle of Italian investors, called the Baganza Group. At one point, we were short of money, so I was forced to sell my big house to invest in the hotel. Eshe and I moved into a much smaller flat in town that she owned from before we were married. Her Danish boyfriend used to work for DANIDA [Danish International Development Agency], and through his connections in government, he obtained a flat for her.

We built the hotel from scratch, until we reached a point in 1987 where we had put in 180 million Tanzanian shillings and had no more money, no more liquidity. That year I traveled to the United States; because I had been a communist for many years, I was a "prohibited immigrant," so I had to get a waiver to allow my entrance. I met my old friend Frank Carlucci in Washington, D.C., who at the time had just been appointed secretary of defense under President Ronald Reagan. I asked Frank to put some money into my hotel project, but he said he did not have any to invest. It was on that trip, however, that he wrote in a memo to me, "Your capitalist success exceeds all my expectations."

On my return, I went to the Chase Manhattan Bank in Nairobi about a loan. The bankers took me to a subsidiary of the IMF [International Monetary Fund], the APDF, or African Project Development Facility.

We came to an agreement in Nairobi that the APDF would come to Zanzibar and have a look. After that, we managed to get a loan from two banks, one in Geneva and one in Germany. We obtained a loan of 1.8 million U.S. dollars that, along with another twenty-five million Tanzanian shillings from the local bank, allowed us to finish the project.

I do not know how Carlucci managed to pull the strings, but he did. I told him, "If you don't want to invest your own money, then try to get us a loan, so I can finish this white elephant." Only God knows, but in my heart, I believe he pulled strings—whether right or wrong, that is what I feel.[2] Ours was the first beach resort hotel in Zanzibar. When the country opened up, we were the first. We started building in 1985 and finished in 1990.

Then in 1994, the Baganza Group sold out to the Venta Club, which owns an international chain of hotels. The new company gave me an ultimatum, saying it would give me $7,000 per share. At the time, I was an 11 percent shareholder, so they offered me $77,000 to sell out completely. Prior to that, however, I had sold a few shares at $15,000, and I thought it funny the price suddenly dropped to $7,000. The company gave me one day to decide; the investors said, "If by tomorrow you don't agree, the price might go down further." I said, "Well, I'll give you my reply tomorrow. Give me time to think; that's reasonable enough."

So I went to the bar and had six beers. Then I went home to my cottage and had a bottle of *gongo*, liquor made from papaya. I decided that, if the Venta Club did not agree to my price I would burn down the whole hotel. I thought, "Let them charge me with arson; I've already been charged with treason."

But before I gave the investors my reply, they said, "We decided last night that you must be with us." They must have gone to their consular officer here who told them not to leave Ali Sultan because I am a local, the land belongs to me, and I can help them. I am not sure, but that is what I believe. So I said, "All right, if I must be with you, you should give me an allowance so I can survive." I negotiated with them from that point of strength, and they agreed to give me an allowance, and we have stayed together ever since. That is where my capitalist success exceeds Carlucci's expectations.

That is my pension, and I do not know how I would have survived without it. As a matter of fact, I am not a businessman, but neither can I any longer call myself a communist. I am now a member of the *petit bourgeoisie*, exploiting the labor of others. But after all, I originally came from the landowning elite, and now I have returned to such aspirations.

But I am giving wages higher than the government does, and if I had been corrupt when in public service, I could have built a palace, I could have made a lot of money, instead of whatever meager income I now have.

I still believe, however, that wherever there is capitalism, there is exploitation. I will die with this idea. There is an essential contradiction between the capitalist and the worker, who has nothing but his labor to sell. The realities of life are still there. But I do not want to talk about those ideological polemics now. They are out of fashion, and there is no hope for socialism. The days of revolution are over, my friend. What can we do? We have no chance, and we are going to be swallowed by globalization whether we like it or not.

In 1994, I was boozing too much, consuming fifteen to twenty beers a day. I had money and did not need to report to an office every day. My ulcers had been operated on, so I was free to indulge myself. I drank so much my hands would shake in the morning when I went to make coffee. So on New Year's Eve, I told my wife I would give up drinking until Ramadhan, when I normally did not take alcohol anyway. I said this almost as a joke. That night we went to the hotel and had dinner. For my New Year's wish, I spontaneously said to Eshe that, after I stopped drinking, I wanted to go on a pilgrimage to Mecca. We had several bottles of champagne with our dinner and then came home to our cottage. By 4:00 a.m., I had finished off two more bottles of champagne.

These were my last drinks, however. I lasted until Ramadhan and for several months after that. Then in October 1995, the elections in Zanzibar took place. I personally brought President Salmin Amour an official letter of congratulations from our company and told him I had quit drinking. He thanked God and offered me a free pilgrimage to Mecca at state expense. Of course, I accepted, but I told him, "If you want to send me to Mecca, you'd better do it this year because anything can happen." He agreed, and my wish came true. I was to be a passenger on a plane full of about 150 pilgrims from Zanzibar.

I was briefly the talk of the town: people asked, "Is it true that Ali Sultan is going to Mecca? The plane will not arrive!"

Before I went to Mecca, I had to ask forgiveness from people whom I had wronged in the past, mainly here in Zanzibar. It was like a ritual; they forgave me in front of my face, but in their hearts, I do not know. I asked forgiveness for personal reasons, rather than for things I did as a government servant, because I still did not believe I did anything wrong when in power. I never took advantage of people because, as a minority, anything I did would have been reported instantly.

I spent eight days in Medina, praying five times a day in the mosque where Muhammed was buried. Outside the city, I put on pilgrimage clothes, known as *ahram*. After that, we were not allowed to kill even a fly, and there was very little talking. We focused instead on asking for forgiveness.

Then we went by bus to Mecca. That year there were four million pilgrims in Mecca, and I almost suffocated from the crush of people. We went to the Plains of Arafat and then to a place where all of us were supposed to stone a *shetani*. There were so many people and it was so hot that I felt hypnotized; my mind was like that of a zombie. I wanted only to perform the next step, which was the circumambulation of the Kaaba.

I went around the Kaaba seven times, and then we went to where the angel gave Hagar a spring of water to feed Ismail. We ran seven times from one hill to another, in the area where she found the water. Then we shaved our heads, took off our garments, washed in *zam zam* water, and we were through. Pilgrimage is one of the pillars of our faith, and I had performed my duty. Whether I came back as an angel or not is another issue.

After Mecca, I traveled to Oman to attend my cousin's funeral. There I saw all my kith and kin. They were so surprised that they said, "How did you manage to come here—did you change your name?" I said, "If I change my name, can I change my face? Wouldn't they recognize me?" For the longest time, the assumption was that I could never obtain a visa to travel to Oman because I had helped overthrow the sultan and the ZNP and because I was a communist.

I went to Oman because I wanted to see the land from where my ancestors came. I had heard a lot, and I wanted to see how primitive the place was. When I arrived in the interior of the country from whence the Ismaili clan originated, I could see it was no wonder some of them went to East Africa. Very backward—the place did not even have a mosque, so we said the Idd prayer in an open space surrounded by a half-wall. I met a blind old man who was a member of my clan, an exile from Zanzibar who remembered my father, my mother, and my grandfather; but I did not even spend the night. I returned immediately to Muskat where I was invited to various friends' houses to be entertained. Every day I would move around to their houses or their clubs, drinking orange juice while some of them drank alcohol. I also made a point while in the Gulf of visiting Ali Muhsin and some of the former ZNP ministers, Muhsin's cronies whom we overthrew in 1964. I joked with them, and there were no harsh words. What could they do to me?

I met a number of Zanzibaris living in Oman. They were ZNP people at heart and preferred to live in exile. Who would stay? If you cannot express yourself freely and you get a chance to leave the country, you will leave. When they came to Oman, they were relatively educated compared to the locals; the old sultan of Oman kept the whole country backward because he himself was backward. He just accumulated all the money for himself and left the people literally in darkness, without electricity. But in the 1970s, Sultan Qaboos began to open Oman up and develop its petrol resources. The Omanis got all their civil service from Zanzibar *gratis* because we trained them here and then they ran away, first to the United Arab Emirates and then to Oman.

Zanzibaris living in Oman work hard and go into debt for their big cars and houses. Now they come back sometimes to Zanzibar and build houses and spend their holidays here. They started returning after 1984 when the islands opened up. They do not come here to invest so much as to enjoy life and show people here their wealth. But they are very helpful since every month they send money to their relatives here.

When I returned to Zanzibar from the pilgrimage, I felt lighter, relieved. Only a week later, I flew to Milan with my wife for a business meeting. I was elected chairman of the Mawimbini Hotel, chosen over the son of a major shareholder because the hotel worried about two bank creditors who might prosecute us in the courts if their loans were not repaid. The board elected me so that, in case of a loan default and prosecution, the European banks would have to go to Zanzibari courts, where they were sure to lose.

From Italy, we flew to London where I took my wife to see Babu. After his release from prison, Babu went to England and then lived in the United States, where he taught university courses, before returning eventually to the U.K. as a journalist and lecturer. We met several times during the years he stayed in London. Babu was a very good cook, and I used to wash the dishes, which, for years in the U.K., had been my profession.

On that particular visit, I was not drinking, but I told Babu to drink some whiskey with my wife. He had had open-heart surgery recently, and I could see his health was deteriorating. When he drove us around, his leg was unsteady as he pushed in the clutch, so I said to him, "Ah, look, man, you are finished." That was the last time I saw him alive. We were friends until the end, and I helped bury him here in Zanzibar in 1996.

In that year, I went to Cuba to attend the World Youth Festival, organized to coincide with the return of Che Guevera's remains from Bolivia. All his old comrades were invited to remember him at a special event, and with so many old friends there in Havana, I felt compelled to drink again. It was a spontaneous decision; I met so many old comrades with whom I used to drink and go to nightclubs. I stayed for free in a Venta Club hotel and went with the youth all day, joining in the festivities, and then at night I came back to my hotel. I spoke a little Spanish, and we sang revolutionary songs. I had forgotten a lot, but I participated somehow. Why not? I shouted what I remembered and hummed what I had forgotten. There were so many young people from all over the world, from Africa, Europe, Latin America, and even the United States. There were very few of us who were old, yet we all sat together and talked, and I felt absolutely free. The theme was friendship, as in the old Soviet period. I really enjoyed my short stay in Cuba, though the country had deteriorated a lot because of the U.S. embargo. But the people still had revolutionary spirit and enthusiasm.

When I was in Havana, a Cuban film company asked me questions about Che, how, when he came to Zanzibar from the Congo, we met and spent hours alone together discussing the struggle. But when the crew interviewed me, I started to cry and continued until they had to stop filming. I think it was his death that made me cry. I thought he could still have been alive had he not been killed, because he died so young. When he was in Zanzibar, I did not think he would go that far to push forward the world revolution, which he believed in intensely. Maybe he was driven because he wanted to liberate Argentina, and in his heart, he thought the spark from Bolivia would travel south. That was what made me emotional, what made me cry.

eighteen

MY LAST DAUGHTER,
Natasha, was born in 1985. I named her after the character in Leo Tol-
stoy's *War and Peace*. So, in total now, I have nine children from my
wives and one from out of wedlock. Except for Natasha and Malik, they
all live in the Gulf, the U.K., or the U.S.

I have been with Eshe for twenty years now, much longer than with
the other wives. Of course, in any marriage you shout at each other, but
I cannot be unhappily married to a woman, and we have stayed together
until now. Eshe is very independent and tries very hard to dominate
me, but I am older than she and just look at her and think, "Look at this
little fool."

Although my first two wives were very simple in their tastes, this one
is extravagant. She is lucky because at least now I can afford her tastes.
At first, we struggled—when we began we had nothing—but she has
been able to replenish all the gold she sold to support us and can afford
to travel and send Natasha to school.

I am less strict with Natasha than I was with my other children. I try
to give her all I can. Sometimes I regret sending her for years to a special private school in Zanzibar run by foreign teachers, most of them
British. That school put into her mind ideas that a child has freedom
and rights. We did not have such ideas; we could not say boo to our
parents. They were always right, and we were always wrong. Here parents only give orders to the child.

But I have tried with this one because she came very late in life. I
have tried to give her the maximum freedom of thought and choice,
thinking she will of her own free will understand her limits. Sometimes,
though, I tell her, "Don't argue with me because I'm your father, and I
know what is good for you." But she says, "I have to know, Daddy, why
it is right," so I take time to explain. When they are more sophisticated,

people explain things to their child. It is good to let your children reason things out, rather than simply to impose your will. You only understand this in later years when you are wiser, but when you are young, you just give orders.

Natasha is very talkative and very popular among her classmates, both male and female. One time I asked Natasha why she needed to speak so much, and she said, "Didn't you know when you gave birth to me I would be like this?" I have warned her of the dangers of politics, but she wants to become a lawyer and then ultimately the first female president of Zanzibar. Whether this aspiration will materialize or not, I do not know—it is up to history.

But she is a rebel, this one, and the more you give her, the more she wants. And I do not like the way she dresses, but it is the fashion. Anyway, let us hope and pray. It is only God who can help, to put fear into her mind, the fear of God. I hope she will not do what will disgrace us as her parents. Chastity in our society is looked upon as a virtue. In my experience in the Western liberal society, it has lost its meaning and is not considered a virtue. A pity, really. Here in our society, at her first marriage, the girl must be found with her virtue. After the end of the first marriage or the death of the husband, the woman is free, but at her first wedding, if she is found not to possess her virtue, the shame goes to the parents.

Eshe is a full member of a very well known women's spirit possession cult in town known as *kibuki*, and she goes quite often to attend their dances. I am not involved and not interested because it is mainly for women and gay men; I do not fit in there. But as a child during colonial times, I would watch the *kibuki* in Vikokotoni because the rites were open for all to see. And whether it is pretense or not, these women do become possessed. They dance with spears; sometimes it is scary. Once when I went to collect Eshe, a woman chased me away with a spear. People say they consume a full bottle of Konyagi [gin], even though some of them normally do not drink, only when they are possessed. When they regain consciousness, they do not even have a hangover.

They believe each individual can be possessed by two *mashetani* [spirits], one male and one female. My wife's female *shetani* is named Ndasalima and has a very high and funny-sounding voice. Her male *shetani* is called Ndamanesi and has a normal voice. But in order to learn the names of their *mashetani*, the women must first be initiated to become a full member. After I married Eshe the second time, she underwent this initiation and it was very expensive; we paid around three hundred thousand shillings [$12,000] for two weeks of food, drink, and music. At some point during that period, Eshe's *mashetani* were enticed to mention their names. I was unable to see her the whole time, so I do not know exactly what happened.

For Eshe, it is a family issue because her auntie, Bibi Ashura, is the head of the group, and when Eshe does not attend, the aunt gets annoyed. Sometimes Eshe does not want to go to *kibuki*, but she must. People say that, if a woman does not go, the *shetani* will get into her head and push her there, even if she is naked. And I have noticed that, if there is a dance, Eshe becomes uneasy, nervous, and uncomfortable. She feels something and must go, unless we are out of town or away from the islands.

Bibi Ashura is very revered and very powerful; she is called "Babu," meaning her *shetani* is the grandfather, the most powerful and respected one. The women obey her and come to the *kibuki* and pay their dues. If someone has a problem, she comes to Babu; she performs certain rituals to invoke the power of the *mashetani*, and the person gets what she wants and afterward gives Babu presents of bottles of liquor.

I do not personally believe in *kibuki* but have to allow my wife because it is part of her family. I think it is backward but do not want to be abusive. These women never interfere in politics, they often say their prayers, and some of them are highly respected around town. Before I married Eshe, my girlfriend at the time warned me, but I said I am not worried about *kibuki* because I may be an even more powerful *shetani*. In the streets, people sometimes even call me "Ali Shetani" as a joke.

When I go to collect Eshe, the women sometimes give me a bottle of brandy. To please them, I let them put chalk on my tongue and temples, and they give me a free bottle! Natasha goes herself to *kibuki* to dance, and I believe she will have a *shetani* later as well. I would not like Natasha to be involved, but if it happens, I cannot stop her.

I do not move around much these days. I am a retired man now and usually just relax at home. I rarely go to the pub or see friends, maybe once a week. Badawi still remains one of my oldest and closest friends. He sometimes comes from Dar es Salaam to see me, but he has given up drinking and smoking, so we sit outside and chat. He sends me Islamic books now and then; I think he is becoming too religious for me.

With my satellite dish, I get over forty television channels, and I can consume as many as twenty beers a day. If I go to my cottage at Chuini to enjoy myself with friends, I take an entire crate of beer. When I get into a stupor, I just go inside and sleep. Since my operation, when I lost three-quarters of my stomach, I never get hangovers. I can drink like a fish and have no problems whatsoever. If I had only known this would happen, I would have had my stomach removed years earlier! Anyway, I am a retired man now, and my only work is as a consultant for the hotel. I do not have to sit in an office and do paperwork. And my liver is perfectly fine—I know because the doctors have checked recently.

Eshe tries to limit my drinking to seven beers a day, three during the day and four at night. I sit at home and drink while I read or watch television, by myself or with my friend Abu Mansoor. I smoke forty cigarettes a day, but I used to smoke even more, around sixty a day. Since my days at sea, I have always smoked American cigarettes, like Winston's, which I like because they are a bit toasted. So far I have experienced no side effects; the doctors have checked my lungs, and they are okay.

I spend about $60 a month on cigarettes and $180 a month on alcohol. I also employ two boys and two girls to watch my cottage in Chuini or to cook and to clean my house. Together, all four earn about $75 a month. I do not think my lifestyle is anything unusual for Zanzibari culture. I am happy since I am not in any distress or material hardship. I do not beg, and my health is all right, even though I drink. I no longer have any ideology; I just look after my interests as a hotelier. But this is my country, and if I see something wrong, I go through the right channels.

Economically, we have not developed much since colonial times, but the biggest change is that we are free. Our greatest achievement of the past forty years is that at least now we can express our opinions without fear of being locked up. And we cannot blame the colonialists now; we are to blame for all our misfortunes and mismanagement.

We wanted to build a socialist paradise here, but the mainland swallowed us after only three months. Had we comrades been given a chance to run the country ourselves, we could have developed into a Hong Kong or a Singapore. We did not have any mineral resources, but we could have instituted a socialist paradise, with the help of the advanced countries in the socialist world. We could have been, as Babu has said, the Hong Kong of East Africa, but now everything is decided on the mainland. The mainlanders have tried to bury our identity completely. For years Nyerere wanted to swallow Zanzibar completely within the union, but we got stuck somewhere in his throat. He could not swallow us, nor could he vomit us up.

We tried to industrialize here and be self-reliant. We produced our own milk, butter, cheese, rice, shoes, cigarettes, and sugar. From sugar, we made molasses, from which we produced our own vodka and whiskey, which was nice and cheap in those days. We tried to change the environment here and the mentality of our people, to bring in machines that would influence human behavior and change habits, in order to create a New Man. We knew that Africa could not develop with the old mentality and that we would always lag behind unless we changed our outlook. But all the factories built in the 1960s through Chinese or East German assistance have collapsed.

We did not get the chance, unfortunately, to employ all the ideas we comrades had and cherished. It was America's fault; the Americans did not want development here. Nyerere at the time did not understand development, and Karume was even more backward than Nyerere. The union was a deliberate move by the imperialists to hamper our progress, and eventually it was capitalist sabotage that was responsible for the failure of socialist industrialization in Zanzibar. The capitalists just want to bleed Zanzibar and keep us down.

We have lost most of our market for cloves. Our biggest market was once Indonesia, but now the Indonesians grow their own. They would mix cloves in with tobacco when making cigarettes, and we would send them eight thousand tons a year. In India now, they use synthetic substitutes. America imports maybe one ton a year, mainly for cooking purposes. Still today our cloves are the best and the most expensive in the world.

Of course, the peasants are normally very conservative, but here they are disciplined and not unwilling to absorb new ideas and technology. It is our fault that we do not mobilize them anymore. We do not push them, do not provide them with new technology, and do not allow them to sell their cloves on the open market. The government gets much of its revenue from buying cloves cheap from the producers and selling high on the world market, but we should allow farmers to sell in a free market.

Tourism is now the main economic activity in Zanzibar and can be the basis for an economic takeoff. Even during colonial times, we had a trickle of tourists; but after the revolution, we stopped tourism, fearing mercenaries would come disguised as tourists, as happened once in the Seychelles where there was a coup. Now there are many hotels that provide employment, but who has built and who owns these hotels? Foreigners. Only a few are owned by local people, and they are mainly Indian. The other ethnic groups own only guesthouses rather than hotels.

Since ours was the first beach resort hotel in Zanzibar, in the beginning, the clerics would complain in the mosques and accuse us of decadence. They would accuse us without having seen for themselves, saying the tourists on the beach were nude. It was not true. We do not cater to all kind of tourists; our guests are mainly middle-class families on package tours. And I do not personally have a problem with Africans learning in the hotels to serve Europeans because whoever can afford it can go there and be served the same way. I do not look at tourism as neocolonialism in Zanzibar. I can say, however, that tourism has had a cultural effect. Prostitution flourishes in our society; the prostitutes come from the mainland because they think they will get more money from the *wazungu* [whites].

Now people call Zanzibar an open and free society, but there is no respect, only decadence, and that is how civilizations fall. In the past, the drug here was mainly grass, but now harder drugs come in from outside. People are mugged in the street—we never had this in my time. Under Karume, we were a highly disciplined society. As a minister, I could have taken any bribe but did not take a penny, and no one dared to entice me.

Now our moral values are eroding, and everyone aspires to be rich. But in terms of religion, society is more conservative because more people go to the mosque now than in the past. There is a religious awakening among young people, perhaps because of the hardships we have endured since the revolution. And the translation of the Holy Book into Swahili has meant that no longer do we read the Qur'an like parrots without knowing its meaning.

In the past, we would say the U.S. was the leader of the imperialist camp, but at least there was another camp to fight for the rights of the downtrodden, the oppressed, and the colonized. But now the world is under a single hegemony; the leader of the imperialist camp has become the leader of the whole world. We can say now that we are under the dictatorship of America. A democracy tolerates different viewpoints, but that is not the policy of the present administration, unfortunately. Instead, it is survival of the fittest. I can say that American foreign policy is wholly under Zionist influence. I am sorry to say that, but I have gradually come to realize this. The movies, the banks, and the media in America are all or mostly run by Zionists.

Multiparty elections came in 1995 under foreign pressure, both here and on the mainland. Now people speak freely, but sometimes we abuse the freedom and go to the extreme. Multipartyism, when you do not understand it fully, becomes divisive. For three days after the elections in Zanzibar in 1995, we had a political stalemate. Eventually, the ruling party reasserted control, but society was badly polarized. I went to Pemba in February 1996 and saw the conditions there, how divided people were along partisan lines. People were beating one another, boycotting the funerals of people from the other side, dumping shit down people's wells, and refusing to send their children to school. Generosity and humanity were forgotten, along with basic services such as clean water and education. The whole fabric of our society broke down, culminating in the shootings in 2001.

I know every damn thing that happens here; you cannot fool me in Zanzibar! Does history have to repeat itself? We have to contemplate the future seriously. I believe in the Swahili saying, *majuto ni mjukuu*, meaning "regret is a grandchild," or regret comes last, after the harm has been done. The situation prevailing today is a result of political manipulation and intransigence. It is self-defeating. The best solution for our country is to maintain peace, tranquility, and amity among the people.

I was born in Pemba, but I do not think the same as an ordinary person there because I have been more exposed to the outside world. After my father passed away in 1989, I lost most of my roots and connections there. I have seen, however, how the Pembans, because of their entrepreneurship, lead the way in social, economic, and political progress in the islands. They are serious, and they help each other. When they send someone into business, he will hire another from Pemba. Now many businesses are in the hands of Pembans.

If the people of Pemba and Unguja do not come together, then we will not survive as an entity. Once we have leaders who are committed ideologically, then we can achieve a bright future. But as long as we have people who only think about their personal gain, we will have a dark future. That prediction applies to all Africa. Each leader who gets into power wants to remain at the cost of the people. As long as we accept leaders who have nothing, who are not content and think they only have five or ten years to enrich themselves before they go back to the bush, there will be corruption and the people will suffer.

It is better sometimes to be poor and to live in peace and harmony than to have rich natural resources and, as a result, experience constant war and bloodshed. This is a materialistic world, after all, and it is the fault of the United States, which has put into our heads ideas like the free market, capitalism, and democracy. So, in response to such influences, we grab wealth, whether rightly or wrongly, but eventually we should institute a system where everything is shared according to the needs of the people. Perhaps this is wishful thinking, but we are all revolutionaries, and each of us must decide his or her own way.

Can all of humanity become capitalist? Can we divide the wealth evenly? There are bound to be those who have and those who do not. A capitalist society is by nature unjust, and there are bound to be clashes; so it is just a matter of time before there is a revolution. Who knows what will evolve after that? To be honest, I personally do not believe we are moving toward a worldwide religious confrontation between Christians and Muslims. Instead, I still believe in Marx's analysis of history and believe that socialism is inevitable, though I am no longer a Marxist.

Forty years ago, I was part of the struggle here in Zanzibar to bring an end to the reactionary rule of the semifeudal sultanate that came centuries ago from Oman. Why should we have a kingdom of that nature, so foreign to us, in every sense of the word? But we knew we first had to free ourselves from British colonial rule before we could remove the sultan. Our revolution came just one month after the British relinquished power, and many people died. I do not know if the nationalists of the ZNP have ever forgiven me for helping to overthrow their government, but I have forgiven them for insulting me and making a mockery of us comrades back in those days. I speak with anyone, yet I defend my stand.

And I can say that the first years of the revolution were very good. The turning point came around 1968, when Karume took over the Ministry of Finance and things began to deteriorate rapidly. The element that killed Karume in 1972 thought that, because of the hardship, the people would spontaneously rise up, given the chance. But the conspirators were unscientific; you cannot expect something that is spontaneous.

Still, I do not regret our period in power after the revolution. We made some mistakes—I will not say we were perfect since perfection is the prerogative of God. We tried our best to be perfect, but as mortals, we made mistakes. Many of the negative things took place without my knowledge; I only learned of them after their occurrence. Deep in my heart, I did not condone what happened, but as a minority, I had to keep my mouth shut in order to survive.

God knows my inner self, more than I know myself. He will judge me on the day of judgment. He will punish me for the wrongs I have done, or He will forgive me. He is merciful, and I resign myself to Him.

Ali Sultan Issa (*far right, second row, wearing bow tie*) attending the Moscow Youth Festival, 1957.

Issa attending with his wife a trade union conference in Hanoi, 1963. *Left to right:* Aisha Amour Zahour, Muhsin Abeid, Ali Sultan Issa.

Issa speaking at a trade union conference in North Vietnam, 1963.

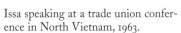

Issa speaking at a village rally in Pemba, 1964.

Abeid Karume officially opening a new primary school, Zanzibar, 1965. *Front row, left to right:* Ali Hassan Mwinyi, Rashid Abdullah, Ali Sultan Issa, Hassan Nassor Moyo, Abeid Karume, Aboud Jumbe. *Courtesy of the Zanzibar National Archives.*

Issa as Minister of Education, 1965. *Courtesy of the Zanzibar National Archives.*

Issa with daughter Moona Ali Sultan,
Zanzibar Town, 1967.

Maria and Issa at their wedding, Zanzibar Town, 1966.

A party at the Chinese consulate, Zanzibar Town, 1969. *Left to right:* Fatma Jinja, Maria Issa, Ali Sultan Issa.

Issa as a cabinet minister,
Zanzibar Town, 1970.

Maria in Retford, United Kingdom, with her children and those of Issa's first
marriage, 1977. *Back row, left to right:* Raissa, Maria, Fidela, Moona. *Front row,
left to right:* Sarah, Salim, Omar, Johanna.

Issa following his release from prison, in Saarbrucken, West Germany, with Gertrude Gutt of Amnesty International, 1979.

Issa traveling with wife Eshe, London, 1995.

part two

AN ENDURING TRUST

The Life Story of Seif Sharif Hamad

I grew up at a time after the war when Zanzibar experienced considerable political turmoil. On one hand, it was a confrontation between various Zanzibari political parties and the colonial government, and on the other, it was a confrontation among the parties themselves. At that time, there was a vibrant free press, so the newspapers reported on all the caustic opinions and accusations of the politicians. Finally, we obtained independence from the British in December 1963, but one month later, we had a revolution. In Swahili, revolution means mapinduzi, *which means to turn things upside-down, and one can say that is what actually happened here. Zanzibar was renowned in the world as a peaceful country, full of tolerance, but the revolution—in which it is said that thousands of people lost their lives—completely changed that image. Although about half the population of Zanzibar welcomed the revolution enthusiastically, the other half was overthrown. They, the supporters of the old regime, suffered a series of atrocities. So, instead of bringing about unity, the revolution sustained divisions in our society. And I saw no efforts made afterward to narrow the schism.*

The objective of the revolution was to bring about equal opportunity for all, but we witnessed a class of people in the Revolutionary Council [RC] and their associates taking the benefits and fruits of the revolution for themselves. During the revolution, the standard and quality of education deteriorated, health services declined, roads were left to decay, and the government administration was in turmoil. Nor was there any freedom of expression, of movement, or of association. For years, we all felt that Big Brother was watching us. We could not say anything that implied we were not totally happy with the way things were going. If we did, we would be taken to task and even arrested and thrown in prison without going through the courts. So really, yes, the revolution had very good objectives, but, unfortunately, these objectives have yet to be realized forty years later.

Politics was not my first ambition, but after I was plunged into it, I gradually got used to it since there was an urge in me to see that the country experienced reforms. And I think being brought into the Revolutionary Council, as well as the highest organs of the ruling party, gave me an opportunity to work from within to bring about some reforms. It has been a long struggle, and I find myself now married to politics. It is difficult for me now to extricate myself because the more I am in the game, the more I feel that leaving would be a betrayal of my fellow countrymen and the nation as a whole, especially the coming generations. I feel I have an obligation to at least lay down democratic foundations on which we can build strong institutions that are, I am convinced, the only way to protect human rights. Through these institutions, it will be possible to check excesses and abuses of power, to ensure that corrupt practices will be controlled, and at least to lay the groundwork for economic and social development in our country. We already have a separation of powers in this country between the legislative, judicial, and executive branches of government; but so far the executive wields almost absolute power. The disadvantaged members of society, if they are wronged, have nowhere to go to seek their rights.

Zanzibar is a very mixed society, with historically large numbers of Shirazi, Africans, Arabs, and Indians. Since my earliest days, I have abhorred racial, ethnic, and religious discrimination. I have always thought race and ethnicity are artificial divisions. All should have the right to exercise their beliefs in their own way. I was brought up a Muslim; my religion abhors discrimination of all kinds. It teaches that we are all brothers and equals. The best person is the one most pious before God, but, otherwise, we are all equals. There is a verse in the Qur'an that says all of us should hold onto the rope of God and should not entertain divisions, so Islam seeks to do away with artificial differences of race and ethnicity. Since Zanzibar is predominantly Muslim, we have the basis on which to employ Islamic teachings to unite the people, as long as non-Muslims are not discriminated against and have their rights protected. Through such unity, we can resist the politicians who try and divide us according to race or ethnicity.

One BEGINNINGS

I WAS BORN ON OCTOBER 22, 1943, ON the island of Pemba in the village of Nyali Mtambwe. Since it is located on a creek that leads to the Indian Ocean, Mtambwe is a fishing village, but it also has many farms and clove plantations. At that time, the village was not very large, with about four hundred homesteads, with no electricity or telephones. There was a road in colonial times, but it has been allowed to deteriorate so now when I visit, I go by canoe, approaching from the creek.

My father did not own much land, only about fifteen acres, but on my maternal side, my grandfather was one of the largest landowners in the village, with more than thirty acres. When he died, my mother and uncle, his only children, agreed that my uncle should take charge of all the land owned by my grandfather, and up to now we have not divided it. When my mother passed away, I could have made some trouble with my uncle since I was my mother's only child and entitled to her third of the land. But I did not because my uncle, whose name is Haji Seif, helped to raise me and was very kind to me.

My father was a highly respected man who served the British colonial government as the local *sheha*, or village headman. In those days, the *sheha* were very well trained, well behaved, and very fair. My father was, in fact, in charge of a large area and often called *Bwana Mtambwe*, or Master of Mtambwe. Anytime a person had a problem or dispute, he or she went to him. He tried to resolve quarrels over property and inheritance, for example. The *sheha* was supposed to know by heart all the boundaries of farms in the area. These were delicate matters, and the *sheha* had to be highly respected because he was like an arbiter and possessed wide powers. For example, when a woman wanted a divorce from her husband due to mistreatment or impotency, she went to the *sheha*. My father sometimes decided such cases by asking the couple to have

173

sex in front of a third person, a witness to determine if the man was actually impotent. Sometimes my mother served as witness since she could be trusted to keep these matters confidential. Sometimes I would sit on the baraza outside my father's office and listen in on such cases. I learned a lot that way. In fact, one of my responsibilities as the son of the *sheha* was to raise and lower the sultan's solid red flag every day at sunrise and sunset.

My family is Shirazi, which means the people indigenous to the islands of Pemba and Unguja, in the sense that my ancestors came here centuries back and settled along the East African coast. According to the legend of the Zenj Empire, our ancestors came originally from Persia, from a town known as Shiraz. The leader was Hassan bin Ali, who had seven sons, each one of whom founded one of the towns on the east coast of Africa, from Lamu in the north to Sofala in the south. Here in Zanzibar, the main evidence remaining of their era is a very old mosque in the village of Kizimkazi and another in Chwaka, in Pemba. The Shirazi remain the most numerous ethnic group in Zanzibar, though as a result of intermarriage between Shirazi, Africans, and Arabs, very few can say they are pure Shirazi. Most Shirazi today, especially among the younger generation, do not know their origin and are partly African and partly Persian.

In Unguja, the Arabs came and took large tracts of Shirazi land for themselves; the Shirazi became either small farmers or fishermen. Arab land alienation, as well as slavery, left a lasting legacy of bitterness in Unguja. I come from Pemba where the population is more homogeneous and where there is less ethnic hatred than in Unguja. A lot of Arabs came and settled in Pemba, but mostly as shopkeepers; there were only a few who owned large plantations. The Arabs intermingled and intermarried with the local people, so now there is not the same racial divide as in Unguja. Nor has Pemba been affected as much by slavery or the slave trade. The Shirazi in Pemba always owned land and were never enslaved, so they used to think their culture was superior. I know for sure my own ancestors were never enslaved, nor did they own slaves.

When I was seven years old, I started studying the Qur'an in the government primary school in Uondwe, about a mile away. The method of instruction was very traditional; we copied down on slates everything the teacher wrote on the board, then learned how to make sounds and to write in Arabic, and later to memorize the Qur'an. In 1951, after one year of this, I started Standard 1 in the same school. The area where I grew up was very green and hilly, and it rained a lot, so it would often take us forty-five minutes or so to walk to school because of the poor road conditions.

In my second year in Uondwe, there was a teacher who beat the students and was very unpopular. One day some older students gathered a certain plant known in Swahili as *upupu,* with leaves that caused severe itching on contact. The students took dried leaves from the plant and ground them into powder and left the powder on his chair. The effect was terrible: the teacher scratched himself everywhere on his body and was completely humiliated. All the students laughed, and when the rest of us heard the story, we laughed as well. Because we celebrated so much, we were all punished together: we were paraded on the school grounds, and each student received three lashes.

Only a year later, the primary school was forced to close over a dispute between the parents and the teachers. A group of parents campaigned against the school, claiming the teachers were arrogant and stealing their wives. These were the allegations, but the real reason was that they thought it un-Islamic to have a colonial school in the village, even though it had been open for a number of years. It was, in fact, one of the oldest state schools in Pemba. The government tried to convince the people to send their children to the colonial school, but they refused.

Fortunately, two of my older brothers were teachers, so they arranged for me to attend Wete Boys' School, located about a mile away, across the creek from my village. Every day I crossed over in a canoe to attend school in what was then the largest town in Pemba, with a population of about eight thousand. One of my favorite teachers there was Omar Haji Dawa. He was very smart and well dressed, a dandy I can say. I admired him very much for the way he taught. He was very friendly, unlike other teachers who beat the students and were very serious. He was more subtle and used psychology to get students not to misbehave. He would talk to you and address you in a way that made you realize you were a fool, which had more effect than any beating. But in those days, there were few disciplinary problems; the student prefect would keep the others under control when the teacher was absent.

I enjoyed school and was at first most interested in art subjects, and later I liked geography. I imagined one day being able to see the different continents. I loved learning about the differences in their formation and was also particularly interested in the origins and development of cities, such as London, Cairo, Beijing, and New York. This was when I was in Pemba, where there were no cities. I wanted to travel, especially to Europe and the Americas, because Zanzibar was a British protectorate and in the schools we were taught a lot about Great Britain. In geography class, we learned mostly about the British Empire, which made us admire the queen, although in Zanzibar we were not her subjects but those of the sultan. Technically, the British came to protect, not to colonize, so they respected the sultan, Seyyid Khalifa bin Haroub. A British Resident was the main advisor to the sultan and the real power behind the throne, however. All government policies came from the British; in areas of customary and Islamic law, however, the sultan's Privy Council had considerable power.

My two brothers both rose to become headmasters of primary schools in Pemba. My elder brother, Hamad, was very keen that I learn and made sure I continued my education. He was my teacher in Standard 5. In class, he usually gave me the most severe punishments to create an impression that he did not favor me at all because I was his brother. He wanted to send a message to the others that, if he could do this to me, he could do it to them as well.

One time while he was teaching, both my legs suddenly swelled up. My brother asked me a question, but because of the swelling, I could not stand up in order to answer. He came toward me to beat me, but I showed him my legs, and he took me to the hospital immediately. He stayed with me for almost the whole day. In those days, he was always very hard on me because he really cared about me. Years later, after his funeral, I cried and cried because I loved him very much. He was my advisor and consultant in all my affairs, and suddenly I had lost him. I was very much aggrieved.

In 1957, the teachers gave all the Standard 7 students a trial exam to enter secondary school. I scored among the top five students in Pemba; when I took the actual entrance exam, I passed and was allowed to skip Standard 8. Because there were no secondary schools in Pemba at the time, I attended school in Unguja. I attended what was then called the Zanzibar Government Boys' Secondary School, located at Beit el Ras, on the ocean shore just north of Zanzibar Town. The first time I ever saw Zanzibar Town was, in fact, when I entered secondary school. In those days. it was not easy for people to travel about, and there were many in Wete who had never been to Mkoani, the town on the southern end of the island. In those days, everyone was in his own small world. When we arrived by boat in the evening, I could see the lights of Zanzibar Town, and I was mesmerized. I was a farm boy coming to the city for the first time.

Students were selected on merit at the time. About 60 to 65 percent of the students in the government secondary schools were from Unguja, and about 35 to 40 percent came from Pemba. Most of us staying at Beit el Ras came from rural areas because the boys from town stayed at home. We were supposed to pay fees of 120 shillings per term, which was too much for most parents, including my own. I filled out a form in which I said I stayed with my poor grandmother, so I only paid twenty shillings. Some students paid less or nothing at all. In those days, there was no chance anyone would be left behind if he could not afford to pay fees. The revolutionary government's rhetoric that poor or African students were segregated in colonial times and not given an opportunity simply is not true. All the students sat for the same exam and were selected according to merit; no one was held back because of poverty or race. Of course, those people raised in educated families had an advantage. Most Indians were educated; the Arabs to some extent were also educated, but educated Africans, the majority of whom lived in the rural areas, were few. Students in town had access to private tuition, libraries, and other facilities, whereas the village boys and girls had no such advantages. In those days, there were also private schools, mostly in town, run by various communities like the Comorians, Ismailis, and Christians. Most students in town passed their exams to enter secondary school, while many in the rural areas did not.

When I first arrived at Beit el Ras, I was very young, only fifteen years old. On the first day, the older boys bullied and intimidated all the newcomers, saying they would come at night and try to screw us. So sometimes I would sleep with three pairs of trousers on. I thought, "These people are dangerous!" There was, in fact, a man who would come from town by bicycle to sell ice cream and shout out to the older boys, "Who wants to buy ice cream for the newcomers?" But I never accepted any ice cream from the older boys, knowing it was a trap.

There were no partitions in the shower room, so there was no privacy at all. I would take showers at night, but slowly I got used to the situation. We were well looked after; we had very good beds with good mattresses and linen. Everybody received eating utensils and soap both for washing clothes and taking a bath. One of the rules at Beit el Ras was that we had to pray, especially in the morning and evening in the mosque the British had built for the students on the school grounds. The British never tried to impose Christianity; instead, they introduced Islamic Studies as one of the school subjects. We were allowed to revise our work until 10:00 p.m., when the lights were put out. Everyone was supposed to be asleep at the time, but we had our own lanterns and had discussions or read by ourselves until very late, and then we would wake up again at five for prayers.

We elected a food committee responsible for deciding on our menu. Every morning we received bread, butter, jam, and eggs. At lunch, we had rice, sometimes potato and meat stew, and at night, we usually had bread and curry and tea. We had a very good diet; but, you know, children are children, so we liked to go in the dead of night to pick young coconuts. Usually four or five were enough to fill us up, but there was one boy who could eat and drink the meat and juice of twenty-five coconuts at a time. Or sometimes during the season, we would wake up early to collect mangos, and in the afternoons, we would look for guava. Of course, the owners of the trees did not like this, and they would chase us away.

It was a very fun-filled time in my life. If a boy fell in love with a girl in the girl's boarding school in the town, we would arrange it so that one of the other girls would write a note to the boy, scent it nicely, and make an appointment to meet on the weekend. The chap would be very happy as he cleaned and prepared himself on the day appointed. We made sure he had transportation to meet her by telling one of the other boys to let him borrow his bicycle. We followed him discreetly from a distance and then enjoyed watching him become increasingly dejected as he waited for half an hour, one hour, two hours. And when he returned to the school, he found all of us waiting for him. All the boys would line up and cheer and congratulate him on his wedding and then show him his bed, which we had prepared with very nice bed sheets and decorated with flowers. Some of the chaps, when the girl never arrived, would know they had been fooled, so they would go to town and not return until the following day.

But, generally, I tried to protect the newcomers, who sometimes came to me for advice and help. I offered them protection so they would not be bullied. Sometimes the students would have fistfights, but after a few hours, they would be friends again.

From my boarding school to town, it was a journey of about five miles, so it was not easy to go there. I either had to get a lift, ride a bicycle, or walk. I was allowed to go out only on the weekends; anyway, I was a *shamba* boy and not used to life in Zanzibar. Nor did I have many relatives in town; I only had my brother's very close friend, Mr. Mdungi Ussi. I visited him regularly because he was like a brother to me.

One of my closest friends at school was Khalfan Salim, who came from a village in the same district of Pemba as I. My best friend was Kassim Ali, who also came from Pemba. In those days, it was fun with Khalfan and Kassim just to roam around the town on the weekends and to visit the shops, though we had no money to buy anything, but just to see what they sold. Sometimes we would go to the café to have tea or some food different from the school meals. It took me about a year or so to see my first movie in Zanzibar Town, which was not a new thing to me since we had cinemas already in Pemba. In Wete, we had two: the Prabhat Cinema and the Novelty Cinema. They were both owned by Asian families and showed mostly Indian films.

My best friend Kassim and I were so close that on vacations either I would visit his family or he would stay with mine. Still to this day, his parents regard me as one of their sons. In Pemba on the holidays, I would meet childhood friends, go swimming in the creek, or roam about the countryside. We would pick any kind of fruit we wanted and nobody cared or ever asked questions, so it was really fun. We would be gone the whole day and sometimes afterward get a lecture from our parents. Actually, my father never beat me; he only spoke to me when I was naughty. My uncle beat me, but my father was more diplomatic.

I picked cloves on my father's plantation in Pemba, or I worked as a tally clerk, measuring and recording the cloves harvested by each worker. Our workers during the harvest were Zanzibari, but we also had some Wanyamwezi from the mainland who came specifically to clear the bush. They enjoyed using the hoe more than climbing the trees and picking cloves. It was hard work, especially after harvesting, to separate the cloves from the stems. In one day, I could finish about eight measures of cloves, known as *pishi,* but the best workers could finish about fifty-four *pishi.* I worked just to have some money to buy clothes and to spend while in school; I was not trying to support a family. Sometimes, of course, I would secretly take dried cloves from my father's or uncle's land and sell it on the side for cash. I would put some aside for myself before it was bagged. Of course, they suspected, but they never caught me. I got a lot of money from selling cloves and from my work as a clerk; so when I came to Beit el Ras, I had a lot compared to other students, and I would help them. Sometimes I would pay for them when we went to town, or sometimes a student could not pay for a uniform, so I would help him.

In September 1958, after two school terms at the Government Boys' Secondary School, I began to attend King George VI Memorial Boys' Secondary School, now called Lumumba College, though I continued to stay at Beit el Ras. I was there until November 1963, when I finished my Form 6 examinations. King George VI was actually the only place in Zanzibar at the time where you could advance to that level of education. The Indians composed about 50 percent of the school population, the Arabs were 30 percent, and the rest were African. Among the Africans, the Shirazi and Comorians were the most numerous. We also had three streams of students: A, B, and C. The best students like myself were sent to Form 2A, 3A, and so on. All the students in Form 4A passed their Cambridge Secondary School Examinations, either in first or second class. I passed in first class, for example. In Form 4C, more than 80 percent got third class, and the rest failed.

People say those were the best times both at Beit el Ras and at King George VI because the facilities were very good and the teachers well qualified. The teachers were British, Indian, and African. One of the African instructors was Mr. Aboud Jumbe, who would later become Zanzibar's second president and would be responsible for so many things in my life. He taught English, Swahili, biology, and chemistry, often as a temporary substitute. He was very good and very friendly. Sometimes on Mondays, he just would not show up; but when he did, he was very bright, a very well-rounded teacher, always able to teach without notes.

TWO STUDENT POLITICS

SOME OF THE STUDENTS AT BEIT
el Ras were very interested in politics in those days. I was not that interested and did not take seriously the politicians who said the British were imperialists who exploited the people of Zanzibar. I would say to myself that at least now we have good schools. I was not against the British, but neither was I against independence; I was just waiting to see what would happen.

Other students liked to argue politics, supporting different sides in the nationalist movement. Some supported the Afro-Shirazi Party [ASP], and others the Zanzibar Nationalist Party [ZNP], or the Zanzibar and Pemba People's Party [ZPPP]. These parties emerged from various groups like the African Association, the Shirazi Association, the Arab Association, the Comorian Association, the Indian Association, and so on. Especially in Unguja, there was the feeling that the Arabs, and to a lesser extent the Indians, exploited the Africans and Shirazi. Not so in Pemba, where the Arabs intermarried and integrated and where there was far less hostility. But in Unguja, the Shirazi and Africans felt they were exploited, and it was easy for them to unite to form the Afro-Shirazi Party. We heard that Julius Nyerere, who was then the leader of the Tanganyikan African National Union, was personally behind the formation of the ASP.

The Shirazi from Pemba eventually formed their own party, the ZPPP, which made an alliance with the ZNP in 1961 in order to defeat the ASP. Africans and Shirazi in Unguja founded the ZNP in 1955 and were later joined by many Arabs and the affluent of Zanzibar Town. That is how the ZNP acquired the reputation of being an Arab party; there were plenty of Africans in the party, but the top leadership was mostly Arab. In 1963, the ZNP also underwent a split; some of their members with socialist convictions, led by Abdulrahman Muhammed Babu, left to form the Umma Party.

My own family was divided; my uncle and older brothers supported the ASP, and my parents were sympathetic toward the ZPPP. Though my family was divided, there were no quarrels. Because my brothers and my father were government servants, they could not publicly state their loyalties. As far as I was concerned, I never attended any public rallies, never voted and, honestly, had no strong convictions that one party was better than another. I thought it was all nonsense because, as a student, I considered my main duty just to learn and not to associate myself with any parties.

I remember that one day some students and I were traveling to Pemba by boat and that Abeid Karume, the president of the ASP, also happened to be on his way to Pemba. I had read about him in the newspapers and heard about him from other people, but that was the first time I actually saw him. He had his own private cabin, but he came out on deck, and all us students surrounded him out of curiosity and asked lots of questions. He answered them very jovially, and that impressed me very much. I liked him that day; he seemed very accessible and down to earth, answering the students' questions with jokes.[1]

One of the major issues in Zanzibar was whether to retain the sultan after independence. At the time, I was not an ardent monarchist, but I felt the monarch could, as in Great Britain, play a stabilizing role, but only if he and the royal family stayed out of politics completely. During Seyyid Khalifa's forty-nine-year reign, from 1911 to 1960, the country was very stable, and he enjoyed the respect of all the people. He was just a figurehead, a symbolic figure; had his successors remained politically neutral, many probably would have tolerated the continuation of this constitutional arrangement. Unfortunately, the sultans who came after Seyyid Khalifa sometimes allowed the brass band of the Youths Own Union, the ZNP youth organization, to perform for them. This made some politicians more antagonistic toward the sultan, who was seen to be partisan.

Sheikh Thabit Kombo, who before the revolution was the ASP's secretary general, once told me that, if Seyyid Khalifa had lived a few years longer, they would have never overthrown the government. He enjoyed the respect of most Zanzibaris. In the late 1950s, Karume said in one of his public rallies that, if the ASP won the elections, the party would make Zanzibar a republic. Seyyid Khalifa invited him to his palace and entertained him and, in passing, gently asked Karume about his statement. Karume said, "My lord, what I meant was, in having a republic we should continue with the wise leadership of you, our sultan." Seyyid Khalifa answered, "Yes, I know. You are my son."

There were a few students at Beit el Ras who, after the formation of nationalist parties, began to bring up the ethnic issue during political discussions. But they were very few and, otherwise, cooperated very much with everyone else. In fact, I never sensed any real ethnic hatred in school, which was very healthy. I did not have a strong personal sense of ethnic identity because in Pemba there was not much of an ethnic divide. I was Shirazi, but I had relatives of African or Arab descent.

Like islanders throughout the world, I was insular; I identified myself as a Zanzibari. I thought the emphasis of some politicians on African identity was brought about through insecurity. Some people wanted to impose their identity as Africans because, in Zanzibar, their own ethnic groups from the mainland were so small. They chose the large umbrella of African identity to collect all of them into a grouping to be reckoned with politically. I was a Shirazi who was especially proud of Zanzibar and its unique culture. I had a strong sense of Zanzibari nationalism because we regarded ourselves in Zanzibar as more civilized than our brothers in the rest of East Africa. We thought we had a better culture, were more educated, and had better customs as a result of the intermingling of races and cultures here. We were unique because, as an island, Zanzibar had a potpourri of influences and peoples from Africa, Asia, the Gulf, and Europe. Ever since the old days of the Zenj Empire, Zanzibaris were more exposed to the world. People came here from different parts of the world with their various experiences and traditions and, through their diversity, formed a unique culture not found in an area where only one racial group predominates, as in Kenya or Tanganyika.[2]

Zanzibar is also unique because of religion. Some people argue that Islam came to the islands even before it arrived in Medina. Some of the earliest companions of the Prophet went to Abyssinia, but the wind took them to Zanzibar first, before they landed eventually in Abyssinia. Their arrival brought about a great awakening and made Zanzibar unique. When the Christian missionaries came in the nineteenth century, they found a very tolerant society and were able to gain the full cooperation of the sultans. Like Islam, Christianity spread from the islands throughout East Africa. Zanzibar was and is a gateway to the whole region.

I read a lot in my high school days about segregation in South Africa and about how black and "coloured" people there were treated as second-class citizens. I also read about slavery in the United States and came to admire President John Kennedy who acknowledged that blacks had the right to have equal access to education. Here was a white man from a wealthy family willing to use the force of the state to ensure equal rights; that appealed to me very much. I thought of him as a courageous and charismatic leader, especially when he stood up to Nikita Krushchev during the Cuban Missile Crisis. I thought he was the kind of man needed to lead the world, and I could not believe the news when he was shot. I thought, "How could this man be killed, who was doing so much good for his nation and the world?" I was really shocked. The other person I admired from the West was Winston Churchill. He was not a success in school but showed his capacity to lead his country in a time of crisis. My teachers would always say that failure in school did not mean failure in life and then give Churchill as an example. I admired his courage and the way he stood firm against the Nazi occupation of Europe.

Of course, I also admired Mahatma Gandhi as a great leader who used peaceful means to fight colonialism in India. Although he lost his life, his philosophy triumphed in the end, and the colonialists were defeated. From the Muslim world, the one I admire most is the Prophet Muhammed, who was illiterate but a wise and true leader who reformed the Arab world. He was a teacher, a soldier, and a father to his followers. Of the current world leaders, I definitely admire Nelson Mandela who, though suffering the oppression of twenty-seven years in jail, could still unite black South Africans to fight against apartheid. After his release, he had the opportunity to have his revenge but was very magnanimous, and for that he earned the respect of the entire world.

If I was involved in politics as a student, it was as a founding member and later president of the Pemba Students Union, or PSU. We had about forty to sixty members, with about twelve sitting on the Executive Committee. Mostly we discussed what actions we should take regarding Pemba's position regarding Unguja. We had certain grievances: we thought Pemba was being neglected in terms of development, and we demanded, for example, electricity, roads, and especially more and better education. After the 1963 elections, we PSU leaders met with the new minister of education, Mr. Maulid Mshangama, who listened to our grievances and promised to give Pemba more development assistance.

I also remember that, in Form 6, I led a student strike at Beit el Ras, though it was just over a small matter. The school principal, Mr. Piggot, changed the stoves in the cafeteria from wood-burning to gas and instructed the cooks to use a very slow flow of gas when they cooked our meals. The cooks warned him the food would take years to cook, but he insisted.

On the day the changes took effect, I was informed we would not eat lunch until very late in the day. I went personally to see Mr. Piggot at his house, but his wife said he was asleep and did not want to be disturbed. I informed her that this was a very serious matter, but she said her husband was not to be disturbed. So I met with the other students, and we quickly organized a procession of about 120 students, to bring pressure on Mr. Piggott. We marched to his house banging our aluminum plates and spoons, shouting, "*Tuna njaa!*" [We are hungry!] We put the smaller kids up front because we wanted Mr. Piggot to know it was a protest from the grassroots. When his wife saw us coming and heard us banging, she woke her husband, who shouted at us to go back to our dormitories, but we refused. He called in the Police Mobile Force, a unit specially trained to handle riots and disturbances. They came with loudspeakers, saying we needed to disperse, but still we refused to move.

Eventually, one very respected teacher came and personally asked us to leave the grounds, and we agreed. The cooking staff decided to do something fast; they bought some bread and increased the flow of gas to the stoves, and within an hour, we were served with curry. The students were very satisfied with the protest because, in the following days, we received our meals at the proper time of 1:30 p.m., whereas before we had waited until 3:00 p.m.

Mr. Piggot and I afterward had a chat, and I informed him that we had tried to appeal to him but that he had refused to listen. Meanwhile, the police launched a criminal investigation to find out who was responsible for the strike. Their objective was to expel the ringleaders, but we had already agreed on what we would say. When they asked the younger boys who had convinced them to strike, they all said, "My hunger." The police never learned who was responsible.

It still had not occurred to me to be in politics; instead, I wanted to be a senior civil servant, heading a ministry. That was my ambition, and in this respect, my father who served as a village *sheha* was a big example to me.

three REVOLUTION

EVER SINCE THE ELECTION riots of June 1961, I had an uneasy feeling about the future. Fighting broke out in Zanzibar Town on polling day due to suspicions between the ZNP and the ASP. Each side accused the other of trying to rig the elections. Some ZNP members were convinced that individuals who did not deserve political rights in the islands came from the mainland to vote. ASP members, meanwhile, felt that the ZNP's aim was to marginalize mainland Africans. As people in Darajani waited to vote, the ZNP accused ASP voters of fraud, and that was the spark that ignited the fire. The violence needed only something small to get it started, and ever since, the mistrust between the two sides has continued; it haunts Zanzibar even now.

The British government sent soldiers to restore peace and order. I was in Form 4; the school officials closed our school and sent all of us home. A British unit known as the Golden Highlanders escorted us on the boat to Pemba. They escorted us to our very homes and personally handed us over to our parents, so much care did the government take to make sure we were safe.

So I worried about what would happen if the British left, with people killing each other like that. Without the British to protect us, I did not know what we would do to each other. We approached independence with some degree of uncertainty. There was a lot of ethnic tension between Zanzibaris of African descent and those of Arab origin, especially in Unguja.

I finished high school in November 1963 and wanted to go to college to study administration, so I could come back and serve in the Zanzibari government. After sitting for the Form 6 exam, I stayed with Abadhar Juma Khatib, the minister of agriculture and a relative of mine from my home village. I was an adolescent with some free time and curious about the handing over of power, so I waited around to attend the Independence

186

Day celebrations. I was there at Cooper's Grounds, later known as Maisara, on December 10, 1963, and witnessed Prince Philip from the United Kingdom give the instruments of independence to Sultan Jamshid. I witnessed the lowering of the Union Jack and the raising of the new Zanzibari flag. I could see those who were enthusiastic about this were mainly supporters of the ZNP and the ZPPP, whose support came mostly from Pemba and Zanzibar Town, as well as from northern Unguja. The ASP, meanwhile, dominated in southern and central Unguja and in the neighborhoods of Zanzibar Town where Zanzibaris of African origin were most numerous. The ASP had won about 44 percent in Pemba and overall 54 percent of the total vote, but it failed to win a majority of seats in parliament and so lost the elections. So, while some celebrated independence, I sensed that the other half did not regard it as a significant day. They felt it was not true independence because, though the British were leaving, the sultan remained. In fact, my brother's friend, an ASP supporter, told me that the new government would not last, that it would be overthrown, though I did not ask why or when.

When I heard the news in Pemba the next month that the government had been overthrown, I was not completely surprised. The first news I received was by radio when I heard John Okello broadcasting from Zanzibar Town. The news spread very fast throughout Pemba, and he really frightened people. He called himself field marshall and threatened some Zanzibaris of Arab origin, saying that so-and-so had been sentenced to jail for 150 or 300 years or that certain individuals must immediately hang themselves. He promised that, if he had to come himself, he would shoot them personally. When he arrived in Pemba a couple of weeks later, the authorities just submitted, they did not resist, and that is the reason fewer died in Pemba than in Unguja, where I am told over thirteen thousand, mostly Arabs, lost their lives.

When Okello arrived in Pemba, he moved with a contingent of heavily armed followers in about three land rovers. They were a mixed group of mainlanders and Shirazi but mostly ASP supporters from Unguja. Okello started the punishment of caning and whipping people; he would give orders, and his protégés would obey. Okello liked, in particular, to humiliate Arabs from Oman, called Manga Arabs. The sultans and the ruling class were of mostly Omani origins, so Okello believed it was their turn to be humiliated. Okello rounded up Arabs and ordered them to sing words like *uhuru na jamhuri*, meaning freedom and the republic, over and over again. They were forced to praise Karume, and then he would order their beards to be shaved without water, just dry. I personally saw this take place in Wete in February 1964.

Even when Okello passed by on the road, all the people had to come out and wave, and often when he saw an Arab with a beard, he would immediately stop his car and start to abuse him. For Arabs from Oman, their beards were a status symbol and a sign of respect; if they were shaved dry and in public, it was a great humiliation. Under normal circumstances, they would have fought to defend their honor, but at the time, they were subdued and forced just to take it.[1]

Karume's government soon appointed new government officers in Pemba. They began to announce public floggings, encouraging people to attend. These were always political floggings: for not standing up when an official passed, for not showing up for nation-building projects, or for not attending public rallies. But if you cannot flog your own child, how can you flog someone older than you? It was especially wrong for a young guy like Ahmed Hassan Diria, district commissioner in Wete, to order the flogging of his elders. Ali Sultan Issa, the district commissioner in Chake Chake, was there for only two months, but in those days, he also really abused his power. His successor, Issa Shariff Musa, never flogged anybody.

I was not personally harmed or humiliated by the revolution, and I tried to keep an open mind. I thought that many of its goals were very good. I wanted to create a New Zanzibar free of ethnicity or racialism. The best way to do so, I thought, would be to give the poor more help in order to encourage them to develop themselves and catch up with the rest of society. I thought children of all ethnic groups should be made to feel proud to be Zanzibari and not to be over occupied by their ethnicity or race. I thought that, in order for Zanzibaris to be united, development assistance should be spread out. Each district should receive the same facilities, so people from one part of the country would not feel neglected or like second-class citizens. It is still my conviction that the best way forward is not to allow any part of the islands to receive special favors. I have had these ideas from my childhood, that we can have a nation of united individuals with the same aspirations, possessing more or less the same religion and culture. Islam can be used to bond and unite the people.

As president of the PSU, I organized a procession of about five hundred students and others in Wete in support of the revolution. We wanted to convince the new authorities that Pembans were not against the revolution. The regional commissioner received our procession in February 1964, and that was where I first addressed a mass rally, an audience of about three thousand people. I said we now had a new government we should support because it had a vision to bring development in Zanzibar, to look after the welfare of all the people. I said we should work with the government to achieve progress and equal opportunity for all. Something like that. My brothers were surprised that I could talk like that in public, yet I was sincere and keeping an open mind.

And it was true: the revolutionaries could have brought the people together, but instead they thought, "Most Pembans supported the former regime, so let's punish them for years. The Arabs enslaved us, so let's make them second-class citizens." They did not understand that Zanzibar is a cosmopolitan place, as are most islands; it is a mixture of different cultures and races, and each one should be used to complement the other in order to come out with something positive and unique.

I am one of those people who, considering what has taken place over the past forty-plus years, wishes the revolution had never taken place. Of course, on paper, the goals of the revolution were very good, and that is the reason some of us were hopeful and enthusiastic; but considering the deterioration in all spheres of Zanzibari life that has taken place, I do not think the revolution has helped the people. Zanzibar has gone back a century in terms of development. Although colonialism is not something to be proud of, the British, to be fair, did a lot of good in Zanzibar. They established an education system that became one of the best in Africa. By 1963, Zanzibar was self-sufficient in terms of doctors, experts, engineers—everything. The standard of education was very high, and the health system was also well equipped and staffed. The roads were well maintained and passable throughout the year. Law and order were enforced, and the whole administration was very efficient, orderly, and fair. In colonial times, one could go to a court to seek justice. Civil servants knew what was required of them, and if they did well, they were promoted. Opportunities were available for further studies. You could see that it was a good system; unfortunately, after the revolution, it was destroyed. The Commonwealth system of legal justice was abolished. People with qualifications in the civil service were humiliated and demoralized because there were no longer any standards based on merit. Instead, they are now based on nepotism; the children of revolutionaries have all the rights to the best jobs.

It is unfortunate that, after the revolution, colonial achievements were not sustained. Of course, no one has the right to rule another people; but colonialism had its good points, and the British in Zanzibar did not allow the torture and killing of innocent people. Perhaps colonialism was less brutal in Zanzibar than elsewhere in Africa; it was a protectorate in which the sultan was maintained, though the British Resident held the real strings of power. But after the revolution, almost everything came to decay and neglect.

What the revolutionaries say is that they liberated us from the sultan's rule, yet the sultan was just a symbol without any power at all. And even if there was widespread feeling among the ASP mainstream that the sultan was an Arab, an alien to the country, with no right to rule or serve as head of state in Zanzibar, the question could have been resolved peacefully through a national referendum, and I am sure the sultan would not have resisted. Yet the revolutionaries claim the sultan's removal was a great achievement, and they never talk about how they overthrew an elected ZNP-ZPPP government.

When I stayed at Beit el Ras, Sultan Seyyid Khalifa would drive by every Friday afternoon from his palace in town to one north of town at Kibweni, in only one vehicle, with only his driver and his *bawab* [butler], and that was all. And all the way along the road, people stood and waved to greet him, and he waved back. But since the revolution, the presidents, along with the thirty-two members of the Revolutionary Council, have been paid and maintained in every way by the state. The presidents only travel with a convoy at a very high speed, and no one comes out to greet them, yet they claim to be popular. During Seyyid Khalifa's rule, there were no excesses, no human rights violations, no misuses of power. If Khalifa's grandsons misbehaved, they were punished. But after the revolution, our new rulers never cared about human rights, and their children could behave any way they liked. Even if they abused or killed people, nothing happened to them.

Julius Nyerere, the president of Tanganyika, is partially to blame for the revolution. He believed Zanzibar should be part of Tanganyika and started interfering in the affairs of Zanzibar as early as the 1950s. He came here in 1957 to oversee the formation of the ASP, and his party went on to help the ASP for the next several years. When the ASP lost the 1963 elections, the Tanganyikan government began to prepare for the overthrow of the ZNP-ZPPP government at the earliest opportunity. Until now, the story has been that the people in Zanzibar organized the revolution, but there is evidence that Tanganyika was very much involved. Some believe, for example, soldiers from Tanganyika actually led the revolution. The Tanganyikans very cleverly disguised an invasion as a revolution, which was the beginning of Zanzibar's problems as a state.

My own feeling is that Nyerere was the brain behind the overthrow. It is difficult to believe stories that the revolutionaries toppled the sultan's government with just *pangas* [machetes] at first; the weapons they used must have come from the mainland. Nyerere shares the blame with Zanzibari politicians on both sides. In 1962 and 1963, the politicians had discussions in Lancaster House in London about the future of Zanzibar.

If they had been able to come together and agree on a number of matters and put aside their party interests and divisions, there would have been no revolution. If the ZNP-ZPPP leaders had vision, they would have done everything possible to woo Karume to their side. Even if Nyerere had his own designs, he would not have been able to undermine the unity of the Zanzibari people. Our own politicians gave Nyerere the opportunity to interfere in Zanzibari affairs.

I was twenty-one years old when it was announced in April 1964 that Zanzibar and Tanganyika were uniting to form one sovereign state. I thought the decision was wrong. The idea of a union was not included in the ASP manifesto or in speeches made by ASP leaders. If the people had elected a party with the union in its manifesto, then the move would have been legitimate. Even when the ZNP accused the ASP of wanting to form a union, the ASP always denied it very strongly, saying it had no such intentions. So from where did Karume have a mandate from the people? He betrayed their confidence.

Karume, however, did not at first want a union, but Nyerere threatened to withdraw the police recruits he had sent to the islands to restore order, leaving Karume exposed to a counterrevolution. Karume was forced to go through with the union, without even consulting his colleagues in the RC beforehand because he knew it was an unpopular idea. It was his own decision, and no one else was involved. When he announced the union, the majority of the RC were as shocked as the man in the street. Senior ministers like Babu, the minister of external affairs, were taken completely by surprise. Karume held a series of public rallies in support of the union, and everyone was forced to cheer out of fear.

Suleiman Mohammed Suleiman, a school friend of mine, told me a few days after the union announcement that members of Babu's Umma Party, who were most opposed to the union, were summoned to the State House. Although Mr. Suleiman was not an Umma member, he joined the crowd going to the State House, where he was shocked by the sight of Wamakonde, Africans of very recent mainland origins who had played an important role in the revolutionary violence. They were armed with spears, machetes, clubs, and bows and were posted all around the walls of the State House, even standing inside. Karume defended his decision to form the union to the crowd, assuring his listeners that they had nothing to worry about, that he could deal with Nyerere. But he also threatened them, saying those opposing the merger would be dealt with promptly, pointing to the armed Wamakonde standing around the State House.

After the signing of the union agreement, the articles of union had to be ratified by the RC and the Tanganyikan parliament. Records show that the Tanganyikan parliament did so, but none records that the RC ever formally ratified the union. When I was chief minister, I went through all the minutes of the RC meetings of that period. Salim Rashid served as secretary of the RC at the time, and he confirms that the issue of ratification was never on the council's agenda. He was the person responsible for inviting the council members to attend, for preparing the agenda, and for recording the minutes. What more authority is required to ascertain that Zanzibar never ratified the union? That is the reason some people question the legality of the union, because this essential requirement never took place.[2]

It is also a fact that the Western powers were very worried that Zanzibar would become the Cuba of East Africa. They feared that Babu and his Umma comrades would launch their own revolution and overthrow Karume. Zanzibar was suddenly a hot spot in the cold war. The West became more alarmed when, only a few days after the revolution, there were army mutinies in Tanganyika, Kenya, and Uganda. Western leaders wanted to find a way to contain the revolution, thinking that, if Zanzibar was left independent, East Africa would be destabilized and communism would spread to the Great Lakes. They imposed a lot of pressure on Nyerere. And as far as Nyerere was concerned, he knew that, if one of the superpowers controlled Zanzibar, the islands could pose a security threat, especially in the cold war. Anyway, Nyerere had the intention all along to try and control Zanzibar.[3]

If the West was afraid that Zanzibar was going communist, it worried about Umma, not the ASP. Before the revolution, the ASP platform had no socialist agenda, and Karume had no socialist ideas. He was impressed by the West but was really turned off when the U.S. and the U.K. waited weeks to offer his regime official diplomatic recognition. Socialist advisors and ministers like Babu influenced him to embark on policies like land reform not originally in the ASP manifesto. It was Umma—which allied with the ASP—that invited the Chinese, East Germans, and Russians to come and establish embassies here. Umma supported radical policies and adopted a hostile stance against the Western powers. Because some comrades already had military training in places like Cuba and elsewhere, they quickly took top positions in the new army and were appointed members of the RC. Umma had a plan before the union agreement to somehow outmaneuver Karume and force him out of power. My sister-in-law, before she married my brother Hamad, was married to someone who was very close to the Umma Party at the time. In February or so, she and her husband went for an outing with some high-level Umma comrades somewhere near the airport.

Babu was there and, after a few drinks, made a statement to the effect that "by this time next year, I'll be president of Zanzibar." In fact, he went on to say, "I'll be god of East Africa." But the act of union with Tanganyika meant Umma was outmaneuvered because most party members were transferred to the mainland, including Babu himself.

four CROCODILE TEARS

AROUND THE TIME OF THE revolution, I applied to a number of universities, and the response from several was very positive, but the government did not allow me to go overseas. This was because, in March 1964, it had decided to expel all the expatriate civil servants from Zanzibar, especially the British. This decision created a lot of vacancies in the government, and the leaders called on secondary school graduates to fill the gaps. Since I had already finished Form 6, I was asked to be a teacher at Lumumba College, though I was only twenty-one years old and without any formal training. We were told we had to wait to obtain further education because the needs of the country came before our own. In 1964, I was sent to Lumumba College and the next year transferred to Fidel Castro Secondary School in Pemba, where I remained until 1968. I taught geography, English, history, and Swahili. I taught five classes a day of twenty-five to thirty students each.

I had been appointed a teacher without my consultation; I had no choice in the matter, yet I felt duty-bound to serve my country in the work assigned me. I was not a trained teacher, but after a few months, I found myself coping with the work and even liking it because it was my chance to educate society. I considered it a calling to impart what little knowledge I had to others and to help build a responsible and accountable society. I found I was very popular because I was young, and the boys and girls found it easy to seek consultation with me about any problems. There were no obstacles—the door of my house at Fidel Castro was always open. At any time, students could come, knock on the door, and seek my advice as an elder brother, and I enjoyed helping them solve their problems.

In those years, I was called *Maalim*, meaning teacher, and today I am still known by everyone as Maalim Seif. I was very serious in class, but at the same time, I paid special attention to students who were not doing well. At Fidel Castro, we employed teachers from Russia and East Germany who did not speak English very well. When they taught geography, the students did not understand anything, so they would come to me for help. The principal even required me to mark all the students' papers for the foreign teachers; I had to correct all my own papers, plus those of the Russian teachers, who would give students a zero if they misbehaved in class, regardless of their test results.

I saw educational standards decline after the revolution, and the destruction has continued ever since. The government had no planning; it wanted to take in as many students as possible with the same number of buildings and teachers. Class sizes increased from twenty-five to as many as eighty students. Teachers were recruited, but there was no training. A student might complete Form 3 and earn poor grades and still be recruited as a teacher. Nor did the government provide proper reading materials. It abolished the colonial system of choosing students based on merit. It allocated each ethnic group a percentage of the total number of seats available in the secondary schools. Africans, including Shirazi, were given 80 percent; Arabs, 15 percent; and all other ethnic groups, 5 percent. Students whose parents were high in government were assured positions in secondary school, whether they performed well or not.

When I first became a teacher, we were paid very good salaries, about 660 shillings a month, but Ali Sultan Issa, as minister of education, reduced our salaries to 440 shillings. He demoralized us because only our salaries were cut and not those of other civil servants. He went to Karume and told him we had voluntarily agreed to reduce our salaries in order to serve the country, but it was all a lie. For these reasons, the standard of education went down, and the single person most responsible for this deterioration was Ali Sultan Issa.

Since I taught at a boarding school in the countryside, most of my social life in those days was with my fellow teachers and students. It was only on the weekends that I went to Wete to meet friends. The evenings were quiet, so usually I would sit on my verandah and talk with another teacher, Abeid Marine, with whom I shared my house. We had a very good cook, a local boy known as Beka, who was very honest, diligent, and hardworking.

There were constant shortages in Pemba in those days. If there was news of a supply of bread, people would queue up at the bakery at midnight and wait until the shop opened at 7:00 a.m. Some people just went hungry and, during the mango season, would eat unripe green mangos or young coconuts, *madafu*. Or they would dig roots known in Swahili as *biye* or *chochoni* and wash them and prepare them very carefully because otherwise they were poisonous. Sometimes when I went home to my village, I ate these foods; but at Fidel Castro, teachers like me depended on smugglers who brought beans, soap, clothing material, and other needs from Mombasa or Tanga on the mainland. We had to maintain personal relations with smugglers in order to be supplied. They brought everything secretly, coming to the back door because if you were caught purchasing from smugglers, you would definitely be arrested. If you were caught smuggling cloves, you faced a death sentence.

Karume caused these shortages because he did not want to spend money on food imports, only on his construction projects. If people were starving, it did not matter. Of course, Karume probably did not know people were suffering because his intelligence system was poor. His cronies were afraid to tell him the truth because Karume would get furious if anyone informed him the people were hungry. He would say in his speeches that Zanzibaris were naturally healthy, saying this in a meeting where people were falling down from hunger. Presidents like him never want to hear the hard truth, that state-owned corporations like the ZSTC [Zanzibar State Trading Corporation] or Bizanje in charge of imports and exports had no leadership or competent staff. Because they were state-owned, nobody really cared. All the retail shops were turned into government cooperatives under the supervision of the *Umoja wa Wanawake* [Women's Union], and led by people who could not handle even basic accounting. Some individuals became very rich, but all the cooperatives eventually collapsed. The only government-owned corporation surviving from those days is the ZSTC because it still has a monopoly on exporting cloves.

In the difficult years when food was scarce, people's habits gradually changed. Zanzibaris had always been a very generous, hospitable, and courteous people; but they soon became selfish since there was not much to share, and each person had to fight to get something for himself and his family. So instead of welcoming others at mealtime and feeling blessed by receiving guests, people hid themselves when it came time to eat.[1]

People also hid themselves in their houses when it came time for political meetings. They would lock themselves inside their homes and pretend not to be there. Unfortunately, if you made a noise or the baby cried, then the Volunteers would come and try to break down the door. The main task of the Volunteers was originally to protect party leaders and to ensure security at public rallies. But because they had little to do, they were given other tasks to perform, like enforcing attendance at meetings and nation-building assignments. They were given the power to arrest whomever they wanted. Mainly ASP Youth League members volunteered for such work; they had more power than the police, and they were despised.

The Youth League also established student committees in all the schools. We teachers had to be very careful about what we said; otherwise, we would be considered enemies of the state, a tool of the sultan and the imperialists. Even among teachers, we had to know whom we could trust if we wanted to speak openly. The committees consisted of students who wanted to show they were always active and vigilant against enemies of the state. They would report a teacher to their district Youth League committee, and from there the matter would be sent to the security forces, who would sometimes come and arrest the teacher. I was never reported, though, because I had a very good rapport with the students and I was very careful; I never said anything critical of the government. I watched my tongue.

It did not take very long to feel disappointed by the new revolutionary government and by all the oppression. I felt angry at the way it treated its own citizens. As students, we had experienced freedom of expression; we could openly criticize the colonial government. Now we could not criticize our own. If someone said there was no salt available, he would be arrested and thrown in jail, given a bag of salt to eat, and told, "Here is salt, so there *is* salt in this country, and you will eat it."

Although more people died in Unguja than in Pemba during the revolution, in the years afterward, the people of Pemba suffered more. We called Rashid Abdalla, our regional commissioner during those years, *Mamba*, meaning crocodile in Swahili. When a mamba eats you, tears come to his eyes, showing his pity as he kills you. Sometimes Mamba would call for a public rally, and if anybody did not attend, the whole village would be punished. Such punishments took place only in Pemba, not in Unguja. The authorities instituted public floggings for the most trivial offenses, for example, if the regional commissioner passed in his car and you did not stand up. After a while, the students in Pemba learned by reflex to stand at attention whenever they saw any car, assuming a party dignitary was passing.

All the colonial *sheha* were terminated, including my father. ASP branch chairmen assumed their administrative duties, and sometimes they would put an entire village under curfew and require every male to go to the marketplace to be flogged, especially if that community formerly supported the ZNP or ZPPP. My own village was once put under curfew, and the police came there and dragged all the men from their homes, including my father. They were led to the school where the police stood in two lines facing each other. Each man was told to pass through the lines, and every policeman beat him with a club or anything that was handy. My father was beaten in this way and afterward was bleeding seriously. Nobody was allowed in or out of the village, so all the beaten men were denied medical treatment. My own brother had to come secretly by canoe to smuggle medicine to my father. Unfortunately, my father never fully recovered from that experience; for him, that was the beginning of years of poor health and sickness.

I asked myself if all these beatings were really the purpose of the revolution. The leaders told us that the revolution was necessary because the colonial government had oppressed and mistreated the people; they said now they were only trying to serve us and to build the nation. But after seeing all these atrocities, I was very disappointed. Zanzibar was once second only to Egypt in Africa in terms of education. We had had specialists in every field; but they were mistreated and abused, and most of them had to leave. How can a qualified medical doctor come to the hospital five minutes late and a political commissar, who has never even been to school, punish him by having him wash dishes? Most left for other countries. In the 1980s, Sultan Qaboos of Oman said frankly that his country had an obligation to help Zanzibar because trained specialists fleeing Zanzibar were the ones who had built Oman and Oman had not spend a single cent on their education. So just imagine: in 1964, we had a ready-made work force the new government never employed for the good of Zanzibar; rather, it was employed for the construction of other countries. Very unfortunate.

We should not just praise the revolution; we should be very critical. I saw the government services deteriorating by the day, and I asked myself, "What kind of a revolution is this?" All the roads in Zanzibar were once very clean and well maintained. Even the public toilets were very clean; you could not see a single fly. Mnazi Mmoja Hospital was one of the best in East Africa. There was a west wing for senior government officials and those who paid, but the other wing was free, and people were never told they had to pay for their drugs themselves. Now look at the hospital: it is filthy—even the bed sheets are dirty. Three or four patients share the same bed. Really, if the revolution has achieved anything, it is only to promote racial differences, disunity, and discrimination.

The revolution abolished the sultanate and established the People's Republic. Once, in a meeting, one of the former presidents of Zanzibar castigated the sultans, the Arabs, and the imperialists and praised the revolutionary government for all the development it had brought. Then one old lady in the back of the crowd asked him politely, "Where are these Arabs? When will they come back? I think they should come back as soon as possible. Under the Arabs, we had a good life; we got whatever we wanted. There were no human rights abuses and no rations. What do we see now? Just hardship." The meeting came to an abrupt end.

At another time, in Pemba, Adullah Said Natepe, a founding member of the Revolutionary Council, was denouncing the Arabs, telling stories of their forcing Africans to climb coconut trees and then using them up there as target practice, or forcing African women to sweep the streets with their bare breasts, or slashing open the bellies of pregnant women. These stories were part of the propaganda given for years in the schools to poison the minds of students. On this particular day, an old man stood up and said, "My son, do you accept that I am older than you, that I can be your father and grandfather?" Natepe answered yes. Then the old man said, "In all my life, I've never witnessed what you have just described, and not even a single elder of mine has ever told me such stories. But what are we witnessing today? People flogged in public, arrested, and never seen again, and a lot of other things. My son, I request that you be true to yourself and not deceive the young people any longer."

After the revolution, all the history books in Zanzibar Town from colonial times were burned. I saw this take place at Lumumba College. The authorities burned mostly colonial publications, especially those that covered the sultans and the real history of Zanzibar. In fact, they completely disregarded history as a subject in the schools. Instead, the late Seif Bakari, chairman of the Youth League, wrote a book used as a textbook in the schools and the youth labor camps. It indoctrinated youth in the philosophy of victimization. The Youth League invented the propaganda that the past was nothing but *dhiki na dhulma:* hardship and injustices. It was all fabricated, the stories that people were treated harshly and enslaved. Yes, there was slavery, but no Shirazi here was ever enslaved. While Africans were enslaved, Arabs were not the only ones involved. These people never mention that it was often Africans chasing and enslaving other Africans, and really, which is the worst sin? And slavery in East Africa was far less atrocious than it was in West Africa. Slavery is wrong, of course; there is no excuse at all for slavery. It is abhorrent and a dark chapter in the history of Zanzibar, of East and West Africa, and elsewhere in the world. But we should not exploit the past now so as to plant seeds of hatred among the population. We should consider slavery a historical event and be aware that it should never be repeated.

This propaganda continues even now. In the 1990s, Omar Mapuri wrote a book about past injustices like slavery in Zanzibar, which made Oman's Sultan Qaboos very angry because it claimed that only Arabs ever owned slaves or enslaved Africans in the region. Sultan Qaboos sent a delegation here to complain to Salmin Amour, then the president of Zanzibar. Salmin welcomed the delegation and said Mapuri was just a troublemaker, that he did not know the real history of the islands, and that he himself, a Shirazi, even had a grandfather who owned slaves.

While I was teaching at Fidel Castro, a colleague of mine beat one of his students very badly. The student was already suffering from fever, and the other students were not happy about the beating. They went secretly at night to stone my colleague's home, which was a very serious incident. The principal came out with his torch and dispersed the students; he then informed the regional commissioner, who wanted to expel all the students. I went personally to see the regional commissioner to say I did not think it would be wise to expel the students since it would mean closing down the entire school. But he was adamant, so I advised the principal to inform the minister of education, Ali Sultan Issa. Ali Sultan paid a visit to the school and spoke to the students, who aired their complaints against the teacher. Finally, he told them this was not the way to deal with their grievances; he gave them a general warning and then closed the file.

During all the time I taught at Fidel Castro, I was still sending out applications to various universities and receiving letters of acceptance, but the government refused to grant me permission to leave. During Karume's time, very few students were sent overseas because he said we had no need of college graduates here in Zanzibar. A Form 6 education was enough, he said. But, really, he wanted to use this opportunity to give his sons senior jobs in the government and to use the public treasury as family property. He gave Amani Karume the job of principal secretary in the ministry of finance, and his second son Ali was posted at the ZSTC, which sold Zanzibari cloves overseas. Karume liked to repeat in his speeches, "We tried to study, but we didn't learn. But we have sought to learn practically, and now we know." By this slogan, he meant that formal education was less important than practical knowledge. After his death, the RC passed a resolution it displayed in every public office, which went something like "Karume has passed away, but we have not forgotten his body, his philosophy, or his thoughts, which will remain with us forever." But now, they have all been forgotten.

Most of my colleagues managed to leave the islands, however, by being smuggled out. It was the only way. After the revolution, one could not even travel between Pemba and Unguja without a permit from the local ASP branch chairman. You had to show that you had a really important reason to travel and that you had already finished all the work needed on your farm. It was even more difficult for any of us to obtain a passport and travel outside the country. You had to undergo a lot of bureaucratic procedures at the local ASP branch, with the district commissioner, regional commissioner, and a special immigration committee organized to scrutinize each applicant. That is the reason many people ran away, because they knew, if they tried to leave legally, they would never manage. They left secretly by boat; unfortunately, between Pemba and Tanga on the mainland, a number of them lost their lives when their boats capsized.

One of my friends, Khalfan Salim Rashid, was publicly flogged until he lost consciousness. Afterward, I heard he left the island. Khamis Juma was another friend and Ali Sultan's cousin, in fact. He rang me once, and we met privately; he told me he was fed up and was leaving. He asked for some money, which I gave, and asked if I wanted to go with him. I said no. He did not tell anyone else he was leaving, just that he was going to visit his sister somewhere. I knew he had left the islands, though, and one week after his disappearance I told his family what had happened.[2]

Many people left, but I said, "No, as long as the country needs my services, I'll stay." Then in 1968, I was transferred from Fidel Castro because, in those days, Ali Muhsin, the junior minister of education, lived in Pemba and one day he noticed a young female teacher, and he fell in love with her. He had a lot of wives already but wanted to marry this one as well. He sometimes came to her school, so he could teach her class; he would ask her to sit down and listen and be impressed. But when he proposed marriage to her, she refused since she was already my girlfriend. In fact, one day I went to visit her in her area of Chanjamjawiri, and on my way back to Fidel Castro, Ali Muhsin gave me a lift in his car. Later, when he came to understand the girl refused him because of me, he told me that my scholarship was ready for an overseas university and that I was needed in Unguja immediately. I traveled to Unguja, hoping I would soon be leaving for overseas studies, but the minister of education at the time, Hassan Nassor Moyo, explained to me that there was no scholarship. Instead, I was assigned to teach again at Lumumba College. Even though Ali Muhsin managed to remove me from Pemba, my girlfriend still refused him and eventually married someone else.

five KARUME THE TERRIBLE

AFTER COMING TO ZANZIBAR TOWN, I got a lot of pressure from my mother to marry one of my cousins. But I resisted, telling her that I should not marry within the family because, if the marriage did not go well, it would provoke quarrels within the family. Secondly, it was not healthy. I had to convince her to allow me to take somebody outside the family. My father was always on my side, saying I had the right to marry a girl of my choice. And after much argument—it took almost a year to convince her—my mother agreed.

At Lumumba, I told my friend Muhammed Said that I was ready to marry a nice and decent girl. He said he would tell his cousins, and they would select someone for me to marry. Eventually, Muhammed informed me that there was a girl I could meet who was well brought up and from a good family. He arranged for us to meet, with Muhammed and his cousins also being present. Her name was Fourtunah Mbamba; she was about twenty-four years old, of Comorian origins, and from Funguni (Malindi) in Zanzibar Town. We talked for less than a half hour, without discussing marriage. She was rather shy, but it was easy for me to talk to her. I just wanted to find out how she looked: I already knew she came from a good family and was of good character, so all that remained was to see how she looked. She was very attractive; she was tall and slim, with a beautiful face.

Afterward, Muhammed asked me what I thought of her, and I said she was all right. His cousins asked Fourtunah whether she was prepared to take me as a husband, and she said yes. The normal practice after that is to send a delegation to the girl's parents; after two weeks, my friends were informed that I had been accepted and also that Fourtunah's family needed a dowry of about five thousand shillings, a lot of money in those days. Usually, you may bargain over the amount, but it is not respectable to do so. The family simply stated the amount, and we agreed.

I had to inform my parents in Pemba that I had found a girl and that I intended to marry her. I explained that she came from a good family and that I sought their blessings. My salary was only 440 shillings a month, so I had to use all my savings and to get contributions from friends and family. When my delegation eventually met the bride's delegation, they handed over the dowry, and her family had a big party. The wedding began with certain religious rites in the mosque, and the next day the bride wore a veil and was escorted by her brother-in-law to a stage in the Municipal Hall, which now houses Television Zanzibar here in Zanzibar Town. She sat waiting for me. I arrived with my best man and uncovered her veil. Our friends and relatives took a lot of photographs, and after a half hour or so, I left with my wife on my arm, and the celebrations continued afterward for about a week. There were many guests and *taarab* music. Comorians like big functions, so it was a big wedding party.

I met Karume only twice, once on the boat to Pemba when I was a student and once when all the teachers at Lumumba and almost all civil servants in Unguja were told to assemble at the port, from where we were told we were to go on a one-day journey. When we reported there, Karume addressed us, informing us that, because the government was bringing so much development, we liked it very much. But there were businessmen in town trying to exploit the country by charging prices that were too high. So he was going to have all of us spend the night on a boat in the harbor and the next day make surprise visits to shops around town. We were given some guidelines and told where to go. We were also told that there were to be no incidents. Each of us had an official letter; when we entered their shops, many of the businessmen were already trembling.

When I first met Karume, he did not seem like the kind of person to take pleasure in another person's suffering. But as they say, dictators are not born—they are made. They surround themselves with people who never criticize and gradually consider themselves superhuman. Or they develop a fear that, if they lose power, they will suffer, so they want to find all means, whether fair or foul, to stay in power.

As a president, Karume was charismatic, ruthless, and whimsical. It all depended on his mood. If he was in a bad mood, everyone was afraid of him. Before approaching him at the State House, people would ask the guards if he was in a good mood. If he was not, they would wait to see him another day; they would avoid him unless they were summoned. He liked to drive his car through town; sometimes if he passed by someone he did not like, he would order his driver to pull over. He would ask the person, "Why are you still outside? Why aren't you in jail?" and order his immediate imprisonment. In prison, a special division was set aside for torture, led by a very notorious officer named Hassan Mandera. He and his colleagues learned their methods in East Germany.

But Karume had another face: generous, kind, and magnanimous. He had a habit of going to the jails every six months, where the prisoners would be paraded before him. Most of the time people sat in prison without any documentation; the prison warden did not even know why the prisoners were there. Karume asked them why they were there, and when they answered that they did not know, he would sometimes announce their release, right then and there. He was very whimsical. He was the law; he was everything. There was an incident just after the revolution when one of the members of the Revolutionary Council, Muhammed Abdallah Kaujore, went to an Indian Ithna-Asheri mosque outside Stone Town and began to fire shots wildly. He killed four persons, injured several others, and got off scot-free. All Karume did was require him to turn over his pistol temporarily. There was no punishment of any kind.

Karume was not educated, but as a younger man, he had traveled a great deal and had ideas for construction. He wanted, for example, to build a ring road around the entire island of Unguja. He was very practical and liked to supervise in the field. Every morning he would be at a construction sight, giving orders. There is a story about how, during the construction of the flats at Kikwajuni, he told the East German experts to make certain design changes, but they answered that his ideas did not meet international architectural standards. Karume responded through an interpreter that we had our own book of standards here in Zanzibar, the Qur'an. The East Germans said it was dangerous to ignore such building standards, but Karume asked them whose side they were on, and they had to give in.

Karume was not a socialist. You never find a socialist amassing wealth or creating a special group by giving them special favors. But he wanted to see that the people had a better life, and he was charismatic; he could at least mobilize the people for nation-building projects.[1] Of course, you had no choice because, if you were a civil servant, your promotion depended on a recommendation by the local ASP branch, a recommendation that depended on how much you made yourself available for voluntary labor.

He was also a person who kept grudges from before the revolution. He did not like Comorians and told them they had to apply for Zanzibari citizenship, no matter how long they had lived in Zanzibar. He told the

Shirazi they had to renounce their Shirazi identity and take that of another tribe. Karume had an inferiority complex and thought the Shirazi regarded themselves as superior. Since he was the boss, since he was the master, he was in control and ready to humiliate them. Many resisted, especially in Pemba; my own father refused to renounce Shirazi identity, saying he would not change until Karume himself came and provided him a new tribe. Nor did I when asked to change my Shirazi identity because the edict was never very well enforced. Only those people who wanted to impress Karume changed their identity.

To an extent, Karume was a racist because, if you read his speeches before independence, he frequently said *"Gozi! Uhuru Zuiiya!,"* meaning that black people should try to stop the drive for independence. And after the revolution, his tendency was to marry Arab women; he only took one African wife and stayed with her only a week before he divorced her. He wanted to feel superior and to order around his Arab wives. It did not matter whether the girl or her parents gave their consent or not. He also encouraged members of the RC to engage in forced marriages with Arab and Asian women. Even though Africans were now masters of the country, they still felt insecure and wanted to demonstrate that they were now dominant and could do what they liked to the other races.[2]

During Karume's time, people had no security in their homes because if they had a beautiful wife or daughter, she could be taken and forced to sleep with a big shot. There was one chap known as Foum, a security officer who drove a special car registered with the license plate KZ1. The people interpreted it as an acronym for "Kuadi [Pimp] Zanzibar Number One." His job was to find a girl every afternoon for Karume, especially an Arab or Asian girl, and bring her to his Kibweni Palace north of town, which had belonged to the former sultans. It did not matter whether she was a virgin or a married woman; the car would pull over as she walked on the street, and Foum would tell the girl to get inside and drive her to Kibweni Palace, whether she liked it or not.[3]

Posterity should know about these things, though nobody usually dares talk about them. Foum approached one woman, for example, whose father the government had killed only a few months earlier. He told her Karume wanted to see her immediately at the State House. She was trembling, fearing for her life. Instead of taking her to the State House, Foum drove her straight to Kibweni Palace. He parked the car and escorted her upstairs, where Karume was seated in a chair. When Karume saw the woman, he immediately pounced on her and tore her *buibui* and her dress, wanting to rape her. The woman thought quickly and said *"Bwana Mkubwa* [Great Master], what do you want? I am your servant;

I am your subject. If you need me, you just need to tell me, and I will come. If you want to make love to me, I will, but I cannot today because I am having my period." Karume listened and told her she would come another day. She said, "Of course, I am prepared to come and satisfy you." And she went away and began to cry.

It was very common in those days for people to hear a knock on the door in the dead of night and to be taken from their homes and never seen again. The government did not kill just the leaders within the ZNP and ZPPP; even some former ASP leaders lost favor and were taken to prison and never seen again. Nobody knows even today where they are buried. Karume did not like people who were educated; he did not trust them, so most of those from the ASP who were imprisoned were educated, like Othman Shariff. Shariff and Karume were rivals within the ASP before independence; after the revolution, Shariff was first appointed minister of education and then Tanzania's ambassador to the United States. It is said that, on a visit to Tanzania, he was seen taking photographs of the State House, and that was enough for the RC to accuse him of being an imperialist stooge and a CIA spy trying to help the Americans take over. The authorities arrested him but released him after Nyerere intervened. He was reduced to serving as a veterinary officer in Iringa on the mainland. Later, some members of the RC were sent to arrest him and bring him back to Zanzibar, but Nyerere intervened again. They eventually convinced Nyerere to hand Shariff over, and once he arrived in Zanzibar, that was the end of him.

Abdallah Kassim Hanga was Russian-educated and very popular among younger ASP members. After the revolution, he was named vice president but, after the union, was transferred to Dar es Salaam. Hanga eventually lost favor with Nyerere because he was very close to Oscar Kambona, Nyerere's minister of foreign affairs and defense. During the Tanganyikan army mutiny of 1964, it was Kambona who went to talk with the soldiers, while Nyerere remained in hiding. After Kambona fell out with Nyerere and went into exile, Hanga lost favor, because he was so close to Kambona. After Hanga was removed from the cabinet, he went to live in Conakry, Guinea, because he had married a Guinean woman. After some time, Nyerere sent a delegation to President Sékou Touré, asking him to convince Hanga to come back to Tanzania, where he would be safe. Unfortunately, when he returned, he was arrested and publicly humiliated. At a rally at Mnazi Moja in Dar es Salaam, Nyerere had Hanga brought there in handcuffs. Nyerere publicly insulted him and then later agreed to send him to Zanzibar, where Hanga was tortured and killed.[4]

The late Saleh Sadaalah was a member of the RC and minister of communications. Karume had a habit of insulting his ministers, and one day Sadaalah was determined that, if Karume insulted him again, he would shoot him. In fact, beforehand he got himself drunk and loaded his pistol but left it on a table while he went to the toilet. His wife found the pistol and saw it was loaded and removed the bullets. When Sadaalah went to the Revolutionary Council meeting and tried to shoot Karume, there were no bullets. The other members pounced, and he was arrested and never seen again.

My brother's friend, Mdungi Ussi, was a regional commissioner when he lost favor with Karume; he was arrested and tortured, going completely blind in the process. Abdulaziz Ali Twala was a member of the RC and minister of health. I am not really clear why he lost favor, but he was also arrested, tortured, and never seen again. There were also many people killed on the pretext that they wanted to overthrow the government. Always the scare was that they were organized from outside the country. There was a group allegedly sent from Mombasa who were brought before a public rally at Maisara where they were denounced. They were sentenced to ten years' imprisonment and condemned to look after the cattle herds of the regime. Later during Jumbe's era, they were killed.

When it comes to human rights, Karume's regime rates very poorly. There was no freedom of expression; all the time you felt as if Big Brother were watching. If you were arrested, you had little hope of obtaining justice. Karume abolished the system of courts established by the British and introduced so-called People's Courts. They were a mockery of justice because most of the magistrates had never gone to school and did not even have an elementary knowledge of the laws of the country. Every magistrate was assisted by two councilors, who together formed a *baraza*. And usually the prosecuting attorney also acted as sort of a lawyer for the defense because Karume despised defense lawyers, saying they were all just liars. He would say, "If they know somebody has stolen something, they'll come to court and say they haven't, so they're liars; and we'll have no liars in our courts."

If a person appeared in court, a prosecuting police officer would read the charge and build up a case against him, and then the accused would be required to say something in his defense. Then the magistrate would instruct the accused to look outside. He would ask the accused what he saw out the window. The man would say he saw people moving around outside, going from place to place. The judge would ask him why they were outside, and the accused would answer he did not know.

"And why are you not out there, with those people?"

"I don't know, your honor."

The judge would then say, "They're outside because they haven't committed an offense, but you have, and that's why you're in here, and that's why I'm sentencing you to six months in prison."[5]

It was like a fairy tale. As I watched these things take place, I felt the revolution was a betrayal of the people.

During Karume's time, especially in the later years, from 1969 to 1972, there were constant shortages, and people were arrested for possessing a tube of Colgate toothpaste. If you were caught owning toothpaste, you were obviously involved in smuggling since that sort of thing was not available in the state shops. It was very different from before the revolution, when everything was available. Depending on your pocket, you could buy anything, but during the revolutionary years, all the shops dried up. The government confiscated some shops and then tried to establish its own, all of which eventually went bankrupt. Instead of a vast array of commodities, all you could find were coconuts, firewood, charcoal, and other locally produced materials.

After Karume took power, we were lucky because we inherited a lot of unsold cloves from colonial times, stored in government warehouses, and the prices internationally were very high. Karume boasted about the government's having a lot of money—when people did not have any food. For one week, a family was rationed to three pounds of rice, one pound of sugar, and two pounds of wheat flour. To get your rations, you had to have a special card, and you could not get that card unless you became an ASP member. Everyone was forced to become a party member and queue up every week for rations. Karume would address public meetings about all this waiting, saying it was a sign of progress since, in developed countries in Europe and other places, they had long lines for different things, so this was a very positive thing for us in Zanzibar.

And then the Youth League committee at Lumumba College forced teachers and students to harvest rice or build new apartment blocks at Michenzani or to line the streets to welcome visiting dignitaries. We had to go; there would be a roll call for every class. If the guest came at about 2:00 p.m., students would begin to line up at 8:00 a.m.; of course, students liked that because classes would be cancelled for the day.

I personally went to the rice fields and to Michenzani.[6] I helped build roads. Government servants reported on alternate Saturdays, and we would work from 7:00 a.m. to 1:00 p.m. At first, I sang revolutionary songs as I worked; I was really enthusiastic because I was doing something for my country. At first, there was a voluntary spirit; people were willing to work together on nation-building projects and came in the hundreds to build a road or new apartments. It was something very exciting, but as the days passed, the enthusiasm slowly dissipated, and then some sort of coercion was necessary. Gradually, morale in the workplace also deteriorated because sometimes a person who had never gone to school would be appointed a political commissar and assume arbitrary powers. People without any qualifications would be promoted over those with experience and ability.

Karume was a charismatic leader and able to mobilize people for nation building, and this is something about his time I do not really regret. But in order to build new apartments, the government demolished many older homes, and even up to now, some people have not been compensated because the distribution of the new flats depended on personal connections and was not fairly decided.

Not only did all the teachers report for work on the weekends, but we marched a group before the president during the annual revolutionary festivals held every January. We spent about three months in preparation for this; starting in October, we trained every day from 3:00 to 6:00 p.m. Trainers from the army drilled us, usually corporals, and they were very rude to us. They would insult us, shouting *goi goi*—meaning "lazy person," or someone who is not smart—and make us run and do push-ups. No respect at all! Even if party leaders went for training, they also had a tough time. They were told, "Here you leave your leadership at the gates. Here you're just a soldier." We accepted the training because we had no choice; there was no resistance. Of course, there were complaints, but you could only whisper to your friends. A few dropped out every year, those with health reasons or those who absconded from the country.

On the final day of the festival, on the anniversary day of the revolution, every one of us would be looking forward to our chance to participate, to be cheered in the stadium as we saluted the president. After all the drilling, I felt some satisfaction at showing my patriotism, and I felt more comradeship with my fellow teachers.

So, in many ways, there was more discipline in Karume's time than today, but it was *nidhamu ya woga,* or discipline emanating from fear.

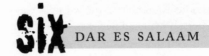

SIX DAR ES SALAAM

WHEN KARUME WAS ASSASSINATED, I was living with my wife in Shangani, near the old post office in Stone Town. On the afternoon of Friday, April 7, 1972, my wife said she was going to visit her brother. I remained at home, preparing my lessons for the next day. Then just after sunset, she came rushing in, telling me shots had been fired at the ASP headquarters where, in the afternoons, Karume played draughts with his colleagues. She said it was not known if he had been shot, but everyone was rushing home. We listened to the radio and heard Aboud Jumbe, minister of state, announcing a curfew and the closure of Zanzibari airspace.

We turned off the lights and looked outside. We saw policemen patrolling in their vehicles. Some members of the Revolutionary Council passed by, like Hassan Nassor Moyo, all of them in a somber mood. The next day Nyerere announced over the radio that Karume had been shot dead and that the burial would take place on the following Monday.

I gathered that most people were happy with the news because at the time the hardship was beyond limits. There was a lot of discontent even within the ASP; people were hungry and suffering from the rationings, and there were many who had disappeared. So there was a feeling of genuine relief in the country. I think the RC sensed this, so, to dampen the enthusiasm and sense of celebration, it began a campaign of arrests, to replace celebration with fear. We began to hear over and over again that so-and-so had been taken away; the news came so often that, on the day of the burial, we lined the streets in a very somber mood as the coffin was taken from the State House to Kisiwandui. Some people were crying, but most, although they were outwardly showing signs of grief, were very happy in their hearts.

The authorities began a house-to-house search of our neighborhood. In this atmosphere of fear, my own neighbor, Mr. Usi Khamis, went to his office one day and did not come back. His wife was worried, and I had to comfort her, saying maybe he was too busy to come home. I looked after their family for a week, and he eventually returned, having been detained and questioned.

One day at Lumumba College a land rover arrived, and a senior inspector walked into the school, asking for me. My principal was a Goan named George Fernandez, and he worried they were coming to arrest me. I already had my toothbrush in my pocket, which everyone carried around in those days in case of arrest. I said my last good-byes to all my teacher colleagues, but the visitor turned out to be only a relative of mine checking up on me. I told him never to come to the school again because he caused such panic among the teachers.

It is still an enigma to me who was behind Karume's assassination. Definitely, it was Colonel Humoud who pulled the trigger, but he could not have acted independently. Former members of the Umma Party were arrested, brought to trial, and sentenced to death for organizing the conspiracy to kill Karume. But after the assassination, Ali Mafoudh, a former Umma leader and army officer, was briefly in charge of the government, when the entire Revolutionary Council was paralyzed. So that is another question: here Ali Mafoudh could have taken over the government but did not; instead, he was at the forefront of those hunting down the conspirators, his former comrades.

Some people think that Nyerere was using Babu and Umma to eliminate Karume because it was well known that he and Karume were not on the best of terms. Karume even said in some of his speeches that he had a different vision of the union than did Nyerere, that he saw it as something temporary, to last maybe ten years. I heard those speeches myself. Around 1971, he uttered the following words: "What is the union? It is like a coat; if you feel it's too tight, you just take it off." Of course, those speeches are not played now. Karume said publicly that we should keep cannons on Chumbe Island to guard Zanzibar against the mainland.

When Nyerere announced the Arusha Declaration, one of the requirements was for all politicians and civil servants to declare their properties. Yet Karume said in a speech that the Arusha Declaration was not for Zanzibaris. "We in Zanzibar have to think of our leaders' future," he said. Karume was also planning on having a separate currency for Zanzibar, different from that of the mainland. In fact, preparations had gone very far but were undertaken very confidentially. There was a councilor in the Tanzanian High Commission in London named Omar Zahran who was from Zanzibar and had the task of preparing a new currency.

So it is a well-known fact the two leaders were not on good terms and that Karume was suspected of preparing to break the union—hence, the theory that Nyerere used Umma comrades to assassinate Karume. It is still an enigma, however; one thing I can say for certain is that with Karume's death there was a tangible sense of relief in the country, even within the ASP. A power struggle then ensued within the ruling party, with Seif Bakari, chairman of the Youth League, claiming to be Karume's natural heir. It was Nyerere's influence, however, that prevailed. He wanted Aboud Jumbe as Karume's successor because Jumbe was educated and was not likely to commit so many atrocities. When I heard the news of Jumbe's selection, I was very hopeful that now Zanzibar would begin to see some changes. Jumbe was the only one on the RC at the time who possessed some university education. I knew him personally from when he was my teacher, and sometimes I wondered how he managed to survive the Karume years when nearly all the other educated people in government were either moved to Dar es Salaam or eliminated. For anything that needed writing, Karume depended on Jumbe's assistance. I think he survived all those years because he was a drunkard; he was not much of a threat to Karume.

It was obvious, however, that some people like Seif Bakari did not respect Jumbe as president and were not happy with the new circumstances. There was an incident when Jumbe was driving to the airport and met Bakari's car along the way. The two cars stopped, and everyone was surprised to see Jumbe get out of his car to greet Seif Bakari, rather than the other way around. Nyerere did not want Jumbe to have any difficulties, so later he arranged for Bakari's appointment as deputy minister for defense in the union government, to remove him from Zanzibar.

I was hopeful for changes under Jumbe's administration, although I knew instituting change would require a lot of courage, diplomacy, and persuasion. When after only three or four months several Zanzibaris, including me, were sent to the University of Dar es Salaam, I became even more hopeful. Jumbe decided it was time to send people outside for higher education, and I finally got the chance to attend the university. For this, I will always thank Jumbe. I studied political science, public administration, and international relations, and after three years, I graduated with flying colors. I found the habit of studying had not died in me since, as a teacher, I had been forced to read and prepare my lessons. During my last series of exams, I was actually hospitalized for about three months for chronic back pain, so I took my final exam in the hospital. I was still able to earn a first-class degree, with honors, and was even informed that I had earned the highest test results in the history of the university until that time.

There were twelve of us in that first group from Zanzibar, no women, only men. All of us did very well except one person who suffered a mental breakdown a month before his exams. I was the leader, and we established our own Zanzibari Club, which met every evening after dinner under a special tree, where we exchanged ideas and any news we had heard from home. We would stay there for about an hour and then return to our various residential blocks. We also had a study group; if someone was good at a certain topic, he would be given an assignment to do additional research and then report back to the group. We organized a schedule of lectures among ourselves, and our instructors liked us a great deal. John Chiligati was very intelligent, hardworking, and helpful; he brought lecture notes to my hospital bed and discussed everything with me, for which I was very grateful.

When I began at the university, I immediately felt free; it was a tangible feeling among all of us that Big Brother was no longer watching. Among our group, there were some who appeared to be staunch Karume supporters, like Juma Duni Haji, for instance, formerly chairman of the Youth League branch at Lumumba College. But even he had his misgivings about Karume's dictatorial rule. All of us praised Nyerere for allowing freedom of expression at the university. Even in government meetings, he would have his own position but would allow others to speak their minds. At the end, he would summarize the discussion and then go ahead with his own ideas.

Because ours was the first group from Zanzibar, Jumbe was very interested in our progress. There was one lecturer named Dr. Ishau Abdallah Khamis who had good relations with Jumbe and would sometimes bring us messages from the president, wanting our views on a number of things. We would discuss the issue among ourselves and then write down our views and present them to Dr. Khamis. In this way we were very favored.

Aside from our Zanzibari Club, I was also a member and eventually president of the Muslim Students Association of the University of Dar es Salaam [MSAUD]. In those days, in comparison to the Christians, there were very few Muslims at the university. This was one reason for MSAUD: a minority must always look after its interests through such associations. On the other hand, there was no hostility between Muslims and Christians, and you could hardly distinguish who was Muslim and who was Christian, except during prayer times. At the time, I did not think Muslims were a disadvantaged community in Tanzania. We did not differentiate so much according to belief and did not sense any favoritism from the lecturers based on religion.

We mainly focused on bringing Muslim students together and organizing lectures by respected Muslim scholars. We discussed our interests with the university administration. We asked that no classes be scheduled during Friday prayers and that, during Ramadhan, special arrangements be made to have our food served before sunrise and after sunset. The administration was very willing to work with us on these matters.

My most formative years intellectually were at the university. I read a lot and was able to compare political systems and philosophies. At the time, the university was very leftist, and most of the students and lecturers thought socialism was the way of the future. The famous Dr. Walter Rodney was very popular; he was a firebrand socialist whose specialization was colonialism. He would explain to us how the Europeans had exploited the colonies, especially in Africa. To a certain extent, he was right: even today African countries only export raw materials, while the processing and manufacturing occur overseas. Rodney tried to show that socialism was the only solution for Africa's economic problems and praised Nyerere a lot for his theories.

The lecturer I liked and admired the most, however, was Goran Hyden because he appeared more realistic than the other ideologues, who were generally far removed from what really happened on the ground. Hyden's analysis was more relevant to the Tanzanian situation. He always matched theory with practice and made comparisons between European and third-world countries. I learned that, in contrast to the developed world, we in the third world often have "soft" states. We may have very good laws, but they are not implemented, allowing some people to live above the law, while in the developed world, the law is the law; it applies to all, exempting no one.

At the university, we read comparative philosophy, authors like Plato and Machiavelli, for example. We were free to make up our own minds, and I thought, naturally, that socialism was not the solution to the problems facing Tanzania. As a Zanzibari, I had a unique perspective because the others often only knew about socialism from propaganda and brainwashing. At least, I had some tools and concrete examples with which to analyze. Not only had I experienced a form of socialism while living under Karume's regime, I also had gone to stay in a village in the Iringa Region during the long vacation after my first year of university studies. I worked with a company constructing a hydroelectric dam at Mtera. During that summer, I came into contact with the realities of "villagization," Nyerere's plan to compel all peasants to adopt socialism. I saw how the villagers lived, how villagization restricted the capabilities of the people, and how the plan generally inhibited rather than promoted rural development. Very little was harvested on the communal farms, and all the proceeds went to the village chairman. From that experience, I had a lot of misgivings about socialism on the mainland as well as in Zanzibar.

As a student, I participated in debates for and against socialism. Yoweri Museveni was there, the future president of Uganda, though he was ahead of me by two years. Haroub Othman and Issa Shivji were also there, who were both young lecturers at the time. I sometimes played the devil's advocate, arguing against socialism, saying that it was good in theory but not in practice, that it was just a grandiose idea, incapable of bringing about the required changes. I would say that if socialism was so egalitarian, then why did members of the Soviet politburo have special roads and other services for their own exclusive use? If socialism worked, then how was it that a country like the Soviet Union, with so many natural resources, was far less developed than the U.S.? The most telling example was that of East and West Germany; it was clear the West was more developed, so something was missing in socialism.

Most of the students were carried along with the tide and went along with socialism. I would air views that were not of the majority and was told to be careful since the teachers might not be happy with what I had to say and label me an imperialist stooge. It was true that some of the teachers, when it came time for examinations, would penalize a student if he had articulated antisocialist ideas. Yet I was not a convinced socialist and did not even like to employ terms like *capitalism, socialism,* and *imperialism*; all these *isms* did not appeal to me at all. I simply wanted to see a system established in Zanzibar that was just and fair. I became a pragmatist who believed in the need to respect human rights, the rule of law, democracy, and complete transparency in the administration of public affairs.

I studied French at the university, and a group of us were eventually able to travel to France, to Lille just north of Paris, to take further language courses for three months at the University of Lille. This was my first trip abroad, and I was very excited. Before we left Lille, we arranged a farewell party for ourselves in my room. There were twelve of us in the group: eight men and four women. I did not know their reasoning at the time, but later I realized they were trying to get me to drink. They bought a lot of wine, and there was music and women; of course, eventually they managed to get me to drink. Though I ended up drinking more than the others, everyone except me got drunk that night. They all fell asleep in my room, and I had to take the key out of the pocket of another student to sleep in his bed.

After the course in Lille, I wanted to see London and visit my brother-in-law who lived there. I went by boat from Calais, but on the way, I somehow lost my passport and was taken to one of the detention centers in Dover. The wardens were very nice, I had a television in my room, and the diet was very good. The wardens would come to my room and talk to me very politely and bring me things to read. In the afternoons, the officials at the center took me around Dover and showed me the castles and all the interesting places of the town. This was my first experience in England: being detained. On Monday, the Tanzanian high commissioner in London contacted the center, and the wardens freed me immediately. They apologized for my detention, but I said, "No, thank you. I enjoyed my stay here." The difference could not have been more dramatic between detention in Dover and in Zanzibar, as I was later to discover.

In London, I was very impressed by the hustle around me, the crowds going here and there. There was a very different pace of life than where I was from. The tall buildings, the traffic, and the nightclubs were all new to me. My brother-in-law Abdallah Saleh Mbamba knew London inside and out and took me to see the nightlife and to dance, though I never took alcohol. We went to SoHo and all over London; I met a lot of other Zanzibaris because Abdallah was very well known. I stayed in London for two weeks and enjoyed the atmosphere very much, then returned to France and stayed in Paris for a few days with my brother's friend, a counselor in the Tanzanian embassy. I attended several diplomatic parties, where we discussed African affairs. What impressed me most there was that real life began at 10:00 p.m., after all the working people had rested and were out again on the Champs-Elysées.

seven SERVING THE REVOLUTION

IN 1972, MY WIFE FOURTUNAH
gave birth to Saadia, our first and only daughter, when I was just beginning at the university. Three years later, after my return to Zanzibar, we
quarreled, and I divorced her. In Zanzibar, all a man needs to do to divorce his wife is to pronounce to her the words, "I divorce you." It is even
more authentic if the words are put in writing. If not, it is better that the
words are pronounced before a witness or witnesses. After our quarrel,
I thought there was no chance we could ever make up, so I wrote in a
letter that, from that day forward, I divorced my wife, without actually
telling her so in person. I then went to her parents, but, unfortunately,
her brother was not there, so I could not deliver the letter. I came home
and continued to stay with my wife, without telling her that I had divorced her. We did not sleep together.

The first person whom I informed about my decision was my brother,
the late Hamad Sharif Hamad. He asked if I was serious. I said yes and
explained why. He said, "I know you love her, so can you really let her
go?" I said that I had made up my mind. When Fourtunah's brother returned, I went to him and said I was very thankful for how his family had
received me in their home and that I still considered myself one of their
family. Finally, I gave him the letter of divorce. Because we did it this way,
I am still close to Fourtunah's family, and there has always been good will
between her relatives and me. Her brother was at first very upset, but he
accepted my decision. Then I went back home and brought the bad news
to my wife, that I had divorced her twelve days previously. She cried, she
really cried, but I had already divorced her. Fortunately, her family home
was not far away, so I took her there. The next day some of her family
members came to collect her belongings. I was also very sad because my
daughter came every day and asked why we were living separately and
why I was cooking for myself. She kept asking why we had separated.

In fact, a lot of people asked me to remarry Fourtunah, but I gave them all very polite answers, saying no. One respectable sheikh called on me, and after some discussion, he said, "I have come to ask you something that is very private." He recited some verses from the Qur'an, and some *hadith* from the Holy Prophet. There is one that says one thing permitted by God but which he hates is divorce. I said, "Sheikh, I respect you very much. My request is that you not ask me to do something that by my refusing would be disrespectful to you. I want to continue respecting you, please." And he understood.

One good thing is that I continue to have very good relations with Fourtunah and her family. We agreed that we should not live in enmity, which is not usually the case when there is a divorce; usually there is much bitterness. But if her family has a celebration or a funeral, I go and participate. When in 1976 she married someone else, I was invited to the wedding; I went and helped serve food to the guests. Everyone was surprised.

I took my second wife in 1977 when I had already been appointed minister of education. I was appointed in February, and I married in September. I told my sister-in-law that I was looking for a wife and that I wanted a woman from Pemba, not Unguja, because I thought a woman from Pemba would be more responsible, honest, and trustworthy. Of course, it also depends on her family and upbringing. My brother's wife said she had a neighbor with a daughter teaching at the Fidel Castro Secondary School in Pemba, where I once taught, so, as a minister, I paid her school a visit. I did not explain the real purpose of my arrival, but I knew what I wanted. All the teachers were introduced to me; she stood up with the rest and said her name. We did not exchange a word, but I later informed my sister-in-law that I wanted to marry the girl. She asked her friends if the girl would accept, and eventually I received the news that, yes, I was accepted.

I never actually spoke to the young woman until after the wedding because others handled all the arrangements. There was not a lot of fanfare or a huge celebration of the wedding; there were just the religious rites. Of course, many people were invited to the mosque and to my in-laws' house afterward, but the celebration was nothing like the first wedding. That was how I married Aweinah Sanani Massoud. She was only nineteen years old and came from a very good family in Wete. We have three daughters together; the first was born in 1979 and is named Time, my mother's name. The second was born in 1981 and is called Salma, the name of my wife's mother. The third, Shariffa, was born in 1985. In my difficult times, my wife has very ably assumed responsibility for rearing our three daughters and has shown patience and understanding when I have stayed away from home for days, weeks, or even months serving the people of Tanzania. She has never complained even in the most difficult times.

Because of my performance as a student in Dar es Salaam, the university authorities asked the Zanzibari government to allow me to pursue a master's degree and be employed as a lecturer. The Ministry of Education refused to let me continue, however, saying it needed me very badly back in Zanzibar. I was posted to the Nkrumah Teacher Training College, but before I took up the new appointment, I received a message that my father was sick in Pemba. I obtained permission to go home to stay with him. One day during this leave, a policeman arrived and gave me a note from the regional commissioner. The note included an air ticket and informed me that President Aboud Jumbe wanted to meet me the following day in Tanga on the mainland. Since by that time my father was recovering from his illness, I went, not knowing why I was summoned.

I waited for Jumbe in Tanga at a state-owned lodge. At sunset, the presidential convoy arrived. Jumbe said his prayers and then called me to the lounge on the first floor. He spoke to me using very few words. He said, "From today, you're in my office." He made me his personal assistant, and when we came back to Zanzibar, I was given an office at the State House and one at the ASP headquarters in Kisiwandui.

I served as Jumbe's personal assistant until 1977. I wrote his speeches, but since one of Jumbe's weaknesses was his habit of changing his mind from time to time, I learned to present his speeches to him the day before he was to speak because, otherwise, he would call for multiple rewrites. Another of my tasks was to do research on the relations between Zanzibar and the union. A group of soldiers in the army had been given the task already, but their text included many mistakes. I found most of what they reported was nonsense because they had not been trained to do research and had no analytical skills.

Another of my tasks was to help turn Beit el Ajaib, the palace built on Zanzibar Town's waterfront by Sultan Barghash in the 1880s and later used by the British as their main administrative building, into an ASP history museum. Jumbe deliberately chose this former palace as part of a psychological strategy to show the permanence of the revolution. The same building that was once a symbol of the sultans and colonial rule could now serve as a museum of ASP rule. I worked with some experts from North Korea, about ten in all. We worked very hard because there was a time limit: the museum was supposed to open for the twenty-year anniversary celebrations of the ASP's founding. Jumbe came to inspect and gave all kinds of last-minute directives, so I spent the whole night there. After finishing everything, I left Beit al Ajaib at eight in the morning. Since the formal opening was scheduled for 10:00 a.m., all I could do was just go home, take a bath, and return. Jumbe, however, was very impressed and in his speech thanked us, saying here were people who, when given orders, implemented them on time.

The ASP museum's exhibition started with the party's history from its first meetings and showed how it had evolved in later years. The North Koreans painted historical murals. The museum included photographs of revolutionaries, some of the weapons they used, and various images of recent economic developments. The exhibits claimed that the revolution had brought advances in education, housing, and roads. As you entered, there was also a life-size photograph of Karume and the car he used to drive. We painted revolutionary slogans on the walls, such as *mapinduzi daima* [revolution forever], or something of that sort.

The Youth League would send ideological classes to the museum, or state guests would be taken there. After Karume's death, the government also built monuments to his memory, in Kisiwandui, at the Bwawani Hotel, and at the Pemba airport. The authorities built a house in Mwera, in a subvillage known as Kiongoni, where they claimed Karume was born in 1904. They put various common household utensils on display and even put a bed in the house, pretending that was where Karume was born. The late Maulidi Makame, who later became minister of health and one of my colleagues in the political struggle, was assigned the task of writing Karume's life history. In his research, he discovered that, although the party had always claimed Karume had attended school in Mwera until Standard 4, the school was not, in fact, established there until 1928, when Karume was twenty-four years old. When this news reached Jumbe, he said that the whole project should be abandoned. Everybody knew, anyway, that Karume was not born in Mwera or anywhere else in Zanzibar. Some think he was born in Malawi, others in eastern Congo.

On the morning of February 27, 1977, I was told I was required at the State House at 10:00 a.m. I rode my bicycle there and was led to a lounge and seated in a row with ministers and members of the Revolutionary Council. I asked someone if there was a mistake because I was only a clerk. He said there was no mistake; that is when it occurred to me that maybe I was being called to be a minister. At exactly 10 a.m., Jumbe arrived and said he had decided to reshuffle the RC. He read out the new appointments, announcing I was now the minister of education. That very day, the former minister of education, Tawakali Khamis, introduced me to his senior staff and handed his responsibilities over to me. I told the staff members that I would be relying on them and that my office door would always be open if they had any questions or concerns. There would be no protocol.

Many people congratulated me, but that night as I visited my sister-in-law, the late Mrs. Fatma Abdallah Totty, I began to cry a little. I knew the task was too big for me because there were problems in every corner of the ministry. The buildings were very old and dilapidated; there were no desks, no trained teachers, and no books. I said it was an impossible task, and I prayed to God to help me. I was really sad because I had not been consulted, and in the political atmosphere of the time, if you refused an appointment, you could be victimized. It was just something imposed on you. I would have been very pleased to continue with what I was already doing, but, nevertheless, I accepted the job wholeheartedly, saying I would try my best.

At first, there was no discipline in the ministry; people came to work whenever they wanted. I made a point of being at my desk at 7:00 a.m. and staying until 3:00 p.m., though the day officially ended at 2:30. After one week, the senior staff began to follow my example, and through our efforts, the discipline of the entire staff improved. In fact, I am happy to say that I received very positive cooperation from the staff and the teachers in general because I knew the first task was to try to fight for better salaries, a very popular move. I also made sure supplies and equipment were evenly distributed between schools in Unguja and Pemba. In fact, I spent a lot of time visiting the schools and discussing their needs; many teachers, parents, and students thought that, for the first time, they had somebody who was really concerned.

After the revolution, the government had allocated secondary-school openings according to the student's ethnic group. I wanted to change this policy to one based on merit. I first had to convince the president, and after that, I prepared a paper for the RC. There was a great deal of opposition, especially from the old guard, from people like Seif Bakari, Abdullah Said Natepe, and Hamid Ameir. But the younger members backed the paper and argued in its favor. We carried the day since what mattered most was the backing of the president himself.

The ministry sent out a circular that announced that students would be promoted to secondary school based on merit, which encouraged both teachers and students. I also tried to secure as many university scholarships as I could for Zanzibari students. I went to speak to Nicholas Kuhanga, the minister of education on the mainland, and the university authorities. We agreed the university would accept a special quota every year of students from Zanzibar, even if their grades were lower than those of some students on the mainland. We felt this policy was justified in light of how Zanzibari students had in the past been deprived of educational opportunities. There was a policy at the time for the distribution of imported commodities like rice—40 percent to Pemba and 60 percent to Unguja. I recommended that this policy be extended to university scholarships. It is unfortunate, however, that while students from Pemba completed their quota, those from Unguja did not. So, when necessary, we filled the quota with students from Pemba.

During my first year as minister, I noticed that, over the previous three years, the capital budget for education was only about five-hundred thousand shillings per annum, the equivalent of twenty-five thousand British pounds at the time. In light of the conditions in which I found the school buildings, most of which needed rehabilitation, I asked for capital expenditure to be raised to 2.5 million shillings. This sum did not include recurrent expenditure. Jumbe was clearly not happy with our request; in a meeting of the RC, he began to shout at us, saying, "There are some people here who are like women, who only like to spend money." I grew very angry and felt his criticisms were unfair. I was fuming and ready to respond, but an old man, the late Mzee Hamdan Muhiddin, restrained me, pulling me back into my seat. I was very young and emotional and did not care if I was thrown in prison. Later in the afternoon, I took my copy of the budget proposal and drove to Jumbe's official residence.

I asked his bodyguards for access, and Jumbe agreed to see me. He was quite jovial at first, asking what had brought me there. I said, "Maalim, when you appointed me to this ministry, you didn't consult with me to know whether I'd accept or not. Out of respect for you, I wholeheartedly accepted, determined to help you and to serve the country. You know the condition of education in Zanzibar; you know how much it has deteriorated. So when I asked for this money, which is not even enough, I did so with the intention to see progress that would earn praise for you and your government, and not for me. I asked for the sole purpose of improving school facilities, but for my efforts I only got insults, which I cannot stomach. So I've come to tender my resignation. And I'd be very appreciative if you'd relieve me of this responsibility, sir."

I was looking at him directly in the eyes for his response. He was in one of his better moods and looked at me and began to laugh and said, "Take it easy, Seif." He asked me to leave my budget proposals with him. The next day at a meeting in the State House, he was very dramatic. While the officials were taking their seats, he instructed a policeman to bring the minister of education immediately. He seemed very angry, and everybody was worried, thinking I would go to jail. When I arrived, everybody avoided my eyes. Jumbe asked how much I wanted for the ministry, and I told him how much; he immediately told the chairman of the finance committee to give me what I requested. President Jumbe had the habit of publicly criticizing his own ministers, even before television cameras, but, for me, that was the first and last time he ever did so.

If Karume had an idea, he would follow its implementation until the end. Jumbe always had new ideas and would want to start a new project, but then not follow through. He would call a meeting and explain his ideas, but after a month or so, he would come up with something new. Another of Jumbe's weaknesses was bringing uneducated people into the government because he was afraid of being accused by the old guard of embracing the educated and ignoring the rest, who for years had been the backbone of ASP support. Nor did I think Jumbe's economic policies were very wise. Many fault him for having inherited a lot of money from Karume and for not investing it properly. When Karume died, our reserves amounted to more than six-hundred million Tanzanian shillings, the equivalent of about $50,000,000, or about $100 per Zanzibari citizen. This was one of the largest government reserves on a per capita basis anywhere in the developing world, which Jumbe squandered in various grandiose projects. For example, the Bububu Road, which seemed a good idea at the time, was unfortunately not made with the future in mind; it could have been built much wider than it was, at almost the same cost. When the government constructed barracks for the army, the original design was to build homes without toilet facilities, and so the builders had to go back and construct toilets later on.

When Jumbe had his ideas, it was really difficult to persuade him of anything else. There was a proposal from the mainland once that the reserves of the two governments be kept in the same account, which would be subdivided into accounts A and B. At the time, our reserves were much greater than those of the mainland, so the majority of the RC was suspicious, thinking it was a trick to steal our money. Jumbe insisted, however. We only deposited a portion of our reserves as an experiment. After a few months, when the government needed those funds, the bank informed us they had already been spent by the mainland. We said to Jumbe, "Didn't we tell you so?"

The Revolutionary Council was also divided over the question of bringing electricity from the mainland. Some of us did not support the idea, feeling it would make us too dependent. We did not want to pay to lay cables across the sea channel when Zanzibar had just ordered and paid for a number of generators, which were on their way from London. They would have provided enough electricity for both islands. We asked, "Why should we join with the mainland, when we have our own source of energy here?" But Jumbe insisted, saying it would not be economical to run the generators ourselves because we would have to maintain them and buy the fuel ourselves. In fact, the generators were actually delivered and one or two installed at Mtoni to serve as a standby. Two were sent to Pemba, and the remainder went to the mainland. And just as we predicted, we are now totally dependent on the mainland for our energy: now TANESCO [the Tanzania Electric Supply Company] can cut Unguja off anytime it wishes. Plans are now under way to connect Pemba to the Tanzanian national grid and make all Zanzibar dependent on the mainland for its electricity.

There have also been accusations that, under Jumbe, corrupt practices increased and that he allowed this to take place. Jumbe, for example, wanted to buy a presidential jet. Most in the RC opposed the idea; when it was first brought up for discussion, Jumbe could see the general mood and did not push the matter further. But he later told the RC's Economic Committee that it was necessary for the president to have his own plane and that if it was not bought now, the price would go up in the future. Under pressure, the members approved the purchase; the jet cost more than building five well-equipped secondary schools. In 1996, the wife of President Salmin Amour flew the jet to Mbeya on the mainland to collect hay for her cattle. It was somehow damaged there, sent to London for maintenance, and never seen again.

After he purchased the jet, Jumbe was often absent from Zanzibar. He would stay on the mainland and visit eight regions in one trip. He would move around with government files, and some of them were lost. He would order ministers in Zanzibar to meet him on the mainland; sometimes, because he moved so fast, they had to follow him all over the mainland, trying to catch him. Once when he called me to the mainland, I rushed to see him in Kibaha. After waiting some time for him to finish his prayers, he came downstairs and asked why he had called me to see him. I replied I did not know, and then he told me to return to Zanzibar since he could not remember himself why he had summoned me.

Of course, Jumbe was not a complete failure. When he became president, he abandoned drinking; he became very pious and religious. He built a mosque within the State House grounds and went on pilgrimage to Mecca many times. He was repenting for what he did when he was young.

Jumbe also made a habit of regularly going to Pemba and staying there several days. He wanted to see that something was done for Pemba. One time he was visiting Wete and asked for some ginger ale. His assistants told him they had forgotten to pack his favorite drink, so they sent a plane to Unguja to collect ginger ale, at a time in Wete when people had no clean drinking water. Eventually, however, Pemba under Jumbe had a new airport, roads in urban areas were reconstructed, and streetlights were installed. He brought more balance between the two islands in terms of government investment. Under Jumbe also, the commodities brought from overseas were now distributed according to population percentages; Pembans received 40 percent of food imports, for example, whereas before they had received only 20 percent, or even less. Jumbe also made a major reshuffle in 1977 in the cabinet and Revolutionary Council, appointing young blood as ministers. Before there had been only one man from Pemba in the RC, out of thirty-two. When Jumbe brought some Pembans into the government, he angered some members of the RC who thought he had gone too far.

Jumbe also tried very hard to end the law of the jungle in the islands and to institute the rule of law. This was very difficult because he faced serious opposition. In the initial years, many were killed, but gradually the atrocities began to disappear. Slowly and surely, with the advice of Nyerere, the human rights situation improved. The so-called Old Guard was very powerful; they were like warlords who, under Karume, had the right to do whatever they pleased. In my opinion, Seif Bakari was the most evil one of them all. He was a very short and stocky chap who had worked as a tailor before the revolution, but afterward Karume gave him a free hand to do whatever he wished. He was a very dangerous man, notorious for having no mercy on his victims.

Jumbe insisted there should be no arbitrary arrests, and gradually the general atmosphere eased. People were able now to move about and at least to whisper to each other, criticizing the government. Forced marriages ended, and forced labor also disappeared. The sense of voluntary service and nation building gradually eroded and was no longer imposed by force, except on young people. One institution that Jumbe established was the JKU, or *Jeshi la Kujenga Uchumi* in Swahili, modeled after the JKT [*Jeshi la Kujenga Tanzania*] on the mainland. It was a form of national service compulsory for a student who had completed Form 3 or 4 who wanted to find government employment or pursue higher education. Those who joined the JKU faced a lot of hardships: temporary dwellings, no beds or mattresses, poor food, hard agricultural work, and military training. Those who did not go into the JKU could earn only 144 shillings a month, which was counted as their national service.[1]

Jumbe ended the food rationing, but there were still constant shortages due to government mismanagement. Jumbe also dramatically curtailed the influence of the Youth League. It was still considered part of the party but mainly as a training ground for future leaders. It was not as active as in Karume's time. The Volunteers still operated but with less enthusiasm. They arrested young people in Zanzibar Town who wore very narrow trousers or bell-bottoms or who had large hair. Young people got these fashion ideas from the mainland or from cinema. I remember that Nyerere was once asked about the campaign against Western fashions. He responded that he did not see the fuss; it was a matter of fashion, and fashions came and went. But the Volunteers, many of them brought over from Pemba because they were seen as no-nonsense people, detained people wearing these clothes. When some youth resisted, there was fighting in the streets.[2]

I personally thought it a waste of time to punish these people. Young people have to be up to date, and they like to dress like the youth in other countries. Instead of chasing youth through the streets, the Volunteers could have been used for nation-building projects. But the party said the Volunteers arrested people because Zanzibar was experiencing a cultural revolution. As part of this revolution, Karume had once banned all *taarab* love songs in the islands. And in order to make our culture more African, Jumbe tried to introduce dances from the mainland. He paid for a mainlander known as Kinati to go around to the schools to teach students how to dance and to sing in political choirs, praising the revolution and party leaders. There was much criticism of this because it was not part of Zanzibari culture. Traditional Zanzibari dances do not involve a lot of movement, but Jumbe wanted to bring in *ngoma* from the mainland that require students to really move and sweat. Many parents complained when they heard about all the time spent on *ngoma* in the schools, but Jumbe insisted because he thought these dances were more African.

Another thing introduced during Jumbe's time was *halaiki,* a Swahili word meaning a large crowd. It referred to the huge flag demonstrations and other mass spectacles that took place every year in January during the revolutionary festivals. Training in *halaiki* lasted three to four months prior to each festival and involved thousands of students and teachers. It was no wonder standards of education declined: all the students were sent to Amaani Stadium every day in the morning until the afternoon to practice *halaiki.* They spelled out words with colored cards, like

TANGANYIKA ZANZIBAR TANZANIA, or MIAKA ISHIRINI YA MAPINDUZI, meaning twenty years of revolution.

We imported Chinese and North Korean experts for this purpose. We definitely copied *halaiki* from China, though I cannot say exactly who initiated the idea. We had a few hundred Chinese experts in Zanzibar in those days. They worked on the rice farms, in the hospital, and in the army. They never wore suits, just Mao shirts with no collars. They kept to themselves and always moved around in groups. Some Zanzibaris praised the Chinese for being good workers, but mostly we did not bother ourselves about them because they kept to themselves. I heard about the wonderful Chairman Mao Tse-tung with his *Little Red Book,* which I never read. My image of China in those days was of a country where the people all looked alike and of a country that sent us commodities of poor quality.

So, for a few years, I marched at the revolutionary festivals with the other teachers. Then, when I went into government, I sat up with the other *waheshimiwa* [honored ones], and I felt patriotic because it was our national day. Most of the students liked training for *halaiki;* they liked the different colored uniforms and often preferred to play rather than to study. To perform for the president made them proud. When they performed well on the festival day, they were cheered. Some ordinary Zanzibaris thought *halaiki* was good, but many thought it a waste because the shows consumed money that could have been used for books and laboratory equipment. For one day's *halaiki,* the government would spend countless hours and millions of shillings. *Halaiki* died out around 1982, and all the Chinese experts were sent home.

 eight ASCENDANCY

IN 1975, NYERERE SUGGESTED IT was time to merge the two ruling parties, the ASP and the TANU, into one for the entire union. He probably thought that, since the hardships were so great on the islands, Zanzibaris would support the move. Life was much better on the mainland at the time than it was in Zanzibar. Jumbe did not immediately refuse or accept the offer. He was clever: he said that ASP members would consider the proposal and make the final decision. Every party branch would be required to discuss the proposal. The idea was overwhelmingly popular in the branches because almost everybody felt it would bring about better conditions in Zanzibar.

I was not very enthusiastic about the merger because, in an environment wherein the party was supreme, Zanzibar would lose some of its autonomy. Final decisions on certain matters would now be made by the national party executive, dominated by the mainland. Yet my sense is that, if at that particular time Nyerere had sought to establish a single unitary government, a majority in the islands would have voted for the idea because of the hardships here. People were hungry; if you were found with a bar of Lux soap, you would be arrested. People were ready for a change, even if it meant a loss of autonomy.

So the proposal was approved on the branch and district levels, and when it went before the RC and the ASP's National Executive Committee, it was reluctantly approved. A constitution was written and adopted for the new party, which was known as *Chama Cha Mapinduzi* [Party of Revolution], or CCM. The official merger of the two parties was scheduled for the ASP's twentieth anniversary celebrations in February 1977. On that day, there were grand ceremonies in Amaani Stadium. The new CCM flag was raised to replace the lowered ASP and TANU flags. People jumped up and down and were very happy. They sang a song saying goodbye to the ASP, "not because you failed us, but because of the new need to strengthen unity within the country." They believed CCM would do away with all the bad things associated with the TANU and the ASP and preserve whatever was good. In his speech, Nyerere said he was very moved by the people's enthusiasm.[1]

Following the merger, there were elections for a new CCM national leadership. I was informed that I should fill out forms to compete for a position on the CCM Central Committee. I said I was not interested. I was told, "Whether you are or not, these are your instructions." As candidates, we had also to appear before the CCM National Executive to say why we should be given an opportunity to sit on the Central Committee. I did not expect to be elected, so I said the absolute minimum and then took a plane to Zanzibar.

That night I received a call from Mr. Pius Msekwa, saying that I was elected to the Central Committee and that I was required to attend a meeting in Dar es Salaam. We were appointed to serve on subcommittees, and I joined one dealing with publicly owned corporations, or parastatals, and was also made a member of the Economics Committee. I now had to divide my time between serving the party on the mainland and the government in Zanzibar. Through my assignments on the mainland, I began to see how a few individuals squeezed the parastatals until they went bankrupt. No action was taken against those responsible for such corruption. If a managing director caused a bankruptcy, he would not be taken to task but simply transferred to another parastatal, to repeat the process of misuse of funds all over again.

In the late 1970s, Zanzibar still had no constitution. Privately I had mentioned to Jumbe that the time had come to think of instituting a separation of powers because the Revolutionary Council was acting both as the executive and legislative arms of government. Jumbe, in fact, worked with a team of legal advisors and in 1979 presented a new draft constitution in the RC. The Old Guard, also known as the Liberators, did not even want to discuss it, saying they did not see the importance of a constitution. I thought the document had a number of shortcomings, but at least we were starting to establish constitutional rule in the country; for that, I commend President Jumbe because it was his idea. The constitution passed by consensus; we never had an actual vote in the RC—if someone opposed a policy, he would just keep quiet.

With the new constitution, for the first time we had an actual separation of powers, with executive, legislative, and judicial branches. A new House of Representatives was established, but it was interesting how the members were chosen. There were no elections; instead, each regional or district development committee appointed two persons to the house. The president also nominated some people to the house. We supported this because it was the first move toward democratization in the country.[2]

The constitution also established the office of chief minister, to be second in power only to the president. Usually, we assumed the minister of state was number two, but now the constitution established an order of succession through the chief minister and then the speaker of the house. The first chief minister was Brigadier Ramadhan Haji Faki, who was from the army and the Committee of Fourteen, a group of men allegedly responsible for organizing and executing the revolution in 1964. It was a wise move because Jumbe needed to show he was not discarding those in the forefront of the revolution. If Jumbe had chosen me—an outsider, a Pemban, and a college graduate—the inner circle would have resented it, especially the revolutionaries.

To be frank, I thought at the time that I had a bright future because I was performing well as a minister and on my committee assignments. Nyerere had a lot of confidence in me; he found me an energetic, able young man. I also got along well with Jumbe, who trusted me very much indeed. I was always diplomatic and respectful to all the RC members, but some Liberator elements like Bakari and Natepe resented me; they could not help it—they saw me as a threat. So, in 1980, some of them went to Jumbe and told him that some of the new persons he had promoted considered themselves pure Zanzibaris, Shirazi with more rights to rule Zanzibar than themselves, who were of mainland origins. They warned Jumbe that we would try to remove him since he and nearly all the Liberators were mainlanders and not Shirazi. Actually, the split within the ASP along ethnic lines was not very obvious, but gradually I came to learn that it had been Karume's policy not to trust anyone who did not have mainland origins. If you did not have either a mother or father who came from the mainland, you could not be entrusted with any important government position. Mainlanders were very conscious that they were outnumbered and feared democratization because they lacked a popular base.

I think that somehow all this entered Jumbe's head and that he began to believe the accusations. One day in 1980, he announced in the RC that there was a plot to overthrow the government. He said, "According to the information we have, some of my ministers here will be in the new government. Our investigations will reveal the truth." I had good working relations with Haji Mlinde, the minister of security, and afterward I asked him privately what it was all about.

He said, "Yes, there is a plot."

"Oh, really," I said, "or do you just want to go back to the old practice of trying to implicate people in plots that do not exist: imaginary plots, fairy tales"?

"No, no really, there is a plot."

"So who are the ministers involved in the plot?" I asked.

He said, "You're on a list of people to be in the new government, but that doesn't mean you're actually in the plot. You may only be earmarked by the conspirators to be part of the plot."

A few months later there was a cabinet reshuffle, and I was dropped along with a few other ministers. Of course, I felt sad, especially because I knew I had been performing very well and was committed to my work. I was bitter and thought I was being victimized. After a few weeks, however, I thought I still had a chance because I was still a member of the Central Committee, so I decided to concentrate on my work on the mainland. That is how I won the confidence of Nyerere and my CCM colleagues and how I came to know the whole of Tanzania.

I was always on the move, visiting different parts of the country. The Central Committee divided mainland Tanzania into economic zones, with each zone's being supervised by one of its members, especially to ensure we always had essential food supplies. I was put in charge of the southern highland regions: Iringa, Mbeya, Ruvuma, and Rukwa. I was responsible for ensuring that all farm inputs were sent in time, that the harvests were transported, and so on. I was very proud that, during my time, those regions were known as the Big Four: the most agriculturally productive regions of the country. I traveled frequently to consult with local leaders and to adopt strategies for food production. I remember that once I had to travel in a Land Rover to four regions in three days.

The 1982 CCM elections were very bitterly contested between two Zanzibari factions. The Liberators resisted change, and the Front-liners wanted to institute reforms such as democratization. We wanted party members at least to be able to elect their own party leaders. We also wanted more freedom of expression because, with Jumbe, it was still blasphemous to criticize the government. The young men who formed the Front-liners chose me as one of their leaders; they always pushed me forward. Throughout my career, in fact, I have been pushed into these positions, and eventually I learn to cope and gain the confidence of those around me.

The real competition was over forty positions in the National Executive Committee [NEC]. The Liberators wanted us Front-liners to lose our seats on the NEC, so we had to campaign very hard. In the end, most of us Front-liners survived the elections because most of the twelve hundred members of the National Congress were from the mainland and more concerned with each person's abilities than with his historical background. I was also elected again to the Central Committee and appointed the CCM's director of economics and planning. Because this was a one-party state, I was more powerful than any minister, although I scarcely used those powers. I would inform ministers that I would be visiting their offices, rather than simply summoning them to my office, so as not to intimidate them or make them hostile.

By 1982, there was a need to amend the 1977 union constitution, to make it more democratic, although still within the one-party system. I served on the committee that proposed amendments that were eventually passed by the Central Committee. We decided to publicize the changes in a green paper and allow people to air their views. Jumbe used this opportunity to have people in Zanzibar who wanted more autonomy for the islands air views critical of the union. In late 1983, for the first time the idea was raised of having three governments: one for Zanzibar, one for Tanganyika, and one for the union. Jumbe's pressure group, including Attorney General Wolfango Dourado, sponsored a private member's motion in the House of Representatives to discuss the idea of three governments. In the heated debates that followed, the chief minister gave his full support to the motion. There were also radio broadcasts from an unknown source in Zanzibar very critical of the Tanzanian government, especially of Nyerere, demanding an end to the union. We never found out where the radio broadcasts came from, only that they came from someone called *Kiroboto*, meaning lice. Along with Kiroboto, other people were invited to air their views about the union in the Zanzibari state media.

Jumbe and Nyerere were now on a collision course over the union. Another issue was an organization for Muslims that Jumbe had established known as BAMITA, or *Baraza la Miskiti Tanzania*, the Council of Mosques in Tanzania. Jumbe established this for the imams of different mosques on the district, regional, and national levels. Nyerere accused Jumbe of mingling religion with politics. I am not sure how Nyerere tolerated BAMITA in the first place. It functioned as a counterassociation to BAKWATA, the National Muslim Council of Tanzania, established by Nyerere years earlier to contain Muslims so that they would not run wild and claim their rights. BAKWATA was seen as a puppet organization of the ruling party and was very unpopular among Muslims. Some people felt that, by establishing BAMITA, Jumbe had overstepped himself and that this contributed to his downfall.

In the same period following the 1982 elections, Jumbe ordered all party and government leaders from Unguja and Pemba to assemble in their respective islands. In these meetings, Jumbe said to us—and I was there—"There are people sowing seeds of discord within the islands, to the extent of bringing about conflicts between Unguja and Pemba, and within Unguja between one region and another, and also in Pemba between one region and another, and between one district and another, and also between one village and another." He said that those sowing such discord would face revolutionary justice.

I interpreted these events as indications of Jumbe's growing political frustrations. During his tenure as vice president of Tanzania, he spent a lot of time on the mainland and expected to be Nyerere's successor, especially when Nyerere indicated to Jumbe that he would not contest the union presidency in the 1980 elections. Jumbe considered himself Nyerere's natural successor, but the war between Tanzania and Uganda in 1979 changed everything. The country experienced very difficult economic conditions, and a lot of pressure was placed on Nyerere not to abandon the ship in such rough waters. Nyerere agreed to stay for another term, dashing Jumbe's hopes.

After the war, Edward Moringe Sokoine was a rising star, a very popular politician and the prime minister. He was not really a party man but was admired by the public for his no-nonsense approach. He was seen as someone who really defended the interests of the disadvantaged. So Jumbe, seeing his chances to succeed Nyerere diminish by the day and failing in 1982 to remove Front-liners like myself from positions in the NEC and Central Committee, instigated demands for more Zanzibari autonomy. If he were successful, his government could do what it wanted to the people in the islands, rather than be restrained by the mainland. And the first to suffer from revolutionary justice would be people like me, people with education. That was my interpretation, at least. He did not want the Central Committee to stop him from reverting to the policies of the 1960s.

We Front-liners agreed that the idea of three governments was good but that the president had sinister motives, so we should not support him. Jumbe could have first consulted Zanzibari members of the NEC concerning the union. We could have brought it for a vote in the Central Committee. It would have been much easier to do it that way; instead, he was very secretive and made us very suspicious through his statements about revolutionary justice. We were convinced that, if Jumbe succeeded, if he won more freedom for Zanzibar or managed to break the union, people would lose their lives. Jumbe would revert to the lawlessness of the first decade of the revolution, when innocent people just disappeared. We felt that if younger politicians like ourselves did not act in time, we would lose our lives.

I discussed these things with Salmin Amour and Salim Ahmed Salim, both from Zanzibar and high CCM officials, and the three of us went to see the secretary general of the party, Rashidi Kawawa. We explained our worries to him, and Kawawa was very sympathetic. He told us to bring our issue before the Central Committee. The Central Committee decided that Jumbe should be temporarily restrained from taking any actions and that two subcommittees should be appointed to investigate the truth of his allegations concerning instigators' wishing to divide the people of Zanzibar. One worked in Unguja and the other in Pemba. Although the subcommittees worked separately, their findings were strikingly similar—that there was no basis to the allegations.

These findings did not please Jumbe, and the political atmosphere continued to be poisoned. Jumbe hired a lawyer from Ghana to make a case for three governments before a court of law. One of my Front-liner colleagues, Khatib Hassan Khatib, managed to collaborate with Jumbe's aide-de-camp to steal, photocopy, and secretly return a document that described the case Jumbe wanted to make for three governments. Khatib was formerly in the Youth League and in the intelligence service and had trained in East Germany, so the Liberators regarded him as their child who was now betraying them. Khatib brought the document to me, and we decided to take it to Sokoine, the prime minister. Sokoine then arranged a trip to see Nyerere in Butiama, his home village, where he was resting. We gave him the document and recommended that the Central Committee meet. Sokoine told Nyerere, "The lives of these young people from Zanzibar are in danger. If you don't act and they lose their lives, you'll be responsible."

When Nyerere convened the Central Committee, with Jumbe in attendance, the main agenda was the polluted political atmosphere in Zanzibar. I was asked to present the case against Jumbe because I knew most of the details and could argue persuasively. Others like Ali Ameir Muhammed, also a Front-liner, spoke after me. Jumbe was then asked to defend himself and was very defiant; he did not know that Nyerere already had a copy of the document. He claimed there was no basis to the allegations. The issue was then referred to a special session of the NEC, which convened on January 28, 1984. I was given the unpleasant honor of opening the debate. I spoke for about forty-five minutes, and afterward some others spoke from both sides, those who backed me and those in defense of Jumbe, now in the minority. Finally, Nyerere asked Jumbe to offer his explanations; again he was very defiant, denying any plan to change the union. But he also said, "We Zanzibaris came into the union of our own free will; we were not forced and have the right to make changes." He then made a case for three governments.

This was a three-day session, and on the final day, Nyerere summarized all the evidence against Jumbe. Then he dropped a bombshell. He said, "*Makamo*," meaning vice president, "what is this?" showing Jumbe the document we had stolen from him. You could see Jumbe freeze, as if all the energy were draining out of him. Nyerere looked Jumbe in the eyes and said, "*Makamo*, you must resign." Jumbe said, "All right, I'm resigning." A member of the NEC, Job Lusinde, raised his hand and asked what position he was resigning from, and Jumbe said all of them. There was a somber feeling in the chamber after that.

Nyerere met privately with Jumbe and asked him to put the resignation in writing and to hand the statement over to him. Jumbe had his private jet and wanted to fly immediately to Zanzibar, but his pilot elected to be sick on that particular day. That is how socialist systems work. There was the fear that he might try to organize a rebellion in Zanzibar, but no one could say what was in Jumbe's mind. As it turned out, he was helpless; he had to remain in Dodoma to offer his resignation in writing. Nyerere said Jumbe would receive his full benefits with a full pension as a retired vice president. Some members of the NEC were not happy about that, since he had put the union in jeopardy, but Nyerere said that, all in all, Jumbe had actually cemented the union. Later, Nyerere said he did not know how they would have managed the crisis, had the two parties remained separate.[3]

Jumbe started very well; in the beginning, he was very popular, and we were hopeful that he had good intentions for the country. All in all, I respected him, though he had his weaknesses. He could have been a very good president, had he been more consistent. But he always changed his mind, and then power went to his head, especially when he surrounded himself with yes-men. He was originally very obedient and supportive of Nyerere, thinking he would succeed him. He was pro-union and cemented closer ties by spending six months of every year on the mainland, whereas Karume would hardly ever sleep in Dar es Salaam. But then he and the Liberators thought it time to fight for more independence for Zanzibar, and had they succeeded, they would have had more powers to do whatever they wanted against their own people.

I respected Jumbe as a man, as my former teacher, as my leader, and as the person responsible for allowing me to gain a university education. I am very grateful to Jumbe because he brought me into politics, because, as I said before, I had no such ambitions. I served Jumbe honestly and to the best of my ability. To a certain extent, we shared the same vision for Zanzibar; I also wanted to restructure the union to provide Zanzibar with more rights to run its own affairs, to protect its identity, to bring about development, and to be able to choose leaders who would serve the people of Zanzibar. It is a pity that later we had sour relations and that he allowed himself to be influenced against me and other Shirazi politicians.

Contrary to what my critics have said, I had no plans to overthrow Jumbe. And even when I stood up with others to lay the case against him, it was not done out of personal hatred but out of the higher interests I felt for Zanzibar and out of a desire to save myself from elimination. I did not want to see the loss of innocent lives, and I thought that removing Jumbe was the only way forward. I did not really betray him, because I saw a real danger facing the country. We had to act to protect ourselves and save the country from further atrocities.

Now that I am fully involved in politics and I enjoy the game, I recognize it was Jumbe who played the greatest role in bringing me into politics, and for that, I will always thank and praise him. Even though later we did not see eye to eye, Jumbe was very kind to me, and I pray God will forgive him for his mistakes as a president. Nobody is perfect; only God is perfect.

# nine REFORM

THE MORNING AFTER JUMBE
resigned, the NEC met to decide who would fill the gap. The constitution
was very ambiguous about the succession. It offered two ways in which
a successor could be appointed. Either the Revolutionary Council or the
NEC could choose a successor for a period of three months before elections were held. Nyerere asked members of the NEC from Zanzibar
which alternative they preferred, and since there was little trust in the
Revolutionary Council, most said it was better for the NEC to name an
interim president, but that Sheikh Thabit Kombo, an ASP veteran and
Karume's close friend, should be consulted. Nyerere sent a plane to Moshi
to fetch Thabit Kombo; the two met privately and agreed upon a name.
Mwalimu [literally "teacher" in Swahili, Nyerere's informal title or nick-
name] then informed the NEC that he wanted to propose Ali Hassan
Mwinyi as interim president. There were wild cheers in the chamber,
and he was appointed by acclamation.

I did not know Mwinyi extremely well, though he was a minister of
state in the union government. He was probably appointed because he
could bring together all the factions; he was educated and had some experience as a minister and ambassador. He came from the mainland but
grew up in Zanzibar. The day following this announcement, Mwinyi
was flown to Zanzibar amid tight security and took the oath of office in
a very low-key function at the State House attended only by high-level
CCM members.

In Dar es Salaam, Mwalimu summoned me to his house in Msasani
and said he had a message he wanted me to give Mwinyi. He told me
that, if Mwinyi thought there were people causing difficulties for him in
the RC, then he should tell him, so he could detain them. He was thinking of the Liberators because, immediately after Mwinyi's appointment,
the government arrested Seif Bakari. When I arrived in Zanzibar, I met

Mwinyi at the State House, congratulated him, and gave him Nyerere's message. He asked what I thought of some of the troublemakers here in Zanzibar, like Hafidh Suleiman. Hafidh was a member of the RC and nicknamed "Sancho," after an actor, because he was very fat and liked to walk around with a pistol.

"Sancho is a hard-liner," I said, "and may cause some problems for you later on," but I left it at that. Eventually, Sancho, like Seif Bakari, was put under house arrest in one of Tanzania's more remote western regions.

I went to Pemba to visit my family. As I was sleeping one afternoon, I suddenly heard knocking on the door. I came out and saw people very happy and jovial, who started embracing me. I asked, "What is it?" They said I had been appointed chief minister. "Me?" I asked. They said they had heard the news over the radio. I was taken by complete surprise because Mwinyi had not indicated that he would even make me a minister. After a half hour or so, the police came and started guarding my house. When I took my meals with my in-laws, about a half-kilometer away, the police escorted me the whole distance by foot, which I found really hard. The next day the minister of state informed me that a plane would come to pick me up. As I was now a big shot, many government leaders came to see me off. The presidential plane came, and I flew away.

When I arrived in Zanzibar Town, the government had already selected my bodyguards. From the airport, they drove me to Kibweni Palace, where I was to stay for some time. Since the revolution, nobody had stayed in that palace; Karume had often used it for his afternoon rendezvous, but that was all. There were rumors the place had devils, or *mashetani,* but after my first night there, everything was okay. In fact, I felt very good and satisfied because I was a farm boy living in what was once the sultan's palace. All the time I asked myself if I deserved this when so many others never had the opportunity. I thanked God. I obtained these things because of God and my destiny, not because I was any better than anybody else. All the time I was praying and thanking God.

Three days later I was sworn in and assumed formal responsibilities. I thought it was now happening—I was being allowed to have a more active role in Zanzibar's affairs. The cabinet consisted mostly of Frontliners; we brought in new people like Hamad Rashid Mohammed, Shaaban Khamis Mloo, Machano Khamis Ali, and Khatib Hassan Khatib. We also retained certain members of the Old Guard like Natepe and Bavuai, who went along with the Front-liners who were now dominant.

But the appointment of Mwinyi did not please everyone in the islands. Because of Jumbe's campaign against the union, Zanzibari nationalism was on the rise, and many felt that Mwinyi was a president imposed on

Zanzibaris by the mainland. CCM's popularity reached an all-time low; when the party called meetings in the branches, the members were so furious that they tore up their CCM cards and would not listen to any leader they regarded as a sell-out.

When party members reported that public opinion was against the new administration, I said, "Leave it to me."

I arranged for TV and radio broadcasts in which I explained the reasons for Jumbe's resignation. I said that he was not sacked, that he had resigned by himself. I defended Mwinyi's appointment as the best man at the time. When the people heard me speak in defense of Zanzibari interests, they became convinced we were not just Nyerere's stooges. For an entire week, I continued to broadcast until public opinion began to turn in our favor. And as soon as we began to introduce our new policies, our popularity grew daily.

We inherited an empty treasury and asked ourselves what we should do. Mwinyi said Zanzibar was traditionally a trading nation, but our policies discouraged trade. So we decided to liberalize trade and allow people to bring in anything they wanted. Very soon the country changed completely, and Zanzibar Town was once again a bustling trading center. People with relatives in the Middle East were the first to take advantage of the trade liberalization; they received commodities to sell from their relatives, and that increased employment and the circulation of money. A lot of entrepreneurs emerged, the port became very busy, and hardships decreased. Food shortages ended, and all the streets of Mbuyuni, Darajani, and Mchangani, once used for selling only kerosene, firewood, and tea, now attracted people from Kenya and Tanzania.

After three months, we held elections, and people went to vote willingly. I campaigned very hard with my Front-liner colleagues, and more than 84 percent voted "yes" to Mwinyi. Afterward, we continued to develop and polish the policies we had already commenced, and people were impressed by what was happening. Every day we visited rural development projects and held meetings with the people to hear their views. Mwinyi coined a slogan, *Zanzibar Njema: Atakae Aje,* meaning, "Wonderful Zanzibar: Whoever Wants to Come Here Is Cordially Invited." Some exiles from the revolution did return to Zanzibar, but, more importantly, the remittances increased from overseas. Businessmen here often depended on such capital from their relatives, mainly in the Gulf.

Some people within the party, however, felt we were going against socialism and criticized us for that reason. The Liberators opposed liberalization, as did most people in the union government. They continually called us on the carpet in the union parliament and in the NEC. Socialism was still vibrant, in theory, so hard-liners interpreted any attempt to bring about reforms as a betrayal of the socialist cause; they labeled us reactionaries. I had to sit with Nyerere and explain why we were liberalizing. I said, "Let us make use of capitalism to build socialism." Later, he picked up on that phrase, and the union government began to liberalize as well.

We lifted passport restrictions and ended police harassment and arbitrary arrests. We sent many people outside the country to study, continuing something I had started as minister of education in the 1970s. We encouraged qualified people to aspire to positions in government, trying to establish a system in the civil service wherein they earned promotions based on merit rather than on family connections. We launched radio programs like *Jicho* where ordinary citizens could air their grievances, to alert us about government abuses and neglect. We discovered problems and followed up on the views of ordinary people. TV Zanzibar also began to visit problem areas in the islands, instead of only just reporting good news all the time. In this way, we tried to make society and government more transparent and accountable.

We also decided to write a new constitution for Zanzibar. I had the honor of presenting the 1984 constitution in the House of Representatives for approval. And, indeed, I am very proud of that because, for example, the new constitution provided for direct elections to the House of Representatives. It returned Zanzibar to the Commonwealth judicial system, abolishing the People's Courts instituted by Karume. For the first time in our history, the clauses in our constitution dealing with human rights were more advanced and in line with the United Nations Human Rights Charter than were those in the mainland's constitution.

The new constitution included provisions to preserve Zanzibari identity and autonomy within the union. Only Zanzibaris born in the islands could be elected to the Zanzibari presidency. The constitution placed the Zanzibari Special Forces under Zanzibari jurisdiction. It made the High Court in Zanzibar the final authority on all matters of constitutional interpretation; such cases could not be sent to the Tanzanian Court of Appeal. The constitution also stipulated that any law passed by the union parliament involving Zanzibar must be tabled in the House of Representatives.[1]

The relationship between Zanzibar and the mainland did not change that much. The only thing we added to union matters was the Tanzania Intelligence and Security Services. We did so because most of our security officers in the islands were sympathetic to Jumbe's regime since most were recruited purely for their connections to members of the RC.

They owed their loyalty to these individuals and not the state, so they were in need of reform. The security service needed, furthermore, to recruit people with education because, in intelligence work, after all, you need to have people with intelligence.

Unfortunately, on April 12, 1984, Prime Minister Sokoine, with whom we had excellent relations, died in a road accident. He was traveling from Dodoma to Dar es Salaam, and at a place near Morogoro, his car was involved in a head-on collision. Unfortunately, he was not wearing a seat belt, so the force of the impact threw him out the windshield. It was a big loss to the country. I took a plane to Dar es Salaam and could see the people were really grieving. Thousands and thousands came to file past his body lying in state in Karimjee Hall. I have never seen such grief for any political figure in Tanzania before or since; it was more even than at Nyerere's funeral. The body was flown to his home, and the whole CCM leadership attended his funeral. Though some suggest Sokoine's death was not an accident, I do not personally subscribe to any conspiracy theories.

Salim Ahmed Salim was appointed the new prime minister. He was forty-two years old, and I was forty-one; we were both from Pemba, both Front-liners, and both popular on the mainland. Salim had actually once been a young member of the ZNP but had broken away when Babu formed the Umma Party. Karume had nominated him as Tanzania's ambassador to Egypt. Nyerere was very impressed by how seriously Salim took his responsibilities in Cairo; although very young, he was one of our best ambassadors. He later became ambassador to India, and then for ten years served as Tanzania's representative in the United Nations, where he played a pivotal role in admitting the People's Republic of China into the UN and gaining the Chinese a permanent seat on the Security Council. Nyerere then recalled him to serve as minister of foreign affairs. He was very hard working, clean, and incorruptible, and that impressed Mwalimu. When he was young, he had socialist convictions but later became more liberal and pragmatic. The two of us had very good relations.

When I was on CCM's Central Committee in the 1980s, I traveled to a number of communist countries, like the USSR, China, Poland, Yugoslavia, Cuba, and North Korea. At the time, these countries were still seen as models for Tanzanian development. In Zanzibar, and in Tanzania in general, China had the most influence, more than the Russians. One time the Russians brought a very old plane as a present to Karume, and he never used it. In fact, he lamented, "These people think we're fools!"

I visited China only once, when I accompanied Rashidi Kawawa for about a week in 1983. The visit was very well managed; all our time was devoted to guided tours and discussions, and we had no free time to go out on our own. Sometimes we would finish the evening banquet at 11:00 p.m. and could not even think of doing anything on our own because we were tired and stayed in guesthouses that were very well guarded. On the first night of our tour, we had a banquet hosted in our honor. We had about seventeen courses, and I asked my host what each course was. I passed on the snail, and Rashidi Kawawa did as well. But we did not tell one lady in our delegation what she was eating, and when Kawawa later announced to all of us what she had eaten, she vomited immediately, right there in the corridor.

I was very impressed with Deng Xiaoping, who had taken over as China's leader after Mao's death and was responsible for initiating their economic liberalization. We asked him, "Don't you think your policies will affect the way the Chinese have lived all these years under Mao Tsetung?" He laughed and said, "When you have a house and open the windows to that house, fresh air will come in, but some harmful insects will come in as well, so it's up to you to find a way to deal with the insects. But fresh air will still come in." I thought that was a wonderful answer.

Among the world leaders I met, I found Kim Il Sung of North Korea very impressive. We attended sessions of North Korea's National Congress, and he called on every delegate by name, though there were over a thousand in attendance. Wherever we went in the country, there were markers listing the dates when the Great Leader had visited and provided "on- the-spot guidance." Kim Il Sung had built a huge palace for himself on the sea front, and in order to meet him, we had to go underground on an escalator. His sitting room was literally in the sea because the windows showed only the ocean. He had a charming and commanding personality. It was very comfortable and easy to talk to him, and he liked to joke a lot. He told our delegation to inform Nyerere that all he had to do to end hunger in Tanzania was to mobilize the people to dig irrigation canals from Lake Victoria all the way to Dodoma. He said, "Here in North Korea, we have a food surplus that'll last us thirty years."

But you could also really feel the iron grip of Kim Il Sung; people were completely intimidated and afraid to speak. Even those escorting us never had anything to discuss about their country, except to praise the Great Leader. Later, I was very disappointed to hear that people were starving in North Korea. We were shown silos and told they were full of food, and yet people were starving. The communists really knew how to play the game of deceit; they would try to impress you with numbers, but when it came to reality, it was very far from the numbers. In Moscow, for example, members of the politburo and other party bosses went to their own shops from which local people were excluded. In Albania, which struck me as very backward, each of the party leaders drove a Mercedes-Benz, every one of them black, when everyone else moved around on donkey carts. Even their medical transport employed donkey carts.

Traveling abroad opened my eyes and widened my experience. In Cuba, I was interested in how the different races intermingled. I did not see any sort of discrimination and thought Zanzibar could learn from Cuba in this regard. One evening Pius Msekwa and I were taken to a nightclub. There were many very beautiful girls performing cabaret style, and I remember Mr. Msekwa said to me, "This is socialism with a human face."

Of course, the standard of living there was very low, but the people still had a strong sense of nationalism because they had stood up to a powerful nation like the U.S. for many years, which takes courage and perseverance. In fact, I thought Cuba was the only example of a socialist country somehow doing good for its people. The government put a high priority on education, and the literacy rate was very high. We visited an island where most young people went to be taught, consisting mostly of colleges and universities. The whole environment was very conducive to learning and study. It is no wonder that, whereas in most countries medicine is not a field many people like to study, Cuba has always produced a surplus of doctors and has sent many overseas; even here in Zanzibar, there have been some very good Cuban doctors.

Another time I went to Cuba with Prime Minister Sokoine, and one day we were to see President Fidel Castro at his residence; we were told to wait in our guesthouse from 2:00 p.m., and at about 4:00 p.m., eight people arrived to search the entire place. Fifteen minutes later Fidel Castro arrived, and he spoke to Sokoine and me for an hour or so. He was very friendly to us and very impressive. He was mesmerizing, in fact. The next day we attended one of his rallies, and he spoke for four hours without stopping, and people were really cheering.

So, definitely, travel widens one's horizons; always there is something new to learn, which you can apply in your own country, modifying it to suit your own conditions. I saw the possibilities for development in different spheres. In North Korea, I saw one street full of tall buildings constructed in only six months. I observed in Beijing how the people relied on bicycles for transport, which I thought a good thing. In East Berlin, we were taken somewhere where young men and women exercised. They played popular songs and danced to the songs as they exercised. I noticed they could go on like this for a long time without feeling tired.

And later, especially after I was released from jail in 1991, I visited a number of countries in the West, in Asia, and the Gulf, and my experience widened further. In countries not historically as developed as those in the West, I wanted to see how they managed to progress so fast. What can we learn from the so-called tiger economies in East Asia or the Gulf? I am interested in how various federal systems work and how they can apply to Tanzania. I am interested in agriculture, industry, education, and in how some countries have shortened the period of study. Here in Zanzibar, we have eleven years of compulsory education until Form 3. Students begin at age seven; by the time they complete Form 6 and are ready to proceed to college, they are twenty-one, when in other countries someone by that age can graduate from university.

I observed in Britain that minorities enjoyed equal rights, which only enhanced my conviction that there are no grounds in Zanzibar for discrimination of any kind. My travels also made me rethink some of my views about women. I must admit that, for many years, I did not think much of gender equality. I had no sister, only brothers. I thought men should shoulder heavier responsibilities, a belief that is part of Islam because there is a verse in the Qur'an that says men should oversee the affairs of women. Only later did I come to think gender equality was a good thing. Only after I entered politics, started to travel, and saw women doing jobs I thought were the domain of men did I begin to think women with proper education could be entrusted with heavy responsibilities.

ten OLD GUARD INTRIGUES

THE HARD-LINERS WERE OBVIOUSLY not happy with political developments in 1983 and 1984, so they began to intrigue. They knew Nyerere would soon retire from politics, so they plotted about who should succeed him. They did not want Salim Ahmed Salim—the new prime minister—and me to continue in our positions or to be considered for further promotion. My sin was that I came from Pemba. They alleged, meanwhile, that Salim was an Arab, and as a former member of the Umma Party, he somehow knew of the conspiracy to kill Karume. They campaigned a lot and managed to convince some party elders that Salim should not be president because he would supposedly avenge the mistreatment of Arabs in Zanzibar during the revolution. History repeats itself because the same arguments were used against him in 2005.

Mwalimu thought Salim was the best candidate; Salim told me that Nyerere called him and said to him openly: "I am leaving, and I think you're the proper person to succeed me." Salim told Nyerere that Vice President Mwinyi should automatically be the candidate for that position. Mwalimu replied, "Don't worry about that because I've spoken to Ali, and he thinks you should take over." After that, Salim went to see Mwinyi, told him what Nyerere had said, and asked for his opinion. Mwinyi said that Nyerere had consulted him, and he was not interested in the union presidency, adding, "I'm satisfied in my present position as president of Zanzibar, and I think you're the proper person to lead Tanzania."

Despite these conversations, the Liberators campaigned very hard for Mwinyi to succeed Nyerere, so we Front-liners appointed a team to see Mwinyi. The team members emphasized that he was doing very well in Zanzibar, that Zanzibaris still needed him, and that it was inappropriate to abandon them when they placed so much hope in him. Mwinyi's response was, "Don't worry. Salim is the best candidate, and even if my name is proposed, I'll withdraw in favor of Salim." I also had a private talk with Mwinyi, and he reiterated that he was not interested in the union presidency. I advised Mwinyi that, if he really was not interested in succeeding Nyerere, he should personally tell him so. If he did not, it would be very difficult, as vice president, for his name not to be considered. He accepted my advice. Yet when the time came in 1985 for the Central Committee to nominate candidates, we had dinner together in his private rooms. and he informed me that he had not gone to Nyerere as I had suggested. It was now clear the man was interested.

The next morning the Central Committee met in the State House in Dar es Salaam to nominate candidates. Nyerere said that, first of all, the committee should spell out the qualities a candidate should possess, and about thirty-five qualities were mentioned. After that, Nyerere said that we had three names to consider: Ali Hassan Mwinyi, Salim Ahmed Salim, and the secretary general of the party, Rashidi Mfaume Kawawa. Usually, those candidates who were mentioned then left while the others discussed their credentials. But before anyone left, Kawawa stood and asked the committee to withdraw his name, giving two reasons. First, he was not a very well man in terms of his health. Second, if he were nominated, people would generally think there would not be any changes, due to his long association with Nyerere since the 1950s. Nyerere said we had to respect Kawawa's views.

After that, Mwinyi and Salim were asked to leave. Really, the discussion was only about Mwinyi and whether the committee thought he had the necessary qualities. We agreed he had most of them, and Salim was not even discussed. Nyerere did not push Salim's name, probably because the Old Guard of both the TANU and the ASP teamed up to oppose him.

So the two candidates were called in and informed of the decision, and I could see the disappointment in Salim's face. Salim was very loyal to Nyerere and did not expect this to happen. Salim never then or later ever uttered a word against Nyerere, but I blamed Nyerere, saying, "Why did he give you all this hope? You had the right to be informed." He said, "No, don't blame Mwalimu because he acted under pressure." He was very magnanimous, really.

In the afternoon, it was time to nominate a candidate for the Zanzibari presidency because now Mwinyi had been promoted. Mwalimu said that we had three names to consider. First was Idris Abdul Wakil, an ASP veteran who had been nominated in two previous elections and each time had asked for his name to be removed from consideration. My name was second, and third was that of Salmin Amour, then minister of home affairs in the union government. We were all asked to leave the room, but Salmin said it was better that the committee select Mzee Idris because he was older than the two of us. I said, "Yes, I agree with you." We then left the room. I do not know what transpired afterward, but we were called in again and informed that the committee had decided to present two names to the NEC: Idris Abdul Wakil and me. This was highly unusual. I stood up and said, "I'm grateful to the Central Committee for the confidence it has shown me, but I request my name be withdrawn. Let us all support Mzee Idris because he has been very generous to others by withdrawing his name in the past. I think it's now his time to be nominated. Second, if two names are submitted to the NEC, I fear it might divide the party."

Nyerere said, "Okay, we've heard you, but it's a constitutional requirement that two names be presented to the NEC." And it was true that two names were supposed to be presented; still, in the past one would always withdraw, but now that was not allowed. The meeting took place on a Saturday, and we agreed that our decisions should remain very confidential and that no one outside the Central Committee should know our decision until Monday when the NEC would meet. I returned immediately to Zanzibar, but the Liberators began to campaign very vigorously, going to member after member of the NEC in support of Idris. The Front-liners heard of this and began also to campaign for me. It was really tense, although supposed to be secret.

In the NEC meeting, the Front-liners' strategy was, first of all, to try to keep Mwinyi in Zanzibar by rejecting the proposal that he be the candidate for the union presidency. People like Ali Haji Pandu, Soud Yusuf Mgeni, and Hamad Rashid Muhammed argued that he should remain the candidate for president of Zanzibar, and they managed to build a very strong case. Even Thabit Kombo was not happy with the idea of Mwinyi's moving from Zanzibar. Nyerere, however, was a clever tactician; when he saw that the majority in the NEC opposed Mwinyi's nomination, he adjourned for tea and took Thabit Kombo aside for a tête-à-tête. Afterward, Thabit stood and gave his support to Mwinyi's nomination, and because he was so highly respected, there were no more debates.

The committee then considered who should be nominated for the Zanzibari presidency. Idris and I appeared before the NEC, just to be seen, and then a secret ballot was taken. In the end, the members announced that Idris won the nomination: out of a total of about 180 votes, he had received 7 more than I. Many people did not believe the results, saying they were just made up. They thought Idris was already old and not well known within the NEC, whereas I was new blood and very well known. The former minister of finance on the mainland, Amir Jamal, lamented after the meeting, "Where is this country going? We leave this energetic young man, and take this old man." Nevertheless, I accepted the results and congratulated Idris on his victory.

When people in Zanzibar heard that Mwinyi was the candidate for the union and Idris for the islands, they were very unhappy and began to condemn the party. Idris was not popular; they looked at his record and were not impressed. Zanzibari nationalism was very high at the time, and people thought of him just as Nyerere's stooge. Many people knew I was working very well and believed mainland politicians were deliberately trying to put a stop to development in Zanzibar. And for me, personally, this period was one of the hardest in my life. As hard as I tried to show support for Idris, I was always accused of campaigning against him. The Central Committee decided that I should open the campaign in Pemba in August 1985. I spoke in Wete on behalf of Idris, and everyone was happy, even Liberators like Hassan Nassor Moyo. They said I had set the pace for the whole campaign; but within only a few days, the same people accused me of having secret meetings to undermine the campaign. When I heard these allegations, I decided to return to Unguja, and the party removed my name from the campaign committees, though everyone knew I was a strong campaigner.

The campaign in Pemba did not go well for CCM; people were rowdy in the meetings and openly challenged Idris. It reached such a level that Nyerere decided to go himself to Pemba. And because he went, I was also required to go to Pemba. Afterward, he said it was the most difficult rally he had ever addressed; whenever he mentioned Idris' name, he was booed, but whenever he mentioned my name, there were cheers. He tried to move the rally in one direction but could not. He said he understood Pembans' concern that Idris was the fourth president of Zanzibar not to come from Pemba, "so I promise the next time we'll take your concerns under serious consideration." The same day he also spoke in the afternoon at a rally in Unguja and clearly played divide-and-rule politics. He said, "Look at these Wapemba. They want their own president, and if you people also want your own president, then how can we run this country?" He said that Idris was their man; whether or not the Pembans liked Idris, they should support him. The next day at a meeting of CCM leaders in Zanzibar, Nyerere castigated all the Liberators. He said, angrily, that the world was changing and that they did not want to change; they were afraid of their own shadows and were bringing all these problems on themselves.

After the voting on October 22, 1985, it was announced that 57 percent of the people had voted "yes" for Idris; on the next day, the number was increased to 62 percent. Pemba had, in effect, rejected him; he also failed to win a majority in the Urban West region, winning a "yes" vote from only 37 percent.

After Idris was sworn in, the Liberators sought to influence him to appoint Salmin Amour as chief minister. Idris faced a lot of pressure to ignore me altogether, and, personally, I did not want the position because I thought it impossible to have good working relations with him. But Nyerere had other views. I believe he thought it was not time yet for me to be pushed aside completely. CCM could not afford just to sack me. So, Mwalimu called me to Dar es Salaam and said he knew I did not want to continue as chief minister after all that had happened: "Yet for the sake of Zanzibar, I request that you continue in that capacity. Zanzibar has recently had two very able and popular leaders. One of them has now been moved to the union government, and we cannot afford to lose the second one. So please, please, think of the greater interests of Zanzibar more than your own interests and be willing to serve with Idris."

I said to Nyerere, "This is very difficult for me. As much as I'd like to offer my services to Zanzibar, Mzee Idris has already been poisoned against me and believes I campaigned against him, which I deny. So, Mwalimu, don't you see that our working relations would be tantamount to an ineffective government?"

He said, "I know, but these are common problems, and I'm sure you can work with him. I know you; you can work with anybody. And if you accept, I'll have a word with Idris about this."

I said, "Okay, if you have a word with him and he genuinely wants me to work as chief minister, then for the sake of my country, I'll do this, but I must first be satisfied he doesn't think I want to undermine him. If that's the case, I'll serve him honestly and loyally."

After two days, I was summoned to the State House in Zanzibar where Idris welcomed me and said, "Seif, do you know I am your elder brother? Your brother was my classmate, and we were very close." I said I did not know that. Then he said, "But why did you campaign against me?"

I said, "Maalim, this is my fear, that you have been poisoned. I assure you I never campaigned against you. It was I who opened the first campaign meeting in Pemba and everybody praised my speech, including those who sought to poison you. They accused me of having secret meetings in the area of Pandani in Pemba, but I haven't visited that village for the last three or four months. I say emphatically I never, never campaigned against you. If you believe me or not, it's up to you."

He said "Well, let's leave it up to God. He knows better." Then he said he had decided to reappoint me as chief minister. I said, "Thank you, but can you really trust me? Two persons in these positions of power must trust one another; otherwise, they can cause a lot of damage." And he said yes, he could, that Mwalimu had spoken to him. I asked him if this was his own decision, and he said it was. "In that case," I said, "I'll serve you loyally."[1]

To the chagrin of the hard-liners, I was sworn in at the People's Palace, and we began to form a new government. In most cases, Idris accepted my advice about who should head each ministry. Some former members of the Revolutionary Council were just ignored; I tried, however, to influence Idris to see that they were at least looked after. I always gave them a lot of respect; they could come to my office anytime, and most of them were very thankful.

Idris and I were initially able to establish very good relations. He realized I was helping him, even though people were always going to him and saying this and that against me. It went so far that once, when addressing a public rally, he exclaimed, "These people want me to quarrel with my chief minister." You could see he was really frustrated, but at the same time, elements with their own agenda found him easy to influence. He was torn: on one hand, he thought I was helping him, and on the other, he could not ignore the party stalwarts.

He was a very kind old man; he had a soft heart and did not want to see anyone hurt. He was originally a teacher by profession, with a degree from Makerere College. He became very active in the ASP before the revolution and afterward was sent to the mainland where he served in a number of positions, such as minister of health. When we established the House of Representatives here in 1981, he served as its first speaker. He was very humble, honest, and religious. He was not much of a socialist; in fact, he had no ideology. He loved Zanzibar and hated corrupt politicians but was unable to provide strong leadership. He could be easily persuaded and usually depended on the advice of his immediate junior. He was the type of leader who, if I sent him a memo or briefed him and gave him a few options from which to choose, he would keep the file for a month or six weeks and do nothing. I would then ask him what had happened with the file, why he had not taken any action, and he would respond that I had not given him my exact recommendation. I learned to recommend one of the options, and he would accept my advice the same day.

Long after he retired from the presidency, when his health was deteriorating, Idris sent one of his best friends, the late Mzee Ali Muhammed, to see me. He said he had a message from Sheikh Idris, asking for my forgiveness for things that happened to me I have yet to describe. I said, "Tell him I've forgiven him for whatever he did to me in this world and in the next." Later, Mzee Ali told me it had taken him a very long time to come and see me, and many times Idris had asked him, "Have you gone to see Seif? Do you want me to die without getting his forgiveness?" Mzee Ali reported Idris' great sigh of relief when he heard my reply.

Unfortunately, the international price of cloves dropped rapidly in the mid-1980s. Our treasury was empty, and there was a serious food shortage in Zanzibar. The foreign reserves we accumulated under Karume were completely gone, all of them squandered during Jumbe's era. All the factories built in the 1960s and 1970s with the help of the East Germans and Chinese had decayed. The Chinese were still interested in Zanzibar and continued to send medical doctors. In these years, donor organizations from Europe also began to have an influence. DANIDA [Danish International Development Agency], FINNIDA [Finnish International Development Agency], SIDA [Swedish International Development Agency, and NORAD [Norwegian Development Agency for Cooperation] were very involved in education, health, forestry, livestock, and electricity. The European Community was involved in road building and port construction. The mainland, however, was not helping at all at the time.

We wanted to continue to reform the economy, and liberalization allowed us to collect revenue from the importation of goods from overseas. With the little revenue we had, we almost balanced the budget, with a small deficit every year. We decided to award agriculture the highest priority and had a very ambitious project called MTAKULA: *mpango wataifa wakujitosheleza kwa chakula*, or "plan to become self-sufficient in food production." We sought to increase food production, especially rice. I was personally very involved in this, always going into the field to be with the farmers to discuss their problems and to hear their proposals for increasing production. We had a tremendous amount of success, and I became very popular with the farmers because I ensured that, at a reasonable price, they got all the materials they needed. We embarked on irrigation schemes, so that a piece of land could produce two or three times a year. We encouraged peasants not to neglect local crops such as cassava, sweet potatoes, yams, and bananas. We encouraged the farming of livestock and poultry and the growing of fruits and vegetables. We revived the use of fertilizers and pesticides, which were common during Karume's time but gradually had been neglected. Also during Karume's time, the government rented out tractors to farmers at low prices, a practice that we revived, along with extension work and agricultural research. During Mwinyi's era, we also ordered a number of vehicles from overseas, mainly Toyota pick-up trucks, and then sold them on credit to individuals here, which eased the islands' transport problems.[2]

We were responding to the stated needs of the people, and I was very happy about what we were doing. I remember that one time Benjamin Mkapa, then Tanzania's minister of foreign affairs, came with a foreign delegation and wanted to see me. Because my schedule in the field always began about 7:30 a.m., I gave him an appointment for a breakfast meeting at 6:30 a.m. Mkapa remarked, "This is Chinese style."

Of course, my problems with the Liberators continued. The Makurunge case in 1986 further alienated me from some of them. Jumbe's government had acquired land in the area of Bagamoyo on the mainland with the intention of establishing a large livestock farm, but there was a lot of embezzlement and mismanagement of the project. This situation came up in a debate in the House of Representatives, and the house formed a committee to investigate the charges. Of course, the investigation found evidence of corruption, and some Liberators' names were mentioned. Some people alleged that I had stage-managed the whole debate to embarrass and implicate the Liberators.

The Liberators accused me of favoring the people of Pemba in terms of university scholarships, saying I was intent on creating a class of educated Pembans who would dominate the highest government positions. I was forced to provide statistics showing they were wrong, demonstrating there was no government preference toward Pembans. As I explained previously, it was our policy that 40 percent of the scholarships would go to Pemba and 60 percent to Unguja. Sometimes, however, the people of Unguja could not fill their quota on merit, so their scholarships were given to Pembans. To be frank, some students in Unguja had family connections and were not interested in studying, while Pembans knew their only chance for survival was through education, so Pemban parents put great effort into seeing that their children were educated. A situation emerged in which many more people from Pemba came with qualifications than came from Unguja. But at most, we distributed the scholarships on a 50/50 basis, or usually 55/45, still in favor of Unguja. Pemban students never received the majority of scholarships.

The problem was that, in the past, there were very few Pembans in government, not because they lacked ability but because the government had a deliberate policy of exclusion. So under Mwinyi, we began to bring them in, and many people in Unguja complained, as if Pembans had no right to these jobs. I had to defend our policy and was able to influence public opinion, yet even now you still hear some people say I favored Pembans. These people are politically bankrupt; they want to find a way to divide our society by appealing to certain groups who believe they are disadvantaged.

The Liberators also accused me of being a former member of the ZNP, but the first time I ever voted was for Nyerere in 1965. They, nevertheless, made accusations, and I had to deny them in TV interviews and radio programs. They even said I wanted to bring back the sultan! At one time in 1987, I did have an official visit to the Gulf States, to Oman, the UAE, Kuwait, and Qatar; my delegation included my principal secretary Muhammed Mwinyi Mzale and a number of ministers, like Taimur Saleh. It was our first official delegation to nations in the Middle East since the revolution, other than Jumbe's visits to Saudi Arabia, and was very promising. Sultan Qaboos of Oman gave me almost two hours of his time and told me that Oman had a real obligation toward Zanzibar because of our long historical ties and family connections. Once in the nineteenth century, Zanzibar had assisted Oman when it was having a hard time. When Sultan Seyyid Said died in 1856, his territories were divided; his son Majid ruled Zanzibar, and another son, Thuwain, ruled Oman. Sultan Qaboos very graciously reminded me of this time of hardship in Oman's history; Majid sent money from Zanzibar to help his brother in Oman, so now that Zanzibar was having difficulties, it was the duty of Omanis to help their brothers. Qaboos said to me, "Muskat and other cities you've visited here in Oman were built by Zanzibaris who came here after your revolution." They came when Omanis were not educated and took most of the senior government positions. "The Zanzibari government educated them, and then they ran away and came here, and Oman didn't spend a single cent on their education."

The two of us agreed we should bring the budgetary requirements of certain ministries, such as for road-building projects, to the Omani government. As long as we knew how much we needed, the Ministry of Construction in Oman would provide for us. In fact, the sultan was very generous; he said that water projects would also be approved and that Oman would pay for an extension of the airport in Zanzibar. I was very pleased by this reception because I knew that, if we wanted cooperation from the Gulf States, Oman had to first accept us because of its close historic relations with Zanzibar. After my meeting with Sultan Qaboos, I went to the UAE and met Crown Prince Khalifa bin Zayed bin Sultan Al-Nahyan. I also had very fruitful discussions with Prince Mohamed bin Rashid al Maqtoum in Dubai and was well received by Sheikh Sultan Mohamed al-Qassemi of Sharja. Similarly, I was well received in

Qatar by Crown Prince Sheikh Hamad bin Khalifa and in Kuwait by Sheikh Jabir, the ruler. All of them indicated they were prepared to help Zanzibar reconstruct itself.

After my return to the islands, there was, however, propaganda that I wanted to bring the Arabs back to rule and oppress Zanzibar. The Liberators said I had private meetings with these leaders and had left out other people like Mzee Hamdan Muhiddin. But I specifically made sure Mzee Hamdan accompanied me wherever I went and even gave instructions that his room be next to mine. Mzee Hamdan personally stood in one of our meetings and defended me, saying the allegations were lies. Unfortunately for Zanzibar, I was sacked from government within a few months of my return, and my successors did nothing to follow up on these opportunities. I am sure that, if after my downfall they had done so, they would have achieved a lot because Oman did not care about personalities, only about helping the people of Zanzibar. The Omanis did not care if their cooperation came through me or someone else. So it was yet another squandered opportunity.

I served Idris faithfully through 1987. In the CCM elections of that year, some of the Front-liners like Ali Haji Pandu were simply left out of the nomination process. I stood for election in Pemba North and nearly lost; the Liberators arranged this to try to demonstrate that I had lost my popularity among the people. Afterward, I went to see Nyerere at the Chamwino State Lodge in Dodoma; although retired from the presidency, he continued as chairman of CCM. Since he had considerable power to nominate candidates for election to the Central Committee, I asked him not to consider my nomination. He asked why, and I said because of the negative campaign against me; I only aspired to continue my membership in the NEC. Nyerere appeared satisfied, yet the next day I still found my name on the list of people to contest positions in the Central Committee. Under such circumstances, I was not surprised when I lost.

During the same period, there was one chap named Dr. Omar Ali Juma rumored to become the next chief minister, in place of me. He actually came to my office once to say, "Mzee, there are rumors they want to make me chief minister instead of you, but this is just a divide-and-rule strategy. I assure you I'm not prepared to accept this appointment. If they want to use me to divide the people of Zanzibar, I'll not accept." I said, "Even if you accept the nomination and are elected, be assured of my cooperation."

In December 1987, I went for medical treatment in London. I underwent two operations for ENT: ear, nose, and throat problems. When I returned, the people on their own initiative organized a big welcome rally for me in Unguja. It was totally spontaneous, and I was completely surprised. State security officials tried to sabotage the event by intimidating people, but they failed. Later in Pemba, the reception was more organized; thousands came to receive me at the airport. It seemed as if half the population of Pemba came to welcome me. They were very aware of the Liberator intrigues against me and came to show their support. They knew I was about to be sacked and were not happy about it. When I descended from the plane, there was a mass prayer on the airport apron, and then I decided to walk with the people from the airport to the Tibirinzi grounds, about seven kilometers away, where I gave a short speech. I thanked the people for their support, and I uttered a sentence that has always been repeated when they talk about me and that has had a very great influence on my decision to stay in politics. It always reminds me that leaving politics at this stage would be a betrayal of the trust of Zanzibaris.

I said, "I am with you now, and I promise to be with you whether I shall be in the government or outside the government. I will be with you whether I am in the party or outside the party." People always repeat this because I have remained with the people until now, and they still give me their support.

CCM had to find a scapegoat for the difficult campaign in 1985. Nyerere thought that I did not respect the party's decision and that I sabotaged party unity. He calculated it wise to ask me to continue for the time being and waited for the proper time to manage my downfall.[3] When the party was about to sack me, it sent auditors to my office to see if I had stolen any money; what they found was contrary to what they expected. When I went for treatment in London, for example, I stayed longer than anticipated but still returned with a lot of unspent money to return to the government—usually people never give back any of the travel funds they receive. My accountant was shocked when I returned two thousand British pounds to the treasury.

The auditors also found that, when I paid a visit to Brunei, the sultan personally gave me a check for about a million dollars. He was also prepared to help Zanzibar in its development projects and only required us to send project write-ups, but, of course, after I was sacked there was no follow-up. When I returned from Brunei, I transferred the million dollars to the treasury. I did not consider it my own, though it was given to me personally. I could have taken it and nobody would have known, but I asked myself whether I received this cash because of myself or because of my official position. This was another surprise for the auditors.

When they came to my office, even my principal secretary, Mohammed Mwinyi Mzale, told them, "If you find fault with the books, it's not the chief minister but I who would be responsible since I act as the chief accounting officer here."

eleven

I RETURNED FROM LONDON
in December 1987, and by January 18, 1988, I was out of the government.
Idris dissolved the entire Revolutionary Council, saying he was taking
charge of all the ministries himself. The army was put on full alert; soldiers were not allowed to leave camp. Four days later, Idris reappointed
all the former ministers except Ali Haji Pandu and myself. People wondered why he went to such trouble if his original intention was just to
sack me. Dr. Omar Ali Juma was appointed as the new chief minister;
it was very unfortunate that, after he was called to Dodoma, he returned
to Zanzibar and at his first public rally rained a tirade of abuses on my
head. I was at first happy he was appointed chief minister because he
was educated and, at least before his appointment, not much of a CCM
stalwart. But he changed completely, and I do not know what Nyerere
and the others gave him to eat to cause such a change. He often abused
me in public, but when we met at functions, he was always very friendly.

I moved from the chief minister's house to where I live now in Mtoni.
It is government property; the state feels an obligation to ensure I have
somewhere to stay. A man named Hamad Haji came with me to Mtoni
and became my private bodyguard; he has remained so ever since. Rashid
Ali Dadi was also very loyal, and I do not know how to thank the two
of them. I could not pay them a single cent, and on their own volition,
they sacrificed their families to be my personal assistants, to keep me
company, and to ensure my security.

I wanted at first to rest and review my achievements and failures. I
was actually rather naïve; I thought at first it was okay, that my sacking
was just a normal change in government, though I knew there was pressure on Idris to get rid of me. When ordinary people found out that I
had moved to Mtoni, from ten to forty came every day to show their
support and sympathy. The government did not like that, so it began to

post security officers around my house to question and intimidate my guests. They kept track of everyone who came there. Even when I went to town, in no time at all crowds of people followed me around. As I walked through the streets people called me "*Seif Mkombozi*," meaning Seif the Liberator, and even carried me once shoulder-high for a distance of twenty meters or so.

After my sacking, people began turning in their membership cards to the party branches or tearing them up. There were other signs of discontent, like the destruction of Nyerere's portrait in various public places in Pemba. The party appointed a committee chaired by Rashidi Kawawa to investigate, especially in Pemba. Kawawa met with CCM cadres who accused me of causing all their problems, saying I was enticing people to reject CCM. So in May 1988, barely four months after my sacking, the NEC accused me and six others of encouraging people to reject CCM and undermine the union. The others were Ali Haji Pandu, Hamad Rashid Mohammed, Khatib Hassan Khatib, Suleiman Seif Hamad, Shabaan Khamis Mloo, and the late Rashid Hamad Hamad. The government accused us of representing an opposing faction within the party. It was clear the authorities had already decided to expel us from CCM, though security officers on the mainland advised Nyerere that our expulsion would bring about disastrous results. They said it was better to keep us in the party, so they could control us.

But the intelligence services here in Zanzibar recommended our expulsion, claiming people would turn against us and stone us in the streets; Nyerere, I am told, decided to heed their advice. At an NEC meeting in Dodoma, a number of CCM officials spoke against us. Mzee Muhammed Mahmud Jecha stood up and said, "First of all, I request, Mr. Chairman and all members of the NEC, that we stand in memory of Seif's brother, Hamad Sharif, a staunch ASP supporter, who contributed a lot to the success of the party. So let us remember him." Then he began to castigate me as an Arab stooge; he said I had been given all of CCM's trust and that I had betrayed that trust and was now poisoning the people to reject the party. He called for stern action against me. Another chap, the late Jamal Ramadhan Nasibu, also accused me, saying the party possessed a tape in which I received instructions from Ali Muhsin, the former ZNP leader who had been imprisoned after the revolution and was now living in exile in the Gulf.

We were given a chance to defend ourselves, and we put up a very strong defense; some fair-minded members of the NEC even said there was no evidence against us. The case went late into the night, but Nyerere was traveling the next day and wanted to resolve the matter before he left the country. Finally, Nyerere summed up the session, trying to be fair, saying some of the evidence presented against us was not true. But all in all, he said, we needed to resign. We stood our ground, however. I said, "As long as I haven't done anything wrong, I'm not going to resign." That was a real challenge to Nyerere. And all my colleagues refused to resign as well because we thought that, if we resigned, it would suggest we were guilty, which might lose us popular support. In response, Nyerere simply said, "Okay, then I'm sacking all of you," and the NEC went along, by a show of hands.

This took place around twelve midnight, on the eve of twenty-seventh Ramadhan, which Muslims believe is a very auspicious night. It is the night, according to the Qur'an, of power, and if you do any good deed on that night, it is as if you have done that deed for a thousand months. If you pray on that night, it is as if you have prayed for a thousand months. Anything happening on that night is very auspicious, so instead of coming out of the meeting grieving, we were very happy. Hamad Haji, my private bodyguard, overheard one former minister named Job Lusinde telling his colleagues, "These young men are leaving here now, but they'll bring us a lot of trouble later on because they won't just accept this and keep quiet." Even Nyerere himself later acknowledged in an interview broadcast over German radio that, along with his recognition of the secessionist Biafran government in Nigeria, our expulsion from CCM was one of his greatest mistakes.

That same day in May 1988, there was a demonstration of Muslims in Zanzibar protesting a statement made by the late Mrs. Sophia Kawawa, the wife of Rashidi Kawawa and chairperson of *Umoja wa Wanawake* of Tanzania, the CCM women's wing. Though she was a Muslim, she said in a speech in front of the NEC that the Qur'an should be amended to allow women to marry more than one husband. A huge protest took place, which the police put down by force, killing one man and seriously injuring some others. One man was forced to have his leg amputated. When Mwinyi came here personally to meet with religious leaders, people were angry with the government for trying to deny that the man had been killed by the police, albeit accidentally. They also considered it blasphemous to suggest the Qur'an should be amended since it is the word of God. Religious sentiments are really something one must be careful about because they touch the emotions of the people. Many thought Mwinyi did not take the matter seriously, and that cost him some respect in Zanzibar.

On August 8, 1988, some close friends and supporters and I held a formal meeting at my residence in which we resolved we would always stick together to bring about the unity of all Zanzibaris. The meeting included myself as the chair, Shabaan Khamis Mloo, Ali Haji Pandu, Machano Khamis Ali, and Juma Othman Juma. I traveled to Pemba in May 1989, and everywhere I went people came in large numbers to see and hear me. If they knew I was passing through their area, they would gather in large numbers. Strictly speaking, these were illegal meetings, but I had already promised the people I would be with them whether in or out of the party, so I could not run away from them now. I traveled from Wete to Chake Chake and had to stop in almost every village along the way to discuss matters with locals, telling them they should not despair as long as they maintained their unity. There were many police roadblocks, but we always passed through, and the police never recognized me. On May 9, I got wind while at Chake Chake that the police wanted to arrest me, so my bodyguards hid me in a safe house. I thought if the authorities arrested me in Pemba, it would lead to bloodshed, so better to be arrested in Unguja. My bodyguards chartered a plane, and we flew out about 6:30 the next morning, and the police did not know.

I drove straight to my home in Mtoni. The same day two Land Rovers full of police arrived with a warrant to search my house. At the end of the search, the authorities arrested me and took me to the Mwembe Madema police station. After formalities, I was taken, barefoot, to a very dirty and wet cell that smelled of urine, with concrete benches around the room. I had to relieve myself into a bucket. The next morning I was taken to the district court at Vuga where I was charged with holding illegal meetings. The magistrate had been instructed not to give me bail, so I was sent straight to the central prison at Kilimani, under heavy escort. I was sent to a special area called "Cottage for Children" set aside for offenders under the age of eighteen. The prison officials reserved a special room for me alone, with a mattress but no bed. I was kept there as a sort of psychological torture, surrounded by children, with no adults to talk to.

Later, the government changed the charge against me, alleging I was found with top-secret government documents. And, indeed, when the police searched my home in Mtoni, they left with a number of files. That was a serious offense; holding illegal meetings could only draw a fine or a one-month jail sentence, maximum, whereas anyone caught possessing secret government documents was liable for up to twenty-five years' imprisonment. My bodyguards went to Kenya and managed to get the services of two very prominent human rights lawyers: Mr. Pheroze Nowjee, assisted by Mr. Murtaza Jaffer. When they arrived in Zanzibar, they faced harassment from security forces; they were searched at the airport and questioned and intimidated in their hotel rooms, but they were very bold.

The prosecutor throughout my trial was a police officer from the mainland named Lawrence Mtembei. His assignment was to ensure that I was kept behind bars and that the case was sometimes heard *in camera*, meaning that no observers and no press should be allowed in the court. When I was called to defend myself, the officials closed the roads leading to the courthouse and chased people on foot away from the area. My defense became a political speech. The judge interrupted many times, saying that I was just making a speech, but I was allowed to continue. I recorded my speech in my cell and had it circulated everywhere in Zanzibar. I said that my trial was just an example of CCM oppression; I said that the people should unite in a common cause and that, if the government killed me, the struggle would still continue. In total, I spent thirty months in prison, from May 1989 to November 1991.

Mwinyi was president of the union during all that time and knew of the injustice done to me. He knew that the NEC elections in 1985 were rigged, giving Idris the nomination for the Zanzibari presidency. In fact, at the time he lamented in confidence to Khatib Hassan Khatib that an injustice had been done to me. But later he danced according to the party tune. When I was detained, Mwinyi addressed a public meeting in Pemba, saying, "We'll catch these fish one by one, and the largest of them has already been caught, and he's already in the freezer." True to his word, in 1990, more of my colleagues were arrested and detained under the president's powers—they were not even sent to court. They were: Ali Haji Pandu, Shabaan Khamis Mloo, Machano Khamis Ali, Juma Othman Juma, Soud Yusuf Mgeni, Suleiman Seif Hamadi, Juma Ngwali Kombo, Said Baes, Hamad Kingwaba, Masudi Omar, Kombo Hassan, Hamid Haji, and Salim Muhammed Jaha. They stayed in detention nearly six months and then were released. After their release, they began in earnest to agitate for multiparty democracy. Eight of them formed a pressure group known as *Kamahuru:* or *kamati ya kupigania vyama huru* [committee to struggle for multipartyism]. Mloo was elected as chairman, Ahmed Seif Hamad as vice chairman, and Ali Haji Pandu as secretary. They agitated in full consultation with me in jail and had all my blessings. They issued press releases and tried to mobilize people and to draw international support.

Around that time, leaflets were distributed throughout Zanzibar Town that really provoked the government. They all said *"Bismilahi rahman rahiem,"* the opening words of the Qur'an and nothing else. The words mean: "In the name of God, the most merciful and the most magnificent."

Kamahuru did not circulate the pamphlets; refugees in Dubai smuggled them into Zanzibar in large quantities. They thought what we really needed in Zanzibar was an Islamic state because, I am told, some were Muslim extremists. People put the messages on their doors and cars as stickers, and the government could not, as a government led by Muslims, ban these messages since they came straight from the Qur'an. Idris was very pious and did not want to be considered an infidel. Yet since the government was so unpopular, it was very insecure and could not tolerate such things. The police tore up the messages and arrested many people arbitrarily, leaving them in police cells for days without sending them to court. They would arrest a man and keep him for forty-eight hours, release him, and then arrest him again. Some detainees were just moved about from one police station to another.[1]

My own treatment in prison could have been worse. The worst part was the isolation. Generally, however, the prison wardens respected me and were never abusive. While the other inmates were required to remove all their clothing during inspections, the guards never ordered me to do so. The wardens even came and sat and played bao with me and gave me all kinds of information from outside, including messages from my family. My family could bring me meals and visit me once a month for half an hour or so, but my advocates could come any time. If I wanted to see somebody, the wardens would summon him or her from outside, but when we spoke, we always did so in front of guards. There was also a "red cap"—a prison monitor and fellow prisoner—who was very trusted and who brought me whatever I wanted, even papers and tape recorders. One of the red caps would smuggle messages out for me.

One day there was a surprise search in the prisons. The guards found some sensitive papers in my room, but the warden was very kind. He found messages that I had been writing to my friends outside, and instead of telling his seniors, he just took them away himself. What really made the prison authorities angry was when Mwinyi appointed a commission to hear the people's view about the possibility of Tanzania's converting to multipartyism, a topic on which I managed to write about seventy pages, which I smuggled out. It was typed, then given to Ali Haji Pandu to present formally to Chief Justice Francis Nyalali, the chairman of the commission. This really angered the authorities. To isolate me further, they transferred me from the juvenile section to a room very close to the kitchen, where all the smoke tended to concentrate. I protested to my lawyers, so they transferred me to the cells on death row. Then I really made hell; I began a hunger strike and said I would not eat until I was moved. So I was moved again, to a very "nice" old place within the prison, with a big garden where, in the daytime, I could walk. I stayed there until I was released.

My brother Abdullah Sharif died when I was in jail in 1990, but nobody told me. Even those who brought me information from outside never mentioned his death. It was only after my release that my relatives informed me. They said that I had enough worries in jail and that they did not want to give me more stress.

While I was inside, Idris stepped down as president of Zanzibar. What has been said is that CCM officials felt he had failed to control the opposition, although it was still underground. When he was on a visit to Germany, the Central Committee met and agreed that Idris should not continue as president and on the day of his return, sent a messenger to inform him that he should not run for another term. After Salmin Amour replaced Idris in 1990, some people advised him to make a fresh start by ordering my release. But Salmin was not willing or bold enough to take that step because he had his instructions from the top. The German ambassador spoke to him, however, and was able to convince him to release me on the condition that I refrain from politics. When she came to me with this news, I told the ambassador that no one could take away my right to participate in politics and that I would never forsake this right, even if it meant staying in prison all my life. She said, "Yes, that is quite reasonable but do not instigate people against the government." I said, "The people have the right to express their grievances, and I have the same right. If they generally accept my views, who is to blame?"

The government continued to receive a lot of pressure from Amnesty International, various diplomatic missions, and some academicians. In the end, the leaders decided to give me bail but under very tough conditions. I needed to provide five million Tanzanian shillings as a standing bond. My passport was confiscated, I was not to travel outside Zanzibar Town, and I was neither to speak in public meetings nor to attend gatherings of any kind.

On the day of my release, I gathered my belongings and was transported in a prison vehicle to my house. As the guards took me home, some people saw me on the way, and word of my release spread immediately; the hordes began soon thereafter to arrive at my home in Mtoni to wish me well. I came out with a big beard because in prison we did not always have the amenities to shave and because it was a symbol of my PG status: prison graduate. After I came out, I decided I liked having a beard, and ever since, it has been part of my brand.

By the time of my release, I had two new lawyers named Dr. Masumbuko Lamwai and the late Yusuf Mchora, who appealed on my behalf to the Court of Appeal in Dar es Salaam. After hearing both sides argue about the conditions of my bail, the judge ruled that the conditions were very oppressive and ordered that I be allowed to travel around Tanzania, that my passport be returned to me, and that I regain permission to address any public rallies. Even the bond was reduced. We then appealed my case; I won the appeal and was set free.

twelve MULTIPARTYISM

I WAS RELEASED IN November 1991, and on February 28, 1992, the CCM National Congress, in an extraordinary session and after a very hot debate, passed a resolution to allow Tanzania to adopt multipartyism. In fact, some members of the congress were not in favor of multipartyism and condemned the new political parties even before they were formed. But after the fall of the Berlin Wall, the donor nations now put emphasis on multiparty democracy. There was also internal pressure, so Nyerere saw that it was better to contain the situation by allowing new parties that could be controlled, rather than just to resist. In fact, he made the famous statement that it was no sin to talk about multiparty politics in Tanzania, and after that, Mwinyi appointed a commission under the then chief justice, the late Francis Nyalali, to collect the views of Tanzanians. In the end, the Nyalali Commission found that more than 45 percent in Zanzibar favored the introduction of multipartyism, while, on mainland Tanzania, the number was only about 20 percent. About 80 percent of those who wanted a one-party system had recommended, however, drastic reforms to the system.

Despite these results, the commission recommended that the country adopt a multiparty system. The National Congress passed a resolution establishing a timetable for the transition: by April 1992, Parliament was supposed to amend the constitution, as well as pass a bill permitting the establishment of political parties. Most CCM congress leaders were not in favor of multipartyism, considering it a threat to their monopoly on power. Salmin Amour, as president of Zanzibar, made it very clear that, if it were not for the union, the islands would never accept multipartyism. In a speech to the National Congress in February 1992, he said, essentially, "We accept this because we are part of Tanzania and have no choice, but if it were our own decision, we wouldn't accept the reform."

So it is no wonder that, when parties were established in Zanzibar, there was considerable state resistance. Yet when my colleagues and I went to explain to Nyerere why we were organizing our own party, his attitude was totally different. He told us it was time to have serious parties in the country apart from CCM; they would check the excesses of the government and of the ruling party. CCM would be kept on its toes and forced to deliver. He said that now it was as if CCM were on holiday. He wished me success and said, "I know you're a serious young man, and I'm sure the country will benefit if you have a good party. But we should refrain from dividing the nation on racial, tribal, or religious grounds, or even which part of the union one comes from." He insisted national unity was still our cherished goal.

Parliament made regulation of the new parties a union matter. I thought this another erosion of Zanzibar's sovereignty, but later I found it a blessing in disguise because if the Zanzibari government had exercised sole jurisdiction over these matters, our party would probably never have even been allowed to register. The bill also made it necessary for each party to be national, to have members in both parts of the union, and not to be religiously, racially, or tribally oriented.

While I was in jail, I had thought about what the party should be called, and I came up with the name ZUF: Zanzibar United Front. My colleagues accepted the proposal. After my release, we held regular secret meetings at my home in Mtoni. We discussed different options: one was to go ourselves to find members on the mainland; another was to look for a group already organized on the mainland with which we could merge. We decided that it would be much easier and quicker to find an established group ready to work with us. We sent a delegation to approach, in turn, the Union for Multiparty Democracy [UMD], the National Committee for Construction and Reform [NCCR], and, finally, the Civic Movement, led by James Mapalala. Of the three, only the Civic Movement responded positively, so we began serious negotiations with it. We agreed we should take the name *civic* from Mapalala's group and *united front* from our own, to call our party the Civic United Front, or CUF.

On May 27, 1992, the leadership of the two groups met secretly in Zanzibar in a house in Kokoni belonging to my sister-in-law. Now the house is known as Beit el-Haq, or the House of Justice, because a slogan of our party afterward was *haki sawa kwa wote*, or equal rights for all. On the day we met, it was raining heavily outside. We signed a contract that divided positions in the party on a provisional basis, with Mapalala serving as chairman, myself as vice chairman, and Shabaan Khamis Mloo as secretary general.

The law stipulated that, in order to gain legal registration, we needed to send a copy of the party's constitution to the government, and if accepted by the authorities, we were then given six months to look for members. The minimum requirement was two hundred members from at least eight regions out of twenty on the mainland and two regions on the islands, one of which needed to be in Pemba. Mr. Mloo and Mussa Haji Kombo did a wonderful job leading the effort to recruit members. We aimed for certification in twelve regions, and in the end, we had fourteen. Our advantage was that most of our leaders were former high CCM officials, so we were experienced. Our representatives found locally influential people and discussed our party's aims with them. We then informed the registrar that we were ready for inspection; he traveled around the regions and was satisfied with our efforts. On January 21, 1993, CUF received permanent registration. We members then held our first party congress in Dar es Salaam, which approved a constitution and elected office bearers, including Mapalala, Shabaan Mloo, and myself.

The enthusiasm and support of the people made me very energetic. Of course, the government still attacked and insulted us. In Zanzibar, we faced the arbitrary arrest of our members, police beatings, and government unwillingness to grant us permits to hold public rallies. Despite these obstacles, the party grew very fast, so much so that at times the government would give silly orders. The regional commissioner from Zanzibar North, Abdallah Rashid, once tried to ban me from entering his region. We took him to the High Court, and after some delays, the court ruled that he had no such powers and that I was free to go wherever I wanted. At another time, the government ordered that no one except the president could travel with escorts, since wherever I went, I was escorted by at least two or three cars. The whole CCM administration regarded CUF as public enemy number one.

When I first came out of jail, I actually wrote a very courteous letter to Salmin Amour, telling him I did not see any reason that we should quarrel since we knew each other very well and had worked well together in CCM in the 1980s. In those years, I often stayed in his house when in Dodoma on party assignments. I said that we were both working for the people, so we should cooperate. For a period of time, we were in contact with each other, though we did not meet face to face. Salmin would send one of his ministers, Saidi Bakari Jecha, as intermediary. He would come in disguise to my house at night to convey messages, wearing a very old and rugged *kanzu* and leaving his car very far from my house so that he had to walk the rest of the way. My bodyguards nicknamed him *Kanzu Bovu* [Ragged Kanzu].

One day Salmin informed me that he was going to a Central Committee meeting in Dodoma and that afterward he would see me. But after his return, he instead held a public rally where he really castigated me. He probably consulted his superiors in Dodoma, and they advised against the meeting. And that is when things really began to sour. I continued to write him letters offering advice when I felt the interests of Zanzibar were being threatened. I would say that CUF was prepared to offer its support, but he never replied and instead just attacked me in public meetings. To make matters worse, there was an incident in Unguja in the village of Mkokotoni during the month of Ramadhan in 1992 when a stone-throwing crowd attacked my party colleagues and me. The police came to escort us to the station, where we spent the night. Afterward, in 1993, as I spent six months abroad, I gave a BBC interview in which I made the allegation that Salmin was involved in a plot to kill me, referring to the incident in Mkokotoni. Salmin sued the BBC, and later the BBC agreed to settle with him out of court.

While abroad, I also heard rumors from Zanzibar that the government wanted to arrest me on my return. One cadre, Omar Aweisi, went to the extent in CCM meetings of showing prisoners wearing shorts, saying I would soon be wearing such shorts. CUF organized a huge rally to receive me on my return; from the airport, I went straight to address a rally at the Malindi grounds, where I challenged the government to arrest me. I also made a pledge that, if CUF came to power, it would bring significant changes to the lives of Zanzibaris in a matter of a hundred days. At every occasion afterward, CCM challenged me, asking how I would do that. Especially Dr. Omar Ali Juma, who said, "My brothers, don't be deceived by this man; the difficulties here in Zanzibar are the same throughout the world. Even in Europe the conditions are the same." When I had the opportunity, I replied, "When the chief minister says conditions in Europe are the same as ours, I think he's referring to Albania."

Salmin disliked Pemba and generally avoided appointing Pembans to his government, with only one Pemban cabinet official in his second administration, the minister of trade and industry. All the rest were from Unguja. In terms of development projects, Pemba was left out. There was also discrimination in education. Salmin said very openly that Pembans had already learned, and now they must mark time. Almost all the students who went to the University of Dar es Salaam were from Unguja, not Pemba. When the government sent eighty students to Malaysia for training, it sent only Ungujans. Unfortunately, they had no qualifications; they were sent only because they helped CCM rig the 1995 elections, and all of them failed. They enrolled in elementary computer and secretarial courses, and yet not a single one passed. As a government leader, Salmin should have tried to unite the country, but instead he claimed that CUF was a party for Pembans and that Pembans were not good people, that they were bent on usurping power, so they should be opposed by all means. He did a real disservice to his country.

As we began to challenge CCM, our party also faced its own internal problems, particularly concerning our first chairman, James Mapalala. He was secretly meeting with the then prime minister of Tanzania, John Malecela, who, we heard, told him that the government had intercepted a letter written to me from people in the Gulf allegedly telling me to depose all of CUF's non-Muslim leaders. Unfortunately, Mapalala believed that nonsense and did not want to discuss it with me. He was a changed man: he expelled party members he thought were sympathetic to us in Zanzibar and even wrote a circular prohibiting the secretary general and me from visiting the mainland regions. We discussed this situation in the party's Central Committee, which met for seven consecutive days in Dar es Salaam in 1994. In fact, it was a very bitter exchange between his group and the rest of the party. He refused our suggestion to adjourn the meeting to allow the two of us to sit down together and find a compromise. He eventually walked out with some of his supporters on the Central Committee, all except five persons from the mainland: Wabu Musa, Pawa Musa, Hassani Omari, Hamisi Hassan, and Ali Hashim Namata. By refusing to walk out that day, those five men saved the party. They withstood pressure from their mainland colleagues, and they deserve our praise.

The Central Committee decided to convene an extraordinary session of the National Congress in Tanga in November 1994 to resolve the matter. After deliberations, the congress decided by secret ballot to expel Mapalala from the party. The vote was unanimous: nearly 750 delegates voted for his expulsion. He did not come to defend himself; he was an arrogant troublemaker who conspired with government leaders to destroy the party.

After that, the Zanzibari government invited Mapalala to Zanzibar and gave him a heavy police escort. They continued to call him the CUF chairman and even organized a public rally on his behalf, in the name of CUF. On the radio and television, speakers all praised him as a wise man. The government convinced him to open a case against us in the Zanzibari High Court, assuring him that the ruling would be in his favor: that he was sacked in contravention of the party constitution and should be reinstated as chairman. Unfortunately for him, the judge presiding over the case was Wolfango Dourado. After all sides had given evidence, Mapalala was required to come to court, but he did not arrive on time. Dourado ruled against him, saying he was expelled in accordance with the party constitution. He even blamed Mapalala for trying to sow seeds of discord within CUF and said that, in doing such, he was an obstacle to the nation's democratization. By the time Mapalala showed up in court, Dourado had ruled against him, and he was very disappointed.

After that first attempt to destroy our party, our task was to find a person from the mainland to replace Mapalala. Shaaban Mloo proposed we approach one old man in Mwanza region named Mr. Musobi Mageni Musobi, who during Nyerere's time was minister of housing, then served two or three times as district commissioner, and had retired. So we went to see him. He accepted our offer but told us, "I'm an old man, so just consider me a ceremonial chairman. You should look for a younger man." The local district commissioner then approached him and began to entice him to leave the party. The district commissioner (DC) promised that the government would build Musobi a multistoried house either in Mwanza or in Dar es Salaam, as he chose. It would appoint him executive chairman of a big parastatal and give him a very nice car.

But Musobi was very sincere and straightforward, and his response to the DC was, "What has happened so that now I've become such an important person? Before becoming the CUF chairman, I'd been retired from government service for more than ten years. And nobody asked me anything or provided me anything, and now suddenly the government is interested in me, and I have all these offers." Musobi told the DC, "Tell your superiors I know you've deceived many people with a lot of attractive promises, but in the end, when you've made them lose the confidence of their colleagues, you just forget them. Even if you give me cash, I'm not prepared to betray my party." They never approached him again.

As the 1995 elections approached, it was well known that I would be CUF's candidate for the Zanzibari presidency, but we had problems finding a capable candidate for the union presidency since Musobi did not want to stand for that office. It was the eve of the National Congress to nominate candidates; we had invited all our delegates but did not even have a candidate for the union presidency! Shaaban Mloo recommended Ibrahim Haruna Lipumba, a professor at the University of Dar es Salaam, and we immediately dispatched a delegation to see him. He agreed at once, saying, "As long as you have confidence in me and want me as your candidate, then I accept." The National Governing Council accepted him, and the National Congress nominated him almost unanimously. I was also nominated for the Zanzibari presidency. After that, in July 1995, we came to Zanzibar Town where a huge crowd put us on their shoulders.[1]

thirteen PRINCIPLES

CUF HAS AN IDEOLOGY known as *utajarisho*, which means something similar to "enrichment." In a nutshell, it means that national resources should be well utilized for the benefit of the public. People should be helped, given a proper education, and then encouraged to make use of Tanzania's abundant resources. The ideology of *utajarisho* is based on the belief that, if you can improve the life of an individual, that individual is like a brick in the construction of a house. Our ideology is based more on individual development than on socialist principles of community development. In fact, our motto, which is very popular and which has attracted a lot of people, is *haki sawa kwa wote*, equal rights for all. It is also *neema kwa wote*, meaning prosperity or a good life for all.

CUF believes that the union should continue but that it needs restructuring. We call for the establishment of three governments, instead of two: one each for Tanganyika and Zanzibar and one for the federal union. We believe the union as it exists today will continue to have problems, so it is better to have an authority responsible for nonunion matters in Tanganyika, another in Zanzibar, and a third responsible only for union affairs. Even the articles of the union, which is the grand norm, established three distinct jurisdictions. Now we have something very confusing: a union government responsible for both union matters throughout the United Republic and for nonunion matters in Tanganyika. Many Zanzibaris feel that this is a way to swallow the islands because we have transferred authority to what is, in effect, a Tanganyikan government. Tanganyika did not surrender anything and only got more power.

CUF's policy is very clear: we do not want to break the union. It would be folly to do so. We cannot afford in Zanzibar to have a giant Tanganyikan neighbor as our enemy. And over the past forty years, bonds and relationships have been created among people from the mainland

and from the islands. Many children have parents from both places, so where would they go? Thousands of Zanzibaris live on the mainland, and some of them have property and businesses there, so what would happen to them if we broke the union? And, after all, the trend in the world is for states to amalgamate rather than divide. Look at what is happening in Europe; even former communist countries are now competing to join the European Union. And in Africa, we now have the East African Community, the ECOWAS [Economic Community of West African States], and the SADC [South African Development Community]. What is important, I believe, is to have an arrangement that ensures Zanzibar's interests and autonomy. The ideal situation would be to revert to how things were in 1964, when Nyerere and Karume agreed that only eleven matters would be under union jurisdiction. CUF stands for an adjusted union, so that both nations feel there is justice. Yet if things continue as they have, in a few years Zanzibar will end up as simply another region of Tanzania, with little autonomy left at all.

CUF has also been portrayed as a party that rejects the revolution, which is not true. Whether we like it or not, it happened; nobody can deny there was a revolution in January 1964. Unfortunately, CCM has invented the allegation that our party does not accept the revolution and wants to break the union. CCM has, in fact, taken these two things— the revolution and the union—as its own personal possessions and has justified its unwillingness to accept defeat on the grounds that it is the only party defending the union and revolution, which is not true. All parties must accept the revolution as an historical fact; the question is whether the revolution achieved its objectives. And about that we are very clear: it has not. The revolution, you can say, went astray, to the extent of devouring its own sons.

It is only CCM propaganda that we want to return the lands redistributed to the people after the revolution. What we say is that many peasants received three-acre plots but never title deeds to their land. We will give them title deeds, so they know it is their property and will help them utilize their lands for their own benefit. After land reform, clove and coconut production declined dramatically, and plantations went to bush; but with personal-property rights, the peasants will be able to obtain bank loans so as to develop their land.

Of course, there are the concerns of those people whose lands were taken to give to the peasants. We have said that we will sit with them and try to find a way so that they will accept what has taken place, even through offers of compensation. Any kind of property that was legally nationalized should have been gazetted; but, unfortunately, ASP branch chairmen and senior government officials took a lot of land for them-selves, and there are no records of these confiscations. People really abused their power, so this is a question that, unfortunately, does not have an easy answer. If CUF comes to power, it will appoint a commis-sion, and the commission will recommend what should be done about these nongazetted confiscations. But there will be no question of taking back from peasants lands given to them legally.[1]

The accusation that CUF is an Arab or non-African party is pure propaganda. I have been asking our opponents in CCM how we could have obtained registration if we are an Arab party. The registrar, appointed by the government, has the power to strike the registration of any party that does not meet the required qualifications. Instead, CUF has united Zanzibaris of different backgrounds, including former ASP leaders and cadres, people like Shaaban Mloo, Ali Haji Pandu, and so on. In fact, the majority of CUF leaders in Zanzibar have roots in the ASP. There are also those in CUF who supported the ZNP, the ZPPP, and the Umma Party; so people of all political ancestries are found in CUF. It is a Zanzibari party in Zanzibar and a Tanzanian party in Tanzania.

Zanzibar includes a mixture of cultures and races, and any political leader needs to bear that in mind. But in the end, we are all Zanzibaris, no matter our racial or ethnic origins. Some people say that there are people in Zanzibar who do not consider themselves Africans, but to my knowledge, it is only those who have come to the islands in the recent past, after World War II, who consider themselves Africans, and they are a minority. The Tumbatu and the Hadimu do not consider them-selves Africans as such. So I ask myself why this issue of African identity is continually raised in Zanzibar; on the mainland, the question is not whether you are African, but whether you are Chagga, Haya, Nywamwezi, or a member of some other ethnic group. If a Tanzanian of African ori-gins goes across the border to Zambia, would he receive equal rights there? No, he would be arrested and returned to Tanzania.

I do not see why people in Zanzibar of African origins should be given more rights than, say, an Indian family that has been here for sev-eral generations. It is wrong to discriminate for whatever reason and a sin to use racialism and tribalism to divide the people, especially in a cosmopolitan place like Zanzibar. The resentment of Africans toward people not of pure African descent, especially Arabs, comes from slav-ery, from the degradation of their ancestors. But in a country like Zanzi-bar, it is folly to think in terms of race because most people in the islands have mixed blood. Those who call themselves Africans should not con-sider those who do not as racists. One of CUF's tasks will be to enact policies that encourage people to think of themselves as Zanzibaris, rather than as Africans, Arabs, or anything else. We want to promote the idea that all Zanzibaris are citizens, united by a common history and destiny, rather than divided according to racial origins. Of course, some Zanzibaris of mainland origin are not comfortable when we say we want to promote *Uzanzibari,* or "Zanzibariness." CCM has been very good at labeling CUF as an Arab party that wants to bring back the sultan, an accusation that is completely absurd. There is no way the monarchy can come back to Zanzibar. The idea is outdated; it would be very queer now to reinstate the sultan. Nor would it be acceptable to the majority of the population. Instead, we need a presidency controlled by a series of constitutional checks and balances.

CCM propaganda has also tried to label CUF as a Muslim party. It is true that, when we first began, we adopted a strategy that would ensure we grew gradually, with Zanzibar as our first priority, a country where the vast majority is Muslim. But Muslims are Tanzanians, and they have the right to join any party they so choose. Our opponents say that most of the leaders in CUF are Muslims, including the secretary general, chairman, and vice chairman. But they stop there; they do not look beyond that. Even if their allegations were true, it would make sense that these people would be Muslims since the party comes primarily from Zanzibar. Look at our main rival in Zanzibar: all the leaders are Muslims. So why does this label apply only to the CUF? And if you look at CCM on the mainland in 2005, the chairman, vice chairman, and secretary general were all Christians. In the union government in 2005, the president, prime minister, speaker of the National Assembly, and chief justice were all Christians. Since that was the case, should we have considered CCM to be a Christian party?

In CUF, we have a Governing Council consisting of twenty-five members from the mainland and twenty from Zanzibar. Of course, those from Zanzibar are all Muslims except one, but from the mainland, thirteen of the twenty-five are Christians, including a reverend. So the allegations that we are a Muslim party have no basis; they only demonstrate CCM's political bankruptcy. Without convincing power or worthwhile policies, CCM resorts to foolish things like religion and racialism.

I want Zanzibar to join the Organization of the Islamic Conference [OIC]. It was unfair that Zanzibar was not allowed to join the OIC in 1993 because, although the union has jurisdiction over foreign affairs, our joining was, instead, a matter of international development cooperation. Zanzibar would have benefited a great deal, as have the Comoro Islands. They have very good roads there, paid for by the OIC. If a country like

Uganda can be a member and benefit, with a population less than 20 percent Muslim, or Mozambique, with a population about 12 percent Muslim, then why not Zanzibar? During Salmin Amour's administration, Zanzibar became a member of the OIC, but the union government objected and forced Zanzibar to withdraw. At the time, we were told that Zanzibar needed to withdraw to make room for Tanzania to join. But what attempt did Tanzania make to join the OIC? None—the government was just deceiving us. After his retirement, Salmin explained to one of his friends why he eventually agreed to withdraw, after he had said he would never back down on the issue. He said Nyerere summoned both him and Mwinyi and told them squarely that, if they did not withdraw [Zanzibar from the OIC], he would order the army to occupy Zanzibar. According to Salmin, Mwinyi was trembling, and the two said they had no choice but to withdraw.[2]

I want to join the OIC in order to obtain the economic benefits that come from membership. Of course, the OIC is a political organization, consisting mostly of Muslim nations trying to influence international relations in the interests of Muslims, which is a legitimate cause. But there is no question here of trying to Islamize the world. President Museveni of Uganda, for example, would never have agreed to that. And I want Zanzibar, of course, to remain a secular state. Zanzibar has been secular since its inception, since the time of the Zenj Empire and during the Omani al-Busaidi dynasty that came in the nineteenth century. The Zanzibari sultans gave missionaries from Europe land on which to build their missions and cathedrals; these Christians used Zanzibar as a base for their proselytizing efforts on the mainland. Zanzibar is a tolerant society; during Ramadhan, even the Christians and Hindus respect local customs and do not eat openly in the streets. Religious pluralism is very healthy in Zanzibari society and should be maintained.

When I say I want to put into practice the teachings of Islam that place great emphasis on unity, I do not mean to suggest that I wish to discriminate against religious minorities. They will have freedom of worship and the same rights and opportunities as everyone else. The mixture of different religions and cultures makes Zanzibar a unique society, a cosmopolitan society, and we want to retain that. Islam teaches that all people are equal, regardless of their ethnicity, and I want to use those teachings to unite Zanzibaris. If the teachings of Islam are followed, there will be no room for segregation or discrimination.

Of course, the mainland faces its own issues when it comes to religion. Traditionally, Christians and Muslims have lived together; even within one family, some members might be Christians, some Muslims.

That is very common, and that is the reason the two religions have co-operated and worked together for so long. But there has been some antagonism of late between Muslims and Christians, which the authorities in Tanganyika should not ignore. Muslims feel that the government under Nyerere deliberately sidelined the Muslims, though it was they, in fact, who supported Nyerere and who were in the forefront of the struggle for independence. The Christians had good jobs and were afraid to antagonize the colonial administration, but the Muslims had nothing to lose.

After independence, the East African Muslim Welfare Society was very powerful and active in education and health projects. But Nyerere banned the organization and replaced it with BAKWATA, a Muslim association with close ties to the ruling party. Muslims have ever since argued that Christians are allowed to do what they want, but Muslims are put under firm government control. Muslims also feel that they have been left out in terms of education and government positions. In twenty-four years of power, Nyerere never appointed a Muslim minister of education. At the University of Dar es Salaam, the Muslims are very few, usually less than 10 percent of the student population. Christians have, therefore, taken most of the important posts in the civil service and parastatals. Muslims have been calling for the government to address these inequalities; even if they are unintentional, the government needs to address the problem, if a large segment of the population feels this way.[3]

Also, on the mainland, there are some Muslims who criticize Christianity in their sermons, and even claim that Islam is the true religion. This has not been taken well by Christians, and seeds of discord have begun to appear. Most Muslim critics have returned from studying abroad in other countries like Saudi Arabia, Iran, and Sudan. Those educated here by local Muslim *ulama* are more traditional, but those who go abroad do not have any loyalty to any religious leader in the region and feel they can criticize Christianity harshly.

To a large extent, however, I think the government has—fortunately—brought this under control. In a secular state that allows freedom of worship, there should be respect for one another; if you insult another faith, you should expect to be insulted as well. People should use their sermons to convince others of the truthfulness of their own faith, rather than to find fault with another. Islam is, after all, a tolerant religion; even under the Holy Prophet, it was ordained that those who belonged to other religions should be defended unless they fought or attacked Muslims. Although it is true that in the Qur'an, there are certain passages that call upon Muslims to fight, it is only in self-defense.

This is what we espouse in CUF, but CCM has, nevertheless, painted us as a terrorist party. CCM propaganda has been very effective, especially in the early years, on the mainland and in some international capitals. We in CUF believe terrorism is illogical because it mainly hurts innocent people. Take the London bombings in 2005; the terrorists bombed the underground, so that those hit were ordinary innocent people of various races and religions who did not necessarily have any position on what was happening in Iraq or anywhere else. We in CUF condemn terrorism in the strongest terms; we have always felt that we should seek solutions to the world's problems through dialogue, yet because we had no resources to combat CCM propaganda against us, their message was initially somewhat effective. Now, however, it is clear that, if we keep having stolen elections in Zanzibar and if those who remain in power by force are unable to reduce poverty in the islands, then we will likely have Muslim extremism in Zanzibar. And on the mainland, if Muslim complaints are not squarely addressed and the Muslim population feels it is being neglected and becoming more disadvantaged, then there will be an opening for Muslim extremism.

Some people have thought our party very rich, that we have a lot of money coming from the Gulf, when, in fact, CUF has always had financial problems. Poor people sell a cock or hen in order to contribute to CUF. Wealthy individuals in Oman or anywhere else in the Gulf have contributed relatively little. The Omani government discourages their people from involvement in the political affairs of other nations and has made it very clear that their overseas relations are government to government. Very few Zanzibari exiles have retained their Tanzanian citizenship; some are CUF members, but they are not very rich. Sometimes members overseas contribute in kind, by providing cell phones, for example. This is one of our weakest points in CUF: we have not been able to learn how to raise funds.

Zanzibari exiles sent money in 2001 to help the families of those killed by the police and army. Sometimes they have held demonstrations in capitals like London and Washington to sensitize the international community to the situation here. They also support our trips abroad. If I travel to the U.S. or Europe, I buy a return ticket from Dar to London or New York. Zanzibaris living overseas pay for my side trips from these cities and provide accommodation, and that is how we can afford to travel, and we thank them for their support. But overall we really do not have much funding from outside. In fact, there was a belief even among our own members that we were being bankrolled by petrol dollars from the Gulf. There were even some opportunistic rogue leaders who left the party once they found they would need to contribute and could not wait for a party hand-out. Our main source of funds in 2005 came from a Tanzania government subsidy, about seventy million shillings a month, or about sixty thousand dollars. This amount was based on the number of parliamentary votes and seats we won in the most recent elections.

Many times CCM has tried to paint CUF as simply the resurrection of the ZNP and has asserted that, before he died, Ali Muhsin had the entire party in his power. If ZNP supporters in the Gulf were actually helping us, then CUF would not be starved for cash. And anyway, most CUF leaders came from the ASP, not the ZNP, and until the 1990s, I had met Ali Muhsin only once, as president of the Pemba Student's Union in 1963. It is true that, starting in 1992 or 1993, I visited Ali Muhsin whenever I traveled through the Gulf. I made a point of seeing him to ask about his health and to gain from his experience. I wanted to know what had gone wrong with the ZNP and how it was overthrown. But I was never very close to him, and only from about the year 2000 was it clear that Ali Muhsin supported the CUF. He instructed his followers here to support us, saying that the CUF was the only hope for Zanzibaris and that we had to learn from their mistakes.

In terms of economic development, it is CUF's position to privatize Zanzibar's clove industry. The government is reluctant to privatize because of the personal financial interests of Zanzibar's top state leaders, but if we were to privatize, the people themselves would find new markets for their crops, and the buyers would bargain directly with the growers; the government would just charge export duties. The industry would benefit the producers themselves and not the bureaucrats holding high positions. This would also stimulate production because the farmers would have a motive to produce more.

During the 2004 clove season, before harvesting started, the government announced a very high price, about four thousand shillings a kilo. That price affected the wages paid to the clove pickers and others who helped with the harvest, so the clove growers had to pay very dearly. Then toward the end of the harvest, the government lowered its price by almost half, and many growers suffered heavy losses. They refused to sell to the government and began to smuggle their harvests to Kenya. The government sent police to stop the smuggling, but in the end, the government realized it was paying the police more than what it reclaimed in terms of revenue. So everyone lost, on all sides; some cloves were never even harvested because the growers were so discouraged.

During the colonial period, the government never interfered like this. The Clove Growers Association [CGA], controlled by the clove farmers, would look for markets overseas and announce its prices beforehand. The CGA gave loans to farmers to maintain their plantations; to buy materials such as mats, bags, and pressure lamps; or to pay workers. After the revolution, the government abolished the CGA and created the Zanzibar State Trading Corporation [ZSTC], and all these services ceased. It is no wonder production has declined. In a good season, Zanzibar once produced about twenty-four thousand tons of cloves; now in some years, it is about six thousand tons. More than 80 percent of the cloves come from Pemba, and because they have not been paid well, many growers have allowed their clove trees to return to bush.

I remember that, when I was chief minister, I personally visited the plantations and met the clove farmers to hear their grievances. We managed to make the ZSTC give loans to farmers before harvesting, and they were very encouraged. They began to take an interest again in maintaining their plantations. I really liked meeting the people because intelligence reports simply delivered to my office always distorted the picture. During our time in the 1980s, smuggling declined dramatically because the farmers said to each other, "The government is now helping us." So if we cultivate the people's confidence, everyone will be surprised by the help the growers are ready to provide, especially if we go to them at their farms and listen to their problems at the source. They even sometimes propose workable solutions.

Unfortunately, now there is a glut in the world clove market. Indonesia was for a long time the biggest buyer of cloves, but now it is producing a lot itself. And when Tanzania recognized East Timor, Indonesia retaliated by erecting protectionist policies, reducing their purchase of Zanzibari cloves. So although privatization will motivate some farmers, we cannot rely solely on cloves because the demand is insufficient. We can, however, look into actually processing the cloves in Zanzibar, rather than just selling them raw. There has been no research in Zanzibar on how to process cloves or what new uses, perhaps in pharmaceuticals, cloves or clove by-products can be put. You cannot leave this research to farmers; it must be the work of the government.[4]

We also have to look into other economic sectors, and my conviction is that we have not utilized our land resources to the maximum. Every kind of tropical fruit can be grown in Zanzibar, very high-quality mangos, for example. All you need to do is train farmers how to grow and preserve them for export. The name *Zanzibar* still has a certain magic and would be a great marketing tool, especially in the Gulf. We would just need extension services to educate farmers to utilize their land to the maximum. Nor have we fully exploited our sea; more than 93 percent of the fish in Zanzibari waters die of old age, of natural deaths. Foreign companies come to our waters to fish and they benefit, but we do not. In the Seychelles, the government helps fisherman with refrigeration equipment and with a harbor fish-processing plant, but we do very little.

Measures to market and promote tourism began after Salmin Amour came to power. Idris did not take such concerted measures. Tourism has had some ill effects. In areas such as Matemwe and Nungwi, people complain that young girls have been let loose in a way that is against Zanzibari culture; they find prostitution an easy way of making money. I do not want to impose the sharia, and I do not want to arrest tourists for wearing bikinis. I just want to advise tourists to respect local culture by not walking through the town, especially women, exposing themselves. They can do what they want on the beach, but they should respect our customs in town. I also want to encourage higher-class tourism in the islands, rather than to depend mostly on backpackers. I want the government to train local people to work in the hotels, rather than outsiders. How much training do you need to make a bed or clean a room? As we move toward an East African federation and the free movement of goods and people across national boundaries when all that matters is one's qualifications, there is a danger that Kenyans and Ugandans will take most of the well-paying jobs in Tanzania. Since we lag behind our regional partners in education, we can arrive at a situation where foreigners take most of the good jobs.

Pemba is still less developed than Unguja, which is the result of a deliberate policy of the ASP/CCM government to punish Pembans for not supporting its party before the revolution. Pemba lags behind when it comes to roads and electricity. It is quite normal to have power rationing in Pemba and for big towns like Chake Chake, Wete, and Mkoani not to have any clean water. Things improved somewhat under Jumbe and Mwinyi, but then Salmin's regime reversed this course through deliberate discrimination. How can you say Pembans should not have access to higher education, that they should just mark time? How, according to official policy, can students with the highest qualifications be left out? How can you sack or demote people in the civil service merely for their Pemban origins? Salmin called himself a national leader yet completely rejected about 40 percent of the nation, whom he treated as second-class citizens. The worst time for divisions between Pemba and Unguja was Salmin's time.[5]

fourteen IMPASSE

IN THE 1995 ELECTIONS, CCM had all the resources it needed because it was state-supported. CUF, however, was starting from scratch; we party members knew we could not go everywhere in the country, but we could start in a few areas and establish ourselves. We wanted to begin in Zanzibar, then take the coastal areas, then move to the Lake Region, where many Tanzanians live. Our campaign meetings attracted thousands of people. I challenged Salmin Amour to a televised national debate, but he refused. I also made a public statement that, if the elections were free and fair, I would accept the results. I challenged Salmin to make the same announcement, but he refused. No CCM leader would make such a statement.

The voting took place October 22, 1995. I remember it was raining heavily, but people stood in very long lines; they were very enthusiastic and full of expectations. The voting went smoothly and peacefully. We were confident, perhaps overconfident, that we would win the elections. That was perhaps one of our weaknesses, overconfidence. We were naïve, especially I, believing CCM would easily accept defeat.

The next day the authorities completed counting the votes, and Aboud Talib Aboud, secretary of the Zanzibar Electoral Commission (ZEC), called together the agents of CUF and CCM. Our agent was Nassor Seif Amour, and Mzee Muumin represented CCM. They were both informed that I had received 56 percent of the vote but were told not to announce the results publicly before the ZEC did. Aboud Talib went to see Salmin at his residence and informed him that he had lost the elections. Salmin was furious. It is alleged that he retorted, "I didn't appoint you commissioner of the ZEC so as to see me lose the election." Salmin was corrupted with power and not prepared to let go. That day the deputy secretary general of CCM in Zanzibar, Ali Ameir Muhammed, gave a CCM written statement that the party rejected the results and wanted another election to be held.

Confident he was going to win, Salmin had planned a very grandiose swearing-in ceremony at the Mnazi Mmoja football grounds, where the party had constructed a huge platform. But on October 24, the workers began to dismantle the platform, and the police outriders for the official motorcade were all sent back to Dar es Salaam. At the time, people were very happy because they thought it meant CCM had accepted defeat. The ZEC still had to make a public announcement, but copies of the election results reached Dar es Salaam Television (DTV), which announced on the same day during prime time that I had won the election in Zanzibar. Later, the Tanzania Media Council, a government organ, reprimanded DTV and fined the network one million shillings for reporting the news.

Also on October 24, a delegation of CCM elders from Zanzibar went to see Nyerere, who was campaigning in Morogoro for Benjamin Mkapa, the CCM candidate for the union presidency, since voting for the union government was scheduled one week after ours in the islands. That evening Nyerere held a meeting with CCM party elders in a hall in Morogoro. One of the elders present in the meeting reported that Nyerere told them that CCM in Zanzibar had been defeated and that Seif had been elected president of Zanzibar. CCM elders from Zanzibar began to plead with Nyerere, saying, "It would be a shame for an old party like CCM to lose to a young party only three years old." They used all the old garbage that we were agents of the sultan, so it was necessary for Mwalimu to intervene. It is alleged that, after listening to these arguments, Nyerere called President Mwinyi and told him to instruct the ZEC to announce that Salmin had won by a very narrow majority.

So, in Zanzibar, the election officials had to make a lot of new computations, and that is the reason it took them until October 25 to give the results. They announced that Salmin got 50.2 percent and that I got 49.8 percent of the vote. Zubeir Juma Mzee, chairman of the ZEC, trembled as he announced the results. Many people were shocked and disappointed. There were women who miscarried; one man in Wete shouted out and then lost his voice and has never regained it since. Some people just dropped dead. Many people who had hoped for a better day felt betrayed. Many were crying like schoolchildren.

The UN observers, under the direction of Kari Karanko, the Finnish ambassador to Tanzania, asked the ZEC to allow them to recount the presidential vote. They were able to check only one constituency, Mlandege, and what they found was very telling. The voting for the House of

Representatives from some voting stations was overwhelmingly for CUF, but the presidential vote was overwhelmingly for Salmin. When they asked for a recount, they found that my votes were given to Salmin. Since in total only about 350,000 votes were cast, the observers requested one day to do a national recount, but the ZEC refused. There was one ZEC consultant, Ms. Judith Thompson from Canada, who could see the results had been doctored; she informed her High Commission, through which the international community was informed of what transpired. That is the reason most Western countries did not recognize Salmin as president and had no relations with his government until 1999.

After the results were announced, a political impasse ensued because I made a public statement saying that CUF did not accept the results and recognized neither Salmin as the duly elected president nor his government. I was cool and composed, but the single biggest regret of my entire political career is that we did not prepare any plans in case this sort of thing happened. I did not anticipate it, assuming I was dealing with honest and civilized people. For four days, I did not capture the moment, to sensitize CUF followers to demand that the results be announced. I simply waited, thinking these people were gentlemen, but they proved to be the worst crooks. We could have marched to ZEC headquarters and demanded nothing less than victory. If the people rose to that, I do not think the state would have used force to suppress the people. Mwinyi would not have ordered the use of the army without Nyerere's assent, and Nyerere would probably not have been willing to use force, especially if the international community was aware of the situation. Perhaps the international community did not act because we ourselves did not act. The international community did not and does not want Tanzania to be destabilized because for so long Tanzania has been one of the only stable countries in the troubled Great Lakes region.[1]

I remained calm during those days in October 1995, but I was very angry. I thought, "How can these people call themselves believers in God and be so unjust? How can they turn against the will of the people?" There were some people on the ZEC whom I respected; one had even been my teacher in secondary school. I knew him as a man of principle, yet he accepted the doctored results. Salmin later as payback appointed him chief secretary based at the State House.

Later we came to learn that many *maskani* youths on election day were given police uniforms, guns, and instructions—probably by Salmin and his hard-line supporters—that, if CCM lost, they were to go on a rampage, attacking CUF supporters, especially those from Pemba. The *maskani* were unemployed CCM youths paid to organize themselves into cells, and each cell was supplied with a television set. Whenever CCM wanted nasty things done to CUF, it would call on the *maskani*. The person financing them was Muhammed Raza, later appointed Salmin's advisor for sports. He forced other Indian businessmen to make large contributions to CCM, threatening overtaxation if they did not. The *maskani* were active only when they were paid and dormant when they were not. They did not have any real political convictions.

Even after Salmin was announced the winner, the *maskani* attacked some CUF supporters and burned their homes, forcing them to move back to Pemba. Surprisingly, when the BBC asked Salmin about the *maskani*, his reply was that he could not stop people from celebrating CCM's victory.[2] Some of CCM's female supporters, including members of the House of Representatives, came to the Michenzani blocks built during Karume's time and walked around the roundabout traffic circle naked. Some of them were very respectable ladies, and this was how they celebrated.

After Salmin's inauguration ceremony took place on October 27, I was very angry but did not lose hope. I did not think it was the end of the world, believing there would eventually be a day of justice. Yet ever since, I have been convinced that we did not capture the moment during those four days, and for that error, I carry the responsibility. As a result, the CUF has been in opposition for ten years, and the country has suffered more and more from oppression, corruption, and poverty.

CCM rigged certain House of Representatives constituencies, including those in Mfenesini, Kikwajuni, and Vikokotoni. Despite losing those seats, CUF won a total of twenty-four seats and CCM, twenty-six. In all, there are seventy-six seats in the house, of which fifty are elected and twenty-six appointed by the president himself and reserved for women, regional commissioners, and so on. To protest the rigging of the elections and to show that we did not recognize the government, CUF house members decided on a boycott. They showed up at house sessions only to be counted the minimum number of times in order to retain their seats. After the sessions opened with a prayer, they would leave. They voluntarily gave up their financial allowances to participate in the boycott, which was a very big sacrifice. CCM continued to conduct government business, but it was very embarrassing because the opposition side was completely empty. They criticized CUF house members for not serving the people yet publicly denied there was a political impasse.

In the years after the 1995 elections, Salmin's regime became more oppressive: arbitrary arrests of our rank-and-file members increased, and people were beaten and intimidated. In Pemba, there was a group of

JKU servicemen who would go around and find people sitting in the *baraza* and chase them, beat them, and arrest them. They were nicknamed "Melody," the name of a popular *taarab* musical group. The ballot papers used in 1995 carried serial numbers, so afterward, CCM conducted an investigation and connected individuals' names with serial numbers, and those in government employment who voted for CUF were often demoted or sacked. At Darajani, the petty traders selling things informally, who were predominantly CUF supporters, were continually chased and beaten by the police and *maskani*.[3]

In 1997, we had by-elections for a vacant house seat in Mkunazini, which CUF won. On the final day of the campaign, some of our people were arrested, charged with sedition, and denied bail, even though sedition is a bailable offense. Eventually, the offense was changed to treason. The case dragged on for almost three years, from 1998 until the defendants were released just after the 2000 elections. The number of the arrested increased from five to eighteen, including Juma Duni Haji. The Court of Appeals eventually ruled that an offense of treason can never be committed against Zanzibar because Zanzibar is not a sovereign state. When Salmin was about to finish his term, he ordered their release.

The problem with Tanzanian police officers is they think of themselves as CCM cadres and not as professional police. In the beginning, CUF had a motto: if you are beaten on one cheek, turn the other cheek. But the police took advantage of that stance, so now we say "a tooth for a tooth," or *jino kwa jino*. If somebody comes to beat you without reason, protect yourself. On the mainland, they also came up with this word *gangari*, a Matumbi word meaning to be very firm, smart, and prepared at all times. Especially in Dar es Salaam, our members did not accept mistreatment by the police; they resisted.

One of the ways we protected ourselves was through the establishment of a voluntary youth group called the Blue Guards, charged with the responsibility of protecting party leaders and property and of maintaining security at public rallies. The Blue Guards are very enthusiastic and committed; some receive allowances as bodyguards or as protectors of party headquarters, but the majority do not receive a single cent. All they ask for is the appreciation of their party leaders. They are very disciplined; if a party leader tells them to do something, they will do it without arguments. Of course, now the party has been joined by many youths, many from CCM, so now sometimes at public rallies, there is a problem with discipline when elements become rowdy. In such circumstances, we leaders say that anyone acting rowdy has been sent by CCM to make trouble for us, and everyone immediately sits down and maintains discipline and order.

After the 1995 elections, Omar Mapuri published his book on the Zanzibari Revolution, a work that I found disgusting because it included so many misrepresentations and because it encouraged ethnic divisions. He blamed slavery entirely on the Arabs, whom he portrayed as evil people. He also tried to justify the atrocities of the revolution in 1964, which was just propaganda and not palatable at all. So CUF organized a rally at the Malindi grounds, and the guest of honor was Machano Khamis Ali, now vice chairman of the party, who spoke against the book and ordered it burned. The crowd set fire to the one copy it had on hand. It was just symbolic, but people were ululating and really celebrating.

Interestingly, after that incident, Salmin's response was to make the book required reading in all the primary schools. But when Oman sent a delegation here to complain formally about the book, Salmin was very apologetic. He said to Professor Ibrahim Noor, who accompanied the delegation, "Who is this Mapuri? He's just a Mnyamwezi from the mainland who doesn't know the history of these islands." In fact, relations between Oman and Zanzibar soured after the publication of Mapuri's book. Nor did they improve when, in the 1990s, during our annual revolutionary celebrations, the government staged ritual reenactments of Arabs in 1964 having their beards shaved off and publicly humiliated.

One of our headaches in CUF is that there are some people who, when they are on the party platform and receive applause, become too emotional and cannot control themselves. They make statements that are used against us and that portray CUF as a party of violence. Usually before a public rally, the main speakers meet to decide what the message will be that day. Each will be assigned an area of concentration. But some people forget about that when they speak, so afterward, I meet with them and show them where they should not have crossed the line. And since I am usually the last speaker, I try to dilute what previous ones have said.

For example, a speaker might say, "You police are doing this to us, but be sure, when CUF is in office, we will sack you." When it is my turn to speak, I say that sometimes police officers are acting under orders and against their wishes. Most policemen are good, but they are not well trained, so a CUF government will not engage in a vendetta; it will retrain the police so that they can cooperate with the general public. The police will have good salaries, transport, and communications, and even live in modern barracks, unlike now, when a family of five or six shares the same room. After listening to me, most of the police become more sympathetic, rather than worrying that a CUF government will cost them their jobs. We have to build their confidence rather than just engage in threats.

In 1996, we began to face another internal crisis in the party. A group of party members on the mainland organized themselves into what they called CUF Bara [Mainland]. They possessed certain grievances, especially against the secretary general at the time, Mr. Mloo, who they claimed was not visiting his office in Dar es Salaam and not holding regular party councils, in violation of the party constitution. Since then, of course, we have learned that, if we convene these councils regularly according to the constitution, then we solve a lot of problems; we nip them in the bud because we bring them forward and solve them right away. As vice chairman at the time, I also shared part of the blame.

Members of CUF Bara attempted to hold a party council that excluded leaders from the islands, which was unconstitutional. Of course, the Zanzibari government funded them to destabilize our party and helped CUF Bara prepare a document printed by the Zanzibari government press, which alleged we were planning to overthrow the Zanzibari government. So we had to convene an extraordinary session of the party's National Congress in Tanga. Fortunately, we had some people from the mainland supportive of the secretary general, people like Shaibu Akwilombe, who managed on the eve of the congress to obtain some copies of the document in question. CUF Bara's plan was to present the document at the National Congress and then to have the police arrest all the top CUF leaders from Zanzibar for treason.

I remember that, at about ten at night, Shaibu came to my hotel room and handed me the document. Together with Mr. Mloo and Mr. Musobi, we went early the next morning to see the regional commissioner for Tanga, presented him the document, and said it was forged. We asked, "How could we print a document so incriminating to us in the Zanzibari government printing press?" Sometimes, when these people are plotting, because they are not experts, they do silly things that expose themselves and their lies.

The regional commissioner said not to worry, that the government would follow up on the matter and that we could continue with the congress without problems. Later that day, our chairman, Mr. Musobi, employed his admirable skills to bring the issue before the assembled congress. We made a case against the CUF Bara leaders, who were then required to defend themselves. We had a secret ballot to decide if they should be expelled from the party, and more than 95 percent of the

National Congress voted for their expulsion. Yet despite their failure in Tanga, the expelled CUF leaders worked hand in hand with the Zanzibari government authorities to undermine us. In the treason case I mentioned earlier, the main witnesses for the prosecution were these people. The government gave them the full VIP treatment, but, of course, once the case failed, CCM completely discarded them.

Thank God we came out of this crisis and others much stronger as a party. That is one CUF characteristic that really stands out: it is able to manage its own internal conflicts democratically, when other parties like the NCCR-Mageuzi become weaker and weaker through such disputes. We can manage this because CUF rank-and-file members really care about their party, and their tendency is to rally around the leadership to make sure the party survives. That is the reason we have succeeded in weathering all these attempts to destroy the party carried out with the full support of the Zanzibari government.

In 1999, we had another party congress, where Mr. Mageni retired as chairman with full honors and respect. In his place Professor Lipumba was elected as chairman, and Mr. Mloo and I switched positions. He became vice chairman, and I was elected secretary general. Mr. Mloo was getting old and the post of secretary general is very demanding, so he proposed that I replace him. In 2003, he retired from the party and was replaced as vice chairman by Machano Khamis Ali.

After the 1995 elections, I told CUF supporters that they should be patient and that we would follow up the election loss with a concrete strategy. We would use all available means, including appeals to the international community. The secretary of the Commonwealth, Chief Emeka Anyaoku from Nigeria, began in 1997 to take a keen interest in our impasse here in Zanzibar. He sent a special envoy named Moses Anafu. Salmin and I met separately with both Anyaoku and Anafu. Salmin and I never saw one another until June 1999, with the signing of *Muafaka*, meaning "an accord" in Swahili. The signing took place in the House of Representatives. Mr. Mloo signed on our behalf, but CCM appointed a member of the house to sign on its behalf, so we knew from the first that party leaders were not very serious about *Muafaka*.[4]

Afterward, Salmin held a reception at the State House for all of us. He had a prepared speech that he threw away and instead spoke extemporaneously. It was a very moving and emotional speech, in which he said, essentially, "I've known Seif for many years. We've worked together and were once best friends, and if there are divisions in the country, it's our responsibility because if we quarrel, it will trickle down to the people." Afterward, he came and embraced me, and the next day all the enmity between CCM and CUF disappeared.

People were so excited that everywhere, both in CUF and CCM branches, they were holding feasts, and sometimes I would be invited to CCM functions and CCM leaders would be invited to CUF functions. I remember I was visiting my branches in Jang'ombe, and CCM members heard I was visiting the area, so they sent a delegation asking me to visit their branch. Jang'ombe is an area where CCM members are very aggressive and hostile to CUF, but, on that day, they gave me a very warm reception. I think, however, this made CCM leaders jittery; they began to make public statements that we should not interfere in another party's affairs.

We agreed that CUF would end its boycott of the House of Representatives and recognize Salmin's government. We fulfilled our part of the bargain, but Salmin was supposed to amend the constitution so that the forthcoming elections would be free and fair and to reform the ZEC so it could be fair and well respected. He was also supposed to reform the judiciary and to instruct the state-owned media to provide equitable coverage to all political parties. All parties were to be allowed to carry out their public activities without state interference, and the president was supposed to appoint two CUF members to the House of Representatives. None of these articles was implemented; instead, CCM ministers ridiculed *Muafaka*. Benjamin Mkapa, Mwinyi's successor as president of Tanzania, was very supportive of Salmin and very arrogant. Once he came to Zanzibar for a public rally and said in Swahili, *wapinzani wanikome*, meaning people of the opposition should just stay away from him.

So the enthusiasm was very high on both sides for three months or so, and then it began to dissipate when it became apparent the government of Zanzibar did not intend to implement *Muafaka*.

fifteen VIOLENCE

AS WE NEARED THE 2000 elections, conditions were worse than in 1995. CCM had yet to accept multipartyism genuinely and sincerely. The party went through with elections only because of pressure from both inside and outside the country, especially from the donor community. The CCM strategy was once again to alienate CUF from the masses, to portray us as a violent party. They tried to identify CCM rule as African rule and CUF rule as Arab rule. At CCM rallies on the mainland, the leaders showed videos of the fighting in Burundi and said that, if the people allow CUF to have power, this will happen to Zanzibar. They scared women by telling them they would be the first to suffer. They claimed that CUF would seek revenge for all the times CCM had mistreated citizens in the past. CCM speakers also indicated that, if they were defeated in the elections, they would bring about violence similar to what occurred in Rwanda and Burundi. Privately, CCM believed that, if CUF won power, there would be rapid development in the islands and that the people would condemn them as politicians who had wasted a lot of time.

We had a very difficult task, but the party was enjoying more and more support. Even most of the women in Stone Town who did not usually go out, were now attending our campaign rallies in large numbers. In fact, we had some rallies that included a thousand to fourteen hundred cars, lorries, and buses; the police would mount roadblocks to try to stop every vehicle, searching each individual, one by one. Even more outrageous, policemen would search women. Many CUF supporters were questioned, and some arrested and later released. The police never stopped me because I had a police escort, but I would wait in my car until all the others had passed. The officers made great efforts to discourage us, yet such harassment actually encouraged more people to attend our rallies.

At a rally once at Kwahani, some hooligans began to stone us, and I had to be taken to a safe house until the police came to escort me away. Later, however, we heard that some police officers had helped organize the stoning. At another rally in the Amani constituency, the police arrived and began to practice judo. We decided to move our rally to the grounds of our district office in Kilimahewa. Even there we could not escape the wrath of the partisan police; they came and began shooting wildly, wounding three people, who were taken to the hospital. Despite the shootings, I told everyone to remain calm and to sit down, and we continued the rally. About ten thousand people were in attendance that day.

Around April 2000, the government denied us permission to hold a rally at Magomeni, so we decided to hold it instead in an enclosed space near our party branch offices in that area. A female police officer and two others in uniform arrived, carrying guns. The officer was drunk and in civilian dress; she wanted to force her way through to where I was speaking, but the Blue Guards did not permit her. A fracas broke out: the policewoman fell down and was stoned by the crowd, another policeman was hit, and they claimed one of their weapons was stolen. From where I was speaking, I could not see or know what was happening. I told people to sit down, but they were panicking and running away in all directions.

On the next day, I was arrested with about twelve other people, including Ismail Jussa, who was at the meeting but had remained in a car because he was sick. We were sent to the Madema police station, where a large CUF crowd gathered and gave the police an ultimatum: if the authorities did not release me that day by 3:30 p.m., the demonstrators would storm the station. So the police took our statements and then, strangely enough, said I was released on my own bail. On the next day in court, we were charged with stealing police weapons and attacking and seriously injuring police officers. All of us were released on bail, and the case dragged on for over a year. We were all acquitted except two, who allegedly had incriminating evidence against them.

The new ZEC chairman, Abdulrahman Mwinyi Jumbe, acted at first as a person who would be fair. Whenever we went to him, he was very friendly, and we were encouraged because of his impartiality and desire for smooth elections. But he was only presenting a false front in order to gain our trust. He began to show his real colors during the time of voter registration, when the ZEC ensured that all the people that CCM brought from the mainland, despite their ineligibility, were allowed to register to vote, when qualified Zanzibaris were not. Police pulled Zanzibaris out of the queues by force, and the *sheha* claimed that these people were not in their books or registries, refusing to recognize them. Meanwhile, CCM arrogantly brought by boat thousands from the mainland to the port, where buses waited to distribute them to various registration centers, some of these centers clandestine. In a constituency like Mwera, for example, normally they have about fifteen thousand to sixteen thousand registered voters, but by the end of registration, Mwera had nearly thirty thousand voters. We reported all this to the ZEC chairman, who promised to take action but did nothing.

In those difficult days, one thing that kept CUF alive was Radio Kifua, which roughly translates as "word of mouth." People were sometimes so demoralized that the only thing that bound them to CUF was hope. After 1995, they had hoped for another election and for Salmin's removal from power. Radio Kifua invented very convincing stories, called *maburungutu*, that very soon Salmin was leaving, and these rumors spread like fire. Whenever I went to America, people would say, "Now Maalim has gone to America and gained the support of the U.S., so CCM has no chance!" Some people were very convincing and told a story as if they had witnessed everything themselves, and some could not help but believe. Word of mouth is often our most effective means of communication: if you say something in Zanzibar Town, within two hours it is known throughout the islands. Radio Kifua helped restore hope in the party, and so I let the stories continue. Very few people ever asked me if they were true; when they did, I would tell them no, but they would say, "Well, let them believe what they want because it helps the party." Of course, at rallies I would try to explain what was really transpiring.

The only real consolation for us before the 2000 elections was the apparent division within CCM. Salmin had managed to alienate CCM on the mainland by gaining Zanzibar membership in the Organization of the Islamic Conference. When some members of the union Parliament asked why Zanzibar joined the OIC, Salmin was very tough and even used the expression, "You're trying to shake the matchbox," meaning "You're testing us in Zanzibar." There was also the question of tariffs: in order to attract trade, which could be taxed, Zanzibar's tariffs were lower than those of the mainland. Salmin did not want to harmonize tariffs; he was very tough on that, and Nyerere called him *mbogo*, or wild bull.

Salmin lost favor with Nyerere and others, and when his staunch supporters tried to change the constitution to allow him a third term as president, they were blocked. Then Salmin wanted to be succeeded by his chief minister, Dr. Muhammed Gharib Bilal. In a vote taken within a special CCM committee in Zanzibar, Bilal received forty-four votes, Abdul Salam Issa received thirteen, and Amani Karume, the son of the first president of Zanzibar, only nine. But when the NEC met in Dodoma, the committee members ignored Bilal and nominated Amani Karume instead. They saw Bilal as Salmin's man and believed that, if he were elected, Salmin would remain the real power. Because of Karume's nomination, a rift developed between Karume's and Salmin's groups, and there were indications that some of Salmin's supporters would decide not to vote.

When the polling day came, the election was very mismanaged. The ZEC made sure the delivery of voting materials was late to those areas in which CUF was strong. At my own polling station, we could not start voting until about twelve noon, yet in CCM strongholds, everything was supplied in time. The people showed great patience, and despite all the frustrations, enthusiasm was high. After the polling stations closed and the vote counting started, it was clear that CCM was losing heavily. In the Raha Leo constituency, historically a CCM stronghold, it was obvious that Ahmed Hassan Diria, the CCM candidate, was losing badly. Even when officials counted the ballot boxes from the prison area, they found that most of the prison officers had voted for CUF.

Realizing their party was losing, CCM elders met at their party headquarters at Kisiwandui and instructed the ZEC to stop the counting exercise throughout the islands. They sent army personnel to the polling stations to collect the ballot boxes at gunpoint. They did not allow our party agents to accompany the ballot boxes and observe the counting taking place. And for the Urban West Region, the ZEC went further: it cancelled the elections, announcing that a new election would take place after a week. Party officials said there were a lot of shortcomings, that, for example, voting materials were not distributed in time. But our argument was, if that was the case, there should be a second election throughout the country.

We CUF leaders made the mistake of permitting the military to snatch the ballot boxes, thinking that the results would be entirely nullified and that another general election would take place. Without party agents present during the vote counting, the government could give us any vote totals it liked. It took the officials more than a week to announce the doctored results. They gave us just one third of the seats in the house and union Parliament and one third of the presidential vote. The government wanted to show that it had made inroads in Pemba because, in 1995, CCM did not win a single seat there. The government held a rerun election in Urban West, which we boycotted, and on the day of the new election, the polling stations were almost empty.

We knew something bad was coming and were not totally surprised by the theft of the elections. This time the shock was not as great as it had been in 1995. I went to the Bwawani Hotel for a press conference and announced that CUF did not accept the results. When I returned to town by car, the people came out on the streets to cheer me, but Tanzanian soldiers, mostly from the mainland, began to beat them. All this was televised on CNN, and that is when the international condemnations began. All the observer teams, including the SADC, did not accept the results. The Commonwealth termed the elections a shambles. After the debacle in 1995, Western nations cut off relations with Salmin Amour's government. NORAD, DANIDA, and others stopped their aid projects in the islands. When we initiated *Muafaka* in 1999, some of the Western countries revived their relations with the Zanzibari government, but after the 2000 elections, they discontinued or never revived their aid projects and cut direct political relations once again. Unfortunately, the mainland government was not punished at all, even though Mkapa was fully involved in the theft of the elections.[1]

We in CUF decided not to recognize or cooperate with the new government and to launch a diplomatic offensive. I traveled to London and the United States, and Abubakar Khamis Bakary and Ismail Jussa went to EU member nations. We decided to hold nationwide protest demonstrations, but the police refused us permission. Our vice chairman, Mr. Mloo, said that we would hold peaceful demonstrations on January 27, 2001, whether permitted or not. In accordance with the law, we would give the police forty-eight hours' notice. The prime minister, vice president, and the inspector general of police said that the state would employ full force to see that the demonstrations did not take place. Professor Ibrahim Lipumba held a press conference and called upon all party members to wear white armbands and not to carry any type of weapons, including stones and knives.

President Mkapa left Tanzania for an international conference a few days before January 27, but we heard he left instructions for the demonstrations not to take place under any circumstances. On January 25, while traveling to address a public rally in Dar es Salaam, Professor Lipumba was followed by the FFU [Field Force Unit]. They stopped him on the road and roughed him up, injuring his hand in the process. They took him to the central police station and stole his watch. Those who traveled with him were also roughed up and arrested and remained there until January 29, when they went to court and received bail. The charge was holding an illegal political meeting.

Throughout Tanzania on January 25 and 26, the police arrested many of our active leaders, including district chairmen, secretaries, and rank-and-file activists. Here in Zanzibar, most of our members hid to avoid arrest until the demonstrations. On January 26, which was a Friday, as people were leaving the Mwembetanga mosque in Zanzibar Town, the police came and shot the imam dead and injured some of the people who happened to be there. They did this to intimidate the opposition, so that people would not come out the following day.

At dawn on January 27, police officers were everywhere around Zanzibar Town; anybody they found on the streets they beat up, arrested, and tortured. By such means, they succeeded in stopping the demonstration here in town. In Dar es Salaam, the inspector general of police, Omar Mahita, had vowed in the media that, if CUF succeeded in holding demonstrations and in marching up to the designated assembly point, he would resign. So the party youth in Dar es Salaam made sure they lured the police here and there until they proceeded to the actual designated grounds and then demanded Mahita's resignation.

The worst situation was in Pemba, especially in the Micheweni and Wete districts. People came out in the thousands. The police were unable to cope, so the officers used live bullets against the demonstrators. In all, they killed more than forty-five people, but there were also many other atrocities. They broke into people's homes and stole anything they could. Many people were afraid that they would be arrested and tortured, so they abandoned their homes to live in the bush. Police officers broke into our party branches and took all they could, destroying our files, party flags, and office furniture, even pulling down doors and windows. Much worse, they raped women and young girls and forced more than two thousand people to take refuge in Mombasa. It was as if a foreign army had invaded the island of Pemba. It was hard to believe that Tanzanian men in uniform could be so inhuman and cruel.[2]

For the first time, the media here in Tanzania were really courageous. They lamented the violence, saying that this has always been a country that received refugees, but now it is creating refugees because of the arrogance of those in power. Professor Lipumba courageously went to Pemba and visited the victims in the hospitals; he visited the bereaved families to give his and the party's condolences and instructed local leaders like Mohamed Shafi to ensure that CUF party flags were raised again in Wete and Micheweni.

I was in London and people in the Tanzanian government threatened me, trying to make me stay away from Zanzibar. I was also getting a lot of messages from CUF supporters worried about my security. Even some organizations like Amnesty International urged me to wait, but I decided to return to my people, to keep the promise I made to them back in 1988. I went first to Mombasa to visit the Zanzibari refugees there, as well as the injured in the hospital, some with their legs amputated. I told the press that I had to go back to Tanzania and meet with the secretary general of CCM, Philip Mangula, which was reported all over East Africa. After his return to Tanzania, Mkapa addressed a rally in Dar es Salaam and publicly instructed Mangula to meet with me to discuss issues and find a solution. So when I arrived in Tanzania, I wrote to Mangula and, to my surprise, received a response the second day, saying he accepted my invitation for talks.

We met at the Sea Cliff Hotel in Msasani in February 2001; I was accompanied by Hamad Rashid Muhammed, a member of CUF's governing council, and Mangula was accompanied by Kingune Ngombale-Mwiru, Mkapa's chief political advisor. We had accused each other in the public rallies beforehand and so were all very grim, serious, and suspicious. We said the door should be kept open in case a physical fight broke out between us. Yet we all expressed sorrow over the deaths of the people in Pemba and discussed the need to investigate the causes of the violence and squarely to address them. We agreed to prepare a statement to remind the people, especially our CUF supporters, that we were all Tanzanians and that we should work together and let bygones be bygones.

In our next meeting, we approved a joint statement and agreed it should be read publicly in Wete, Chake Chake, and Zanzibar Town. Of course, my people in CUF did not like that I traveled with Mangula on the same plane to Pemba and Unguja; they thought I would die. The grassroots repeatedly challenged me, saying that CCM people were not to be trusted. And when the leaders of the two parties, from the executive to the grassroots level, assembled together, it was very tense. When we entered the hall in Chake Chake, each side sang its party songs. When we read the statement aloud, it was very tough because most CUF members did not take it well, shouting I was a sell-out.

After that, we organized a public rally at Mnazi Mmoja in Zanzibar Town, and it was the most difficult rally of my life. For the first time, I faced a hostile crowd of my own supporters, who were not in favor of my policy of reconciliation. The party rank and file wanted to continue to resist the government and to think of revenge toward CCM members. But I was convinced that this policy would not be effective in achieving our aims because our stronghold was in Pemba, where our people were demoralized and intimidated. I explained to the audience that our people in Pemba were living in forests, there were no functioning party branches, and most CUF leaders were in Mombasa or in hiding. So under such circumstances, how could we continue the stalemate and who would benefit?

I was a leader, and I had to take a leadership role; I could not be led by the emotions of the people. Even if it cost me my own popularity, I knew I had to pursue the right course to the end. Things were made worse for me when the newspapers published photographs of Mangula and me eating chicken together at the Sea Cliff Hotel, when most of our leaders in Pemba North were refugees, as if I had betrayed the party. It was very clear to me, however, that, without having a dialogue with CCM, it would be very difficult to rebuild the party. I think that both CCM and CUF needed reconciliation at the time. CCM wanted to restore national and international confidence in its government, and we wanted to create an atmosphere conducive to the continuation of our political struggle. We both agreed to refrain from inflammatory language and not to use the police as a weapon against one party or another. The government was embarrassed by the presence of thousands of refugees, so in our joint statement, we called on them to come back without fear of harassment. Most of them eventually returned and resumed their local leadership positions, though fewer than a hundred stayed and eventually crossed the border into Somalia, where they remain today.

Each side sent six representatives to negotiate what later came to be known as *Muafaka* II. The CUF team included me as co-chair, Ali Haji Pandu, Hamad Rashid Mohammed, Abubakar Khamis Bakary, Hamisi Hassan Hamis, and Ismail Jussa as joint secretary. Eventually, we built up a very comfortable rapport with our CCM counterparts. We began to trust one another, and after about seven months, we produced *Muafaka* II. We decided to form a special body to supervise the implementation of the agreement, called the Joint Presidential Supervisory Commission (JPSC), which we insisted be given legal powers by an act of Parliament. We also agreed on an amendment to the Zanzibari constitution that we drafted as an appendix to the *Muafaka* II accords to make them legally binding. *Muafaka* II was signed with a lot of fanfare at the State House. This time CCM's top leadership attended, including Mkapa and Karume, both of whom gave speeches pledging their support. Ibrahim Lipumba, our party chairman, pledged CUF support but at the same time, reminded the others that CCM had ignored *Muafaka* I.

I staked my whole reputation on *Muafaka* II because I believe dialogue is the best way to resolve conflicts. CUF leaders supported my position, and we managed to maintain party unity. Unlike in CCM, we always went to our members and explained matters and asked for their views. That is how CUF functions: we take the lead but at the same time involve the people, though sometimes we have long debates. Even the party hard-liners could see that the mainstream was with the leadership and were compelled to follow the path of reconciliation.

And what was achieved? We gained the cooperation of the police and were free to hold rallies throughout the islands and to criticize the government. Our party became stronger than ever. The CUF's image in the international community improved dramatically. Other nations understood us more than they had before and considered us a serious alternative to CCM. The CCM image of me as an uncompromising power monger also changed. Initially in the *Muafaka* negotiations, there was a lot of mistrust, but through months of frank discussions, everyone was able to speak his mind. We accused CCM, and CCM accused us. We started with positions very far apart, but over the course of discussions and hot exchanges, reason eventually prevailed over emotions. In some instances, the co-chairman and I met alone to iron out some of the most difficult points, and that created an atmosphere in which we could trust each other.

That is my philosophy, really, not to treat the other side like monsters. If you avoid dialogue, you allow conflicts to exacerbate, and then eventually people kill each other. Only afterward do people come to the negotiating table. But why do we not come to the table *before* people die? That is my simple philosophy. Look at Mozambique: thousands died in the fighting between FRELIMO [the Liberation Front of Mozambique] and RENAMO [the Mozambican National Resistance], and then the two sides came to the table. Why wait until lives have been lost? Even for a long time before 2001, we had been calling for negotiations, but Mangula refused, saying I was a terrorist. After the people in Pemba lost their lives, CCM realized we had to meet.

So until 2001, CCM thought I was very obstinate and inflexible, but party leaders witnessed that most of the time, when CUF leaders resisted making concessions, I met with them separately and persuaded them. I created an impression that I was genuine and sincere, that I really wanted a solution, and that what mattered to me most was not my personal or partisan interests but the nation's interests. That caused them to respect me and regard me with a different perspective. Omar Mapuri, once a CCM extremist, became a reasonable and understanding man and very supportive of the reconciliation process. In fact, he, the author of the book we symbolically burned back in the 1990s, was attacked within his own party and in the newspapers as a sell-out to CUF. Now he is serving as Tanzania's ambassador to the People's Republic of China.

Mkapa also appeared to change. From 1995 to 2000, he was very supportive of Salmin Amour; he came to Zanzibar and gave speeches just to intimidate the opposition. He was very arrogant, not a negotiating partner. But after the events of January 2001, it appeared as if the seriousness of the violence had sunk into his head, and for years afterward, I believed he genuinely wanted reconciliation. It was always Mkapa who pushed *Muafaka* II, not Karume, who was and is only interested in remaining in power.

It is widely believed that Amani Karume's main motivation as president of Zanzibar is personal gain. It is alleged that, since his election in 2000, he has transformed the Zanzibari government into a family affair. Most of the government deals are not conducted in a transparent way, and he presides over a very corrupt regime. He is not a symbol of the revolution; he is simply Abeid Karume's son, who represents his family dynasty, which only stands for personal gain. It is doubtful that Karume understands the peoples he rules, for as a young man, he grew up in Malawi, where he went to school. When he came back his father was already president, so he lived in the State House, with little interaction with ordinary people.

While deriving maximum personal benefits from his position, Karume has all but killed trade in Zanzibar by accepting the harmonization of tariffs with the mainland. Salmin received about six billion shillings per month in tax revenue from imports and exports, but since 2002 when Karume harmonized tariffs, Zanzibar gets less than 500 million per month. A CUF government would negotiate with the mainland to change the tariff situation.

Another issue is the relationship between Unguja and Pemba. Karume originally criticized Salmin for encouraging serious divisions, yet since he has been in power, he has been doing the same thing. Out of twenty-one ministers and deputy ministers, Karume has only appointed two from Pemba. Out of twenty-three principal secretaries and their deputies, only two come from Pemba. Out of 117 directors, commissioners, and managers, only seventeen come from Pemba. Of the eighteen senior positions in the police force, none is filled by Pembans. In short, Karume's performance as president has been very dismal, and by 2005, it was clear that he was the most unpopular president in Zanzibari history. Yet he wanted to continue for another five years; if others had completed their two terms, he would say, why should he not complete his own? As if the people had no say in the matter.

sixteen

PRIOR TO THE 2005 elections, in the spirit of *Muafaka* II, we in CUF presented a peaceful image to the public. Representatives from the Liberal Democratic Party in the U.K., including their secretary general, came to Tanzania and advised us in this respect. I also told our party leaders we had to stop using a popular chant at rallies in Dar es Salaam that, in effect, suggested we would use machetes to defend ourselves and seek justice. Yet once at a rally in Kinondoni, the speakers before me used the same chant, so when I took the stage, I said this was not the time for machetes—it was time to show our strength through the ballot box. Another time in Dar es Salaam, one of our speakers said the machetes must be kept out because CCM cannot be trusted and because all our success so far in the struggle was due to machetes. When I spoke, I said I did not agree; I said that CUF was a nonviolent party, and we should not deceive ourselves by thinking we could defeat CCM through violence. CCM would be very happy if we used violence because it could use that violence to oppress us. I said that people should not listen to politicians trying to get cheap popularity. The papers afterward reported very straightforwardly that CUF's secretary general warned his people against violence.

Yet despite our efforts to conduct ourselves in accordance with the letter and spirit of *Muafaka* II, it was very clear Karume and his government were not prepared to have free and fair elections. In fact, from 2003 on, he began to strengthen various Zanzibari special forces, like the prison guards, the KMKM—an antismuggling unit—and the JKU, a sort of national service for young people. The *maskani* cells mobilized during Salmin's time had died out almost completely because Mohammed Raza, who had paid them and provided them with television sets, did not support Karume. Nearly all the *maskani* meeting places were covered with weeds, so Karume's government formed new forces, such as a fire

300

brigade and an association of former military personnel, known as *Umawa*. He also established various camps in the rural areas to train a new generation of CCM youth, whom we nicknamed *janjaweed*, to commit acts of violence against the opposition. CCM officials were clearly preparing to win the elections by hook or crook. In one of his campaign speeches, Karume even threatened us, saying the weapons used in the revolution in 1964 were still available and, if necessary, would be cleaned up and used.

The government appointed CCM zealots as members of the new and supposedly impartial ZEC. We complained, but nothing happened. And instead of an impartial media, Zanzibar's state-owned television station came out with special programs painting CCM as the party of peace and CUF as the party of violence and revenge. Another key provision of *Muafaka* II was the creation of a credible and permanent voter register, but it soon became very clear once the registration process began that Karume's government was prepared to use all means to ensure that register did not happen. On several occasions during registration, *janjaweed* intimidated and attacked people with steel bars and clubs and looted and burned down their houses. CCM frustrated the work of, and even for a time expelled from the country, the company from South Africa, Waymark Infotech, contracted to provide computerized verification of the Permanent Voter Register (PVR). Local *sheha* arbitrarily denied CUF members the right to vote. TEMCO (Tanzania Election Monitoring Committee), based in Dar es Salaam, censured the *sheha*, reporting that "discrimination against people thought to be CUF members was rampant." The *sheha* had "soured" the whole registration process. For example, in the Urban West region alone, they denied more than twelve thousand Zanzibaris the right to vote.

CCM added as well as took away. In areas where CCM support was strong, in Unguja North and South, the number of people registered far exceeded the number of eligible residents—according to the 2002 census—by a combined total of more than thirty-thousand. For these reasons, the PVR in our view stands for "Permanent Vote Rigging." We lodged many complaints, which the ZEC either brushed off or ignored, accusing us of dishonesty.

I attempted many times to have an audience with Mkapa to discuss the situation. At a breakfast meeting at the State House in August 2005, Mkapa told me that one problem in Zanzibar was that CUF people feared CCM and that CCM feared CUF. I retorted that I did not fear CCM in Zanzibar, and Mkapa said yes, but they fear you: *Wanakuogopa bwana*. I brought up the issue of the twelve thousand people denied registration, and he asked me to submit a full list to him, saying he would take action.

I gave Mkapa a list of seventy-four hundred people denied registration, and I also identified the *janjaweed* camps by name and location, and he said he would make sure the camps were removed, but nothing happened.[1]

So we in CUF made it very clear that, if we were denied our victory once again, we would emulate the example of other countries and adopt a people's power campaign as a way of ensuring that the popular will would be respected. We had no secret agenda—we announced it publicly and for months tried to educate our followers in the branches on the importance of engaging in peaceful demonstrations. Perhaps it was a mistake to announce it beforehand because Mkapa and his government decided to occupy Zanzibar militarily. Starting in July 2005, they sent thousands of Tanzanian soldiers from the mainland to assist actively in the theft of the election and to crush any organized dissent. They made it clear that they would cling to power by force of arms, even if a thousand people died. A few days before the election, Mkapa came to Zanzibar and said in a speech that CCM would never allow antirevolutionary elements to rule the islands.

We in CUF did not expect this from a man who promised to ensure the implementation of *Muafaka* II. This was, in fact, the last straw—our confidence ended in Mkapa as an honest negotiator. It was now clear that, ever since 2001, he had been negotiating in bad faith. Apparently, CCM decided in 1995 and 2000 that it had been caught unprepared to lose the elections, forcing the leaders to use the most obvious methods to keep themselves in power. In 1995, they changed the numbers at the last minute, even after the ZEC informed agents from both parties that CCM had lost. In 2000, when they saw they were losing, they sent soldiers to end the vote-counting process at gunpoint. This time CCM did not want to face the condemnation of the media and election observers or risk the anger of the international community, so party leaders planned years in advance how to steal the 2005 elections with a minimum of protests.

Responsibility for this campaign of deceit rests firmly with Benjamin Mkapa, who betrayed CUF and the people of Zanzibar and treated the goodwill and financial assistance of the international community with contempt. After three years of dialogue and rhetoric committing each side to uphold the principles of *Muafaka* II and considerable international engagement, Mkapa made sure the law was broken as often as necessary to produce a CCM victory in the islands. The people in my party who argued all along that CCM was never to be trusted were sadly proved right.

One of the main tasks of the ZEC was to publish the PVR weeks in advance of the election, to allow CUF and Waymark Infotech time to verify the authenticity of the register. This did not happen. Only on the day before the election did CUF receive a list on CD-ROM, about eight-thousand pages long, of random names, not sorted by either district or polling station. This made analysis of the PVR impossible. On voting day, however, we noticed that an organized copy of the PVR was displayed outside some polling stations in Pemba and that it had been distributed to all ZEC members. Clearly, CCM did not intend anyone to look too closely at the PVR since it contained thousands of names that did not belong there and did not contain thousands of fully qualified Zanzibari citizens.

Election day on Pemba was quiet and saw few irregularities, probably because CCM thought it easier to steal the election in places where its own supporters were more numerous. After 2:00 p.m., CUF agents in Unguja began reporting on busloads of nonresidents and *janjaweed* in nearly all constituencies. The *janjaweed* were transported in vehicles owned by the armed forces from one polling station to another, voting as many times as they possibly could, under the protection of the armed forces. In many cases, men and women in uniform were themselves observed voting repeatedly and often armed. TEMCO said the large numbers of army trucks on the roads carrying CCM youth around during voting day posed a serious question about whether the elections were free and fair. Most of this escaped the attention of the media and international teams of observers, who were concentrated in Zanzibar Town. Even there, however, CCM had the nerve to bus in people from outside to vote illegally, right in front of the TV cameras, in a CUF stronghold, no less. Of course, a riot ensued, as covered by various news organizations.

In about one-tenth of the total number of polling stations, the ZEC deliberately withheld the results from our CUF agents. This alone threw the outcome of the whole election in doubt. You cannot have an election when there is no actual agreed-upon historical record of how many people voted for either side. To make matters worse, CUF agents were prohibited from entering the areas where the ZEC tallied the results.

On the morning following the election, CUF supporters in Zanzibar Town began celebrating what they thought would be a CUF victory, when security forces attacked them with water cannons, tear gas, and clubs. Many were arrested. Ultimately about five thousand CUF youth assembled at party headquarters in Mtendeni and waited to take orders from party leaders. They came from various parts of Zanzibar Town and from the countryside, even though the government established roadblocks on all the roads leading to town. They had no weapons and did not even carry a stone. The police eventually sealed off all the roads to Mtendeni and put us under siege for three consecutive days; the officers allowed only a few of us leaders to leave the area. They arrested about two hundred CUF supporters for unlawful assembly, and we heard that they were forced to strip off their clothes and were beaten and humiliated.

Because it was Ramadhan, people were already fasting, and there was no food in Mtendeni for the thousands trapped there. We asked the police to allow food to be sent in, but it took ages and happened only after a lot of argument. The Red Cross attempted to transport a sick youth from Mtendeni to the hospital, but the police led the vehicles to the police station instead and arrested the youth.

The CUF crowds assembled in Mtendeni shouted to us that they were ready to launch "People's Power" and were prepared to lose their lives, but we thought it foolhardy to send them out to confront the army and police. We could not just allow them to go where they would surely die; we had to be responsible leaders and not allow a bloodbath, so we made the decision *not* to go ahead with People's Power. At first, Professor Lipumba was against the decision, but the vice chairman, Machano Khamis Ali and I said no, and we ultimately convinced him.

We first identified respected youths and invited them to the party headquarters and explained the dangers that lay ahead with a demonstration. We told each to go to his group to try to sell the idea. Some faced stiff opposition, but when we felt the message had reached every part of the crowd, we came out onto the street with loudspeakers to address our supporters. Some were very hostile; they called us names like cowards and sell-outs. They were shouting and very emotional. We had to explain our position, and in this instance, Professor Lipumba showed tremendous boldness and courage in trying to cool the tempers of the youth.

Our decision to call off People's Power was very unpopular that day and continues to be among certain elements of the party, but I have no regrets. In today's world, the use of violence is out of the question; you can apply pressure, but it must be done very cautiously. And anyway, for People's Power to succeed, you need armed forces that are actually patriotic to their country, who support the people when a wrong has been committed and who are reluctant to kill their own brethren. But most of the armed forces sent to Mtendeni were not Zanzibaris; they had no relations here; to them, Zanzibar was just a foreign country.

We could have invoked People's Power in Pemba, but it would have been ineffective because all the press coverage was in Zanzibar Town. The security forces were tough in Pemba because they considered the island a renegade province. Even though the military presence was not as heavy there as in Unguja, CCM could have been very brutal. Karume's special forces consider anyone who opposes CCM a public enemy and act ferociously.

Fortunately, during the siege, Mtendeni residents shared their food and took care of the crowd. When we heard the police might come at night to rough up the crowd, the residents invited the young people inside for their own safety and for that of their premises. None was left on the street. It was a blessing that we had our headquarters in an area where our support was 100 percent. Also the streets are very narrow in Mtendeni, so the police officers were very careful about entering, not wanting to be surrounded completely.

The UN delegation in Zanzibar eventually stepped in and ended the siege. The delegates came to Mtendeni and took three sick CUF youth away; the police stopped their vehicle and tried to arrest the youths inside, but the senior UN official called his superior, who told the police that the UN would not surrender the youths for arrest. After a few minutes, the Tanzanian government ordered the police to let them go, and that signaled the end of the siege. The entire convoy of police and military vehicles left the area, which provoked a huge celebration.

I have been frustrated by the international community's lack of response to our problems here in Zanzibar because, prior to the elections, a number of foreign delegations came and met with me and the other side, insisted the elections be free and fair, and indicated they would not accept any stealing this time. They also called on us to restrain our supporters and not to use violence. One delegation was led by the Danish prime minister, Anders Rasmussen; the American assistant secretary of state for Africa, Jendayi Frazier; and the British minister for Africa in the foreign and Commonwealth office, Lord Triesman. All assured me that, if CUF was robbed of victory and if we employed nonviolent methods of protest, then the international community would support us.

We took heed, but while we restrained our supporters, the other side used violence, and not a single country condemned CCM. The international community ignored the actions of the Tanzanian government, pretending it did not know what was happening. We thought that perhaps some countries had their own agendas and that they felt, because Tanzania was a big country with many resources, Zanzibar did not matter. And most of the election monitors who came in 2005 did not actually monitor the elections. The worst were the ones from the African Union and the SADC, who just seemed ready to give a rubber stamp to the whole exercise, in the spirit of "I scratch your back today, and you scratch mine tomorrow." African states that are not themselves democratic or have a weak commitment to democratic values should not decide the worthiness of Tanzanian elections. But neither were the ones from the

West always reliable. Only the Norwegian and American monitors criticized the elections in a way that suggested that they had examined the evidence. The Commonwealth observers at first gave their approval to the elections, until we shared our information with them, and then they redrafted their report.

For a long time, the U.S. did not show much interest in African affairs, and when it did, it sometimes backed the wrong horse, as in the case of Jonas Savimbi in Angola. America needs a clear-cut policy for Africa and needs to stick to it. It cannot support dictators in any way. It should use its persuasive powers and influence to steer African governments to build and strengthen democratic institutions, to uphold the rule of law, to respect human rights, and to eradicate poverty. Unfortunately, because the British and French colonized most of Africa, the Americans have seemed willing to let them exercise more influence. But in Bill Clinton's second term, the U.S. began to show more interest in Africa; the U.S. Congress passed AGOA [the African Growth and Opportunity Act] to encourage trade between America and Africa, which President George W. Bush fortunately extended. AGOA has helped, according to the principles of free trade, to open the door to American markets for African commodities and to ensure that globalization works for Africans as well as for the rest of the world. And through British influence, Bush agreed to debt cancellation for some African countries, under certain conditions.

The U.S. is good at expressing its support for democratic regimes in Africa but does little to encourage Tanzania to abide by internationally accepted democratic norms or to respect human rights. The U.S. should stand by President Bush's statement made during his 2004 inauguration, when he emphasized that America would help all nations struggling to uphold democratic values, the rule of law, and respect for human rights.

I think American officials have gradually learned to see through CCM's rhetoric and lies that CUF is a party of Arab terrorists. And CUF supporters were very happy the superpower did not, immediately at least, recognize Karume's government in 2005, the only country not to do so. But Americans and the international community in general still do not realize that, if they stand by and watch the popular will flouted in Zanzibar, the people could easily, out of complete frustration, turn away from democracy. This would strengthen the hand of religious extremists who have been arguing for years that no changes can come through democratic means. Extremists exploit the deep frustrations of the people with CCM rule by calling for an Islamic state in Zanzibar and implementation of sharia law.

If CCM continues to resist democratic changes that would establish a new government able and willing to combat poverty, then the situation could become much worse than it is today. We need to remember always the root causes of religious extremism and terrorism: poverty and political discontent. Right now, CUF leaders are moderate and respected, and our people listen to what we have to say. But if other countries ignore Zanzibar and if CCM continues to steal elections with impunity, then the people might think their leaders too moderate and take matters into their own hands. If the religious extremists convince a great proportion of the population that change cannot come through the ballot box, that CUF has failed to deliver on its promises, it will open the door for further violence in Zanzibar, which will have a destabilizing effect on the whole of Tanzania and East Africa.

What was my personal reaction to the election? Of course, I was frustrated and despondent that, after all we had done for *Muafaka* II, this could still happen. At the same time, I thought we must persevere in looking for peaceful means to end the impasse with CCM for the benefit of future generations of Zanzibaris. We need to look beyond our noses and to shape a future in which our children grow up in a more amicable atmosphere. We need to persevere and stay true to our principles.

If we manage the party well, it has a good future, but we have to admit that, particularly on the mainland, we sometimes have poor leadership. Some of our CUF leaders in the wards and districts are neither honest nor competent; they are guided mostly by self-interest. Realizing we have these problems, we have prepared a strategic plan to identify and vet corrupt people when they apply for nomination to leadership positions and to train officials intensively after their election. We started having competitive local party elections on the mainland only in 2003, and since then, we send people from our headquarters to inspect local party activities, to check on their performance.

We have tried also to impose financial discipline and to hold national party councils regularly, according to the constitution. In a party like CUF, you are bound to have dissident voices, but in our case, the culture we have built within the party allows people to speak their minds. When I visit the branches, I usually give members the chance to air their views. I listen to what they say, while also explaining the benefits of adhering to the party line. Tolerance has its limitations, but, so far, I think we can handle the situation. In fact, people are saying that CUF has arrived now as a real party, the leading opposition party in Tanzania. In the next few years, there is every possibility that CUF will win more seats in Parliament, control more district councils, and so on. But we must also admit that, in the mainland, we have performed very poorly during all three general elections. We were especially stunned by our losses in 2005 and believe there was some rigging involved. Even in areas where we controlled village leadership, we lost heavily, at least according to the official results.

What success we have had on the mainland comes from Professor Lipumba, who has been crisscrossing the country trying to show CCM's failures while explaining CUF's alternative policies. Lipumba has been able to galvanize the party by exposing government corruption, especially when it comes to the mining economy. In Botswana, the government receives 47 percent of revenue from gold exports, but in Tanzania, the government receives a small fraction of that, which can only be explained by corruption. And when it comes to the privatization of public corporations, the contracts are secret and end up costing Tanzania a lot of revenue. As a professor, Lipumba analyzes well and then brings the issues down to the layman's language.

I have not decided whether to run for president of Zanzibar again. I find myself in a fix. I command the confidence of the majority of Zanzibaris, with whom I promised I would be throughout my life. A time will come, however, when I will have to go to the grassroots and explain the need for my standing aside and allowing somebody else to take over as party leader in Zanzibar.

The reason given for the Tanzanian union, which has been repeated again and again, is that it encourages African unity. Two African states freely, by themselves, decided to unite—that is the story. Zanzibaris and Tanganyikans were brothers and sisters; they had long ties and deep associations, and the union was formed in the spirit of Pan-Africanism. The idea of unity is good, but Tanganyika has borders with eight countries, and there are ethnic groups that overlap such borders, like the Maasai, the Wadigo, and so on, meaning there are actually closer natural ties between Tanzania and her mainland neighbors than between Tanganyika and Zanzibar.

Also disturbing is that the union was formed in such a hurry. Remember that Zanzibar attained its independence in December 1963; one month later, there was a revolution and hardly three months after that, a union agreement. Normally, informed peoples in both countries would be involved and give their ideas, but we do not have any evidence that anyone in Zanzibar other than Abeid Karume was involved, even though it was a matter of national sovereignty.

The revolution was hatched in Tanganyika and executed in Zanzibar with Tanganyikan help. The union enhanced the sovereignty of Tanganyika at the expense of Zanzibar. People in Zanzibar cannot be blamed if they think the mainland has an agenda for Zanzibar when union affairs have been increased from eleven in 1964 to twenty-four today.[2] Tanganyikans are determined to keep Zanzibar under their firm grip, and CCM makes economic decisions as if to squeeze Zanzibar. CCM leaders do not trust CUF because they know we would promote Zanzibari development more vigorously than they do. They fear that, if Zanzibar obtains more autonomy, we will identify ourselves more closely with the Gulf than with Africa, probably because CUF emphasizes the historic relations between Zanzibar and the Gulf. This is a serious problem for African nationalists, who fear that Zanzibar would seek closer relations with Muslim countries and organizations and ignore the rest of Africa. Many Zanzibaris, meanwhile, think the intention of the mainland is to swallow Zanzibar.

So what do we do about these mutual suspicions? We have to put everything on the table and discuss it openly. There should be good will on all sides, with each side being willing to express what it thinks of the other and then to try to allay suspicions and fears. I sincerely believe that, despite the shortcomings in the formation of the union, it is an historical fact, and it is here to stay. I believe that it is in the interests of both Tanganyika and Zanzibar to continue the union. But we have to boldly address certain topics that people are afraid to discuss. I believe, in fact, the union relationship should be put to a public referendum. It is impossible to predict the results of such a referendum since the voting would depend on the efforts of opinion makers. But if we went straight to the people right now, without any campaigning, I believe that a majority in Zanzibar would vote to renegotiate the terms of the union, rather than to secede.

My vision for a future Zanzibar is one where there is unity, yet people will have their own political convictions and feel free to express themselves. We will have unity in diversity; everyone will be proud to be Zanzibari, regardless of his or her ethnic background or religion. We must heal the scars of history by not allowing any discrimination and by ensuring equal opportunities for all. All of us should promote the idea that all Zanzibaris are united by a common history and destiny. We need a harmonious and tolerant society, in which democracy and mutual respect are fully established.

I want to see a Zanzibar that is economically developed, where all have employment and can afford the essentials of life. I would like to call on the people to engage in nation-building projects, on a strictly voluntary basis. I want to see a more literate society than we have now. It is time we really fought AIDS and, if possible, eliminate it from our society. The most effective way to combat the epidemic is through the inculcation of morals among our young men and women. We can encourage people to marry and emphasize that most world religions specifically condemn adultery and homosexuality. The moral decay of society is, in fact, the major reason for the spread of the epidemic in the first place.

We can make everyone aware of the causes and effects of AIDS, and we can also eliminate malaria, which is the main killer in Zanzibar. I would like to see well-equipped hospitals, clean and safe water for everyone, electricity in every household, reliable and cheap communications, and a road network that is passable all year round. I would like to see our people more computer literate than they are now. I would like to see Zanzibar as developed as Mauritius because, twenty years ago, Mauritius was just like Zanzibar. When I visited there in 1987, they depended on sugar plantations, but now the islands have been industrialized and have even leased and developed sugar cane farms in Mozambique. They have almost full employment and have to import workers from India. The standard of living has improved significantly.

I also want to see a Zanzibar where the law is enforced and respected, even by the highest authorities. No one should live above the law. As we say in Swahili, *sharia ni msumeno,* or "the law is like a sword; it can cut anybody." Since the 1990s, Zanzibar has been one of the transit points for drugs coming from Asia to southern Africa and elsewhere, and the people behind the drug business are believed to have close connections with influential persons in government. That is the reason that the government just pays lip service to the fight against drugs. I am told that the drug dealers come to the Zanzibari airport and that some police officials help them carry their briefcases. There have been times when special dogs sniffed drugs in someone's luggage, but the bags were allowed to pass because the owner was well connected. The effects of the drug trade can be seen locally; young men in Zanzibar Town get addicted and are willing to rob and steal to get drugs. The places where drugs are sold are well known, but the police just turn their backs.

This is a very crucial time in Zanzibar. The direction in which the islands move depends on how Tanzanian President Jakaya Kikwete handles the situation. He made a statement in Parliament after his election in 2005 that the problem of Zanzibar pains him. If he is sincere, then his own conscience will push him to find a solution. We will see if he is just someone who wants a positive public image or if he really feels what he says and is prepared to take action. He has all the power he needs to bring about an amicable and permanent solution. If he walks on his words and seeks to resolve Zanzibar's political crisis, there will be reconciliation and reconstruction and measures taken to rebuild the people's confidence. It all depends on Kikwete, and CUF has pledged to cooperate with him to find a lasting solution. If there is any opposition to reconciliation, it comes from CCM in Zanzibar, not from CUF.

But we know Kikwete has difficulties within his own party, and if like Mwinyi and Mkapa he supports an unpopular dictatorial regime, there is the danger of a resistance movement's developing among the youth. We have recently had a very difficult task within CUF trying to cool down tempers and convincing party youth to give Kikwete more time. On the surface, things appear normal, but there is an undercurrent of discontent. If Kikwete seeks to have his party remain in power whatever the circumstances, I am sorry to say that the political future of Zanzibar is very, very bleak. The people cannot wait forever.

The dialogue that Kikwete initiated hit a snag in 2007 and was about to collapse. Thanks to concerted efforts by Professor Lipumba and other CUF leaders, Kikwete intervened to rescue the talks. While the dialogue continues, we keep our fingers crossed about the final outcome.

(*top left*) Seif Sharif Hamad as a student at Beit el Ras Boarding School in 1960.

(*top right*) Hamad and Fourtunah Saleh Mbamba on their wedding day, Malindi, Zanzibar Town, 1968.

(*right*) Aweinah Sanani Massoud on her wedding day with Hamad in Kizimbani, Wete, 1977.

(*top left*) Hamad returning
to Zanzibar from medical
treatment in London,
Chake Chake, Pemba,
1987.

(*top right*) Hamad being
interviewed by a journalist
at home in Mtoni immedi-
ately following his release
from prison, 1991.

(*left*) Hamad with James
Mapalala, first CUF na-
tional chairman, Dar es
Salaam, 1993.

Hamad addressing a crowd in Ogoni Province, Nigeria, as
chairperson of the UNPO, 1994.

Hamad at the Mkwajuni residence of President Salmin Amour
immediately following *Muafaka* I in 1999.

Hamad at a press conference during the 2000 presidential campaign. The placard translates as "Together we shall build a new Zanzibar."

Hamad with President Amani Karume at the State House, Zanzibar Town, after signing of *Muafaka* II, 2001.

Hamad with Professor Ibrahim Lipumba at the CUF National Congress, Dar es Salaam, 2003.

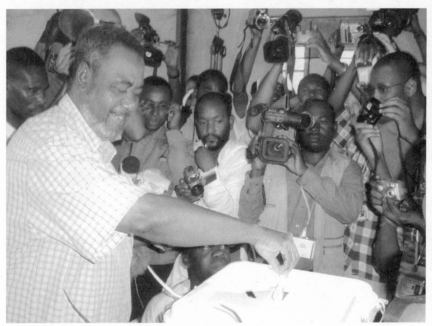

Hamad voting during the 2005 elections.

INTRODUCTION: COSMOPOLITANISM AND ITS DISCONTENTS

1. Salmin Amour, "The Participation of the Masses and the Role of the Leadership in the National Economic Development, 1964–1984" (PhD thesis, Karl Marx Party College, East Berlin, GDR, 1986), 23.

2. For Tanzania, see Jan-Georg Deutsch, *Emancipation without Abolition in German East Africa, c. 1884–1914* (Athens: Ohio University Press, 2006); and John Iliffe, *A Modern History of Tanganyika* (Cambridge: Cambridge University Press, 1979).

3. Amour, "Participation of the Masses," 24.

4. Ibid., 77.

5. See Jonathon Glassman, "Slower Than a Massacre: The Multiple Sources of Racial Thought in Colonial Africa," *American Historical Review* 109, no. 3 (June 2004): 720–54.

6. Liisa Malkki, *Purity and Exile: Violence, Memory, and National Cosmology among Hutu Refugees in Tanzania* (Chicago: University of Chicago Press, 1995), 54.

7. Mohammed Ali Bakari, *The Democratisation Process in Zanzibar: A Retarded Transition* (Hamburg, Germany: Institute of African Affairs, 2001), 254n5.

8. Omar Mapuri, *The 1964 Revolution: Achievements and Prospects* (Dar es Salaam, Tanzania: Tema Publishers, 1996), 4.

9. Ibid, 8, 23. Such an argument is much easier to make for the period extending through World War II than the far more decisive nationalist era of the mid-1950s through 1963. For the earlier period, see Laura Fair, *Pastimes and Politics: Culture, Community, and Identity in Post-Abolition Urban Zanzibar, 1890–1945* (Athens: Ohio University Press, 2001).

10. Mapuri, *The 1964 Revolution,* 45. See also Amour, "Participation of the Masses," 59.

11. B. F. Mrina and W. T. Mattoke, *Mapambano ya Ukombozi Zanzibar* (Dar es Salaam, Tanzania: Tanzania Publishing House, n.d.). Mapuri claims the "most frustrating and offensive" British tactic was the way the British demarcated two key constituency boundaries (*The 1964 Revolution,* 36–37, 48). Such alleged favoritism could not have changed the election results, however, since they were decided by more than the two seats in question. Mapuri's overactive imagination extends also to the United States, as when he claims

the U.S. disputed the outcome of the 1995 elections as revenge for Zanzibar's closure of a U.S. "military base" at Tunguu in 1964 and "extradition" of a U.S. consul in 1965. Ibid., 83.

12. Ibid., 59.

13. Ibid., 66.

14. Ibid., 56–57.

15. Omar Mapuri, *Zanzibar under Siege of Externally Motivated Political Fantasy* (Zanzibar Town, Tanzania: CCM Secretariat, 1997), 22, as cited in Bakari, *Democratisation Process in Zanzibar,* 279n56.

16. Mapuri, *The 1964 Revolution,* 83. This view accords with official historical narratives from the 1960s, which can be easily accessed through hundreds of speech transcripts appearing in two government organs, *Kweupe* and *Kweli Ikidhihiri Uwongo.*

17. Issa Shivji, *Pan-Africanism or Pragmatism? Lessons of Tanganyika-Zanzibar Union* (Dar es Salaam: Mkuki na Nyota Publishers, 2008), 62n63.

18. Mapuri, *The 1964 Revolution,* 71.

19. Ibid., 45.

20. Abdulrazak Gurnah, *Admiring Silence* (New York: New Press, 1996), 135.

21. Abdulrazak Gurnah, *By the Sea* (New York: Free Press, 2001), 228–29.

22. Abdulrazak Gurnah, *Desertion* (New York: Pantheon Books, 2005), 246–47.

23. A. M. Babu, "The 1964 Revolution: Lumpen or Vanguard?" in *Zanzibar under Colonial Rule,* ed. Abdul Sheriff and Ed Ferguson (London: James Currey, 1991), 240.

24. Haroub Othman, ed., *Babu: I Saw the Future and It Works, Essays Celebrating the Life of Comrade Abdulrahman Mohamed Babu, 1924–1996* (Dar es Salaam, Tanzania: E&D Limited, 2001), 18, 28.

25. Babu, "Lumpen or Vanguard?" 244.

26. David Reed, "Zanzibar: Laziest Place on Earth," *Reader's Digest* 81, no. 487 (November 1962): 302, as quoted in Don Petterson, *Revolution in Zanzibar: An American's Cold War Tale* (Cambridge, MA: Westview Press, 2002), xvi.

27. Frantz Fanon, *The Wretched of the Earth* (New York: Grove Weidenfeld, 1963), 203.

28. Petterson, *Revolution in Zanzibar,* 182.

29. Ibid., 269

30. Donald Donham, *Marxist Modern: An Ethnographic History of the Ethiopian Revolution* (London: James Currey, 1999), 123.

31. Adolpho Gilly, Introduction to Frantz Fanon, *A Dying Colonialism* (New York: Grove Press, 1965), 1, 2.

32. Abdellah Hammoudi, *Master and Disciple: The Cultural Foundations of Moroccan Authoritarianism* (Chicago: University of Chicago Press, 1997), 41.

33. Shivji, *Pan-Africanism or Pragmatism?* 149–50.

34. See "'The Bullets Were Raining': The January 2001 Attack on Peaceful Demonstrators in Zanzibar," *Human Rights Watch Report* 14, no. 3 (A) (April 2002): 3–45, http://www.hrw.org/reports/2002/tanzania/.

35. *Guide to Zanzibar* (Zanzibar Town: n.p., 1931). Accessed in the Zanzibar National Archives, Zanzibar Town, Tanzania, BA 109/6.

36. Michael Pearson, *Port Cities and Intruders: The Swahili Coast, India, and Portugal in the early Modern Era* (Baltimore: Johns Hopkins University Press, 1998), 20.

37. Abdul Sheriff, *Slaves, Spices and Ivory in Zanzibar* (London: James Currey, 1987), 48–60.

38. Fair, *Pastimes and Politics*, 28–41.

39. Abdul Sheriff, "The Peasantry under Imperialism," in *Zanzibar under Colonial Rule*, 109–40.

40. Jonathon Glassman, "Sorting Out the Tribes: The Creation of Racial Identities in Colonial Zanzibar's Newspaper Wars," *Journal of African History* 41 (2000): 398.

41. Thomas Burgess, "An Imagined Generation: Umma Youth in Nationalist Zanzibar," in *In Search of a Nation: Histories of Authority and Dissidence from Tanzania: Essays in Honor of I. M. Kimambo*, ed. Gregory Maddox, James Giblin, and Y. Q. Lawi (London: James Currey, 2005), 216–49.

42. Fair, *Pastimes and Politics*, 46–53.

43. In this introduction, I often refer to the Shirazi as Africans, fully cognizant of the disputed nature of such categories.

44. Michael Lofchie, *Zanzibar: Background to Revolution* (Princeton, NJ: Princeton University Press, 1965), 72. Asians, however, as artisans, merchants, and civil servants, were overwhelmingly concentrated in Zanzibar Town. In 1948, they comprised over 27 percent of Zanzibar Town's population of approximately 50,000; Africans and Arabs accounted, respectively, for 49 and 16 percent of the city's population (A. H. J. Prins, *The Swahili Speaking Peoples of Zanzibar and the East African Coast* [London: International African Institute, 1967], 19).

45. Shirazi repudiation of African identity and nationalism may be contrasted to the situation on the mainland, where, despite continuing coastal condescension toward upcountry immigrants, assimilation into an emerging African racial identity is advanced. James Brennan, "Realizing Civilization through Patrilineal Descent: The Intellectual Making of an African Racial Nationalism in Tanzania, 1920–50," *Social Identities* 12, no. 4 (July 2006), 410.

46. Gurnah, *Admiring Silence*, 66–67. The quote also suggests that ethnic relations in Zanzibar may at times be better described as multicultural rather than cosmopolitan. For a useful discussion of the differences between the two terms, see Steven Vertovec and Robin Cohen, eds., *Conceiving Cosmopolitanism: Theory, Context, and Practice* (Oxford: Oxford University Press, 2002). Cosmopolitanism, as used here, is meant to emphasize the transnational ties of the islands' communities, in particular, the reception in Zanzibar of people, ideas, and commodities from overseas.

47. Amour, "Participation of the Masses," 71.

48. Ibid., 70.

49. Lofchie, *Zanzibar: Background to Revolution,*183–84.

50. Burgess, "Imagined Generation," in *In Search of a Nation,* 225–35.

51. See British National Archives, DO 185/59, which includes corroborating official statements by several British expatriate officers, written a week after the uprising began.

52. Abdul Sheriff, "Race and Class in the Politics of Zanzibar," *Afrika Spectrum* 36, no. 3 (2001): 314–15.

53. For the political intrigues of this period, see Thomas Burgess, "A Socialist Diaspora: Ali Sultan Issa, the Soviet Union, and the Zanzibari Revolution," in *Africa in Russia, Russia in Africa: 300 Years of Encounters,* ed. Maxim Matusevich (Trenton, NJ: Africa World Press, 2006), 263–92.

54. CIA memorandum, 9/29/64, URT-Zanzibar Memos, vol. I, 4/64–1/65, National Security File, Africa-Tanganyika, Box 100, Lyndon Baines Johnson Library, University of Texas, Austin, Texas.

55. Ali Mazrui, *Cultural Engineering and Nation Building in East Africa* (Evanston, IL: Northwestern University Press, 1972), 206.

56. Shivji, *Pan-Africanism or Pragmatism?* 109.

57. Bakari, *Democratisation Process in Zanzibar,* 132. The years since have not seen any improvement.

58. Ibid., 127.

59. Muhammed Seif Khatib, "EID-EL-KUFA?" *Mzalendo,* November 8, 2005; quoted in Shivji, *Pan-Africanism or Pragmatism?* 4.

PART I

WALK ON TWO LEGS: THE LIFE STORY OF ALI SULTAN ISSA

Four: London

1. In 1955, there were about a hundred students and seamen from Zanzibar in the United Kingdom, mostly Arab and South Asian males.

2. Communist Youth Festivals were regular events in the Eastern Bloc in the post–World War II years. The Moscow festival of 1957 was the sixth of these and attracted approximately thirty thousand youths from 131 countries.

3. A *kanzu* is a full-length, ankle-to-wrist white gown worn by Muslim males. In this context, a *kofia* refers to circular flat headwear worn by Muslim males.

4. Issa recorded his experiences at the festival in a series of articles in the Zanzibari weekly *Mwongozi* from December 1957 to February 1958. He described performances, exhibitions, tours of industrial sights, and visits to the tombs of Lenin and Stalin.

Five: The Struggle

1. In 1957, the ZNP earned 21.6 percent of the total vote, compared to the ASP's 60.1 percent.

Six: Cairo

1. The students were of varying ages and went mostly to primary and secondary institutions. They studied in Cairo through a personal agreement forged between Ali Muhsin and Colonel Nasser.

2. Muhsin wrote that Ahmad Rashad "created dissatisfaction and instigated open rebellion among some students over whom he obtained an evil influence. . . . It is a thousand pities that it was these very students whom Rashad set to undermine [that were] lured by his mischievous [*sic*] nephew Comrade Ali Sultan to various Eastern bloc countries." Ali Muhsin Al-Barwani, *Conflict and Harmony in Zanzibar (Memoirs)* (Dubai, UAE: n.p., 1997), 110, 142.

3. Literally "The Rooster's Voice," the rooster being the official symbol of the ZNP.

Seven: Expulsion

1. Lancaster House conferences were a typical feature of the decolonization process among British territories in Africa. In 1962, the negotiations included failed British attempts to encourage the ASP and ZNP-ZPPP alliance to put away their mutual hostilities and form a coalition government.

2. Issa related this conversation to me at least a dozen times; each time the memory aroused intense feelings of betrayal.

3. Habana Libre, like the Riviera Hotel, was by 1962 a striking holdover from the Batista regime. "These great hotels of Havana, built only two or three years previously, with their air-conditioning beginning to falter, the service and the food in decline, seemed like splendid ruins of a past civilization amid a new discordant one as yet unclearly defined. The Habana Libre presented the greatest contrast, since with its paintings by Wilfredo Lam, its ballroom, swimming pool and tinkling music, its several casinos, it had become the main international conference centre, the hotel for delegations from friendly socialist nations, for sympathetic Communists from the western hemisphere and fellow travelers from Europe. A bookstall in the foyer sold the latest revolutionary literature and the works of Marx and Marti. . . . Whole floors of this and other palaces were given over to country people for courses in sewing or domestic hygiene." Hugh Thomas, *The Cuban Revolution* (New York: Harper and Row, 1977), 566–67.

4. Issa's conviction that Babu was detained as part of a British and ZNP conspiracy to remove him from politics was shared by all former Umma comrades I interviewed. Wolfango Dourado, who served as the leading government prosecutor at Babu's trial, confirmed this interpretation. Interview, Zanzibar Town, 7/20/05.

Eight: The Vanguard

1. British intelligence reported in April 1963: "Threatening letters have been sent to the Ministers. It was suspected that the originator of such letters was Ali Sultan when the police searched his house but found no evidence to

substantiate the allegation." Zanzibar National Archives 31/16 District Intelligence Committee, no. 11.

2. The ASP won thirteen constituencies, all but two located in Unguja. The ZNP-ZPPP won eighteen seats, twelve of them in Pemba, three by fewer than three hundred votes.

3. Michael Lofchie observed that Umma "was highly disciplined and tightly integrated; it possessed a powerful, unifying marxist ideology and enjoyed considerable *espirit de corps*. Umma's activist element included several of Zanzibar's most effective propagandists and organizers; Babu himself was universally acknowledged as the organizational genius of Zanzibar politics, and in a very brief time had placed Umma at the head of practically all the militant opposition groups. . . . Had Umma been an African political party rather than predominantly Arab and Comorian, it might well have completely undermined the ASP by recruiting substantial sectors of its leadership and popular following." Lofchie, *Zanibar: Background to Revolution*, 262.

Nine: Revolution

1. Those who trained in Cuba were highly visible due to their use of such Spanish revolutionary expressions and their adoption of Castro-style beards, giving rise briefly to Western reports the revolution was the work of Cuban agents.

2. For an assessment of Umma's role in the revolution, see Shivji, *Pan-Africanism or Pragmatism?* 63–66.

3. The Tanganyikan government had a military agreement with the British, whereas Zanzibar did not.

4. Anthony Clayton, Don Petterson, and Michael Lofchie all, for example, accept Okello's claim of having been the sole mastermind and executor of the Zanzibari Revolution.

5. Issa's position is between two extremes—that of the victors who regard the loss of life as both minimal and justified and that of supporters of the former regime who consider it neither. That Issa would say revolutionaries worked both "whimsically" and in consideration of prevailing standards of justice is particularly interesting.

6. For the 1964 Tanganyika mutiny, see Nestor Luanda and E. Mwanjabala, *Tanganyika Rifles Mutiny January 1964* (Dar es Salaam: University of Dar es Salaam Press, 1998).

Ten: Maria

1. Soon after his arrival, Carlucci befriended Karume and was at the very center of the heated Cold War diplomatic contests of the time. Petterson provides an interesting portrait in *Revolution in Zanzibar*, 147–254.

2. Telegram, Carlucci to Secretary of State, 3/26/64, no. 1376, Zanzibar Cables and Memos, vol. II, 2/64–4/64, National Security File, Country File; Africa-Zanzibar, Box 103, Lyndon Baines Johnson Library, University of Texas, Austin, Texas.

3. Such humiliations actually began as early as January and February 1964.

4. Nyerere was deeply disturbed by the growing communist presence in Zanzibar and by rumors of an Arab counterrevolutionary training somewhere in the Middle East. By initiating the union agreement with Karume, he was pursuing his own interests, which coincided with those of the West.

5. Carlucci constantly strategized, along with mainland American embassies, over how to prevent Zanzibar from "going communist." Babu gained Karume's trust while working to undermine his authority and push his socialist agenda. Umma army officers as well as several cabinet ministers generally looked to Babu for leadership. In Carlucci's cables, Karume comes across as either unaware or unconcerned about a situation in which Babu and his comrades utilized any opportunity to consolidate their political position and build up their paramilitary forces. The union agreement had the immediate effect of dissipating Umma's influence and strengthening Karume's position. Babu and others were reassigned to positions in the union government and army.

6. In the 1950s, Vergès coedited with Babu the *Afro-Asian American Revolution*. Vergès later notoriously defended "Carlos the Jackal" (Ilich Ramírez Sánchez) in Paris courts.

Eleven: Nation Building

1. The First Tricontinental Conference took place in Havana in January 1966, attracting delegates from over eighty states.

2. In late 1964, Guevara gained Castro's consent to lead a Cuban military mission to assist in an anti-imperialist struggle in Africa, the exact location of which had yet to be determined. Guevara's visit to Zanzibar took place prior to his legendary intervention in the Congo.

3. Issa's remarks would have pleased Chou En-Lai who, in the mid-1960s, articulated "The Eight Principles" of Chinese assistance to developing nations. These included focusing on projects that encouraged self-reliance and that did not require large capital investment. Chinese advisors were to share local living conditions.

4. In gratitude for diplomatic recognition, the East Germans provided more aid to Zanzibar than to any other African nation. Eventually by 1970, Karume grew disenchanted with East German experts and limited their assistance to the training of state security officials. By the 1970s, the Chinese were clearly Zanzibar's leading patrons, with hundreds of advisors in the islands.

5. According to Ministry of Education reports, prior to the revolution, there were 19,106 students in seventy-two primary schools in Zanzibar. By 1967, there were 39,759 students in ninety-five primary schools.

6. In the late 1950s Asians comprised 5.8 percent of the population, but 41.4 percent of secondary school enrollment. Arabs comprised 16.8 percent of the population and 32.1 percent of secondary school enrollment. Comorians accounted for 1 percent of the population and 7 percent of secondary school students. Although Africans (mainlanders and Shirazi) represented 75.7 percent

of the population, they accounted for 19 percent of secondary school enrollment. Lofchie, *Zanzibar: Background to Revolution*, 71, 92.

7. The flight of Islamic scholars has, for some, been one of the most lamented results of the revolution.

Twelve: Discipline

1. Despite their dependence on state subsidies and serious problems with low productivity, the camps were regarded as showcases of socialist development and received ample attention in the official media.

2. Karume's government was heavily dependent on "voluntary" labor. In addition to persuasion, the state convinced students and state employees to perform labor through threats of dismissal, nonpromotion, or the imposition of fines.

3. Something of the extreme care taken by Issa to avoid life-threatening mistakes comes through in Dr. Charles Swift's memoir. In a meeting, the minister "sat sphinx-like, inscrutable." He was "slender, taut and restless, . . . [and] gave no suggestion as to what he thought about the issues discussed, so I had no idea what was going on behind those dark glasses and his programmed smile which he turned off and on." During one meeting, however, "a curious thing happened. His façade dropped and he spoke candidly and at length about his precarious position in the government. This was his way of explaining why he would take no action on my recommendations." Charles Swift, *Dar Days* (New York: University Press of America, 2002), 84, 91.

Thirteen: Power

1. In November and December 1968, Comorians were declared noncitizens and sacked from government service. Eventually recognizing the manpower shortage that would result if this policy were maintained, Karume allowed Comorians to apply for citizenship by naturalization. Some Comorians, however, left the islands permanently.

2. Karume claimed that Shirazi identity was merely a British invention to divide Africans. In 1970, his government convinced over fifteen thousand people to sign documents disavowing their Shirazi identity. Bakari, *Democratisation Process in Zanzibar*, 71.

3. Karume's "encouragement" of such marriages became one of his most notorious policies, drawing international condemnation. Young women were coerced, and protesting family members were beaten and imprisoned.

4. Swift recalled about Zanzibar in 1969: "It was such a relief to be back in Dar after two days in Zanzibar; right away I breathed more easily. The atmosphere had been so heavy with suspicion and apprehension: among the shopkeepers who were caught between making a living and being accused of over charging; passers-by on the street who didn't know whether or not to answer my greeting; the minor officials in customs and immigration at the airport who were afraid they might make a mistake. About the only people who spoke their minds were the patients at the psychiatric hospital." Swift, *Dar Days*, 98–99.

5. Ali Muhsin recorded his not-altogether-impartial impressions of Zanzibar Town upon his release from prison in 1974. The islands had become "the embodiment of the nightmarish dreams that used to haunt me in prison. . . . Everything was numb and robot-like, no human emotion of any kind. Everybody seemed deflated, everything insipid, like soda water of last night which had lost its effervescence. The euphoria of assuming power and property seemed to have dissipated after ten dreary years, and there remained only the dullness of a dying economy." Muhsin, *Conflict and Harmony*, 245–46.

Fourteen: Arrest

1. The government arrested approximately eleven hundred individuals considered critical of Karume's regime. Hank Chase, "The Zanzibar Treason Trial," *Review of African Political Economy* 3, no. 6 (May–August 1976): 20.

Fifteen: Imprisonment

1. Dourado claims in personal interviews that he voiced opposition from the beginning to the idea of replacing the British court system, but Issa was among its most outspoken opponents. Personal Interview, Zanzibar Town, 7/22/05.

2. Dourado denied the nine had in any way plea-bargained with the prosecution. All the defendants other than the nine retracted their written statements, citing torture. Dourado, however, argued their forced testimonies should still be admissible.

3. Aboud Jumbe's succession was a victory for relative moderates among the ASP elite. Karume had, in fact, favored Bakari, who wanted to rigidly maintain Karume's policies. Jumbe and the moderates feared a wave of public dissent if some of those policies, food rationing in particular, were continued.

4. Twenty-four were sentenced to death and twenty-nine to terms of imprisonment.

Seventeen: Pilgrimage

1. Tourism had slowly revived after the Karume years. However, the only hotels were located in Zanzibar Town, not on the islands' many beaches.

2. Carlucci said in a personal interview that he played no role in the hotel project but was pleased to be remembered in this way. Personal Interview, Washington, DC, 9/23/04.

PART 2

AN ENDURING TRUST: THE LIFE STORY OF SEIF SHARIF HAMAD

Two: Student Politics

1. For another firsthand description of Karume's personality, prior to consolidating power in the mid-1960s, see Petterson, *Revolution in Zanzibar*, 34–36.

2. The assertion that coastal East Africa was "civilized" by waves of foreigners, Arabs in particular, is somewhat common in Zanzibar today and partially derived from colonial-era textbooks such as *Milango ya Historia*. Glassman, "Slower Than a Massacre," 736–47.

Three: Revolution

1. John Okello's hatred of Arabs as oppressors of Africans is loud and clear in his memoir, *Revolution in Zanzibar* (Nairobi, Kenya: East African Publishing House, 1967).

2. For a lengthy discussion of the formulation and ratification of the Articles of Union between Tanganyika and Zanzibar, see Shivji, *Pan-Africanism or Pragmatism?* 76–99.

3. See Haroub Othman and Chris Peter, eds., *Zanzibar and the Union Question* (Zanzibar: Zanzibar Legal Services Center, 2006).

Four: Crocodile Tears

1. For rationing, shortages, and smuggling in Pemba, where deprivation was much more acute than in Unguja, see Esmond Martin, *Zanzibar: Tradition and Revolution* (London: Hamish Hamilton, 1978), 60–62, 116–18. Hamad's account coheres with numerous Pemban oral histories.

2. Martin reckons that thirty-five thousand, or one-tenth the population of Zanzibar, fled in these years. He also quotes Karume, who estimated that 2,800 secondary students left the islands from 1964 to 1969, a significant drain, given that in 1966 there were only 1,681 secondary students total in Zanzibar. Martin, *Tradition and Revolution*, 71, 130.

Five: Karume the Terrible

1. For another portrait of Karume after the revolution, see Anthony Clayton, *The Zanzibar Revolution and Its Aftermath* (Hamden, CT: Archon Books, 1981), 116–18.

2. Regarding forced marriages, see, for example, Martin, *Tradition and Revolution*, 69–71.

3. Zanzibari women's oral histories confirm Hamad's assertions. Wolfango Dourado, Karume's Attorney General, estimates that Karume forced himself on various women at Kibweni Palace twice a week for several years. Interview, Zanzibar Town, 7/20/05.

4. Chachage claims Karume threatened to break the union if Nyerere did not hand over Shariff and Hanga. C. S. L. Chachage, *Environment, Aid and Politics in Zanzibar* (Dar es Salaam, Tanzania: DUP, 2000), 74. See also Clayton, *The Zanzibar Revolution*, 132–34.

5. For the dismantlement of the judiciary in Zanzibar, see Shivji, *Pan-Africanism or Pragmatism?* 110–12.

6. For the (un)popularity of these modern flats among Ng'ambo residents, see Garth Andrew Myers, *Verandahs of Power: Colonialism and Space in Urban Africa* (Syracuse, NY: Syracuse University Press, 2003), 106–34.

Seven: Serving the Revolution

1. For accounts of Jumbe's reforms of the mid-1970s, see Chachage, *Environment, Aid and Politics*, 76–81; Martin, *Tradition and Revolution*, 130–35; Bakari, *Democratisation Process in Zanzibar*, 112–16; Shivji, *Pan-Africanism or Pragmatism?* 143–201.

2. A decade of official repression of Western youth styles is examined in Thomas Burgess, "Cinema, Bell Bottoms, and Miniskirts: Struggles over Youth and Citizenship in Revolutionary Zanzibar," *International Journal of African Historical Studies* 35, no. 2 (2002): 287–313.

Eight: Ascendancy

1. For discussion of the merger of TANU and ASP, see Shivji, *Pan-Africanism or Pragmatism?* 152–63.

2. Ibid., 186–201.

3. For an account of Jumbe's fall, see Shivji, *Pan-Africanism or Pragmatism?* 201–25; David Throup, "Zanzibar after Nyerere," in *Tanzania after Nyerere*, ed. Michael Hodd (London: Printer Publishers, 1988), 186–88. For Jumbe's perspectives on the union, see Aboud Jumbe, *The Partnership: Tanganyika Zanzibar Union 30 Turbulent Years* (Dar es Salaam, Tanzania: Amana Publishers, 1994). Hamad, in making his case against Jumbe, called his actions "treasonous" and prayed for Jumbe's punishment. Shivji, *Pan-Africanism or Pragmatism?* 215.

Nine: Reform

1. Shivji faults the 1984 constitution for legally codifying the control of CCM's Central Committee over the nomination of Zanzibari presidents. Shivji maintains that prior to Jumbe's fall there was no clear constitutional wording on the issue, yet through the 1984 constitution, "a political expediency became an entrenched position striking a severe blow to Zanzibar's right to determine who would lead them." Shivji, *Pan-Africanism or Pragmatism?* 230.

Ten: Old Guard Intrigues

1. These events are summarized in Throup, "Zanzibar after Nyerere," 188–92.

2. For Zanzibar's uneven economic performance since the 1980s, see Bakari, *Democratisation Process in Zanzibar*, 127–35.

3. For a fictionalized account of Hamad's fall from power, see Abdulrazak Gurnah, *Admiring Silence* (New York: The New Press, 1996). Wolfango Dourado remembered Hamad from this period as "ambitious, very firm, but not vindictive. He could harm anyone who stamped on his toes, and get him out of the way. . . . There was no fooling with him. People said he was an Arab, but it wasn't true; he only had a tinkling [of blood]. He was humble, with a certain amount of self-effacement. . . . Nyerere told Ali Hassan Mwinyi that Seif should rise no further than Chief Minister, because Nyerere thought he would be trouble for the union. He would want reforms." Interview, Zanzibar Town, 7/22/05.

Eleven: Prison Graduate

1. For an overview of these events, see Chachage, *Environment, Aid and Politics*, 87–90.

Twelve: Multipartyism

1. For Zanzibar's transition to multipartyism prior to the 1995 election campaign, see Bakari, *Democratisation Process in Zanzibar*, 153–64.

Thirteen: Principles

1. Citizens were supposed to receive three-acre plots. Acrimony, bitterness, and litigation marked the redistribution process, which took place over several years. The size and value of land allotments depended on an individual's access to patronage. See Ibrahim Focas Shao, The *Political Economy of Land Reform in Zanzibar* (Dar es Salaam, Tanzania: Dar es Salaam University Press, 1992); Zinnat Kassamali Mohammed Jan Bader, "The Social Conditions and Consequences of the 1964 Land Reform in Zanzibar" (PhD diss., London University, 1984); and Chachage, *Environment, Aid and Politics*, 40–47. Zanzibaris who today do not accept the legality of the redistribution have been rather outspoken, asserting that, according to Islamic tradition, the confiscations are *haram* (sinful) in the sight of God. Muhsin, *Conflicts and Harmony*, 34–37.

2. OIC membership has aroused serious controversy in other African states. See Toyin Falola, *Violence in Nigeria: The Crisis of Religious Politics and Secular Ideologies* (Rochester, NY: University of Rochester Press, 1998), 93–102.

3. For the history of the East African Muslim Welfare Society, and Muslim grievances in Tanzania in general, see Roman Loimeier, "Perceptions of Marginalization: Muslims in Contemporary Tanzania," in *Islam and Muslim Politics in Africa*, ed. Benjamin Soares and René Otayek (New York: Palgrave, 2007), 137–56.

4. For declining clove production in Zanzibar, see K. I. Tambila, "Aspects of the Political Economy of Unguja and Pemba," in *The Political Plight of Zanzibar*, ed. T. L. Maliyamkono (Dar es Salaam, Tanzania: Tema Publishers, 2000), 83–93; and Chachage, *Environment, Aid and Politics*, 48–56. For a contemporary survey of Zanzibar's economy, see F. P. Mtatifikolo and R. B. Mabele, "Zanzibar's Economy: Background and Current State of the Economy," in Maliyamkono, *Political Plight*, 177–212.

5. For discrimination against Pembans, see Bakari, *Democratisation Process in Zanzibar*, 136–41.

Fourteen: Impasse

1. For the 1995 campaign and election, see Tanzania Election Monitoring Committee (ZEMCO), *The 1995 General Elections in Tanzania* (ZEMCO: Dar es Salaam, 1997); C. A. Rugalabamu, "Electoral Administration during the 1995 General Elections in Zanzibar," in Maliyamkono, *Political Plight*, 105–32; Chachage, *Environment, Aid and Politics*, 90–98; and Bakari, *Democra-*

tisation Process in Zanzibar, 209–47. Bakari and Chachage quote the report of the "International Observation Team" funded by the donor community, which announced "serious discrepancies in the compilation of the votes for the presidency. The figures announced by the Zanzibar Electoral Commission do not correspond with the figures recorded at polling stations. . . . The authorities have proceeded to inaugurate the President while the outcome of the election remains unclear."

2. For the *maskani* phenomenon, see Bakari, *Democratisation Process in Zanzibar,* 179–84.

3. This is no exaggeration; see U.S. State Department, Bureau of Democracy, Human Rights, and Labor, *1999 Country Reports on Human Rights Practices,* February 25, 2000; Bakari, *Democratisation Process in Zanzibar,* 249–68.

4. For the genesis of *Muafaka,* see Bakari, *Democratisation Process in Zanzibar,* 284–95.

Fifteen: Violence

1. For an excellent study of both the drama of the 2000 campaign and CCM vote rigging in Zanzibar, see Greg Cameron, "Zanzibar's Turbulent Transition" *Review of African Political Economy* 29, no. 92 (2002): 313–30.

2. For the most systematic account of the violence in 2001, see "'The Bullets Were Raining,' *Human Rights Watch Report.*

Sixteen: People's Power

1. For the demise of *Muafaka* II and the CCM's rigging of the PVR, see Ben Rawlence, "Briefing: The Zanzibar Election," *African Affairs* 104, no. 416 (2005): 515–23.

2. For a complete list of areas of union jurisdiction, see Legal and Human Rights Center, *Tanzania Human Rights Report 2006: Progress through Human Rights* (Dar es Salaam, Tanzania: Legal and Human Rights Center, 2006), 157.

SELECT BIBLIOGRAPHY OF PUBLISHED SOURCES ON ZANZIBAR

Al-Barwani, Ali Muhsin. *Conflict and Harmony in Zanzibar (Memoirs)*. Dubai, UAE: n.p., 1997.

Ayany, S. G. *A History of Zanzibar: A Study of Constitutional Development, 1934–1964*. Nairobi, Kenya: East African Literature Bureau, 1977.

Bakari, Mohammed Ali. *The Democratisation Process in Zanzibar: A Retarded Transition*. Hamburg, Germany: Institute of African Affairs, 2001.

Bennett, Norman. *A History of the Arab State of Zanzibar*. Cambridge, UK: Methuen and Co., 1978.

Burgess, Thomas. "A Socialist Diaspora: Ali Sultan Issa, the Soviet Union, and the Zanzibari Revolution." In *Africa in Russia, Russia in Africa: 300 Years of Encounters*, edited by Maxim Matusevich, 263–92. Trenton, NJ: Africa World Press, 2006.

———. "An Imagined Generation: Umma Youth in Nationalist Zanzibar." In *In Search of a Nation: Histories of Authority and Dissidence from Tanzania: Essays in Honor of I. M. Kimambo*, edited by Gregory Maddox, James Giblin, and Y. Q. Lawi, 216–49. London: James Currey, 2005.

———. "The Young Pioneers and the Rituals of Citizenship in Revolutionary Zanzibar." *Africa Today* 51, no. 3 (April 2005): 3–29.

———. "Cinema, Bell Bottoms, and Miniskirts: Struggles over Youth and Citizenship in Revolutionary Zanzibar." *International Journal of African Historical Studies* 35, no. 2 (2002): 287–313.

Cameron, Greg. "Zanzibar's Turbulent Transition." *Review of African Political Economy* 29, no. 92 (2002): 313–30.

Chachage, C. S. L. *Environment, Aid and Politics in Zanzibar*. Dar es Salaam, Tanzania: DUP, 2000.

Clayton, Anthony. *The Zanzibar Revolution and Its Aftermath*. Hamden, CT: Archon Books, 1981.

Cooper, Frederick. *From Slaves to Squatters*. New Haven, CT: Yale University Press, 1987.

Fair, Laura. *Pastimes and Politics: Culture, Community, and Identity in Post-Abolition Urban Zanzibar, 1890–1945*. Athens, OH: Ohio University Press, 2001.

Glassman, Jonathon, "Slower Than a Massacre: The Multiple Sources of Racial Thought in Colonial Africa." *American Historical Review* 109, no. 3 (June 2004): 720–54.

———. "Sorting Out the Tribes: The Creation of Racial Identities in Colonial Zanzibar's Newspaper Wars." *Journal of African History* 41 (2000): 395–428.

Gurnah, Abdulrazak. *Admiring Silence*. New York: New Press, 1996.

Human Rights Watch. "'The Bullets Were Raining': The January 2001 Attack on Peaceful Demonstrators in Zanzibar." *Human Rights Watch Report*, April 2002. http:/www.hrw.org/reports/2002/tanzania/.

Ingrams, W. H. *Zanzibar, Its History and People*. New York: Barnes and Noble, 1931.

Jumbe, Aboud. *The Partnership: Tanganyika Zanzibar Union 30 Turbulent Years*. Dar es Salaam, Tanzania: Amana Publishers, 1994.

Lofchie, Michael. *Zanzibar: Background to Revolution*. Princeton, NJ: Princeton University Press, 1965.

Maliyamkono, T. L., ed. *The Political Plight of Zanzibar*. Dar es Salaam, Tanzania: Tema Publishers, 2000.

Mapuri, Omar. *The 1964 Revolution: Achievements and Prospects*. Dar es Salaam, Tanzania: Tema Publishers, 1996.

Martin, Esmond. *Zanzibar: Tradition and Revolution*. London: Hamish Hamilton, 1978.

Mrina, B. F., and W. T. Mattoke. *Mapambano ya Ukombozi Zanzibar*. Dar es Salaam, Tanzania: Tanzania Publishing House, n.d.

Myers, Garth Andrew. *Verandahs of Power: Colonialism and Space in Urban Africa*. Syracuse, NY: Syracuse University Press, 2003.

Okello, John. *Revolution in Zanzibar*. Nairobi, Kenya: East African Publishing House, 1967.

Othman, Haroub, ed. *Babu: I Saw the Future and It Works: Essays Celebrating the Life of Comrade Abdulrahman Mohamed Babu, 1924–1996*. Dar es Salaam, Tanzania: E&D, 2001.

Othman, Haroub, and Chris Peter, eds. *Zanzibar and the Union Question*. Zanzibar: Zanzibar Legal Services Center, 2006.

Petterson, Don. *Revolution in Zanzibar: An American's Cold War Tale*. Cambridge, MA: Westview Press, 2002.

Rawlence, Ben. "Briefing: The Zanzibar Election." *African Affairs* 104, no. 416 (2005): 515–23.

Shao, Ibrahim Focas. *The Political Economy of Land Reform in Zanzibar*. Dar es Salaam, Tanzania: Dar es Salaam University Press, 1992.

Sheriff, Abdul. "Race and Class in the Politics of Zanzibar." *Afrika Spectrum* 36, no. 3 (2001): 314–15.

———. *Slaves, Spices and Ivory in Zanzibar*. London: James Currey, 1987.

Sheriff, Abdul, and Ed Ferguson, eds. *Zanzibar under Colonial Rule*. London: James Currey, 1991.

Shivji, Issa. *Pan-Africanism or Pragmatism? Lessons of Tanganyika-Zanzibar Union*. Dar es Salaam: Mkuki na Nyota Publishers, 2008.

Throup, David. "Zanzibar after Nyerere." In *Tanzania after Nyerere*, edited by Michael Hodd, 184–92. London: Printer Publishers, 1988.

INDEX

Abdulaziz Twala, 77, 120, 131, 207
Abdullah Said Natepe, 86, 199, 221, 230, 238
Abdulrazak Gurnah, 7, 20
Afro-Shirazi Party (ASP): and competition with the ZNP, ZPPP, 19–21, 55–56, 69, 74–75, 80, 181, 186–87, 317n1; and Julius Nyerere, 190; museum, 219–20; and revolution, 85; and socialism, 192; and Umma Party, 92, 99, 192; and union with Tanganyika, 191; and union with TANU, 149, 228–29. *See also* Karume, Abeid
Afro-Shirazi Party Youth League, 99, 112, 197, 226; and clothing, 119; and memory, 199; and revolution, 21, 85–87, 92; and "voluntary" labor, 208; and youth labor camps, 114–16. *See also* Seif Bakari; Volunteers
agriculture, 251, 279–80
Ahmad Rashad, 41, 63–65, 317n2
Ahmed Rajab, 145, 151
Ali Haji Pandu, 140, 247, 254, 257, 258–60, 261, 262, 297
Ali Hassan Mwinyi, 259, 261, 275, 282–83; and 1985 elections, 245–48; as president of Zanzibar, 13, 153, 154, 237–40
Ali Mahfoud, 66, 72, 101, 103, 132, 146, 211
Ali Muhsin Barwani, 59, 65, 78, 81, 85, 101, 157, 317nn1–2, 321n5; and Babu's detention, 70, 72, 73, 80; and Civic United Front (CUF), 258, 278
Ali Mzee, 132–33, 145

Amnesty International, 143, 145, 148, 263, 295
Amour Zahor, 100–101
Arabs, 1, 3–6, 17, 20, 22, 31–33, 36–37, 56, 87, 109, 124, 126, 187, 199, 273–74, 319n6; and clove industry, 50, 56
Argentina, 52, 159
ASP. *See* Afro-Shirazi Party (ASP)
atheism, 50, 56, 64, 81, 142
Aysha Amour Zahor, 57–58, 76, 82–84, 88, 99, 100, 103, 111–12, 118, 122, 144

Babu, Abdulrahman Muhammed, 37, 41–43, 49, 59, 60, 61, 82, 96, 101, 132, 144, 158, 163; and arrest, detention (1962), 69–70, 72, 77; and assassination of Karume, 136–37, 139–40, 211; and relationship with Karume, 22, 92, 191–93, 319n5; and Umma Party, 21, 79–80, 92, 182; and union with Tanganyika, 98, 101, 191–93; and Zanzibari Revolution, 9, 86, 88, 89; and Zanzibar Nationalist Party (ZNP), 55, 79. *See also* socialism
Badawi, Ahmed Quillatein, 45, 76, 78, 80, 81, 82, 86, 130, 132, 139, 162
Blue Guards, 285
British Communist Party, 8, 49–51, 53, 54, 61, 81

Cairo, 61, 63–68, 72
Carlucci, Frank, 96, 99, 106, 154, 155, 318n1, 319n5, 321n2
Castro, Fidel, 77, 102, 243, 319n2
Castro, Raul, 72, 77
CCM. See *Chama cha Mapinduzi* (CCM)